UKRAINIAN BIBLIOGRAPHICAL REFERENCE CENTER — CHICAGO
Ukrainian Reference Series, No. 1.

UKRAINE

SELECTED REFERENCES IN THE ENGLISH LANGUAGE

Second Edition Enlarged and Up-to-Date

by

ROMAN WERES

Ukrainian Research and Information Institute, Inc.

Chicago, 1974.

To

My Wife Eugenia and Son Oleh.

Author

Library of Congress Catalog Card Number: 74-84403

FOREWORD

FOREWORD

Since World War II the tremendous growth of interest on problems of Slavic and East European nations spread throughout the world. It became an important fact on international arena not only from the political standpoint but from the historical and economical, as well as cultural point of view. These vital questions have found their recognition and deep consideration especially in the English-speaking countries. Hence, the studies of Eastern Europe established their citizenship and tradition among other significant subjects at Western European and American universities and learned societies as well.

In the development of Slavic and East European studies problems of the Ukraine as the second largest Slavic nation, it occupies an important place mainly because of its central geographical location among other East European nations, its old history and rich culture which played a distinguished, influential role in development of its neighbors, and finally, its constant opposition toward Moscow-Communist rule, evidence of which one can observe even today. Particularly at present, the movement of Ukrainian dissidents, mainly university and college students, scholars, and literary authors, who defend national rights of Ukraine, have been recognized throughout the world.

In order to meet the demand of growing interest and to provide one of the most important keys to studies of the Ukraine for English speaking people, Dr. Roman Weres presents his Ukraine: Selected References in the English Language. In fact, this is the second, revised and enlarged edition of his work,* preparation of which lasted several years.

Dr. Weres, a leading Ukrainian bibliographer, has been highly recognized among distinguished Ukrainian scholars and librarians in particular. Besides this work he compiled eight volumes of the Index to Ukrainian Serial and Periodical Publications, covering the years 1951-71, issued by University Microfilms in Ann Arbor, Michigan, 1966-72. He also published a number of articles regarding reference and bibliographical work. Among other of his professional and cultural activities, Dr. Weres has been President of the Ukrainian Librarians' Association of American for seven years. At present he is President of the Ukrainian National Museum in Chicago and Director of Ukrainian Bibliographical-Reference Center of the U.S.A.

Dr. Weres' Ukraine: Selected Reference in the English Language* is one of the most comprehensive bibliographies on the subject and the only one which presents retrospective and

up-to-date materials with critical annotations. Thus, it
represents a significant contribution to studies of this vital
area, providing a description of monographic publications and
important articles in scholarly periodicals as well.

   We are certain that this reference publication will
become a valuable item in libraries and private collections
since it will serve as a guide to students and scholars of
East European studies in general and Ukrainian problems in
particular.

                              Dmytro M. Shtohryn
                              Head of Slavic Cataloging
                              University of Illinois Library
                              President of Ukrainian Librarians
                              Association of America

*Ukraine. Selected References in the English Language . . .
Kalamazoo, Western Michigan University. School of Graduate
Studies, 1961 .

To The User of The Bibliography

Many older titles have been listed in this bibliography, which might be out of print but can very probably be found in some Ukrainian libraries or collections of Ukrainica in American or Canadian libraries.

This bibliography includes references to: complete book about Ukraine and Ukrainians in the English language; parts of books containing information concerning certain aspects of the Ukrainian problem; pamphlets and articles from periodicals or serials when they are of permanent rather than ephemeral value.

In a few cases monographs listed here, which cover more than one aspect of the Ukrainian problem have been analyzed.

In addition to the books and articles in the English language there are also listed a few publications in Ukrainian and other languages: bibliographies, sources to the history of Ukraine, reference works and some works of exceptional importance, which have an English abstract.

Only references to books and parts of books have been annotated. References to pamphlets and articles have been annotated in exceptional cases only, when the title is not self-explanatory.

This bibliography has been arranged by broad subjects with subdivisions. The entries in most subdivisions have been arranged in two sections: Books, parts of books and pamphlets in one, articles in another one.

But there are some exceptions. In all sections including biographies, all biographies are arranged by name of the bio-graphee, and all biographies of the same person alphabetically by author or title.

The same concerns all entries in the section: Monographs on single authors and, Monographs on single kinds of works.

All titles concerning Ukrainian-Jewish relations have been listed in the chapter: Ukraine - Minorities.

Besides published items a few unpublished doctoral dis-sertations, masters and bachelors theses on Ukrainian topics have been listed.

The English language series of Ukrainian scholarly institutions have been analyzed.

In the case of the Ukrainian and other Cyrillic entries the rules of transcription of the Ukrainian and other Cyrillic

alphabets, established by the Library of Congress minus
diacritical marks, have been applied.

Terminological problems in the search
for Ukrainica in English language sources.

In all American library catalogs and book selection aids
such as: bibliographies, indexes, abstracts, a.o. we can
find the subject headings: "Ukraine," "Ukrainian,"
"Ukrainians" standing alone or with subdivisions and entries
keyed to these with see also references. But despite this
much information on Ukrainian topics, they can also be found
under other headings.

Therefore, in this bibliography, the reader will find:
"History of Russia," "Kievan Russia," "History of Early
Russian Literature" and other similar titles as Ukrainica.

The reason for this is that English-language authors
sometimes use the term "Russia" in cases which do not concern
Russia proper but rather present-day Ukraine. They very
often use the term "Russia" or "Russian" for designating the
medieval Kiev state which was called "Rus" but situated on
the territory of present-day Ukraine.

Therefore, in most cases one can find works concerning
the medieval history of Ukraine and Medieval Ukrainian literature under the term "Russia" and "Russian."

The use of "Russia" instead of "Rus" is misleading.

The name "Rus" was used from the very beginning of the
medieval period until its end exclusively for the territory
of present-day Ukraine. The forms "Rusyn" and "Rus'kyi"--
in the Latin language "Ruthenian" and "Ruthenus"--derivations
of the word "Rus" remained among the backwood people of the
Western Ukraine until recently with meaning identical with
the term "Ukrainian" as the name of a group of people and as
an adjective. This term is still in use in this meaning among
Ukrainians in Yugoslavia and Eastern Slovakia standing alone
or as compounded into the name "Rusyn-Ukrainets" (Ruthenian-
Ukrainian).

Ukrainian and also Muscovite chronicles of the twelfth
century use the term "Rus" referring only to the present
Ukraine. In these sources princes, clergymen and other prominent people from the Great Novhorod, Moscow and other
Russian cities and territories--visiting Ukraine "go to Rus."
In other words, their cities and territories were not considered "Rus."

Foreign sources from this time stress this difference.
In documents of the Vatican from the beginning of the thirteenth
century the term "Rus" is used for present-day Ukraine while

for Russian principalities, their names, such as "Suzdal" or "Moscovia" are used.

Inhabitants of Moscovite principalities like Suzdal or Moscow used adjectives derivated from their capitals "Suzdalskii," Moskovskii for their designation. Only in the time of the Peter the Great was the term "Russia" introduced for the whole empire, also including Ukraine.

Therefore, the terms "Russia" and "Russian" referring to a political and not ethnic entity can be used for all territories of the pre-revolutionary Russian Empire only for the period from Peter the Great to the Revolution of 1917.

This explains why one can find a wealth of material concerning Ukraine and Ukrainians under the headings or titles "Russia" and "Russian."

In older bibliographies and indexes much information on Ukraine and Ukrainians can be found under the headings "Little Russian" and "South Russian," which are translations of obsolete Russian territorial designations for Ukraine.

Much information on Ukraine and Ukrainians can be found under the heading or title "U.S.S.R." This especially concerns various reference tools such as bibliographies, directories, indexes and gazetteers, in which information on Ukraine is included in chapters on the USSR.

Much material about Ukraine can be found under the headings "Galicia," "Curzon Line" a.o.

Information concerning Carpatho-Ukraine can be found also under the headings and titles "Carpathia," "Carpatho-Ruthenia," or "Carpatho-Russia," used in various non-Ukrainian publications.

Because parts of Ukraine belongs to Austro-Hungaria and later to Poland, Czechoslovakia, Rumania and Hungaria during various intervals, much material concerning Ukraine and Ukrainians can be found under the headings "Austro-Hungaria," "Poland," "Czechoslovakia," "Rumania," "Hungaria" in works on these countries.

All this makes searching for Ukrainica in English language sources difficult for certain degrees. Therefore, somebody not too familiar with these problems should use works written by experts on the Ukrainian problem as checklists in his research.

Acknowledgments.

Following publications, articles and typescripts have been used in compilation of this bibliography.

Canadian Ethnic Studies: Bulletin of the Research Centre for Canadian Ethnic Studies. Calgary, Alberta, University of Calgary. 1st- 1969-

Danko, Joseph. "West European and American Doctoral Dissertations on the Ukraine (1945-1960) in Annals of the Ukrainian Academy of Arts and Sciences in the U.S. IX (1-2/27-28) 313-333.

Goy, Petro. Bibliography of Reference Materials for Russian Area Studies. New York, New York City College, 1962.

Gregorovich, Andrew. Canadian Ethnic Groups Bibliography . . . Toronto, Department of the Provincial Secretary and Citizenship of Ontario, 1972.

Horak, Stephan. Junior Slavica: a Selected Annotated Bibliography of Books in English on Russia and Eastern Europe. Rochester, N. Y. Libraries Unlimited, Inc., 1968.

Knyzhkova Palata Ukrains'koi RSR. Derzhavna Bibliohrafia na Ukraini, 1922-1962. Kharkiv, Vydavnytstvo Knyzhkovoi Palaty URSR, 1962.

Sokolyszyn, Aleksander. Ukrainian Selected and Classified Bibliography in English. New York-Munich-Chicago, Ukrainian Information Bureau, 1972.

Weres, Roman. Index of the Ukrainian Essays in Collections Published outside the Iron Curtain in Year . . . Chicago, Ukrainian American Library Association, 1967-

Weres, Roman. Ukraine: Selected References in the English Language. Kalamazoo, Western Michigan University. School of Graduate Studies, 1961.

Wynar, Lubomyr. "Ukrainoznavchi Dysertatsii v Amerykans'kykh Universytetakh" in Ukrains'kyi Istoryk 5(1-4/17-20): 142-145, 1968.

Besides that I used till certain grade some of the bibliographies and indexes listed in Part I of this Bibliography.

I would like to express my thanks to all persons who helped me with their advice and with their materials

and other information, and who made language edition
of typescript.

    I would like to express special gratitude to the
Ukrainian National Museum of Chicago and the University of Chicago, whose libraries enabled me to com-
pile this bibliography, and to the Prof. Dr. Bohdan
Wynar for his advice concerning selection and arrangement of material in this bibliography.

    Roman Weres.

Outline of History
of Ukrainian Bibliography.

Modern Ukrainian bibliography starts around the middle of the 19th century. The first known Ukrainian bibliography was published in a literary supplement to the Russian magazine "Ruskii Invalid" (Russian War Disabled) in 1837 and listed publications on the Ukrainian historical ballads called "Dumy."

Ukrainian historian Mykola Kostomariv published in 1843 bibliographical essay "Obzor sochynenii pysanykh na malorossiiskom iazyke" (A review of publications written in Little Russian (i.e., Ukrainian) language)--a review of Ukrainian publications--in a magazine.

In Western Ukraine--being then a part of the Austro-Hungarian Monarchy, the first bibliographies recording Ukrainian publications were published in 1863 and 1865.

In 1883 Mykola Komarov published in an Almanac and later as a separate reprint "Pokazchyk Novoii Ukrains'koii Literatury 1798-1883" (A list of the New Ukrainian Literature Published in 1798-1883)--a retrospective bibliography of the Ukrainian publications published in 1798-1883.

The same bibliographer published later some smaller subject bibliographies. Other bibliographers also published supplements to his bibliography.

In 1901 the Ukrainian author, lexicographer and ethnographer, Borys Hrinchenko, published a large and extensive bibliography of and on Ukrainian folklore: Literatura Ukrains'koho Folklora, 1777-1900. Opyt bibliograficheskoho Ukazatela (Literature of the Ukrainian Folklore published in 1777-1900. A bibliography.)

In this time any publishing in Ukrainian language was prohibited by the Russian regime. Therefore all of the above mentioned bibliographies were published in the Russian language.

A very extensive bibliography of Ukrainian publications, published in Halychyna (a part of the Western Ukraine which was under Austro-Hungarian domination during the years 1772-1918) compiled Omelan I. Levyts'kyi under the title: "Halytsko-Russkaya Bibliografiia XIX st." (Galician-Ruthenian Bibliography of the 19th century)--Term russkyi or ruskyi was used in this time in Western Ukraine as equivalent of "Ukrainskyi"--Ukrainian and is translated in the English as "Ruthenian." It was a bibliography of Ukrainian publications published in Halychyna during the years 1800-1886. This two-volume (over 900 pages) work was published in 1888-1895.

Besides these larger bibliographies, there were a number of smaller compilations published both in Austrian-occupied Western Ukraine and Russian-occupied Eastern Ukraine, during this period.

But all of these were the uncoordinated efforts of single individuals. Systematic work on Ukrainian bibliography started in 1909, when Shevchenko Scientific Society at Lviv established a Bibliographic Commission. This Commission started systematic work on Ukrainian bibliography.

In 1909-1932 this Commission published 6 volumes of the "Materialy do Ukrains'koii Bibliohrafiii" (Source Materials to the Ukrainian Bibliography).

Volumes 1-3 of these materials, published in 1909-1911, included three volumes of Omelian I. Levytskyi "Ukrains'ka Bibliohrafiia Austro-Uhorshchyny za roky 1887-1900" (Ukrainian Bibliography of the Austro-Hungarian Empire for years 1887-1900) a continuation of the previously mentioned "Halytsko-Russkaia Bibliografiia XIX. st" by the same author. These three volumes (761 pages altogether) recorded all Ukrainian books published in Austro-Hungaria in 1887-1900.

In vol. 4 of this series the Bibliographic Commission published a bibliography of works by and about the prominent Ukrainian writer Ivan Franko, compiled by Volodymyr Doroshenko and in vol. 5: "Ukrains'ka Istorychna Bibliohrafiia za 1914-1923" (Bibliography of Ukrainian Historical Studies published in 1914-1923) by Ivan Kalynovych. Vol. 6 has been: Doroshenko Volodymyr. Goethe v Ukrains'kykh perekladakh, Perespivakh ta Nasliduvanniakh.

The Russian revolution of 1917 and the short-lived period of Independence of Ukraine gave impulse to the flourishing of bibliographic work. This work started in 1918 with the organization in August 1918 of the National Library of the Ukraine. After the collapse of the independent Ukrainian State and the establishment on the eastern territory of the Ukraine the Ukrainian Soviet Republic, first a satellite of the Soviet Russia and after 1923 a constitutent Republic of the USSR, this work was continued.

In March, 1919 in Kyiv the Ukrainian Book Chamber was organized. Its purposes were collecting specimens of all printed matters published in Ukraine, recording, bibliographic description and exchange of books with other institutions. In the same year district Book Chambers were organized in other larger cities of Ukraine. A bibliography of books published in 1919, entitled "Knyzhkovyi Visnyk" (Book Herald) was published.

In connection with transfer of the capital of Ukraine from its historical capital Kyiv to Kharkiv--a new center for bibliographic work was established. It was the Central Department of Bibliography, organized as a section of the Central Ukrainian Publishing House. Ukrainian Book Chamber became a Kyiv Branch of the Central Department of Bibliography.

Programs of this Department included: Collecting of obligatory copies (In all European Countries all publishers are obliged to give a certain library or another institution a certain amount of copies of every publication for distribution to scholarly libraries) of all books published in Ukraine, their bibliographic description, distributing books to scholarly libraries and publishing of bibliographies.

The Central Department of Bibliography planned to publish a monthly bibliography of works published in Ukraine: "Litopys Ukrains'koho Druku" (A Chronicle of Ukrainian Printing). It was planned for 1922. But this exceeded possibilities of the Center and became a dead project.

In 1922 in Kyiv Ukrainian Booklore Institute was organized. The Central Department of Bibliography was not able to fulfill its tasks. Therefore, in 1922, Ukrainian Book Chamber was reinstated as the Central Bibliographic Institution of Ukraine. Its seat was moved to Kharkiv.

In 1923 Ukrainian Book Chamber started publication of the above mentioned "Litopys Ukrains'koho Druku," beginning as a monthly, becoming a semi-monthly and eventually a weekly.

Bibliographic work in Ukraine flourished. All printed output of Ukrainian publishing houses, also Ukrainian publications issued outside the Ukraine was carefully registered and described. General and subject bibliographies were published.

In 1930 Stalin started his crackdown on Ukrainian political, economic and cultural life. Hundreds of thousands of Ukrainian scholars, writers and also bibliographers and librarians were executed, perished in Soviet penal camps or were silenced for decades. All bibliographic work in the Ukraine stopped. So, as before the revolution of 1917, the only systematic sources of the Ukrainian bibliography in Russian-dominated Eastern Ukraine, were central Russian bibliographic publications "Pravytelstvennyi Vistnyk" (Governmental News) and starting from 1907 "Knyzhnaia Letopis" (Book Chronicle). So now, after destroying the entire bibliographic apparatus of the Ukraine, the only source for Ukrainian bibliography was the central Soviet bibliographies, which also registered Ukrainian publications.

In 1934 some bibliographic work had been resumed in the Ukraine. In 1935 the Ukrainian Book Chamber resumed publishing of the Litopys Ukrains'koho Druku. In the same year it started publication of Book Review Index entitled, "Litopys Retsenzii," (A Chronicle of Reviews). It started as a semi-annual and in 1936 changed its frequency to a monthly. In 1936 the Ukrainian Book Chamber started publication of a monthly Index of magazine articles, entitled "Litopys zhurnalnykh stattei" (A Chronicle of Magazine Articles) and in 1937 a similar monthly Index of newspaper articles entitled "Litopys Hazetnykh Stattei." (A chronicle of newspaper articles.) In the same year the Ukrainian Book Chamber started publication of the quarterly "Litopys Obrazotvorchoho Mystetstva" (A Chronicle of the Painting)--an art Index which stopped publication in 1938.

To fill gaps in registration of Ukrainian print in the time of Stalin's purges, 1930-1934, retrospective annual issues of "Litopys Ukrains'koho Druku" for years 1931, 1932, 1933 and 1934 were issued.

Another setback in development of Ukrainian bibliography was the outbreak of the Germany-Soviet war 1941-1945. Entire Ukraine became a battleground. All Ukrainian bibliographic work stopped. Ukrainian book chambers stopped registration of Ukrainian publications and publishing of bibliographic periodicals. Registration of Ukrainian publications issued on Soviet side of battlelines was done by the Book Chamber of Soviet Union in Moscow.

In November, 1943, when the frontlines moved west, the Ukrainian Book Chamber resumed its activities, including receiving and distributing prints issued in Soviet occupied part of the Ukraine (part of the Ukraine was still under German domination) and started renewal of its bibliographic publications.

To fill gaps in Ukrainian bibliography caused by the war, some retrospective annual bibliographies for the years 1941-1943 were published.

In 1948 the Ukrainian Book Chamber renewed publication of its "Litopys Retzenzii." A section of reviews of films and stage performances was added to it later. In 1952 the Chamber renewed publication of its Art Index "Litopys Obrazotvorchoho Mystetstva." In 1954 they started publication of a semi-annual musical index: "Litopys Muzychnoii Literatury" (A chronicle of musical publications.)

Beginning with 1956 the Ukrainian Book Chamber started registration of Ukrainica published in other Soviet Republics and publication of a semi-annual bibliography of these publications entitled "Ukrains'ka RSR u vydanniakh Respublik

Radians'koho Soiuzu" (Ukrainian Soviet Republic in publications of (other) Soviet Republics). In 1957 the Chamber started an annual bibliography of recent books which appeared in the Ukraine, entitled "Knyhy Vydavnytstv Ukrainy" (books published by the Ukrainian Publishing Houses) and in 1959 a popular bi-weekly "Novi Knyhy Ukrainy" (New Books of the Ukraine).

Besides these current bibliographies, many subject bibliographies tied up to specific campaign or propaganda themes also have been published. Many retrospective biblio-graphies have been tied up to the anniversaries of establishing of the Ukraine Soviet Socialist Republic (40th and 50th). There are many bibliographies of works of and on single Ukrainian authors.

But despite all, Ukrainian Soviet bibliography has serious handicaps. It listed only Ukrainian publications published in the Ukraine, and only in 1956 added those published in other Soviet Republics. It excludes publications which are unorthodox from the point of view of the party and government. Bibliographies are published in very limited editions, are kept in files and never published, and some are published only in typed editions. For instance, retrospective bibliography of Ukrainian publications for the years 1917-1923, including more than 10,000 items, was published in 5 typed copies.

Also, outside of the Ukrainian Soviet Republic some bibliographic work has been done--predominantly registration of works published outside the Ukraine. The center of this bibliographic work has been Czechoslovakia, which was a serious center of Ukrainian scholarship abroad. (There have been two Ukrainian schools of higher education: Ukrainian Free University in Prague and Ukrainian Husbandry Academy in Podiebrady.) There they published many subject bibliographies in the form of monographs, articles and parts of books. There have also been efforts at publishing periodical current bibliography. Other centers of Ukrainian bibliography abroad were Germany, with the Ukrainian Scientific Institute in Berlin during the period between two world wars, and in Poland-occupied Western Ukraine, with two scholarly centers--Shevchenko Scientific Society in Lviv and Ukrainian Scientific Institute, outside Western Ukraine, in Warsau.

There had been published two bibliographical periodicals "Ukrains'ka Knyha" (Ukrainian Book) by Shevchenko Scientific Society in Lviv, and "Knyzhka" (Book) published by the very active bibliographer Ivan Chepyha in Stanyslaviv (that city's name at the present: Ivano-Frankivs'ke).

Among other bibliographic publications there appeared a bibliography of Ukrainian Bibliography "Bibliographia Bibliographiae Ukrainicae" compiled by Euhen Julian Pelensky and published in 1934 by the Shevchenko Scientific Society at Lviv.

As in the Ukrainian Soviet Republic, so also outside the Ukraine the second world war caused a setback to Ukrainian bibliography. But pretty soon after the end of the war bibliographic work was resumed in Germany and Austria in the Displaced Persons camps.

One of the most important works of this period was bibliography of Ukrainica in West-European languages compiled by the previously mentioned Euhen J. Pelensky and published in 1948 by the Shevchenko Scientific Society (in Munich) entitled: "Ukrainica v Zakhidno-Europeis'kykh Movakh" (Ukrainica in West-European languages.) It includes 2,600 entries (books and articles in English, French, German and Spanish).

After resettling of most displaced persons from Austria and Germany, bibliographic work started again, predominantly in the U. S. and Canada.

Here have been published many bibliographies, in most cases retrospective and subject bibliographies. Among these are so serious bibliographies as bibliography of the Ukrainian historical literature by Dmytro Doroshenko listing publications from the very beginning to 1917 and by Oleksander Ohloblyn listing Ukrainian historical publications from 1917 until 1953--both published in one volume by the Ukrainian Academy of Arts and Sciences in the U. S. Jurij Lavrinenko published as extensive bibliography of literature on Ukrainian communism entitled: Ukrainian Communism and Soviet Policy toward Ukraine.

There have been published also many other bibliographies like bibliographies of single Ukrainian military formations, Ukrainian memuaristic and others.

There is a bibliography of the Ukrainian periodicals and serials published outside the Soviet Union by Oleksander Fedynskyi: Bibliohrafichnyi pokazhchyk Ukrains'koii Presy poza mezhamy Ukrainy (Bibliography of the Ukrainian Periodicals Published outside the Ukraine) issued annually or bi-annually by the Ukrainian Museum of Cleveland. Until time being issues for the years 1966, 1967 and 1968-69 have been published.

There is a bibliography of the Ukrainica in English by the compiler of this bibliography: "Ukraine: Selected References in the English Language . . ." including not only books but also essays in collections and certain periodicals. Listed are publications issued predominantly outside the Iron Curtain.

The compiler of this bibliography is working also on an "Index of the Ukrainian Essays in Collections, Published outside the Iron Curtain." Up to the present time, the years 1951-62, 1963-64, 1965, 1966, 1967, 1968, 1969 and 1970-71 have been covered.

There are efforts to establish a current bibliography of Ukrainica. The Ukrainian Academy of Arts and Sciences in the U. S. issued in 1960 the first volume of the bibliography of Ukrainica Americana covering 1957, entitled, Ukrains'ka Akademiia Nauk v SShA. Bibliohrafichna Komisiia. Richnyk Ukrains'koii Bibliohrafii za rik 1957. Zladyly Osyp Danko i Myroslav Labunka. This publication was planned as an annual but as yet nothing more has been published.

More successful was the Ukrainian Free Academy of Sciences in Canada, which started in 1952 its annual publication "Slavica Canadiana"" recording publications in Slavic languages issued in Canada, concerning Canada or where at least one author or editor was Canadian.

In 1953 the same Academy started publishing of an annual "Ukrainica Canadiana" based on the same principles as those of the "Slavica Canadiana." Both these publications have been discontinued after issue for 1972.

Systematic sections on certain aspects of Ukrainian bibliography are published in certain American bibliographic publications such as "Bibliographia Americana" published annually by the Modern Languages Teachers Association" or in bibliographic publications like those of the University of Indiana at Bloomington, Indiana.

In the U. S. and Canada some of the bibliographies published before the 1930's in the Soviet Ukraine have been republished. These were bibliographies listing works expurgated during Stalin's purges, which have been out of print or withdrawn from circulation in the USSR.

Some bibliographic work listing Ukrainica Slovakiana is also done in Slovakia where the universities of Bratislava and Preshov are centers of Ukrainian studies.

Bibliographic work done in Ukraine and abroad complement each other to a certain extent, but it is handicapped on both sides of the Iron Curtain --in the Ukraine, by restrictions imposed by party and government and abroad by lack of money necessary to finance bibliographical work, and to publish the compiled bibliographies.

I. SELECTED BIBLIOGRAPHY OF UKRAINIAN BIBLIOGRAPHY.

1. Bibliographies in Ukrainian Language.

1. Akademiia Nauk URSR. Bibliografichna Komisiia. Ukrains'ka Bibliohrafiia u Kyiivi, 1928-1929. Kyiv, 1929- 3v.
   Issued by Bibliographic Commission of the Ukrainian Academy of Arts and Sciences in Kyiiv. Includes subject bibliographies and articles on theory and practice of bibliography.

2. Akademiia Nauk URSR. Kyiv. Biblioteka. 40 rokiv Radians'koii Vlady na Ukraini. Bibliohrafichnyi pokazhchyk. Sklaly V.P. Tytarenko ta inshi. Zahalna redaktsiia O.M. Matviienko. Kyiiv, Vydavnytstvo Akademii Nauk URSR 1958. 445 p.
   Published by the Library of the Ukrainian Academy of Arts and Sciences in Kyiiv. Bibliography of publications concerning the first forty years of the Soviet rule in Ukraine. Chronologically arranged. Author and title index. Supplement.

3. Akademiia Nauk URSR. Derzhavna Publichna Biblioteka. T.H. Shevchenko. Bibliohrafiia Literatury pro Zhyttia i Tvorchist', 1939-1959. Kyiiv, Vydavnytstvo Akademii Nauk URSR, 1963. 2 v.
   Bibliography of publications on the life and works of the prominent Ukrainian poet Taras Shevchenko, issued in years 1939-1959. Published by the Library of the Academy of Arts and Sciences of the Ukrainian Soviet Republic. 5,575 entries. Arranged chronologically by years of publication and chronologically within single years.

4. Andrievskii, Aleksander. Bibliohrafiia Literatury z Ukrain'koho Folkloru. Kyiiv. Vseukrains'ka Akademiia Nauk. Etnohrafichno-Folklorna Komisiia., 1930. 821 p. (its publication no. 17)
   Bibliography of the literature concerning Ukrainian folklore, published by the Commission of the Ethnography and Folklore of the Ukrainian Academy of Arts and Sciences in Kyiiv.

5. Boiko, I. comp. Ukrains'ki Literaturni Almanakhy i Zbirnyky XIX. i pochatku XX. stolittia. Sklav I. Boiko. Kyiiv, Naukova Dumka, 1967. 300 p. facsims.
   Bibliography of Ukrainian literary almanacs and collections published in XIXth and beginning of XXth century. Lists 206 entries. Contents of every almanac or collection is added. Indexes of authors, titles and geographical index supplement bibliography.

6. Chervinska, L.F. and A. I. Dykyi. Pokazhchyk z Ukrains'koii Movy po 1929 rik. Kharkiv, Akademiia Nauk Ukrains'koii RSR, 1929.

Bibliography of works concerning Ukrainian linguistics, published up to 1929. Published by the Ukrainian Academy of Arts and Sciences which was at that time in Kharkiv. It includes two thousand six hundred and sixty-nine entries.

7. Derzhavne Vydavnytstvo Ukrainy. Ukrains'ka Knyha. Systematy-chyni Pokazhchyk Vydan' Ukrains'koiu Movoiu. Kharkiv, Derzhavne Vydavnytstvo Ukrainy, 1926- v.
   Subject arranged bibliography of books published in the Ukraine in the Ukrainian language.

8. Doroshenko, Dmytro. Pokazhchyk Novoii Ukrains'koii Literatury v Rosii za 1798-1897 roky. Chastyna persha. Chernivtsi, Rus'ka Rada, 1917. 68 p.
   List of Ukrainian books published in Russian empire in the years 1798-1897. Chronologically arranged by year. Alphabetically within each year. Eight hundred and ninety-three items listed. Sources and reviews added to almost every item.

9. Fedyns'kyi Oleksander. Bibliohrafichnyi Pokazhchyk Ukrains'-koii Presy poza mezhamy Ukrainy za 1966- rik. Cleveland, Ohio, Ukrains'kyi Muzei-Arkhiv, 1967- v.
   Serial bibliography of Ukrainian periodicals and serials published outside the USSR. Arranged by countries: U. S., Canada and other countries alphabetically arranged by name of country. Periodicals in each country arranged alpha-betically by titles. Included also are periodicals and serials in other languages than Ukrainian. These are arranged in separate alphabet following alphabet with Ukrainian titles. All supplements and pages enumerated.
   Included is information concerning editors, publisher, business office, price, frequency and other.
   Published annually or bi-annually.

10. Ihnatienko. V. Bibliohrafiia Ukrains'koii Presy. 1816-1916. Kharkiv, Akademiia Ukrains'koii RSR, 1930. 2nd facsimile ed. State College, Pa. Nova Ukrainska Knyha, 1968. 285 p.
    Bibliography of Ukrainian periodicals for century 1816-1916.

11. Kataloh Vydan' Ukrains'koii Akademii Nauk, 1918-1930. Pryhotovyv i vydav Dmytro M. Shtohryn. Chicago, Tovarystvo Ukrains'kykh Bibliotekariv Ameryky, 1966. 280, 74 p. (Slovians'ki Bio-Bibliohrafichni Materialy, t.1)
    Offset reproduced catalogs of publications of the Ukrainian Academy of Arts and Sciences in Kyiiv for years 1918-1929 and for the year 1930.
    Contents of each listed entry are included. Added indexes: author and subject, and lists of sections and institutions of Academy and listed titles added.

12. Knyzhkova Palata Ukrains'koii RSR. Khudozhnia Literatura
Vydana na Ukraini za sorok rokiv, 1917-1957. Bibliohrafichnyi pokaznyk. Sklaly O. O. Maiboroda, H. D. Ruban, O. O.
Starchenko. Vidp. redaktor H. O. Kravchenko. Kharkiv,
1958- v.
    Publication of the Book Chamber of the Ukrainian Soviet
Republic. Bibliography of the Ukrainian fiction published
in years 1917-1957. Arranged alphabetically by authors and
titles.

13. Knyzhkova Palata Ukrains'koi RSR. Ukrains'ka Radians'ka
Kultura za 40 rokiv 1917-1957. Vidpovidalnyi Redakt r H. O.
Kravchenko. Kharkiv, 1957-1960. 2 v.
    Publication of the Ukrainian Book Chamber. Bibliography
of publications concerning Ukrainian culture issued in the
years 1917-1957. It includes works on literature, art,
music, societies, recreation, theatre, films, a.o. Subject
arranged. Arranged alphabetically by authors and titles in
the subdivisions.

14. Korolevych, N.F. and F. K. Sarana. Slov'ians'ks Filolohiia
na Ukraini, 1958-1962. Bibliohrafiia. Kyiiv, Vydavnytstvo
Akademii Nauk Ukrains'koii RSR, 1963. 611 p. processed.
(On head of title: Akademiia Nauk Ukrains'koii RSR.
Ukrains'kyi Komitet Slavistiv. Derzhavna Biblioteka.)
    Publication of the Slavistic Committee of the Ukrainian
Academy of Arts and Sciences. Materials predominantly
Ukrainian. Subject arranged bibliography of Ukrainian
Slavistics. Divided in sections: Linguistics, Literature,
folklore, conferences, slavistic general, slavistic
Ukrainian, Russian and other.

15. Lazarevskii. Al. Ukazatel Istochnikov dla Izucheniia
Malorossiiskykh krain. Vypusk I. St. Peterburgh, 1858. 121 p.
    Bibliography of materials for study of Ukraine (called
here: Malorossia--Little Russia). Lists 554 entries--
monographs and articles.

16. Levitskii, Ivan E. Halitsko-Russkaia Bibliografiia XIX-ho
stoletiia z uzhladneniem russkikh izdanii poiavivshikhsia v
Uhorshchini i Bukovine, 1801-1886. Lvov, Iz Typ. Stavropi-
hiiskoho In-ta. 1888-1895. 2v. Reprint: Vaduz, Kraus
Reprints, 1963. 2v in 1
    Bibliography of Ukrainian publications issued in years
1801-1886 in part of Ukraine belonging then to Austro-Hungarian Empire. According to terminology prevailing then in
that part of the Ukraine, he calls his bibliography Ruska
(Ruthenian--equivalent to: Ukrainian.)

17. Litopys Knyh. 1st- 1924- Kharkiv, Knyzhkova Palata
Ukrains'koii RSR, 1924- Monthly.
    Bibliography of all monographic publications published on
territory of the Ukrainian Soviet Republic. Subject

arranged. Full bibliographical description of each entry.
Information about number of issued copies included. Classification number according to decimal system used in
libraries of the USSR added. Author and subject index in
each issue. December issue has cumulative indexes for the
year. Subject arranged list of theses and dissertations
added.

18. Ryeznikov, V. Demohrafiia Ukrainy za 1914-1928 rik: Chastyna
Persha: Knyzhka. Bibliohrafichnyi pokazhchyk. Kyiiv,
Akademiia Nauk Ukrains'koi RSR, 1931. 275 p. (Monographs of
the Social-Economic Department number 33.)
      Publication of the Ukrainian Academy of Arts and Sciences.
Bibliography of works on demography of Ukraine published
in the years 1914-1928. Includes one thousand two hundred
seventy-six entries.

19. Santsevych, Anatol Vasylych. Problemy Istorii Ukrainy Pisla-
voiennoho Periodu v Radians'kii Istoriohrafii. Kyiiv,
Naukova Dumka, 1967. 213 p. (On head of title page:
Akademiia Nauk Ukrains'koii RSR. Instytut Istorii.)
      Bibliography of monographs and articles concerning the
history of the Ukraine in the years after the Second World
War. Publication of the Institute of History of the
Ukrainian Academy of Arts and Sciences in Kyiiv. Added
indexes of authors subject lists of analyzed collections
and listed monographs.

20. Shpilevych, Vira. Bibliohrafiia Ukrains'koii Literatury ta
Literaturoznavstva za 1928 rik. Kharkiv. Ukrains'kyi
Naukovo-Doslidnyi Instytut Knyhoznavstva, 1930. 302 p.
(Pratsi Bibliohrafichnoii Sektsii t.2)
      Bibliography of the Ukrainian literature and works on
Ukrainian literature published in 1928. Published by the
Bibliographic Section of the Ukrainian Research Institute of
Booklore in Kharkiv. Includes three thousand nine hundred
and ninety-five entries.

21. Spysok Literatury Vypushchenoi Vydavnytstvamy Ukrainy. 1st-
1955- Kharkiv, Knyzhkova Palata Ukrainy, 1955- v.
      An annual list of publications issued by the Ukrainian
publishing Houses. Publisher: Book Chamber of Ukraine.
Title varies: Knyhy Vydavnytstv Ukrainy.

22. Ukrains'ka Akademiia Nauk v SShA. Bibliohrafichma Komisiia.
Richnyk Ukrains'koi Bibliohrafii za rik 1957. Zladyly Osyp
Danko i Myroslav Labunka. New York, 1960. 61 p. English
t. p. added.
      Bibliography of Ukrainian books published in the U. S. in
1957. Annotated. Published by the Ukrainian Academy of
Arts and Sciences in the U. S. Planned as annual but only
the issue for 1957 has been published.

2. Bibliographies in Russian Language.

23. Akademiia Nauk SSR. Istoria SSSR-Ukazatel Sovetskoi Litera-
    tury za 1917-1952 gg. Moskva, Izdatelstvo Akademii Nauk SSSR,
    1956. 2 v.
         Publication of the Academy of Arts and Sciences of the
    USSR. Bibliography of publications on the history of the
    USSR and the constituent republics--including Ukrainian
    Republic, published in the years 1917-1952.

24. Akademia Nauk URSR. Kiev. Biblioteka. Knigi Grazhdanskoi
    Pechati 18 Veka; Katalog Knig Khraniashchikhsia v Gosuda-
    stvennoi Publichnoi Biblioteke Ukrainskoi RSR. Sost. S.O.
    Petrov. Kiev, 1956. 300 p.
         Catalog of books--predominantly Russian-and journals con-
    tained in the Ukrainian State Library in Kyiiv. Arranged
    by authors. Indexes. Published by the Library of the
    Ukrainian Academy of Arts and Sciences in Kyiiv.

25. Akademiia Nauk URSR. Biblioteka. Knigi Pervoi Chetverti
    XIX Veka; Katalog Knig Khraniashchikhsia v Gosudarstvennoi
    Publichnoi Biblioteke Ukrainskoi RSR. Sost. S. Petrov. Kiev,
    1961. 398 p.
         Catalog of publications published predominantly in
    St. Petersburg and Moscow during the first quarter of the
    19th century contained in the collection of the Ukrainian
    State Library in Kyiiv. Lists 2,800 works. Arranged al-
    phabetically by authors. Indexes. Catalog published by
    the Library of the Ukrainian Academy of Arts and Sciences
    in Kyiiv.

26. Bibliografiia Sovetskoii Bibliografii. Moskva, Izdatelstvo
    Vsesoiuznoi Kniznoi Palaty, 1946-
         Bibliography of Soviet bibliography. Published by the Book
    Chamber of the Soviet Union. First issue in 1939. Starting
    from 1946 published annually. Classified arrangement.
    Indexes. Includes also Ukrainian bibliographies.

27. Ezhegodnik Knigi SSSR; Sistematicheskii Ukazatel. Moskva,
    Izdatelstvo Vsesoiuznoi Knizhnoi Palaty. 1927-
         Annual selection of the books listed in Knizhnaia Letopis.
    Includes Ukrainian books.

28. Gosudarstvennaia Ordena Lenina Biblioteka SSSR imeni V.I.
    Lenina. Gosudarstvennaia Publichnaia Istoricheskaia Biblioteka
    RSFSR. Istoria SSSR. Annotirovannoi perechen' Russkikh bib-
    liografii Izdannykh do 1965 g. Izdanie 2. pererabotannoie i
    dopolnenoe. Moskva, Izdatelstvo Kniga, 1966. 426 p.
         Bibliography of Russian bibliographies concerning the his-
    tory of Russia and the USSR. Also includes a bibliography
    of the history of the constituent Republics of the USSR.

Ukrainian entries listed under subject headings: <u>Ukraina</u>,
<u>Kuban'</u>, <u>Drevnoie Russkoe Gosudarstvo</u>,--<u>URSR</u>. Included also
bibliographies of single Ukrainian historians entered under
their names.

29. Gosudarstvennaia Ordena Lenina Biblioteka SSSR imeni V.I.
Lenina. <u>Svodnyi Ukazatel Bibliograficheskikh Spiskov i Karto-
tek Sostavlennykh Bibliotekami Sovetskogo Soiuza v Godu</u> . . .
Moskva, Izdatelstvo Kniga, v.
     Annual publication. Arranged by subjects. Within sub-
jects arranged by locations and names of libraries. List
of bibliographies and book lists compiled by libraries of
the USSR. Includes also bibliographies compiled by the
libraries of the Ukraine. So as item number 28, published
by the Central Library of the USSR.

30. <u>Knizhnaia Letopis</u>. Moskva, Izdatelstvo Vsesoiuznoi Knizhnoi
<u>Palaty</u>, 1907-
     A current bibliography published weekly by the Book Chamber
of Soviet Union. Arranged by subjects. Within the subjects,
entries are arranged alphabetically by authors and titles.
Includes all publications issued in the USSR. When publication is in language other than Russian, its language of
publication is indicated in parentheses. Includes all
Ukrainian book production of the USSR.
     There are two annual cumulations of the above mentioned
weekly.

31. <u>Ezhegodnik Knigi SSSR</u>. Sistematicheskii Ukazatel. Moskva,
Izdatelstvo Vsesoiuznoi Knizhnoi Palaty, 1927-
     Annual selection of the books listed in Knizhnaia Letopis.
Includes Ukrainian books.

32. <u>Knizhnaia Letopis</u>. 1st- 1907- Moskva, Izdatelstvo Vsesoiuznoi Knizhnoi Palaty, 1907-
     Annual cumulation of the weekly issues of Knizhnaia Leto-
pis. Starting from 1934, it lists all publications in all
languages published in the USSR. Continuous numbering of
all entries in annual volume. Indexes.

33. <u>Letopis Gazetnykh Stattei</u>. 1st- 1936- Moskva, Izdatelstvo
<u>Vsesoiuznoi Knizhnoi Palaty</u>, 1936-
     Weekly publication of the Book Chamber of the USSR.
Registers articles, essays and documentary materials from
eighty central, republican and provincial newspapers. Includes
Ukrainian newspapers. Subject arranged.

34. Moscow. Publichnaia Biblioteka. <u>Ukrainskaia Literatura Dook-
tiabrskii Period</u>. Rekomendatelnyi Ukazatel. Sostaviteli.
N.Z. Boiko i dr. Moskva, 1957. 179 p. ports.
     List of works of the Ukrainian pre-revolutionary authors
recommended by the Moscow Public Library to its readers.
Lists 22 authors. There is a biography of every listed

author and a list of his recommended works with annotations. Index added.

35. <u>Novi Knigi Ukrainy</u>. Moskva, Mezhdunarodnaia Kniga, 1967- v.
Catalog of new books published in Ukraine. Issued annually by an organization promoting Soviet books and phonorecords abroad.

3. Bibliographies in English Language.

36. Chicago. University. Division of the Social Sciences. <u>Bibliography of Ukraine</u>. New Haven, Human Relations Area Files, 1956. 20 p.
Bibliography of Ukrainica in the area of behavioral sciences.

37. Gregorovich, Andrew. <u>Books on Ukraine and Ukrainians</u>. Toronto, Stadium Research Institute, 1963. 32 p.
Subject arranged selection of 200 titles of Ukrainica in the English language. Brief annotations. Some fiction included.

38. Horak, Stephen M. <u>Junior Slavica</u>. <u>A Selected Annotated Bibliography of Books in English on Russia and Eastern Europe</u>. Rochester, N. Y., Libraries Unlimited, Inc., 1968. 244 p.
Annotated bibliography of books in English language on the Soviet Union and the countries of East and Mid-Eastern Europe. Annotated.
Arranged by broadly subdivided subjects. Includes a separate chapter on Austro-Hungaria (until 1914) and the chapters on European constituents of the USSR (Ukraine, Belorussia and the Baltic and Caucasian Republics). Some material on the Ukraine and Ukrainians included also in some publications listed in Austro-Hungaria and other Eastern and Middle-European states.

39. Jamieson, A. F. ed. <u>A Selective Bibliography of Canadiana of the Prairie Provinces</u>. Winnipeg, Winnipeg Public Library, 1949. 33 p.
This includes publications by inhabitants of the Canadian Prairie Provinces and concerning the ethnic components of the population of Manitoba, Alberta and Saskatchewan. The Ukrainian section compiled by Prof. Dr. Paul Yuzyk.

40. Pelensky, Euhene Iulian. <u>Ukrainika v Zakhidno-Europeis'kykh Movakh</u>. Vybrana Bibliohrafiya. Munchen, Naukove Tovarystvo imeny Shevchenka, 1948. 111 p. (Zapysky ch. 158.)
English t.p. added. A selected bibliography of Ukrainica in Western-European languages. (English, French, German, Italian) without annotations. Includes books, periodicals

and pamphlets. Divided in Twelve broad subject areas.

41. Sokolyszyn, Alexander. Select Bibliography on Ukraine and other Non-Russian Nations in the Soviet Union. New York, Ukrainian Congress Committee of America, 1962. · 7 p.
        Reprint from Congressional Record vol. 108 no. 111, Monday July 2, 1962. Alphabetically arranged by authors and titles. Without annotations. Includes books and pamphlets. Later reprinted a few times in different collections issued by the Ukrainian Congress Committee of America and other publishers.

42. Sokolyszyn, Alexander. Ukrainian Bibliography in the English Language.
        See entry number 1770 in Supplement.

43. Ukrainian Books Recommended to the Public Libraries. Part 1. Fiction. Winnipeg, Ukrainian Free Academy of Sciences, 1957.
        A selected list of Ukrainian fiction recommended for public libraries.

44. Ukrainica Canadiana. Winnipeg, Ukrainian Free Academy of Sciences, 1953-1973.
        Published annually by the Ukrainian Free Academy of Sciences in Winnipeg, Man. A bibliography of Ukrainian books and Ukrainica published in Canada or by Canadian authors. Arranged by broad subjects. Lists books and pamphlets. In the second part of each issue there is a list of new Ukrainian-Canadian periodicals which started publication in current year.
        Published in series: Bibliography, of the Ukrainian Free Academy of Sciences.
        Editor: Prof. Dr. Jaroslav B. Rudnyckyj, Discontinued after 1972 issue.

45. United States Library of Congress. Selected List of Books on Ukraine Published in English, French, German and Italian. Comp. by Sergius Jacobson and Francis J. Whitfield. Washington, D. C., U. S. Govt. Printing Office, 1941. 13 p.
        One hundred books about Ukraine are listed.

46. Weres, Roman. The Ukraine: Selected References in the English Language. With a brief introduction about the Ukraine and Ukrainians. Kalamazoo, Western Michigan University. School of Graduate Studies, 1961. 233 p.
        An enlarged master's thesis submitted through the Department of Librarianship at Western Michigan University to the School of Graduate Studies. An introductory article on Ukraine's history, geography, literature and Ukrainians in the U. S. Bibliography of Ukrainian bibliography in Ukrainian, English and other languages. A review of

Ukrainica in American encyclopedias. Listed are books,
parts of books and articles. In the annex is added a
list of Ukrainian-English language periodicals, a list of
more important Ukrainian libraries and collections of
Ukrainica, a list of Ukrainian Museums and English language
films on Ukrainian topics. The author, title and subject
index in one alphabet.

4. Bibliographies of Ukrainica in other Languages.

47. Buchynsky, Dmytro. Bibliografia Ucrainiana, 1945-1961. Com-
plementaria del "Catalogo de la Exposition de la Obra Impresa
Ucrainana en al Extraniero 1945-1955" del mismo author.
Madrid, Diana, 1962. 311 p.
    At head of title: Ministerio de Education National.
Direction General de Archives y Bibliotecas.

48. Buchynsky, Dmytro, ed. Biblioteca Nacional: Exposicion de la
Obra Impresa Ucrainiana en la Etranjero, 1945-1955; catalogo.
Madrid, Direccion General de Archives y Bibliotecas, 1956.
225 p.
    Subject arranged catalog of the exhibition of Ukrainian
publications in Ukrainian and other languages, published
abroad in 1945-1955. Ukrainian names and titles in Spanish
transliteration with Spanish translation of titles in
parentheses.

49. Hnatyshak, Mykola. Katalog der Ukrainika im der Abteilung
"Ukraine" im Lichte der deutschen Presse und Literatur der
International Presseausstellung 1928 in Koeln. Berlin,
Ukrainisches Wissenschaftliches Institut, 1928. 28 p.
    Catalog of the Ukrainian Section of the International News-
paper and Periodical Exhibition in Koeln, Germany, 1928.
Includes three hundred and sixty-four titles of Ukrainica in
German language.

50. Kral, Jirzi. Geographicka Bibliographie Podkarpatske Rusi
za rok 1923-1926. Universite Charles. Institute Geo-
graphique Tcheque. Praha. Carls University Press, 1928.
54 p.
    Bibliography of travel and geography concerning Car-
pathian Ukraine with two thousand one hundred and seventy-
five titles in Bohemian language, published in 1923-1926,
listed.

51. Neverly, Mikulas. Bibliografia Ukrainik v Slovenskej reci,
1945-1964. Cesko-Slovenska Komisia pro Ukrainsku Filologiu
pri Ustave Svetovei Literatury a Mov Slovenskei Akademii
Vedy. Bratislava, 1965. 197 p.
    Bibliography of Ukrainica published in Slovakian language
in 1945-1964, issued by Commission for Ukrainian filology of
the Institute of World Languages and Literatures of the Slovakian Academy of Arts and Sciences in Bratislava.

52. Sto-padesat let cesko-ukrainskych literarnych styku, 1814-
1964. Vedecko-bibliograficky sbornik. Redakce zborniku a
vedeni bibliografickych praci: Orest Zilynskyj. 1. vyd.
Praha, Svet Sovetu, 1968. 477 p. facsim., plates, ports.
Ukrainian t.p. added.
    Bibliography of Czech-Ukrainian Literary contacts for the
years 1814-1964, published on occasion of the VI International
Congress of Slavists in Praha.
    Lists 3,023 translations from Ukrainian in Bohemian,
4,316 original items in Bohemian language, 571 archival
items. In bibliography have been included: monographs and
articles published in Bohemian language or translated from
Ukrainian, articles and monographs in Ukrainian and Russian languages on Czech-Ukrainian relations and articles on
Ukrainian culture published in Bohemian periodicals.

                Bibliography of Ukrainian Bibliography.

53. Pelenskyi, Ievhen Iulian. Bibliohrafiia Ukrains'koii Bibliohrafii. L'viv, "Biblos," 1934. 198 p.
    A survey of Ukrainian bibliographies in different languages.

II. UKRAINICA IN ENGLISH LANGUAGE BIBLIOGRAPHIES, CATALOGS, UNION
    CATALOGS, INDEXES, ABSTRACTS AND LISTS OF PERIODICALS.

        1. Ukrainica in Bibliographies of Bibliographies.

54. Bibliographic Index: A Cumulative Bibliography of Bibliographies.
    New York, The H. W. Wilson Co., 1937-
        Books, parts of books and articles including bibliographies
    of Ukrainica are listed under the heading "Ukraine."

55. A World Bibliography of Bibliographies and Bibliographical
Catalogues, Calendars, Abstracts, Indexes and the like.
Third and final edition revised and greatly enlarged throughout. Theodore Besterman, ed. Geneva, Societas Biblio-
graphica, 1955-56. 4 v.
   This publication lists books and articles including
bibliographies of Ukrainica--without difference of language--
under the heading "Ukrainian."

2.   Ukrainica in English Language Bibliographies.

56. The American Bibliography of Slavic and East-European Studies.
Languages, Literature, Folkore and Pedagogy. 1st- 1957-
Bloomington, Ind., Indiana University Press, 1957- v.
(Indiana University Publications. Slavic and East-European
Series.)
   In the chapter: Ukrainica monographs and articles on
various aspects of the Ukrainian problem are listed. One
can also find some Ukrainian entries in other chapters.

57. Byrnes, Robert F. Bibliography of American Publications on
East and Central Europe, 1945-1957. Bloomington, Ind.,
Indiana University. Graduate School, 1958. 213 p. (Slavic
and East European Series, XII)
   Subject arranged. A few Ukrainian English language
periodicals analyzed.

58. The Cumulative Book Index. World List of Book in the English
Language. New York, The H. W. Wilson Company, 1898-
   Ukrainica listed under the heading "Ukraine" or under
headings keyed to this heading with cross references. In
the first volumes Ukrainian entries were indexed under the
heading "Ruthenians" with cross references from "Ukraine"
and "Ukrainians" to "Ruthenia."

59. Dossick, Jesse John. Doctoral Research on Russia and the
Soviet Union. New York, New York University Press, 1966(?).
   Arranged by subjects. Lists doctoral dissertations on
USSR and related subjects submitted at American, Canadian
and British universities. Includes dissertations on
Ukrainian topics.

60. Horecky, Paul L. Basic Russian Publications. An Annotated
Bibliography on Russia and the Soviet Union. Chicago, University of Chicago Press, 1962. 313 p.
   Predominantly publications in the Russian language. There
are some entries concerning non-Russian Soviet Republics,
among others Ukraine. Some entries concerning Ukraine are
under the heading "Kyiiv Rus."

61. Institute for the Study of the USSR. <u>Institute Publications,</u>
    <u>1951-1968</u> Munich, 1969, 160 p.

    This is a list of all the Institute Publications. There
    is an author Index and Subject Index (by broad subjects) of
    all monographic publications and articles in the Institute's
    periodicals, serials and collections.

62. Kaye-Kysilevs'kyj, V. J. <u>Ukraine, Russia and other Slavic</u>
    <u>Countries in English Literature</u>; a selected bibliography of
    books, pamphlets, articles, etc., published in English between
    1912-1936. Winnipeg, Ukrainian Free Academy of Sciences,
    1961. 47 p. (Slavistica no. 40)
    Materials arranged by year of publication. Most of the
    included material concerns Ukraine and Ukrainians.

63. Lewanski, Richard C. <u>Bibliography of Slavic Dictionaries.</u>
    New York, Philosophical Library, 1963. 3 v.
    In vol. 2, there is a section listing Ukrainian diction-
    aries.

64. Maichel, Karol. comp. <u>Guide to Russian Reference Books.</u>
    J.S.G. Simmons, ed. Stanford, Hoover Institution on War,
    Revolution and Peace, 1962. 6 v.
    Arranged by subjects. In all volumes numerous Ukrainian
    reference books are listed, predominantly bibliographies.
    There are listed mostly books published in the USSR.
    There are some from outside the USSR. All Ukrainian entries
    are listed under the subject heading "Ukrainian RSR" or
    other Ukrainian entries.

65. Morley, Charles. <u>Guide to Research in Russian History.</u>
    Syracuse, N. Y., Syracuse University Press, 1951. 227 p.
    In the chapter "Regional and ethnographic bibliographies"
    there is a list of Ukrainica, and also some other references
    to Ukrainian problems.

66. New York Public Library. Reference Department. <u>Dictionary</u>
    <u>Catalog of the Slavonic Collection.</u> Boston, G. K. Holland
    Co., 1959. 26 vols. folio.
    This catalog of Slavic collection includes also Ukrainian
    holdings of the New York Public Library.

67. Peel, Bruce Baden. <u>Bibliography of the Prairie Provinces</u>
    <u>to 1953.</u> Toronto, University of Toronto Press, 1956. XIX,
    680 p.
    Also includes Ukrainian publications and Ukrainica.

68. Roberts, Henry, comp. <u>Foreign Affairs Bibliography</u>; a se-
    lected and annotated list of books on international relations.
    New York, Harper and Brothers, for the Council on Foreign
    Relations.

In this bibliography is a list of Ukrainica in different
languages. From subject-heading "Ukraine" there are also
cross-references to different titles in the chapters about
minority problems in Poland and Rumania. The main list of
Ukrainica is in first edition on pages 514-516 and in the
second edition on pages 564-566. Some Ukrainian books are
listed in the chapters about Poland and about the United
States' Foreign Policy.

69. Ruggles, M. J. and V. Mostecky. Russian and East European
Publications in the Libraries of the United States. New York,
Columbia University Press, 1960. 396 p. (Columbia University.
Studies in Library Service.)
     Collections of Ukrainica in the Libraries of the United
States listed on pages 314-316. The number of books and
periodicals available in certain collection arranged by
ranges. F. ex.: From 1,000 to 2,500 volumes or: From 50
to 100 titles.

70. Slavica Canadiana 1st-20 1952-73 Winnipeg, Ukrainian Free
Academy of Sciences, 1952-1973   (Slavistica Series)
     Published annually. A list of publications in Slavic
languages or about Slavic peoples published in Canada or by
authors living in Canada. Includes an extensive treatment
of Ukrainica. Editor of the Ukrainian part Prof. Dr. Jaroslav B. Rudnyckyj from the University of Manitoba. Discontinued after 20th issue.

71. Subject Guide to Books in Print. New York, RR. Bowker.
     Published annually. Lists English language Ukrainica in
print, published in the United States or Canada or imported
from other countries under the heading "Ukraine" with
various subheadings. Many titles concerning Ukrainian problems can be found under headings "Russia," "Soviet Union."
a.o.

72. The United States Catalog: Books in Print January 1, 1928.
New York, The H. W. Wilson Company, 1928. 3,164 p.
     Lists several Ukrainian titles in English and other lan-
guages printed in the United States or Canada or imported,
under the heading "Ruthenians" with cross-references from
the heading "Ukrainian."
     A continuation of the above mentioned Catalog: Cumula-
tive Book Index a World List of Books in the English
Language. New York, N. W. Wilson--lists Ukrainica printed
in the English language under the subject heading
"Ukraine," "Ukrainians" with subdivisions or under other
headings with subdivision: "Ukrainian" with cross-
references from "Ukraine" or "Ukrainian."
     One can find under "Russia" and other similar subject
headings some Ukrainian entries.

73. U. S. Library of Congress. Processing Department. East European Accession List. v. 1- Sept. 1951- Washington, D. C. 1951- v.
   List of publications from ten East European countries other than USSR added to the collection of the Library of Congress. Ukrainian publications listed under the heading "Ukraine" with subdivisions.

74. U. S. Library of Congress. Processing Department. Monthly Index of Russian Accessions. 1st- 1948- Washington, D. C.
   Every issue consists of three parts. Part Al lists monographs. Part B2 lists periodicals. Part C is a subject index to the parts A and B with English subject headings.
   List all publications from the USSR, regardless of languages, added to the collection of the Library of Congress. Includes Ukrainian books published in the USSR.

75. U. S. Library of Congress. Reference Department. Russia; a Checklist Preliminary to a Basic Bibliography of Materials in the Russian Language. Washington, D. C., 1944-1946. 10 pts.
   Also includes non-Russian books among others also Ukrainian.

76. U. S. Library of Congress. Reference Department. Soviet Geography; a bibliography. Washington, D. C., 1951. 2 v.
   Union list of publications on the geography of the USSR. Part 1 is arranged by subjects, part 2 by natural, administrative and economic regions. Ukrainica is listed in both parts.

77. Vertical File Index. A Subject and Title Index to Selected Pamphlet Material. New York., H. W. Wilson. 1932-
   Issued monthly. Lists Ukrainica under the headings "Ukraine," "Ukrainian" with subdivisions and with cross-references to other headings. Sometimes there is valuable material to be found through this source.

3. Ukrainica in Catalogs and Union Catalogs.

78. U. S. Library of Congress. Cyrillic Union Catalog. New York, Readex Microprint Corporation, 1963.
   On microcards. 1,244 cards in 7 boxes. All entries arranged by authors, subjects and titles in separate sections. Includes Ukrainian holdings of the Library of Congress and associated Libraries.

79. United States Library of Congress. The National Union Catalog. A Cumulative Author List Representing Library of

Congress Printed Cards and Titles reported by other American Libraries. Washington, D. C., 1956-

4. Ukrainica in Lists of Periodicals.

80. Ayers, N. W. and Sons. Directory of Newspapers and Periodicals. Philadelphia. N. W. Ayers and Sons, Inc.
    Annual. Ukrainian titles are listed like all others in some places with comment that they are in Ukrainian language.

81. Bruhn, Peter. Gesamtverzeichniss Russischer und Sovietischer Periodika und Serienwerks hrsg. von Werner Philipp. Wiesbaden in Kommission bei O. Harrasowitz, 1960.- v.
    Union Catalog. Includes Ukrainian periodicals and serials available in German libraries.

82. Gazety i Zhurnaly SSSR. Moskwa. Mezhdunarodnaia Kniga.
    Annual publication listing periodicals and serials published in the USSR. Published by Soviet official agency promoting sales of Soviet books and phonorecords abroad. Arrangement: All-Union and published in RSFSR. Separate sections for periodicals published in single Soviet Republics including Soviet Ukrainian Republic. Lists of All-Union and RSFSR publications in languages: Russian, English, French, German and Spanish. Prices for different countries indicated.

83. Institute for the Study of the USSR. Ukazatel Sovetskoi Periodicheskoi Pechati.
    1,208 Nazvanii Sovetskikh Gazet i zhurnalov v alfavitnom poriadke po mestu vykhoda, po znacheniiu i rozprostraneniu, po nazvaniu. Munich, 1954. 151 p.
    Index of 1,208 most important Soviet periodicals and serials arranged alphabetically by place of publication, importance, circulation and by titles. Published by the Institute for the Study of the USSR. Ukrainian periodicals and serials published in the USSR included.

84. Knyzhkova Palata Ukrains'koii RSR. Periodychni Vydannia URSR, 1918-1950. Zhurnaly. Bibliohrafichnyi Dovidnyk. Vidpovidalnyi redaktor: Kravchuk. Kharkiv, 1956, 461 p. illus.
    Bibliography of periodicals published in Ukraine in 1918-1950. Includes 2,877 items. Alphabetically arranged. Added indexes: subject, geographical and chronological. Published by the Bookchamber of the Ukrainian Soviet Republic.

85. New Serial Titles. A Union List of Serials. Washington, D.C., U. S. Library of Congress, 1949-

Published irregular. List new titles of periodicals and serials added to the periodical collections in American and Canadian Libraries, not included in previous issues. Ukrainian periodicals and serials listed in general alphabet by titles. Subject index arranged according to the Dewey classification. For Ukrainica look in corresponding Dewey Classes.

86. Presa Ukrains'koii RSR. Statystychnyi Dovidnyk. Ukladachi: M. I. Bryzhunova, M. A. Nyzovyi, Yu.B. Medvediev. Vidp. redaktor V. M. Skachkov. Kharkiv, Knyzhkova Palata Ukrains'- koii RSR. Komitet po Presi pry Radi Ministriv URSR, 1967. 147 p.
    Bibliography of periodicals published in Ukraine in 1917-1966. Published by the Book Chamber of the Ukrainian Soviet Republic.

87. Ukrainica Canadiana. 1st- 1952- Winnipeg, Ukrainian Free Academy of Sciences. 1952-1973 (Its series: Bibliography.)

88. Ulrich's Periodical Directory: a Classified Guide to a Selected List of Current Periodicals, Foreign and Domestic. 1st- New York, R.R. Bowker. 15th ed.--1973-74. 2,706 p.
    Published irregularly. Subject arranged. Alphabetical index. Lists some Ukrainian periodicals published in the English language in the United States and abroad.

89. Union List of Serials in Libraries of the United States and Canada. Second edition by Winifred Gregory and an Advisory Committee appointed by the American Library Association. New York, H. W. Wilson, 1943. 3,052 p.
        1st Supplement: January 1941-December 1943. New York, H. W. Wilson, 1945. 1,365 p.
        2nd Supplement: January 1944-December 1949. New York, H. W. Wilson, 1953. 1,365 p.
    Lists holdings of the Ukrainian periodicals and serials in the Libraries of the U. S. and Canada in common alphabet.

90. United States Library of Congress. Cyrillic Bibliographic Project. Serial publications of the Soviet Union, 1939-1957. A bibliographic checklist compiled by Rudolph Smith. Washington, D. C., 1957. 459 p.
    Among periodicals published in all of the European languages of the Soviet Union lists periodicals published in the Ukraine and elsewhere in the Ukrainian language.

91. United States Library of Congress. Slavic and Central European Division. East and East Central Europe Periodicals in English and other West European Languages. Comp. by Paul Horecky. Assisted by Janina Wojcicka. Washington, D. C., 1958. 126 p.

Ukrainian periodicals belonging to this category included.

92. U. S. Library of Congress. Slavic and East European Division. Russian, Ukrainian and Belorussian Newspapers, 1917-1953. A Union list compiled by Paul L. Horecky. Washington, U. S. Government Printing Office, 1956. 218 p.

Includes Ukrainian newspapers published in the Ukraine during the above mentioned period, available in American and Canadian libraries. Arranged alphabetically by titles in one common Soviet list.

93. United States Library of Congress. Slavic and East European Division. The USSR and Eastern Europe: Periodicals in Western Languages. Ed. by Robert G. Carlton. Washington, The Library of Congress, 1965. 204 p.

Lists Ukrainian periodicals in English and other western languages.

94. World List of Scientific Periodicals Published in the Years 1900-1960. Fourth Ed. Washington, D. C. Butterworth's, 1965. 3 v.

Alphabetically arranged. Lists many Ukrainian periodicals and serials. As all other similar lists with alphabetical arrangement, it is difficult to use because of the lack of any subject indexes. It is easiest to locate Ukrainian titles beginning with such distinctive words as "Ukrainskyi." "Zapysky" (Reports), "Annaly" (Annals), "Pratsi" (Works), etc., indicating that it is an Ukrainian publication.

5. Ukrainica in Indexes and Abstracts.

95. Bulletin of the Public Affairs Information Service. 1st- 1915- New York, Public Affairs Information Service, 1915-

Subject arranged. Lists articles, pamphlets, books and parts of books. Lists Ukrainica under the subject heading "Ukraine" and other similar headings or under subject headings keyed to these by cross-references.

96. Dissertation Abstracts: A Guide to Dissertations and Monographs Available in Microfilm. 1st- 1952. Ann Arbor, Mich., University Microfilms, Inc., 1952-

Abstracts of doctoral dissertations and other monographs microfilmed by publisher. Subject arranged. Indexes. Annual cumulations. Cumulative indexes. Ukrainica listed under subject headings "Ukraine" and other similar.

97. Historical Abstracts, 1775-1945. Bibliography of the World Periodical literature. Erich H. Boehm, ed. v. 1. no. 1- March, 1955- Santa Barbara, Cal., Clio Press with the International Social Science Institute, 1955. Quarterly.

An abstract journal with signed abstracts contributed by scholars mainly from the United States. Some Ukrainica abstracted. Five annual indexes.

98. Index of the Ukrainian Essays in Collections Published outside the Iron Curtain in Year . . . Roman Weres, comp. Chicago, Association of Ukrainian Librarians in America, 1967-
   v. (Ukrainian bibliography. Microfilm series.)
   Analyses collections of essays, the Festschrifts, and serial publications of the Ukrainian scholarly institutions. Also includes calendars, almanacs and more important Ukrainian periodicals. Analyses only non-fiction material without regard to the language of publication. Alphabetically arranged by English subjects. The transliteration system of the Ukrainian alphabet of the New York Public Library is used.
   Available in microfilm or Xerox from the University Microfilms, Inc., Ann Arbor, Michigan. To date years covered are 1951-1971.

99. International Index. A Quarterly Guide to Periodical Literature in the Social Sciences and Humanities. New York, The H. W. Wilson Company, 1907-
   Indexes a few Ukrainian periodicals.

100. Litopys Hazetnykh Stattei 1st- 1937- Kharkiv, Knyzhkova Palata Ukrains'koii RSR, 1937- Bi-weekly.
   Index of articles in newspapers published on territory of the Ukrainian Soviet Republic. Completely analyzes only "Republican" (central) newspapers. From district (Oblast) newspaper lists only articles of literary value and articles concerning district of publication. Subject arranged. List of analyzed newspapers and author index added to each issue. Last issue of each year has cumulative indexes.

101. Litopys Zhurnalnykh Stattei. 1st- 1936- Kharkiv, Knyzhkova Palata Ukrains'koii RSR, 1936- Bi-weekly.
   Index of the magazine articles. Published same as Litopys Hazetnykh Stattei by the Book Chamber of the Ukraine. Lists articles of permanent or literary value from magazines, scholarly serials, almanacs and other collections. Subject arranged. List of analyzed titles, author and geographical index included in each issue. Cumulative indexes added to last issue of each year.

102. Readers Guide to Periodical Literature. New York, The H. W. Wilson Company, 1900-
   Does not index any periodical devoted chiefly to Ukrainian problems, therefore, does not have many Ukrainian entries, except during periods when the Ukrainian problem was a center of interest such as in the years 1918-1920 and 1939-1945. Ukrainian entries listed under subject

headings "Ukraine," "Ukrainians," their subdivisions and
headings keyed to these.

103. Ukrainian Quarterly. 1st- 1944- New York, Ukrainian Congress Committee of America, 1944-
     Has chapter on "Ukrainica in foreign periodicals" in
each issue with abstracts of articles in English language
periodicals.

6. Ukrainica in Book Review Digests.

104. The Book Review Digest. New York, H. W. Wilson Company,
1905-
     Reviews concerning Ukrainica are entered under subject
heading "Ukraine," "Ukrainian" and similar.

105. Litopys Retsenzii. Kharkiv, Knyzhkova Palata Ukrains'koii
RSR, 1936-
     Index of book reviews. Published by the Book Chamber of
the Ukrainian Soviet Republic. Reviews of films and stage
performances included. Indexes of authors of reviewed
items, reviewers and reviewed titles added. Numbering of
entries annual.

Ukrainica in Reference Books.

1. Ukrainica in English Reference Books.

Education.

106. UNESCO. International Yearbook of Education. Paris, UNESCO,
1948-
     In each issue contains information about the Ukrainian
educational system, based on official Soviet figures, under
the heading "Ukraine."

107. The World of Learning. 1st- 1947- London, Europa Publications, Ltd. 1947-
     Ukrainian colleges, universities, research institutes,
museums, libraries, etc. are listed among other Soviet
institutions in section about the USSR, arranged alphabetically by cities in one Soviet alphabet.

Folklore.

108. Frazer, Sir James George. The Golden Bough: a Study in Magic
and Religion. Third ed. London, Macmillan, 1907-1915. 12 v.
St. Martin's Press, 1955. 13 v.

109. Frazer, Sir James George. <u>The New Golden Bough</u>; a new
abridgement of the classic work. Ed. with notes and foreword by Theodore H. Gaster. New York, Criterion, 1959.
738 p.
    Both works deal with folklore of all times and peoples.
There are some Ukrainian entries under the headings
"Ruthenians," "Ukrainians," "Galicia," a.o.

Gazeteers.

110. <u>Columbia Lippincott Gazeteer of the World</u>. Ed. by Leon E.
Seltzer with the Geographical Research Staff of the
Columbia University Press and with the cooperation of the
American Geographical Society. Also 1961 suppl. New York,
Columbia University Press, 1962. 2,148 p. 23 pl.

111. <u>Websters Geographical Dictionary</u>: A Dictionary of Names
of Places with Geographical and Historical Information and
Pronunciation. Rev. ed. Springfield, Mass., G. and C.
Merriam Publishing Company, 1962. 1,293 p. Maps.
    Both gazeteers contain information about Ukrainian
cities, rivers, mountains, counties and districts. The
name of the country is given as The Ukrainian Soviet
Socialist Republic. The transliteration of the geographical names is partly Russian, partly Polish.

Libraries.

112. <u>World Guide to Libraries</u>. Compiled by Klaus G. Saur. 2nd
ed. Part 1. Europe. New York, R. R. Bowker Co.,
Muenchen-Pullach, Verlag Dokumentation, 1968. 861 p.
    T. P. in English and German. Ukrainian libraries
listed under USSR. Libraries arranged alphabetically by
cities. No libraries of Lviv or of other West Ukrainian
cultural centers listed.

Language and Literature.

113. <u>Cassells Encyclopedia of Literature</u>. Ed. Siegfried Henry
Steinberg. London, Cassell, 1953. 2 v.

114. <u>Cassell's Encyclopedia of World Literature</u>. New York, Funk
and Wagnalls Company, 1954. 2 vols.
    Both editions include in vol. 1 a brief article with
a survey of Ukrainian literature from the 14th century.

115. <u>Columbia Dictionary of Modern European Literature</u>. Ed. by
Horatio Smith. New York, Columbia University Press, 1947.
899 p.

Contains a short outline of the history of Ukrainian literature beginning with the 19th century.

116. Guide to Slavonic Literatures. Ed. by Reginald de Bray. London, Dent & Sons, Ltd., 1951. 979 p.
    On pp. 69-128 there is a brief outline of Ukrainian history, Ukrainian language, the alphabet and the principles of Ukrainian grammar. Contains selected Ukrainian texts. The author implies that the Ukrainian language came into existence after 1240.

Music.

117. The International Cyclopedia of Music and Musicians. Revised ed. New York, Dodd, Mead and Company, 1952, 2,385 p.
    Contains an article on Soviet music which includes information on many Ukrainian composers.

Slavistics.

118. Strakhovsky, Leonid. A Handbook of Slavic Studies. Cambridge, Harvard University Press, 1949. 753 p.
    Separate chapter on studies of the Ukrainian language and literature.

2. Ukrainian Reference Books.

119. Entsyklopediia Ukrainoznavstva v dvokh tomakh. Pid holovnoiu redaktsiieiu Dra. Volodymyra Kubiovycha i Dra. Zenona Kuzeli. Muenchen, Naukove Tovarystvo imeny Shevchenka, 1949. 2 v.
    Arranged by broad subjects covering all aspects of the Ukrainian problem.

120. Entsyklopedia Ukrainoznavstva. Slovnykova chastyna. Holovnyi Redaktor Prof. Dr. Volodymyr Kubiovych. Muenchen (Dla Naukovoho Tovarystva imeny Shevchenka) Vydavnytstvo: Molode Zhyttia, 1955.
    Issued in parts. In progress. Dictionary arrangement by small subjects.

121. Petrovskyi, Oleksander. Pysmennyky Radians'koi Ukrainy. Bibliohrafichnyi Dovidnyk. Kyiv, Radianskyi Pysmennyk, 1966. 798 st.
    Alphabetically arranged by names of authors. Besides the bibliography of author's works, his biography and portrait are added. Revised ed. 1970.

122. Plevako, Mykola A. Statti, Rozvidky i bio-bibliohrafichni
     materialy. New York-Paryzh, 1961. 808 p. (Ukrains'ka
     Vilna Akademiia Nauk v SShA. Seria: Z nashoho mynuloho
     ch. 2)
         Articles on Ukrainian authors and bibliographies of
     their works. Includes the period of 1940. (Author died
     in exile in 1941.) Biography and bibliography of author.
     French resume .

123. Ukraine: A Concise Encyclopedia. Prepared by Shevchenko
     Scientific Society. Ed. by Volodymyr Kubijovyc. Foreword
     by Ernest J. Simmons. Published for the Ukrainian National
     Association. Toronto, University of Toronto Press, 1963-
     1970. 2 vol.
         Arranged by broad subjects dealing with all aspects of
     Ukrainian problem. Bibliographies added to all more
     important articles.

124. Ukrains'ka Radians'ka Entsyklopedia. Kyiiv, Akademiia
     Nauk Ukrains'koii RSR, 1959-1964. 17 v.
         General Encyclopedia published by the Ukrainian Academy
     of Arts and Sciences. Alphabetically arranged. Vol. 17
     deals with all aspects of the Ukrainian Soviet Republic.

125. Ukrains'ki Pys'mennyky. Bio-bibliohrafichnyi slovnyk u
     p'yaty tomakh. Red. O. I. Bilets'kyi. Kyiiv, Derzhavne
     Vydavnytstvo Khudoznoii Literatury, 1960-1965. 5 v.
         In volume 1 are arranged alphabetically in two separate
     alphabets works of original Ukrainian literature from
     11-14 and 15-18 centuries. Conforming to the official
     Soviet theory editor stresses in preface that literature
     of 11-14 centuries shall be considered as common good of
     the three East-Slavic peoples: Ukrainian, Russian and
     Belo-Russian. Translated works of 11-18 centuries are
     arranged in separate alphabets. In separate alphabets
     are arranged notes describing old manuscripts and old
     prints. A list of works on history of literature of this
     period completes this volume.
         Volumes 2-5 contain alphabetically arranged entries for
     Ukrainian authors of the 19 and 20 centuries.

I. UKRAINE: NAME.

126. Rudnyckyi, Jaroslav B. The Term and Name "Ukraine."
Winnipeg, Ukrainian Free Academy of Sciences, 1951. 32 p.
(Ukrainian Free Academy of Sciences. Onomastica no. 1)
    Explanation of name: Ukraine.

127. Simpson, George W. The Names "Rus," "Russia," "Ukraine"
and Their Historical Background. Winnipeg, Ukrainian Free
Academy of Sciences, 1951. 22 p. (Ukrainian Free Academy
of Sciences. Slavistica, 10.)
    The author discusses the meaning of these terms and
    states that the term "Rus" was never used in medieval
    time as the name of "Russia."

128. Smal-Stocki, Roman. The Origin of the Word "Rus." Winnipeg, Ukrainian Free Academy of Sciences, 1949. 24 p.
(Ukrainian Free Academy of Sciences. Slavistica no. 6)
    The author discusses the origin of the name of the
    Ukrainian medieval state "Rus."

129. Chubatyj, Nicholas. "The Meaning of 'Rus' and 'Ukraine'."
Ukrainian Quarterly 1:351-354. September, 1945.
    Author discusses terms "Rus" and "Ukraine." He states
    that "Rus" was used exclusively for Ukraine. Term
    "Russia" was introduced by Peter the Great.

130. Horbay, Dimitri. "Names of Nations and Imperialistic
Intrigue." Svoboda-Ukrainian Weekly nos. 205, 214, 219,
224, 229, 234, 239- 1958.
    The author states that the imperialistic neighbors of
    the Ukraine use different names for the Ukraine for their
    imperialistic purposes.

131. Kovaliv, Panteleymon. "Name of Ukraine in Foreign Languages." Ukrainian Quarterly 6:346-351. August, 1950.
    Author traces names of Ukraine in foreign languages up
    to the establishment of the present name "Ukraine."

132. Smal-Stocki, Roman. "Terminological Problems of Eastern
European History" Svoboda-Ukrainian Weekly 1957, nos. 66,
71, 76, 80, 85, 90, 100, 104, and 109.
    The author compares the historical and geographical
    terminology in the East European, especially Ukrainian
    and Byelorussian area and makes his proposals for the
    establishment of a simplified but more accurate termi-
    nology.

II. UKRAINE - GEOGRAPHY.

1. Geography - General.

133. Chicago. University. Division of Social Sciences. Aspects of Contemporary Ukraine. Prepared at the University of Chicago. Faculty Committee: Beet F. Roselik and others. Director. Abraham A. Hurvich. New Haven, Conn. Human Relation Files, 1955. 505 p.
    Fully up-to-date information on contemporary Ukraine.

134. Great Britain Foreign Office. Historical Section. The Ukraine. London, His Majesty's Stationary Office, 1920. 110 p. (Great Britain Foreign Office Handbook no. 52.)
    Handbook of data concerning Ukraine compiled for the use of British officials.

135. Lviv: A Symposium on Its 700 Anniversary. New York, published under the sponsorship of the Alumni of Higher Education in Lviv, 1962. 397 p. 29 plates.
    At head of title: Shevchenko Scientific Society. Editor in chief: Wasyl Mudry. English editor: Roman Olesnicki.
    Includes articles dealing with different aspects of Lviv as: archeology, history, economics, cultural life, population a.o. written by prominent Ukrainian scholars.

136. Mirchuk, Ivan, ed. Ukraine and Its People. Munich, Ukrainian Free University Press, 1949. 280 p.
    Handbook about Ukraine: population, characteristics of the Ukrainian people, Ukrainian culture, history of the Ukraine, the social structure of the Ukraine. Physical, political and economic geography of the Ukraine. The causes and the present status of the Ukrainian emigration.

137. Rudnitsky, Stephen. The Ukraine, the Land and Its People. New York, Rand McNally Co., 1918. 4, 1, 369 p. maps.
    Physical, political and economic geography of Ukraine. Anthropogeography, bibliographies, maps.

138. Ukrainian Economic Bureau. Ukrainian Statistical Annual 1st. Warszawa, 1933.

139. ----- Second Ukrainian Statistical Annual. Warszawa, 1934. 173 p.

140. ----- Third Ukrainian Statistical Annual. Warszawa, 1935. 269 p.

141. ----- Fourth Ukrainian Statistical Annual. Warszawa. 1937.

All of these annuals deal with all aspects of Ukrainian economic and cultural life. Captions under statistical tables in Ukrainian and English.

142. Koenig, Samuel. "Geographic and Ethnic Characteristics of Galicia." Journal of Central European Affairs. I:55-65. 1941.
   The name, history and population of the Eastern Halychyna (Galicia).

143. Kubiyovych, Volodymyr. "The Ukraine and the 1959 Census." Ukrainian Review (Munich) 9:19-25. 1960.

144. Lenkavskyi, Stepan. "Changes in the Population Statistics of Ukraine." Ukrainian Review (London) 6:21-33. 1959 no. 3. Bibl. footn.

145. Ukrainian Congress Committee of America. Facts about Ukraine and the Ukrainian People. Published on the occasion of the 50th anniversary of the Ukrainian national revolution, March, 1917-March, 1967. New York, 1967. Folder.

2. Ukraine - Description and Travel.

146. Guillaume Le Vasseur Sieur de Beauplan. A Description of Ukraine. Ed. Oleksander Sokolyszyn. New York, Organization for the Defense of Four Freedoms of Ukraine., 1958. 29 p.
   Translation of a description of the Ukraine by a French engineer who built fortifications in the Ukraine during the 17th century.

147. Heisler, J. B. and J. E. Mallon. Under the Carpathians: Home of the Forgotten People. London, Drummond, 1946. 123 p.
   Description of Carpathian Ukraine.

148. Kumar, Padma Sinansankar Menon. Russian Panorama. London-Bombay, Oxford University Press, 1962. 278 p.
   Author--an Indian Ambassador to the USSR during the years 1952-1962, describes the USSR on the basis of his extensive travels and shows excellent understanding of nationality problems of the USSR.
   He gives a good description of the Ukraine, of its most important cities, and of the Ukrainian antiquities and architecture.

149. McBride, Robert Medill. Romantic Czechoslovakia. New York, Robert M. McBride and Company, 1930. 220 p.

History and description of Carpathian Ukraine in a
separate chapter. Because of the official Czechoslovakian term "Podkarpatske Russko" author considers inhabitants of the Carpatho-Ukraine to be Russians.

150. MacDuffie, Marshall. The Red Carpet. New York, Norton and
Co., 1955. 330 p.
Former head of the UNNRA mission in the Ukraine has
many references to the Ukraine in his book about the USSR.
Stresses the friendliness and hospitality of the
Ukrainians.

151. Mothersole, Jessie. Czechoslovakia Land of the Unconquerable Ideal. New York, Dodd, Mead and Company, 1926.
296 p.
In the chapter about the Carpatho-Ukraine there is a
short history of the area. Descriptions of the capital
city--Uzhhorod and other cities and towns, of the mountains, costumes and customs. Illustrated.

152. Sichynsky, Volodymyr. Ukraine in Foreign Comments and
Descriptions from the Sixth to the Twentieth Century.
New York, Ukrainian Congress Committee of America, 1953.
236 p. illus., maps.
References to the Ukraine from the works of foreign
writers. Illustrations and maps contemporary to writers.
Includes index, maps and bibliography.

153. Van der Post Laurens. A View of All the Russias. New York,
William Morrow and Company, 1964. 364 p. map.
Travelogue through all parts of the USSR. Some chapters deal with Ukraine. Description of some parts of
the Ukraine and of life in the Ukraine. Author does not
distinguish clearly between the Ukrainians and Russians.

154. Mladenovic, M. "An Unnoticed Description of Kiev in 1812-
1813." New Review: 290-294, no. 4/37, 1969.

155. Procko, Bohdan.P. "Ukraine 1967. A Historian's Personal
Impression" Ukrainian Quarterly 24:253-264. Autumn, 1968.

156. Shulgin, Basil. "Kyiv Mother of Russian Towns." Slavonic
and East European Review. XIX:62-82 (Slavonic Yearbook)
A description of Kyiv. The author, a Russian, considers Kyiv to be a Russian city.

157. Sichynsky, Volodymyr. "Edward Daniel Clarke's Journey in
the Crimea." Ukrainian Quarterly 11:264-269, Summer,
1965.

158. Wacyk, Nicholas. "Edward Gibbon on Ukraine." Ukrainian
Quarterly 26:69-72, 1970.

3.   Ukraine - Atlases, Maps and Pictorial Albums.

159.   Boretsky, M. ed. Ukraine in Pictures. New York, M. Boretsky, 1954. 255 p.
    About twelve hundred two-tone pictures, concerning
    Ukrainian history, geography, culture and the arts. The
    captions under the pictures are in Ukrainian and English.

160.   Kubijovvch, Volodymyr. Atlas of Ukraine and Adjoining
    Countries. Lviv, Ukrainskyi Vydavnychyi Instytut, 1937.
    LXII, 62 p.
    Maps concerning physical, political and economic geo-
    graphy of the Ukrainian ethnographic territory.

161.   Kubijovych, Volodymyr. Etnichni Hrupy Pivdenno-Zakhidnoii
    Ukrainy (Halychyny) na 1.1. 1959. Ethnic groups of the
    South-Western Ukraine (Halychyna-Galicia) on the 1st
    January, 1939. London-Munich-New York-Paris, Association
    of Ukrainians Former Combatants in Great Britain. 15 p.
    (Text in pamphlet form) (Memoirs of the Shevchenko Scien-
    tific Society vol. 160)
    Scale 1: 250,000. Includes pamphlet with text in
    English.

162.   League of Americans of Ukrainian Descent; Chicago, Ill.
    The Map of Ukraine compiled and drawn by William Karpa.
    Chicago, 1955.
    A political map of the Ukraine with an extra ethno-
    graphic map added. Ukrainian geographic terminology
    used. Information about Ukraine by Professor Lev E.
    Dobriansky of Georgetown University added.

163.   "Lviv in Pictures." In Lviv (See entry no. 135.) 29 plates.
    An illustrated supplement to monograph: Lviv (see
    entry no. 135).

164.   Simpson, George W. Ukraine: a series of maps and explana-
    tions indicating historic and contemporary geographical
    positions of the Ukrainian people.
    Fifteen historical maps of the Ukraine from the very
    early times to the present. Two-tone maps with histori-
    cal notes for each.

III. UKRAINE - ECONOMY.

1. Ukraine - Economic and Social History.

165. Czyrowski, Nicholas L. Fr. Old Ukraine--Its Socio-Economic History Prior to 1781. Madison, Florham Park Press, Inc. 1963. 432 p.

   In his book the author depicts the socio-economic history of Ukraine from its very beginning until 1781 when the territory of the Ukraine was incorporated into Russia and during the period from 1917-1918 to the present.

   The author proves that the Ukraine strove all the time for economic independence and that its economic potential was always adequate enough to enable the Ukraine to lead an independent state existence.

166. Lyashchenko, Peter J. History of the National Economy of Russia to the 1917 Revolution. New York, MacMillan Company, 1949. 880 p.

   Many references to the Ukraine concerning the history of the Ukrainian economy, especially Polish and Russian colonialism in the Ukraine, peasant unrests and the development of Ukrainian industry.

167. Ohloblyn, Oleksander. "Study of Ukrainian Economic History." New Review. 3:13-18. 1963, no. 6.

168. Prociuk, Stepan Y. "Economic Development of the City of Lviv" in Lviv (see entry no. 135). p. 370-395.

169. Shcherbakivsky, Vadym. "The Early Ukrainian Social Order Reflected in Ukrainian Wedding Customs" Slavonic and East European Review. 31:325-351. June, 1953.

   The early Ukrainian social order reconstructed from present-day Ukrainian wedding customs. The author stresses differences between Ukrainian and Russian social conceptions.

170. Vernadsky, George. "On Feudalism in Kievan Russia." American Slavic and East European Review. 7: 1-14, 1948.

   According to the author the Kievan medieval state was not a feudal but rather a capitalistic state. Feudalism developed in the Suzdal Principality and in the Western-Ukrainian (Halych-Volynia) Principality.

171. Vernadsky, George. "Royal Servs (Servi Regales) of the Ruthenian Law and Their Origin." Speculum 26: 255-265. April, 1951.

   Concerns the semi-free population of certain villages in Western Ukraine, who in the 15th century were in the immediate service of the Polish kings as border guards, mail carriers, etc.

172. Vernadsky, George. "Three Notes on the Social History of the Kievan Russia." Slavonic and East European Review. 22: 81-92. December, 1944.
     The author deals with the special classes of society in the Kyivan medieval state: Kolopy and Vdakhy (slaves) smerdy and khopy (semi-slaves) and Ishoii (free slaves and outcasts).

2. Ukraine - Economy General.

173. Koval, Lubomyr M. "Mykhailo Ivanovych Tuhan-Baranovsky; his political, teaching, scientific and cooperative activity in Ukraine, 1917-1919." Ukrains'kyi Tekhnichno-Hospodars'kyi Instytut. Naukovi Zapysky. 18: 52-168. 1968-1969. Bibl. footn. Ukrainian resume' p. 66-68.
     Concerns prominent Ukrainian economist. Two chapters from unpublished doctoral dissertation of author: Economic Doctrines of M. I. Tuhan-Baranovsky. Urban, University of Illinois, 1965.

174. Marchenko, V. "The Role of Ukraine in the Recent Five-Year Plan." Ukrainian Quarterly. 5: 122-134. Spring, 1949.

175. Melnyk, Z. L. "Financial Relations Between Ukraine and Moscow in 1959-1961." Ukrains'kyi Tekhnichno-Hospodars'kyi Instytut. Naukovi Zapysky. 18: 21-58. 1968-1969. Charts, bibl., footn. Ukrainian resume' p. 48-51.

176. Olesnicki, Roman. "The Ukrainian Cooperative Movement." Ukrainian Quarterly. 2: 36-42. Autumn, 1945.

177. Pavliuk, Mykhailo. "Failure of Moscow's attempt to depreciate the economic importance of the Ukraine." Ukrainian Quarterly. 16: 234-262, Autumn, 1960. Bibl., footn.

178. Pidlusky, Bohdan J. "Analysis of the Economic Growth of the Ukrainian Socialist Soviet Republic since World War I." Horizons 3: 68-80. 1962, 1-2.

179. Prociuk, S. Yu. "Planned Economy in the Ukraine." Ukrainian Review (Munich) 1: 29-37. 1955. Bibl., footn.

3. Ukraine - Agriculture.

180. Baclawski, Joseph Andrew. The Soviet Conservation Program for Steppe and Wooded Steppe Regions of the European Part

of the USSR. Ann Arbor, Michigan, University of Michigan,
1951. 194 p.
   Unpublished doctoral dissertation, available in microfilm or Xerox from University Microfilms, Inc., Ann Arbor,
   Mich. Abstract in dissertation Abstracts vol. 11, 1951,
   p. 639. (no. 2,571).

181. Below, Fedor. History of a Soviet Collective Farm. New
York, Frederick Praeger. Published for the Research Program
on the USSR, 1956. 237 p.
   The history of a Ukrainian village: the administrative
   system of a collective farm as depicted by a former
   chairman.

182. Field, Neil Collard. The Role of Irrigation in the South
European USSR in Soviet Agricultural Growth; an Appraisal
of the Resources, Base and Development Problem. Seattle,
University of Washington, 1956. 229 p.
   Unpublished doctoral dissertation. Available in
   microfilm or Xerox from University Microfilms, Inc., Ann
   Arbor, Mich. Abstract in: Dissertation Abstracts vol.
   17, 1958. (Publication no. 20.378.)
   Deals with the irrigation problem, predominantly in
   the Southern Ukraine.

183. Frank, Andrew Gunder. Growth and Productivity in Ukrainian
Agriculture and Industry. Chicago, University of Chicago,
1957. 229 p.
   Unpublished doctoral dissertation. Available in
   microfilm and Xerox from University Microfilms, Inc.,
   Ann Arbor, Mich. Abstract in Dissertation Abstracts.

184. Nikitin, P. The Organization and Utilization of Forests
in the Ukrainian RSR. New York, Research Program on the
USSR, 1955. 85 p. (Institute for the Study of the USSR.
Mimeograph Series no. 78.)
   Discusses the administration and utilization of the
   Ukrainian forests.

185. Nuttonson, Michael J. Ecological Crop Geography of the
Ukraine and the Ukrainian Climatic Analogues in North
America. Washington, D. C. American Institute of Crop
Ecology, 1947. 24 p.
   Discusses the climate and agricultural ecology of the
   Ukraine and compares the climate of the Ukraine with
   North America.

186. United States Office of Foreign Agricultural Relations.
The Agricultural Climatology, Vegetative Cover, and Crop
Ecology of the Ukraine and the Ukrainian Climatic
Analogues in North America. Washington, D. C., United

States Government Printing Office, 1946. 23 p.
    Comparison of the climate and agricultural ecology of
the Ukraine and North America.

187. Archimovych, Alexander. "Botanical-Geographical Changes
in the Distribution of the Field Crops of the Ukraine
During the Last Fifty Years." Annals of the Ukrainian
Academy of Sciences in the U. S. XI, 1-2:32-68. Bibl.
Footn.

188. Archimovich, Alexander. "The End of Cotton Cultivation in
the Ukraine." Shevchenko Scientific Society. Proceedings
of the Section of the Mathematics, Natural Sciences and
Medicine. 4(32): 47-51.

189. Archimovich, Alexander. "Grain Crops in the Ukraine."
Ukrainian Review (London) 2:21-34, 1956.

190. Arkhymovych, Alexander. "Selective Breeding of Sugar Beets
in Russia and the USSR" Botanical Review. January, 1956,
pp. 1-37.
    About the breeding of the sugar beets in the Ukraine
which is the chief area for their cultivation in the USSR.

191. Bandura, Ivan. "The Problem of the Land Ownership in the
Ukraine." Ukrainian Review (London) 2:52-56. September,
1955.
    The author discusses the form of the land ownership in
the Ukraine after the liberation of the Ukraine from
communism anticipated by him.

192. Bespalov, Ivan. "Varieties of Cereals Bred in the Ukraine
before World War II." Annals of the Ukrainian Academy of
Arts and Sciences in the U. S. 6, 3-4(21-22): 1420-1428.

193. Biloz, Michael. "The Repercussions of Soviet Agricultural
Policy in Post-war Ukraine." Ukrainian Quarterly. 11:310-
325. Autumn, 1955.

194. Birko, P. "Saline Soils of Southern Ukraine." Annals of
the Ukrainian Academy of Arts and Sciences in the U. S.
3(3): 839-859.
    Origin of the saline soils of Southern Ukraine and
methods of their melioration.

195. Bobykevych, Ostap. "Forestry in the USSR During World War
II and the Early Postwar Years." Ukrainian Review (Munich)
7:93-101, 1959. Bibl., footn.

196. Davydenko, Viacheslav. "Another Crisis of the Collective
Farm System in the Ukraine." Ukrainian Quarterly 17:60-
65. Spring, 1961. Bibl., footn.

197. Frank, Andrew Gunder. "General Productivity in Soviet Agriculture and Industry; the Ukraine 1928-1953." _Journal of Political Economy_. 66:498-515, December, 1958.
    The Impact of the Soviet economic policy on Ukrainian agriculture and industry.

198. Glowinskyj, Euhen. "Agriculture in Ukraine." _Ukrainian Review_ (Munich) 2: 5-20, 1956.
    Author discusses Ukrainian agriculture before the revolution, between two world wars and after the second World War.

199. Ivanytsky, Borys. "Ukrainian Forestry." _Annals of the Ukrainian Academy of Arts and Sciences in the U. S._ 3: 553-570, 1953.
    The characteristics of the Ukrainian forests, conditions and trends in wood cultivation, meliorative and experimental forestry.

200. Jalovic, A. "Polesye and the Problem of Reclamation of the Peat Bogs in Belorussia." _Belorussian Review_ 8: 65-74, 1960.
    Polesye it is part of the Ukraine included now in the Belorussian Soviet Republic.

201. Kononenko, Konstantine. "Liquidation of M.T.S. Riscy Maneuer." _Ukrainian Quarterly_. 14: 137-148. June, 1958.
    The author discusses the role of the state-operated Machine-Tractor Stations and Ukrainian agriculture and the possible development of the collective farming after their liquidation.

202. Korol, Nestor. "New Agricultural Plants as Soviet Self-efficiency Policy." _Ukrainian Quarterly_ 9:121-129, Spring, 1953.

203. Makhiv, Gregory. "The Agrarian Policy of the USSR." _Ukrainian Quarterly_ 7:219-232, Sumer, 1951.
    The author states that despite abolition of serfdom by the czarist regime in 1861 and despite semi-collective land use in the Ukraine enforced by the czarist regime until the revolution of 1905, despite Soviet collectivisation and the continuing of the collective system during the German occupation of the Ukraine, Ukrainian farmers remain individualists.

204. Makhiv, Gregory. "Agricultural Sciences in the Ukraine." _Ukrainian Quarterly_. 5:52-61. Winter, 1949.

205. Makhiv, Gregory. "The Cultivated Crops in the Ukraine" _Ukrainian Quarterly_. 5: 318-323. Autumn, 1949.

New cultures tested at the experimental stations but not produced in bulk.

206. Makhiv, Gregory. "A New Soil Map of the Ukraine." Annals of the Ukrainian Academy of Arts and Sciences in the U. S. 1: 43-56.
    The author describes the map of the Ukrainian soils submitted by himself to the First Congress of the Ukrainian Soil Specialists in 1923; he also describes Ukrainian soils.

207. Makhiv, Gregory. "The Problem of Irrigation." Ukrainian Quarterly. 9: 309-312, Autumn, 1953.
    Discusses the necessity of irrigation in dry Southern Ukraine.

208. Makhiv, Gregory. "Soil Fertility and Crop Production in the Ukraine." Ukrainian Quarterly. 6: 306-312. Autumn, 1950. Charts and tables.

209. Makhiv, Gregory. "The Ukraine in the Fourth Five-Year Plan of the USSR." Ukrainian Quarterly. 8: 320-327. Autumn, 1952.
    In Soviet planning the Ukraine shall produce only large amounts of grain and semi-fabricates. It shall be Soviet raw material base.

210. Makhiv, Gregory. "The Ukrainian 'Chernozem'--Its Economic Possibilities." Ukrainian Quarterly. 7: 134-143. Spring, 1951.

211. Marchenko, Vasyl. "The Basic Features of the Development of Farming in the Ukraine under the Soviets." Ukrainian Quarterly. 4: 348-355. Bibl., footn.

212. Newth, J. A. "The Kolkhoz Household: Ukraine 1950-1955." Slavic Studies. 11: 307-316. January, 1960.

213. Paramonov, Pantelejmon. "Forest Depletion in the Ukrainian RSR." Ukrainian Review (Munich) 5: 99-108. 1957.

214. Pavlyuk, Mykhaylo. "Economic and Strategic Importance of the Kakhivka Irrigation." Ukrainian Quarterly. 11: 213-218. Summer, 1955.
    Author states that the Soviet Government had military interests in building the irrigation system in the arid Southern Ukraine.

215. Rozhin, Ivan. "Animal Husbandry in Soviet Ukraine." Ukrainian Quarterly. 9: 218-228. Summer, 1953.

216. Rozhin, Ivan. "The Veterinary Organization of Soviet Ukraine." <u>Ukrainian Quarterly</u>. 9: 27-35. Winter, 1953.

4. Ukraine - Natural Resources and Mining.

217. Holubnychy, Vsevolod. "The Present Status of the Ukrainian Ferrous Metal Industry." <u>Ukrainian Review</u> (Munich) 4: 5-14, 1957. Bibl., footnotes.

218. Kornilow, Alexander. "Natural Building Materials of the Ukraine." <u>Shevchenko Scientific Society Proceedings of the Section of Mathematics, Natural Sciences and Medicine</u>. 2: 51-64. 1954.
      A geological description of all the natural building materials available in the Ukraine. Includes bibliography and maps.

219. Protsiuk, Stephen. "The Kakhovka Hydroelectric Project and the Greater Dneper Scheme." <u>Ukrainian Review</u> (Munich) 4: 33-66. 1957.
      Discusses Russian and Soviet plans for developing Dnipro during the past two hundred years and the present Kakhovka project.

220. Protsiuk, Stephen. "The Metalliferous Base of Ukrainian Industry." <u>Ukrainian Quarterly</u>. 8: 52-59. Winter, 1952.

221. Protsiuk, Stephen. "Ukrainian Donbas at the Close of the Fourth Five-Year Plan." <u>Ukrainian Quarterly</u>. 6: 219-228. Summer, 1950.
      Concerns the coal deposits in the Donec Basin and Soviet methods of production.

5. Ukraine - Industry.

222. Holubnychy, Vsevolod. <u>The Industrial Output of the Ukraine, 1913-1956</u>. A Statistical analysis. Munich, Institute for the Study of the USSR, 1956. 64 p.
      About the industrial potential of the Ukraine beginning with the year 1913.

223. Koropeckyj, Iwan Swiatoslaw. <u>The Economics of Investments in Ukrainian Industry</u>. New York, Columbia University, 1964. 371 p.
      Unpublished doctoral dissertation. The author points out that investment in Ukrainian industry was smaller in the Second than in the First Five-Year Plan. The economic growth of the Ukraine was faster than in the entire USSR. The capital was more productive.

224. Kysil, I. "The Sugar Industry in the Ukraine." *Ukrainian Review* (Munich) 3: 152-159, 1956. Bibl., footn.

225. Myronenko, M. O. The Growth of Ukrainian Industry." *Ukrainian Review* (London) 3:40-45. December, 1955.

226. Poplujko, A. "The Economy of the Ukraine Today." *Ukrainian Review* (Munich) 3: 54-87. 1956.
    Ukrainian industry and its production.

227. Protsiuk, Stephen. "The Evacuation of Industry in 1941 and the Postwar Economy of the Ukraine." *Ukrainian Quarterly* 5: 210-218. Summer, 1949.

6. Ukraine - Transportation.

228. Fedorovsky, N. N. *Autoguzhevnye Dorogi Ukrainskoi SSR*" Munich, Institute for the Study of the USSR, 1957. 98 p. mimeo.
    Russian with English resume . Concerns highways of the Ukraine.

7. Ukraine - Commerce.

229. Harvey, Mose L. *The Development of Russian Commerce on the Black Sea and Its Significance*. University of California, 1938.
    Unpublished doctoral dissertation.

230. Revyuk, Emil. Trade with Ukraine; *Ukraine's Natural Wealth, Needs and Commercial Opportunities, the Ukrainian Cooperative Societies and Their Influence*. Washington, D. C., Friends of Ukraine, 1920. 24 p.
    A description of the Ukrainian economy and its needs brought about by the war.
    Primarily of historical value.

231. Timoshenko, Volodymyr. *Ukraine and Russia. A Study of Their Economic Relations*. Washington, D. C., 1919. 16 p.
    Rebutting the Russian Assertions that the Ukraine cannot survive without economic ties with Russia and accusation of Russian colonialism.

8. Ukraine - Labor and Labor Relations.

232. Protsiuk, Stephen. "Labor Conditions in the Metalurgical Industry of the Ukraine." *Ukrainian Quarterly* 6: 38-48. Winter, 1950. Bibl. footn.

IV. UKRAINE - POPULATION.

1. Ukrainians

233. Koenig, Samuel. The Ukrainians of Eastern Galicia. A Study in Their Culture and Institutions. New Haven, Yale University, 1935.
     An unpublished doctoral dissertation.

234. Bilinsky, Yaroslav. "Drahomanov, Franko and the Relations between the Dnieper Ukraine and Galicia." Annals of the Ukrainian Academy of Arts and Sciences in the U. S. 7(1-2/23-24): 1542-1566. Bibl., footn.
     The history of relations between the Eastern and Western Ukrainians in the time before the first World War and the role Mykhailo Drahomanov played in these relations.

235. Makhiv, Gregory. "The Nature of Ukraine and Its Influence on Material Culture of the Ukrainian People in Prehistoric Time." Shevchenko Scientific Society. Historical and Philosophical Section. Proceedings. 1: 26-47.
     The author discusses the influence of the climate, soil, flora and fauna of the prehistoric Ukraine on the material culture of the Ukrainian people.

236. Mironenko, Y. "Ethnic and National Changes in the USSR." Bulletin of the Institute for the Study of the USSR. October, 1958. p. 14-24.

237. Shumeyko, Stephen. "The Ukrainians" in the Jubilee Book of the Ukrainian National Association in Commemoration of the Fortieth Anniversary of Its Existence. Jersey City, Svoboda, 1936. p. 460-498.
     The history and present status of the Ukraine, Ukrainian religious life, culture, literature, language, music, dances, costumes. References to the Ukrainians in America.

2. Ukraine - National Minorities.

238. Dushnyk, Walter, ed. Ukrainians and Jews; a Symposium. New York, Ukrainian Congress Committee of America, 1966. 199 p.
     A collection of articles discussing different aspects of Ukrainian-Jewish relations, written by Ukrainians and Jews. Memories, testimonies, laws and ordinances of the Ukrainian Government concerning Jews.

239. Goldelman, Solomon I. Jewish National Autonomy in Ukraine, 1917-1921. Chicago, Ukrainian Research and Information Institute, Inc., 1968. 140 p.
    A Jewish scholar from the Ukraine, a former member of the Ukrainian government and diplomatic corps and professor of the Ukrainian Free University at Vienna and Praha, discusses the legal status of the Jews in the Ukraine of 1917-1921.

240. Jewish Pogroms in Ukraine. The authoritative statements by Julian Bachynskyi, Dr. Arnold Margolin, Dr. Mark Vishnitzer, Izrael Zangwill and others. Washington, D. C., Friends of Ukraine, 1919. 14 p., map.
    A statement by prominent Ukrainians and Jews concerning Jewish pogroms in the Ukraine. They state that Ukrainian government was against pogroms which were perpetrated by criminal elements.

241. Keller, P. Konrad. The German Settlements in South Russia, 1804 to 1904. Saskatoon, A. Becker, 1968. 251 p.
    Concerns German settlements in Southern Ukraine, called by author South Russia.

242. Materials Concerning Ukrainian-Jewish Relations During the Years of the Revolution, 1917-1921. Collection of documents and testimonies by leading Jewish political workers. Munich, The Ukrainian Information Bureau, 1956. 102 p.
    Selection of official Ukrainian documents concerning Jews; includes testimonies of Jewish leaders relating to the Jewish population in the Ukraine, 1917-1921.

243. Mierau, Eric. A Descriptive Grammar of Ukrainian Low German. Indianapolis, University of Indiana, 1965.
    An unpublished doctoral dissertation concerning the language of the German colonists in the Ukraine.

244. Smal-Stocki, Roman. Shevchenko and the Jews. New York, Shevchenko Scientific Society, 1959. 11 p. (Shevchenko Scientific Society. Papers no. 8)
    Concerns the attitude of the prominent Ukrainian poet Taras Shevchenko to the Jews.

245. Waten, Judah L. From Odessa to Odessa. Melbourne, Cheshire, 1969. 198 p.
    A travelogue by an Australian author. Concerns the situation of the Jews in the USSR, including the Ukraine.

246. Friedman, Philip. "The First Milennium of the Jewish Settlement in the Ukraine and in the Adjacent Areas."

Annals of the Ukrainian Academy of Arts and Sciences in
the U. S. 7(1-2/23-24): 1483-1516. Bibl. p. 1511-1518.

247. Friedman, Philip. "Ukrainian-Jewish Relations during the
Nazi Occupation." Yivo Journal of Jewish Social Science.
1958-59, p. 259-296.
     Deals with the friendly attitude of the Ukrainian
     population to the Jews during the German occupation of
     the Ukraine. Available also in reprint.

248. Goldelman, Solomon. "Patterns in the Life of an Ethnic
Minority." Annals of the Ukrainian Academy of Arts and
Sciences in the U. S. 7(1-2/23-24): 1567-1585. Bibl.
footn.
     Concerns life of Jews in the Ukraine.

249. Heiman, Leo. "They Saved Jews." Ukrainian Quarterly. 17:
32-332. Winter, 1961.
     Tells about Ukrainians who saved Jews during the German
     occupation of the Ukraine.

250. Heiman, Leo. "Ukrainians and the Jews." Ukrainian
Quarterly. 107-116, Summer, 1961.
     About Ukrainian-Jewish relations in the Ukraine.
     Reprinted also in: Ukrainians and Jews. p. 55-64 (see
     entry no. 238).

251. Heiman, Leo. "We Fought for Ukraine." Ukrainian Quarterly.
20: 33-44, Spring, 1964.
     Author retells the stories of the Jews who were mem-
     bers of the Ukrainian Insurgent Army.

252. Lichten, Joseph A. "A Study of Ukrainian-Jewish Relations."
Annals of the Ukrainian Academy of Arts and Sciences in
the U. S. 5: 1160-1177.
     About Ukrainian-Jewish relations in the past. The
     unselfish attitude of some Ukrainians toward the Jews
     during the German occupation of the Ukraine.

253. Mackiw. Theodore. "Jews, Khmelnyckyj and the Treaty of
Zboriw." Ukrainian Review, (London) 15: 63-70. December,
1968.

254. Pigido-Pravoberezhny, Fedir. "Ukrainian-Jewish Relations,
1917-1921." Ukrainian Review (Munich) 5: 84-98, 1957.

255. Rudnytsky, Ivan. "Mykhailo Drahomaniv and the Problem of
Ukrainian-Jewish Relations." Canadian Slavonic Papers. 11:
182-198. 1969, 2.

The author says that Drahomaniv states that there is no possibility of assimilation of Jews with Ukrainians because Jews are interested in assimilating with the ruling class which was not Ukrainian. Therefore, he sees the only solution in the coordination and coexistence of Ukrainians and Jews.

256. Shankovsky, Lev. "Russia, the Jews and the Ukrainian Liberation Movement." Ukrainian Quarterly. 16: 147-163. Spring, 1960 and Ukrainians and Jews (see entry no. 238). p. 65-96.

257. Stakhiv, Matthew. "Why the Jewish Problem has been connected with Ukraine." Ukrainians and Jews (see entry no. 238) p. 11-153. Bibl., footn.

258. Thielman, George G. "The Mennonite 'Selbstschutz' in the Ukraine during the Revolution." The New Review. 10: 50-60. 1970. 1/38. Bibl., footn. p. 59-60.

259. Ukraine. Laws, Statutes, etc. "Laws Concerning Jewish Community Self-government," in Ukrainian-Jewish Relations . . . " (see entry no. 246) p. 78-102.

260. Vetukhiv, Mikhael (a.o.) "Arnold Davydovych Margolin." Annals of the Ukrainian Academy of Arts and Sciences. 7: (1-2/23-24): 1871-1876.
    Concerns the prominent Ukrainian statesman and diplomat of Jewish origin.

V. UKRAINIANS - ABROAD.

1. Ukrainians in the USSR outside the Ukrainian SSR.

261. Kolarz, Walter. The Peoples of the Soviet Far East. Hamden, Conn., Archon Books, 1969. 193 p. illus., maps.
    Reprint of a 1954 ed. Includes interesting information on Ukrainians in the Soviet Far East. Author gives the number of Ukrainians in the Soviet Far East according to the Soviet census of 1926 as 315,000 and indicates their main areas of settlement and points out that Ukrainians consider that area (Green Wedge) as Ukrainian territory.

262. Chaplenko, Vasyl. "The Ukrainians of the Russian Soviet Republic." Ukrainian Quarterly. 7: 66-75. Winter, 1951. Map.

263. Sweet, John V. "The Problem of Nationalities in Soviet Asia." Ukrainian Quarterly. 9: 229-235. Summer, 1953. Bibl. footn.

264. Sweet, John V. "The Trial in Chita." _Ukrainian Quarterly_ 10: 135-144. Spring, 1954. Bibl. footn.

2. Ukrainians outside the USSR
(Except in the U. S. and Canada).

265. Association of Ukrainians in Great Britain. _Ukrainians in Great Britain._ London, 1954. 40 p. illus.
   About Ukrainians--former displaced persons in Great Britain.

266. Kubiyovych, Volodymyr. _Demographic Problems of Ukrainians in Exile._ Munich, Shevchenko Scientific Society, 1949. 16 p.
   A study of the Ukrainian displaced persons by a prominent Ukrainian geographer and demographer.

267. Mandryka, Mykyta. _Ukrainian Refugees._ Winnipeg, Ukrainian Canadian Committee 1946. 45 p.
   The background of Ukrainian displaced persons; legal and moral aspects and the solution of the displaced persons' problem.

268. Rudnyckyj, Jaroslav. _Slavic and Baltic Universities in Exile._ Winnipeg, Ukrainian Free Academy of Sciences, 1949. 16 p. (Ukrainian Free Academy of Sciences. Slavistica no. 4.)
   Concerns universities organized by the refugees of the various national groups in exile, including the Ukrainians.

269. Kubiyovych, Volodymyr. "The Ukrainians Outside Ukraine." _Ukrainian Review,_ London 5: 62-77. Winter, 1958.

270. Stewart, John P. "The Ukrainians in Scotland." _Ukrainian Review,_ London. 2: 86-92. June, 1955.

271. "S.U.B." 1946-1955. _Ukrainian Review, London_ 2: 65-80, December, 1955.
   S.U.B. is an abbreviation for the "Soyuz Ukraintsiv Velykoyi Brytaniyi." (Association of Ukrainians in Great Britain.) A pictorial history of this organization.

272. World Congress of the Free Ukrainians. "Documents of the First World Congress of Free Ukrainians." _Ukrainian Quarterly._ 23: 354-372. Winter, 1972.
   Materials concerning an Ukrainian Congress held in New York City in the Fall, 1967.

3. Ukrainians in the U. S. and Canada.

A. - History.

273. Alaska Herald and Free Press (Sloboda) Newspaper. (Vols. 1-6, 1868-1874.) Reprinted. San Francisco. R and E Research Associates, 1968-1970.
    Reprint of a newspaper published by an Ukrainian immigrant, Father Ahapius Honcharenko, a revolutionary and defector from Czarist Russia. Published in English, Russian and partially in Ukrainian.

274. Association of United Ukrainian Canadians. Tribute to Our Ukrainian Pioneers in Canada's First Century. Winnipeg, 1966. 106 p., illus.
    Proceedings of a special convention of the Association of United Ukrainian Canadians and the Workers' Benevolent Society on the occasion of the 75th anniversary of the beginning of the Ukrainian immigration to Canada. Included are lectures, address of a representative of the Soviet Embassy in Canada and a text of a special program of Radio Station Kyiv welcoming this convention.

275. Bayley, C. M. The Social Structure of the Italian and Ukrainian Immigrant Communities in Montreal. Montreal, McGill University, 1939.
    An unpublished master of arts thesis. Gives a picture of social composition of the Ukrainian community in Montreal before the large wave of Ukrainian immigrants after the World War 1939-1945, which changed social structure of the Ukrainian community in Canada.

276. Brown, Francis J. and Joseph Slabey Rouchek. Our America: the History, Contribution and Present Problems of Our Racial and National Minorities. New York, Prentice Hall, 1952. 764 p.
    Information about the Ukrainian Americans, history of their emigration, their occupation, cultural life, economic achievements on pages 127-134.

277. Byrne, Timothy C. The Ukrainian Community in North Central Alberta. Edmonton, University of Alberta, 1937.
    Unpublished masters' thesis.

278. Chyz, Yaroslav. The Ukrainian Immigrants in the United States. Scranton, Pa., Ukrainian Workingman's Association, 1932. 32 p.

279. Darcovich, William. Ukrainians in Canada--the Struggle to Retain Their Identity. Printed under the auspices of the Ukrainian Self-Reliance Association, Ottawa Branch. Ottawa, 1967. IV, 38 p.

History of the three phases of the Ukrainian immigration to Canada, an analysis of the figures of the Canadian
census of 1961 concerning the Ukrainian group, their
achievements and underachievements in comparison with
other ethnic groups of Canada. Author separately
analyzes the figures concerning the Ukrainians in
Ottawa.

280. Davidson, Gordon A. The Ukrainians in Canada; a Study in
Immigration. Montreal, 1947. 23 p.

281. Dubinski, Walter. History of Ukrainians in the Sudbury
Basin. Sudbury, Ont., University of Western Ontario, 1962.
Unpublished master's thesis.

282. Halich, Wasyl. Economic Aspects of Ukrainian Activity in
The United States. Iowa City, University of Iowa, 1934.
Unpublished doctoral dissertation dealing with the
activity of Ukrainian immigrants before the Second World
War.

283. Halich, Wasyl. Ukrainians in the United States. Chicago,
University of Chicago Press, 1937. 173 p. Reprint: New
York, Arno Press & New York Times, 1970. 174 p.
Second printing of the study published in 1937. The
historical background of Ukrainian immigrants in the
United States; the settlements, occupations, religious
and cultural life of the American Ukrainians.

284. Hunchak, N. J. Population: Canadians of Ukrainian Origin.
Winnipeg, Ukrainian Canadian Committee, 1945. 164 p.
History and present status of the Canadian Ukrainians.

285. Ignasiak, Robert Leonard. Ukrainians in Lansing, Michigan.
The Adjustment of a Small Ethnic Group. East Lansing,
Michigan State University, 1949. 79 p.
Unpublished master's thesis. A study of Ukrainians
living in Lansing, Mich., their history, origin,
occupations and living habits; includes bibliography.

286. Kaye, Vladimir J. Early Ukrainian Settlement in Canada,
1895-1900. Dr. Joseph Oleskow's Role in the Settlement of
the Canadian Northeast. Toronto, University of Toronto
Press, 1964. 472 p., illus., plates.
The author pictures the role of an Ukrainian teacher in
a teacher's college in Western Ukraine, who became
interested in opportunities for Ukrainian farmers to
immigrate to Canada, and then became enthusiastic propa-
gator of emigration and was instrumental in causing mass
immigration of Ukrainian farmers to the north western
provinces of Canada.

Biographies and photos of Dr. Oleskow and other persons
involved in that resettlement of Ukrainian farmers,
bibliography and index supplement this volume.

287. Kaye, Volodymyr J. Slavic Groups in Canada. Winnipeg,
Ukrainian Free Academy of Sciences, 1951. 30 p. (Ukrainian
Free Academy of Sciences. Slavistica no. 12.)
    Concentrates predominantly on Ukrainian immigrants to
Canada.

288. Kupchenko, Volodymyr. Progress of Ukrainian Pioneers in
Alberta in Their First Sixty Years. Ottawa, University of
Ottawa, 1960.
    Unpublished doctoral dissertation.

289. Luciw, Theodore. Father Agapius Honcharenko, First Ukrainian
Priest in America. New York, Ukrainian Congress Committee
of America, 1970. 223 p.
    A story of an Ukrainian Orthodox Priest who disregarding
a brilliant career in the czarist Russian diplomatic service (was a chaplain in the Russian Embassy in Athens,
Greece) defected, and in 1867 came to the U. S. Author
analyzes bilingual (Russian-English) and partially also
Ukrainian paper Alaska-Herald-Svoboda, published by
Ahapius Honcharenko for inhabitants and administrators of
the newly acquired Alaska by the U. S.

290. Luciw. Wasyl. Ahapius Honcharenko "Alaska Man," by Wasyl
Luciw and Theodore Luciw. Toronto, Slavia Library, 1963.
120 p.
    Concerns the above mentioned Ahapius Honcharenko--one of
the first, historically documented Ukrainian immigrants
to America--and his publication "Alaska Herald - Svoboda"
and the role of Honcharenko as liason person between the
American administration of Alaska and its population in
the transition period.

291. Lysenko, Vera. Men in Sheepskin Coats; Study in Assimilation. Toronto, The Ryerson Press, 1947. 312 p.
    A history of the first Ukrainian settlers in Canada.
Also a short history of Ukrainian culture in the Ukraine
and in Canada.

292. Lysenko, Vera. Yellow Boots. Toronto, Ryerson Press,
1954. 314 p.
    The folklore of Canadians of Ukrainian origin; short
stories revealing the blending of old beliefs with the
customs of Canada.

293. MacGregor, J. G. Vilni Zemli--Free Lands; the Ukrainian
Settlements in Alberta. Toronto-Montreal, McClelland and

Stewart Limited, 1969. IX, 274 p.
A history of Ukrainian settlements in Alberta.
Author mentions the first families, the growth of
Ukrainian colonies. His story is based on the diary of
one of the Ukrainian settlers, Theodore Nemirsky. He
discusses the history of the two Ukrainian Churches,
Ukrainian Catholic (Uniate) and Ukrainian Orthodox, and
the conflict between the two on Canadian soil; the problem
of married Ukrainian Catholic clergy and the attitude of
the Congregation de Propaganda File headed by Cardinal
Ledochowski which opposed married Ukrainian priests.
He discusses establishing of the Ukrainian Catholic
hierarchy in Canada and the growth of the Ukrainian
Orthodox Church.
The author stresses pioneering role of Ukrainians in
the settlement of the Canadian West.

294. Mamchur, Stephen W. The Economic and Social Adjustment of
Slavic Immigrants in Canada with Special References to the
Ukrainians in Montreal. Montreal, McGill University, 1935.
Unpublished masters thesis. The economic and social
growth of the Ukrainian group in Montreal before the
World War, 1939-1945.

295. Mamchur, Stephen W. Nationalism, Religion and the Problem
of Assimilation Among Ukrainians in the United States. New
Haven, Conn., Yale University, 1942.
Unpublished doctoral dissertation. About Ukrainian
immigrants in the U. S. and their adjustment.

296. Marunchak, Mykhaylo. The Ukrainian Canadians; a History.
Winnipeg, Historical Publications, 1970. 729 p. illus.
This book is a complete history of the Ukrainian group
in Canada in English. It describes the national and
social processes occurring inside the Ukrainian-Canadian
community. In separate chapters the author describes
the identity of the Ukrainian Canadians, Ukrainian-
Canadian art, problems of the Ukrainian Churches in
Canada, Ukrainian schools, journalism, literature, organizations, the part played by the Canadian Ukrainians
in the Canadian Armed Forces, administration, courts and
politics. He discusses the history of the contacts of
the Ukrainian-Canadian community with the Mother Country
and the development of this community from a group of
immigrants to a member of the Canadian mosaic of peoples.
Numerous illustrations and a bibliography of works in
Ukrainian and English complete the work.

297. Panchuk, John. A Sketch of Wasyl Zahara, the First Ukrainian Settler in Gardentown and the First Ukrainian Immigrant

from Bukovina to Canada and St. Michael Church, the First
Ukrainian Orthodox Church in Canada. Winnipeg, privately
printed by the author, 1956. 11 p.
   Biography of one of the earliest Ukrainian pioneers in
Canada.

298. Piniuta, H. The Organizational Life of Ukrainian Canadians,
with Special Reference to the Ukrainian Canadian Committee.
Ottawa, University of Ottawa, 1952.
   Unpublished master's thesis. About Ukrainian organizations in Canada: religious, cultural and political
with their superstructure, Canadian Ukrainian Committee,
and the role played by these organizations in life of
the Ukrainian-Canadian community and Canada.

299. Prokop, Petro. Change and Challenge in the Ukrainian
Ethnic Group, by P. Prokop, W. Harasym and M. J. Says.
Toronto, Association of United Ukrainian Canadians, 1967.
31 p., illus., ports.
   Selected papers presented at a meeting of the National
Executive Committee and Advisory Council of the Association of United Ukrainian Canadians, Toronto, February
25-27, 1967. The authors of the paper discuss the
changes in organizational life and the changes in the
attitude to the Soviet Ukraine and Canada.

300. Romaniuk, Gus. Taking Roots in Canada. An Autobiography.
Winnipeg, Columbia Press, 1954. 283 p.
   Autobiography of an Ukrainian immigrant, Augustin
Romaniuk, describing experiences typical of Ukrainian
immigrants to Canada.

301. Royick, Alexander. Ukrainian Settlements in Alberta. 18 p.
   Reprint from Canadian Slavonic Papers. Vol. 10, no. 3,
1968. Pp. 278-297. About the origin of the Ukrainian
settlements in Canada. A map of Ukrainian dialects used
by Ukrainian settlers in Canada included.

302. Slavs in Canada. Proceedings of the First National Con-
ference of Canadian Slavs. Editorial Committee, Yar
Slavutych, Chairman. Vol. 1. Edmonton, Alta. Interuni-
versity Committee on Canadian Slavs, 1966. 171 p.
   Four of the included papers concern Ukrainians in
Canada: V. J. Kaye. "Three phases of Ukrainian Immigration,"
E. D. Wangenheim. "Problems of Research on Ukrainians in
Eastern Canada," Warren R. Kalbach. "Demographic Aspects
of the Ukrainian Population in Canada," and Charles W.
Hobart "Adjustment of Ukrainians in Canada: Alienation and
Integration." Also a few other papers in this volume are
written by Ukrainians or concern Ukrainians in part.

303. Stefanov, Marlene. A Study of Intermarriage of Ukrainians in Saskatchewan. Saskatoon, University of Saskatchewan, 1962.
    Unpublished master's thesis. The problem of mixed marriages in Ukrainian group in Saskatchewan.

304. The Ukrainian Pioneers in Alberta. By the Editorial Committee in Edmonton. Editor in Chief M. Lazarenko. Edmonton, Alta, 1970. 384 p.
    History of the Ukrainian immigration to Alberta.

305. Ukrainian Yearbook and Ukrainians of Distinction. Compiled by F. A. Macrouch. 1st- 1944- Winnipeg, The Ukrainian Business Directory, 1944-
    An illustrated annual. Includes biographies of prominent Canadians of Ukrainian origin.

306. Wangenheim, E. D. The Ukrainian Community in Toronto. Toronto, University of Toronto, 1961.
    Unpublished doctoral dissertation.

307. Wichorek, Michael. Ukrainians in Detroit. Detroit, privately published by the author, 1955. 96 p., illus.
    History of Ukrainian immigration to the United States and especially to Detroit; Ukrainian organizations, publications, customs in Detroit; includes photographs and business directory.

308. Malycky, A. "Ukrainian-Canadian Periodical Publications: preliminary checklist." in Canadian Ethnic Studies. Bulletin of the Research Center for Canadian Ethnic Studies. Calgary, Alberta, University of Calgary. 1: 77-142, 1969.
    A list of Ukrainian Canadian publications.

309. Mudryi, Wasyl. "Ukrainian Immigration in the United States," in: Weres, Wasyl. Guide to the Ukrainian-American Institutions. p. 5-17.
    Contains a brief history of the Ukrainian immigration to the United States of America especially of the large new group of Ukrainian immigrants who came to the United States after World War 1939-1945.

310. Prokopiv, Orysia (et al.). "Ukrainian-Canadian Creative Literature: a Preliminary Checklist of Authors and Pseudonyms" in Canadian Ethnic Studies Bulletin of the Research Center for Canadian Ethnic Studies. Calgary, Alberta, University of Calgary. 1: 143-160, 1969.
    List of Ukrainian-Canadian authors and their pseudonyms.

311. Rasky, Frank. "Ukrainian New Canadians: Black Bread and Easter Eggs," in Liberty Magazine (Toronto) November 1, 1958.

Reprinted in Svoboda-Ukrainian Weekly, nos. 216, 221, 224, 229, 234, 239, 245 and 250, 1958. Concerns the life, customs and activities of the Canadian Ukrainians.

312. Yuzyk, Paul, "Canada—a Multi-cultural Nation," in Zhinochyi Svit, (English Section) 1964, nos. 4, p. 12-13, 5, p. 13, no. 7-8, p. 18-19, no. 9, p. 13-14, no. 10, p. 14.
Concerns ethnic mosaic in Canada.

313. Yuzyk, Paul. "75th Anniversary of Ukrainian Settlement in Canada," Ukrainian Quarterly. 23: 247-254, Autumn, 1967 and in Ukrainian Review, London 14: 81-86. March, 1967.

Fiction.

314. Bloch-Halun, Marie. Marya of Clark Ave. New York, Coward-McCann, 1957. 190 p.
A child's story of the ancestral and American cultures, their conflicts and ultimate blending. For grade school children.

315. Cornish, John. Olga. Toronto, MacMillan, 1959. 174 p.
A Canadian novel with an Ukrainian heroine.

316. Kiriak, Illia. Sons of the Soil. Toronto, Ryerson Press, 1959. 369 p.
Condensed translation of a three-volume Ukrainian story of the Ukrainian pioneers in Canada.

B. - Culture and Education.

317. Bilash Borislav Nicholas. Bilingual Public Schools in Manitoba 1897-1916. Winnipeg, University of Manitoba, 1960.
An unpublished master's of education thesis. The history of Ukrainian-English public schools from beginning of the Ukrainian immigration to Canada until the year 1916 when bilingual schools have been abolished.

318. Czuba, Natalie N. History of the Ukrainian Catholic Parochial Schools in the United States. Toronto, Basilian Press, 1956. XI, 76 p. bibl.
A master's thesis in education. The author discusses Ukrainian parochial schools in the U. S.

319. Deverell, Jessie Marion. The Ukrainian Teacher as an Agent of Cultural Assimilation. Toronto, University of Toronto, 1941.

An unpublished master's thesis. Author discusses the
role of the Ukrainian teacher in Canadian public and
private schools in acculturation of the children of the
Ukrainian immigrants to Canada.

320. Fishman, Joshua A. Language Loyalty in the United States.
The Maintenance and Perpetuation of Non-English Mother
Tongues by American Ethnic and Religious Groups; with an
introduction by Elnar Haugen. Den Hagen, Mouton, 1966.
478 p., illus. (Janua lingarum. Ser. maior 21.)
    Book deals with efforts of Ethnic groups in the U. S.
to preserve their language and national heritage. On
pp. 318-357 author discusses Ukrainian group in the U. S.
and its efforts to preserve the language and national
identity under foreign domination in the home country,
history of Ukrainian immigration to the U. S. and its
national and linguistic consciousness.

321. Hunter, Edward. In Many Voices. Norman Park, Ga., Norman
College, 1960. 190 p.
    Author discusses the foreign language press in the
U. S. and its importance. A Separate chapter discusses
the Ukrainian daily "Svoboda," the "Ukrainian Quarterly,"
and one Ukrainian communist newspaper. He mentions also
deceased Ukrainian newspaperman, former head of the
Foreign Press Division of the Common Council, Yaroslav
Chyzh.

322. Kirkonnel, Watson. Canadian Toponymy and the Cultural
Stratification of Canada. Winnipeg., Ukrainian Free Academy
of Sciences, 1954. 16 p. (Ukrainian Free Academy of
Sciences Onomastica no. 7.)
    Also discusses Canadian place names of Ukrainian origin.

323. Klymash, Robert B. A Bibliography of Ukrainian Folklore
in Canada, 1902-1964. Ottawa, National Museum of Canada,
1969. 53 p. (Anthropology Papers, no. 21.)
    This bibliography describes 453 items in languages
Ukrainian, English and French. An article on Ukrainian
folklore in Canada has been included. All items in
Ukrainian have been transliterated.

324. Klymash, Robert B. A Classified Dictionary of Slavic
Surname Changes in Canada. Winnipeg, Ukrainian Free
Academy of Sciences, 1961. 62 p. (Ukrainian Free Academy
of Sciences. Onomastica no. 22.)

325. Mandryka, Mykyta I. History of Ukrainian Literature in
Canada. Winnipeg, Ottawa, Ukrainian Free Academy of
Sciences, 1968. 248 p.

Following a brief survey of the Ukrainian history and literature in general, the author discusses the pioneer period of Ukrainian literature in Canada, the period before the European war 1914-1918, the period between the wars, and the period after the World War, 1939-1945.

The work covers over 100 Canadian-Ukrainian authors, poets, novelists, playwrights, including literary critics and non-fiction writers. He stresses differences between the English-language and the French-language literatures and Ukrainian-Canadian literature, pointing out that Ukrainian-Canadian literature is aimed at the well-being of the Ukrainian people.

He states that the future of the Ukrainian-Canadian literature will depend upon the constitutional admission of the Ukrainian language to the Canadian schools.

326. Manning, Clarence A. History of Slavic Studies in the United States. Milwaukee, Marquette University Press, 1957. 128 p.
    Includes also the history of the Ukrainistic studies in the United States.

327. Paluk, William. Ukrainian Cossacks: Essays, Articles and Stories on Ukrainian-Canadian Life. Winnipeg, privately printed by the author, 1943. 143 p.
    Concerns the life of Canadians of Ukrainian origin.

328. Piniuta, H. Cultural Adjustment of the Ukrainians in Manitoba. Winnipeg, University of Manitoba, n. d.
    Unpublished bachelor's of education thesis.

329. Robinson, Claude Hill. A Study of the Written Language Errors of 1238 Pupils of Ukrainian Origin. Edmonton, University of Alberta, 1934.
    An unpublished bachelor's of education thesis. Concerns bilingualism of Canadian students of Ukrainian origin and its influence on their proficiency in the English language.

330. Royick, Alexander. Lexical Borrowings in Alberta Ukrainian. Edmonton, University of Alberta, 1965.
    Unpublished master's thesis. Concerns the language of an Ukrainian group in an English environment.

331. Rudnyckyj, Jaroslav B. Canadian Place Names of Ukrainian Origin. 3rd ed. Winnipeg, Ukrainian Free Academy of Sciences, 1957. 32 p. (Ukrainian Free Academy of Sciences. Onomastica no. 2.)
    Discusses Ukrainian pioneers as founders of Canadian communities.

332. Saruk, Alex. "Academic Performance of the Students of Ukrainian Descent and the Cultural Orientation of Their Parents. Edmonton, University of Alberta, 1966.
Unpublished masters of education thesis. Inter-relation between the cultural level of parents and the academic achievements of their children among the Ukrainian group in Canada.

333. Skwarok, Josaphat J. The Ukrainian Settlers in Canada and Their Schools; with References to Government, French-Canadian and Ukrainian Missionary Influences 1891-1921. Toronto, Basilian Press, 1959. 157 p.
Ukrainian schools in Canada during the first thirty years of Ukrainian immigration to Canada. Also an un-published doctoral dissertation under the same title: Edmonton, University of Alberta, 1958(?).

334. Slavutych, Yar. Ukrainian Literature in Canada. Edmonton, Slavuta, 1966. 15 p.
A brief outline of the history of Ukrainian-Canadian literature.

335. Sullivan, David Malcolm. An Investigation of the English Disabilities of Ukrainian and Polish Students in Grades IX, X, XI, XII of Alberta Schools. Edmonton, University of Alberta, 1946.
Unpublished master of education thesis. The influence of bilingualism of the Ukrainian and Polish students in the four upper grades of the Alberta high schools on their knowledge of the English language.

336. Ukrainian Cultural and Educational Center, 1944-1954. Winnipeg, Manitoba. Ukrainian Cultural and Educational Center, 1954(?). 11 p.
Published on the occasion of the 10th anniversary of that Center becoming a Museum with a library and archives.

337. Voycenko, Olha. Canada's Cultural Heritage: Ukrainian Contribution. Winnipeg, Ukrainian Free Academy of Sciences, 1964. 16 p. (Ukrainian Free Academy of Sciences. Chronicle no. 22.)
The role of Ukrainians in the cultural development of Canada.

338. Voycenko, Olha. Ukrainian-Canadian Letters. Winnipeg, Ukrainian Free Academy of Sciences, 1967. 32 p. (Ukrainian Free Academy of Sciences. Slavistica, no. 65. Slavic Literature in Canada I.)
Short outline of Ukrainian-Canadian literature.

339. Voycenko, Olha. The Ukrainians in Canada. A Concise History of a Major Canadian Group. Ottawa-Winnipeg,

Trident, 1967. 271 p. (Canada Ethnica IV.)
A definition of Ukrainians, a history of Ukrainian immigration to Canada, Ukrainian achievements in agriculture and in other fields, Ukrainian-Jewish relations in Canada, their churches, schools, the part of Canadian Ukrainians in the political life of Canada, their literature, scholarly institutions, art, political organizations. Bibliography, list of Ukrainian periodicals, and indexes and maps added.

340. Warzeski, Walter. Religion and National Consciousness in the History of the Rusins of Carpatho-Ruthenia and the Byzantine Rite Pittsburgh Exarchate. Pittsburgh, University of Pittsburgh, 1964. 395 leaves.
Unpublished doctoral dissertation. Abstract in: Dissertations Abstracts. Xerox or microfilm copies available from University Microfilms, Inc., Ann Arbor, Mich.
Concerns Ukrainian immigrants from the Carpatho-Ukraine referred to by author as "Rusins" and "Carpatho-Ruthenia." The author states that those immigrants preserved their national and religious identity. After the European War of 1914-1918 they influenced the fate of their native country Carpatho-Ukraine by plebiscite asking for Union with Czecho-Slovakia. The deprivation of privileges granted to their church by the Church Union with the Roman Catholic Church led to the revival of the orthodoxy among them.

341. White Paper on the Final Report of the Royal Commission on Bilingualism and Biculturalism. First volume. Winnipeg, The Ukrainian Canadian Committee, 1968. 11 p.
Argues that Canada is not a bicultural but a multicultural country and that other ethnic groups of Canada should also have constitutionally granted privileges for their languages.

342. Young, Charles. The Ukrainian Canadians: a Study in Assimilation. Toronto, Nelson Company, 1931. 327 p.
A study of the Ukrainian immigration to Canada, including history, territory, distribution, religion, organizations, education, health and political affiliations.

343. Yuzyk, Paul. Ukrainians in Manitoba: a Social History. Issued under the auspices of the Historical and Scientific Society of Manitoba. Toronto, University of Toronto Press, 1953. 232 p.
History and all other aspects of Ukrainian immigration to the Manitoba; participation of the Ukrainian immigrants in the defense of Canada, their political affiliations and their adjustment to Canadian culture.

344. Zadrozhny, John Thomas. The Differences of Opinion in Chicago in Regard to the Soviet Ukraine: a study of the Opinions, Attitudes and Beliefs of a National Minority in the United States. Chicago, University of Chicago, 1946. 202 p.
   An unpublished master's thesis based on a survey among Chicagoans of Ukrainian ancestry.

345. Zhmurkevych, Stephanie (Janovych). Ukrainian Canadian Poetry, an Attempt to Define General Ideas. Ottawa, University of Ottawa, 1952. 204 p.
   Unpublished doctoral dissertation.

346. Black, J. L. "European Historical Studies in Canadian Universities Since 1945." New Review. 5: 46-58 no. 4, 1965.
   Also concerns studies of the history of the Ukraine.

347. Buynyak, Victor. "Slavic Studies in Canada: a Historical Survey" in Canadian Slavonic Studies. IX, 1: 3-24, 1967.
   Author discusses also Ukrainian studies in Canadian universities.

348. Dobriansky, Lev E. "Ukrainian Rivulets in the Stream of American Culture." Ukrainian Quarterly. 4:55-62. Winter, 1948.
   About the contributions of the Ukrainian immigrants and their progeny to the general American culture; the author lists prominent American educators of Ukrainian origin.

349. Kirkonnel, Watson. "Ukrainian Poetry in Canada" Slavic and East European Review. 13: 139-146. July, 1934.
   The author discusses three groups of Ukrainian Canadian poets; those who came to Canada as grown ups, those who came as children and those who were born in Canada.

350. Malycky, Alexander. "A Preliminary Checklist of Studies on Ukrainian-Canadian Creative Literature, Part I. General Studies," in Canadian Ethnic Studies. Bulletin of the Research Center for Canadian Ethnic Studies. Calgary, Alta, University of Calgary, 1969. I: 161-163.
   A bibliography of studies on Ukrainian literature in Canada.

351. Mamchur, Stephen. "Ukrainian cultural change," in Jubilee Book of the Ukrainian National Association in Commemoration of the Fortieth Anniversary of Its Existence. Jersey City, N. J., Svoboda Press, 1936. p. 498-512.
   About the cultural change in the life of the American Ukrainians, the problem of preserving the native culture, and of social integration without loss of native culture.

352. Nagurney, Michael S. "The Teaching of Ukrainian in the United States," in American Slavonic and East European Review. 4: 186-194, 1944.
     Concerns the teaching of the Ukrainian language in the Ukrainian Catholic schools in the United States and a history of St. Basil's College in Stamford, Conn. and its library.

353. Panchuk, John. "A Story of Ukrainian Canadians," Ukrainian Weekly, 1956, nos. 111, 117, 123, 129, 135, 141, 147, 153 and 159.
     The history, life, customs and achievements of Ukrainian Canadians.

354. Sawczuk, Marta. "Federation of Ukrainian Student Organizations of America: a Short Sketch." Horizons. 6: 53-57, no. 1/19.

C. - Church.

355. The Directory of the Ukrainian-Catholic Archieparchy of Philadelphia, Byzantine Rite. Philadelphia, Ukrainian Catholic Archieparchy of Philadelphia, 1952-
     Annual. Statistics, hierarchy, priests, faithful, schools, organizations, etc.

356. Eastern Orthodox Church. Directory of the United States 1968. San Francisco, R & R Research Associates, 1969. 32 p.
     Covers also Ukrainian Orthodox Church.

357. Scott, W. L. Eastern Ukrainians with special reference to the Ruthenians in Canada. Toronto, The Catholic Truth Society of Canada, 1930. 47 p.
     Predominantly concerns Ukrainians of the Eastern Catholic Rite referred to as "Ruthenians."

358. Trosky, Odarka Savella. A Historical Study of the Development of the Ukrainian Greek-Orthodox Church of Canada and Its Role in the Field of Education, 1918-1964. Winnipeg, University of Manitoba, 1965.
     Unpublished master's thesis. Educational work of the Ukrainian Orthodox Church of Canada and its Historical Development.

359. Trosky, Odarka Savella. The Ukrainian Orthodox Church in Canada. Winnipeg, Bulman Brothers, 1968. 87 p.
     The history and present status of the Ukrainian Orthodox Church in Canada.

360. Wenstob, Murray. The Work of the Methodist Church among Settlers in Alberta up to 1914, with Special References to the Formation of New Congregations and Work among the Ukrainian People. Edmonton, University of Alberta, 1959.
Unpublished bachelor's of divinity thesis, concerning missionary work of the Methodist church among Ukrainians in Alberta before the First World War.

361. Yuzyk, Paul. The History of the Ukrainian Greek-Catholic (Uniate) Church in Canada. Saskatoon, University of Saskatchewan, 1948.
Unpublished master's thesis.

362. Yuzyk, Paul. Ukrainian Greek-Orthodox Church of Canada, (1918-1951). Minneapolis, University of Minnesota, 1958.
Unpublished doctoral dissertation dealing with the history of the Ukrainian Orthodox Church in Canada.

D. - Organizations.

363. Almanac of Ukrainian Canadian Professional Federation. Toronto, Ukrainian Canadian Business and Professional Federation, 1953-
Biennial publication. Classified directory of the businessmen and professionalists of Ukrainian origin of Toronto and Montreal. Articles in English and Ukrainian (with English resume') concerning Ukrainian business life in the past and present in the home country and the Canada.

364. Burianyk, W. S.U.S.--Its Meaning and Significance. Toronto, Ukrainian Self-Reliance League of Canada, 1967. 40 p.
About the "Soyuz Ukraintsiv-Samostiynykiv"--a League of the Ukrainians demanding independence of Ukraine-- a political organization of the Canadian Ukrainians.

365. Ukrainian Congress Committee of America. The Story of the Ukrainian Congress Committee of America. New York, Ukrainian Congress Committee of America, 1951. 64 p.
The story of the Ukrainian Congress Committee of America and of its work on behalf of the Ukrainian cause.

366. Ukrainian Congress Committee of America. Twenty Years of Devotion to Freedom: Survey of Purposes and Activities of the Ukrainian Congress Committee of America. New York, Ukrainian Congress Committee of America, 1960. 104 p.
The aims of the Ukrainian Congress Committee of America and its work during the first twenty years of its existence.

367. Ukrainian National Association: Its Past and Present,
     1894-1964. Antin Dragan, ed. New York, Ukrainian National
     Association, 1964. 162 p.
          The history and present status of the Ukrainian
     National Association, an Ukrainian fraternal organization.

368. United Ukrainian American Organizations Committee of New
     York. Ukrainian Congress Committee Branch. Golden Jubilee
     Book Commemorating Organized Ukrainian Life in New York,
     1905-1955. Alexander Sokolyszyn, ed. New York, Peter
     Kuchma, 1956. 192 p.

369. Weres, Wasyl, ed. Guide to the Ukrainian-American Insti-
     tutions, Professional and Business. New York, Carpathian
     Star Publishing Company, 1953. 336 p.
          A directory of Ukrainian business and professional
     organizations and periodicals; includes some periodicals
     and articles on various aspects of the Ukrainian life in
     the United States.

370. Dobriansky, Lev E. "Report of the President for the
     Period of October 15, 1962-September 1, 1966," in IXth
     Congress of Americans of Ukrainian Descent, 1966, p. 11-69.
          A report of the President of the Ukrainian Congress
     Committee of America for a period of four years to the
     Ninth Congress of the American Ukrainians in 1966,
     published in Proceedings of this Congress.

371. Dobriansky, Lev E. "Ten Years of the Ukrainian Quarterly."
     Ukrainian Quarterly. 11: 108-117. Spring, 1955.

372. "Important Anniversaries." Ukrainian Quarterly. 26: 5-
     11, 1970.
          Concerns 30 years jubilee of the Ukrainian Congress
     Committee of America.

E. - Their Part in Political Lives of Their Countries.

373. Grady, Joseph P. O. The Immigrants' Influence on Wilson's
     Peace Policies. Lexington, University of Kentucky Press,
     1967. 329 p.
          One chapter deals with the influence of Slovaks and
     Carpatho-Ukrainians referred to as Carpatho-Ruthenians,
     on Wilson's peach policy.

374. Kaye, Volodymyr J. Participation of Ukrainians in the
     Political Life of Canada. Ottawa, 1957. 24 p. port.
     bibl. p. 15-16.
          Reprint in Golden Jubilee Almanac of the Ukrainian
     Benefit Association of St. Nicholas of Canada. Winnipeg,

1957, p. 112-133.

375. Kirkonnell, Watson. The Ukrainian Canadians and the War.
Toronto, Oxford University Press, 1940. 30 p.
About the loyal attitudes of the Canadian Ukrainians
during the war of 1939-1945.

376. Kirkonnell, Watson. Our Ukrainian Loyalists. Winnipeg,
Ukrainian Canadian Committee, 1943. 28 p.
The author rejects the statements that the Canadian
Ukrainians are pro-communist on the basis of their war
activity when they revealed pro-Canadian and anti-com-
munist convictions.

377. Luchkovich, Michael. A Ukrainian Canadian in Parliament:
Memoirs. Foreword by Alexander Gregorovich. Toronto,
Ukrainian Canadian Research Foundation, 1965. 128 p.
Illus (Canadian Centennial Series).
Memoirs of a member of the Canadian Parliament of
Ukrainian origin.

378. Yuzyk, Paul. Ukrainian Canadians: Their Place and Role
in Canadian Life. Toronto, Ukrainian Canadian Business and
Professional Federation, 1967. 104 p., port., map, tables.
The author discusses the role of the Ukrainian churches,
the achievements of the Canadian Ukrainians in different
sectors of Canadian life, the part of Canadian Ukrainians
in politics, in the life of Canada and their place in
multi-cultural Canada. He also tells about the literature,
Newspapers and organizations of the Canadian Ukrainians.

4. Soviet Regime and Ukrainians Abroad.

379. Bergh, Hendrik Van. Murder to Order, by Karl Anders,
pseud. New York, Devin Adair, 1967. 127 p., illus.,
ports., facsims.
A story of the killing by a Soviet agent Bohdan Stashyn-
skyi of the Ukrainian political leaders Lev Rebet and
Stepan Bandera, and story of the killer. Based on the
records of Stashynsky's trial.

380. Murdered by Moscow: Petlura, Konovalets, Bandera. London,
Ukrainian Publishers, 1962. 73 p.
Biographies of Ukrainian political leaders who became
victims of Soviet-arranged assassinations.

381. Raschhofer, Hermann. Political Assassination: the Legal
Background of Oberlaender and Stashynsky Cases. Tuebingen,
Fritz Schlichtenmeier, 1964. 231 p.
This book includes the material in the book: Murder
to Order by Bergh, dealing with the killing of the

Ukrainian political leaders Lew Rebet and Stepan Bandera. The rest of the book deals with the Oberlaender case, blamed with responsibility as the commander in chief of the Ukrainian batallion Nachtigall (within the German army), for the deaths of thousands of Ukrainian prisoners found murdered in prisons in Lviv after the Soviet army left Lviv in June, 1941. Investigations conducted by the authorities of the German Federated Republic found that the murder of those above mentioned Ukrainian prisoners was done by the Soviet authorities before the Ukrainian Batallion Nachtigall entered Lviv with the German army.

382. United States Congress. Senate. Committee of the Judiciary. Murder International, Inc. Murder and kidnapping as an instrument of Soviet policy. Washington, D. C., G.P.O. 1965. 176 p.
    This is a transcript of Senate hearings. It inquires into the case of Bohdan Stashynsky, convicted murderer of the Ukrainian political leaders Lew Rebet and Stepan Bandera. Also included is a list of 40 persons to have been assassinated by Soviet agents.
    Among those listed are also Symon Petlura and Euhen Konovalets--both prominent Ukrainian political leaders.

383. "The Trial in Karlsruhe: Documents and Testimonies." Ukrainian Quarterly. 19: 24-44. Spring, 1963.
    Excerpts from the records of the trial of the confessed killer of the Ukrainian political leaders Lev Rebet and Stepan Bandera--Bohdan Stashynskyi.

384. Yendyk, Rostyslav. "Petlura and Konovalets." Ukrainian Review. London 15: 15-21, June, 1968.
    The stories of their assassinations.

VI. UKRAINE - HISTORY.

1. Ukraine - History - Historiography.

385. Akademiia Nauk Ukrains'koii RSR. Instytut Istorii.
Pokazhchyk Prats' Opublikovanykh Naukovymy Spivrobitnykamy
Instytutu Istorii. 1956-1967. Kyiv, Naukova Dumka, 1969.
295 p.
   Arranged by authors. The works of any author chronologically by year of publication. A list of used
abbreviations and an alphabetical index of authors added.

386. Chubatyj, Mykola D. Problems of Modern Ukrainian Historiography. New York, 1944. 16 p.

387. Hrushevsky, Michael. The Traditional Scheme of "Russian"
History and the Problem of a Rational Organization of the
History of the East Slavs. Ed. Andrew Gregorovich. Winnipeg, Ukrainian Free Academy of Sciences, 1965. 24 p.
(Ukrainian Free Academy of Sciences Slavistica 55.)
   Also in the Annals of the Ukrainian Academy of Arts
and Sciences in the U. S. 2/2: 355-364. A translation
of an article of a prominent Ukrainian historian which
became a fundamental work in the new conception of the
history. of Eastern Europe.

388. Krupnytsky, Borys. Ukrainian Historical Science under the
Soviets, 1920-1950. Munich, Institute for the Study of
the USSR, 1951. 122 p. (Research materials, series II,
no. 51.)
   Ukrainian with an English summary. The situation of
Ukrainian historical research under the Soviets.

389. Polonska-Vasylenko, Natalia. Two Conceptions of the History
of Ukraine and Russia. Ed. by Volodymyr Mykula. London,
Association of Ukrainians of Great Brittain, 1968. 79 p.
   The author discusses the Ukrainian conception, developed
by Prof. Mykhailo Hrushevskyi, that the Kyiiv Principality was an Ukrainian state, and the Russian conception
that it was a Russian state or a common state of the pre-
Russian people, from which Ukrainians, Russians and
Belorussians later developed.

390. Doroshenko, Dmytro. "Drahomaniv and the Ukrainian Histo-
riography" Annals of the Ukrainian Academy of Arts and
Sciences in the U. S. 2: 23-32.
   The influence of the prominent Ukrainian scholar
Mykhailo Drahomaniv on Ukrainian Historiography.

391. Doroshenko, Dmytro. "A Survey of Ukrainian Historiography,"
in Annals of the Ukrainian Academy of Arts and Sciences

in the U. S." 5-6: 1-291.
Survey of the Ukrainian historiography up to 1917.

392. Dubrovskyi, V. "The Current Soviet Approach to Ukrainian History," in Ukrainian Review, Munich 3: 122-145, 1956.

393. Fedenko, Panas. "Hetman Ivan Mazepa in Soviet Historiography," in Ukrainian Review, Munich 9: 6-18, 1960 Bibl., footn.
About how Soviet historiography presents Hetman Ivan Mazepa as a traitor.

394. Horak, Stephan M. "Ukrainian Historiography, 1953-1963." Slavic Review, 24: 257-272. June, 1965.
Also available in reprint: discusses both historiography in Ukraine and abroad.

395. Hornovy, Osyp. "In Defense of Truth." Ukrainian Review, London. 1: 13-20, 1954.
Concerns the falsification of the history of Ukraine by Russians to prove eternal Ukrainian-Russian amity.

396. Krupnycky, Borys. "Bohdan Khmelnitsky and Soviet Historiography," Ukrainian Review, Munich. 1: 65-75, 1955.
Author discusses the contrasting attitude of Free World and Soviet historians toward Bohdan Khmelnytsky.

397. Krupnycky, Borys. "Critique from the Ukrainian Point of View of the Traditional Division in Periods of Russian History." Ukrainian Review, London. 1: 5-12, March, 1954.
The author criticizes the approach of Russian historians who consider the medieval Kyiv state a Russian state.

398. Krupnycky, Borys. "Mazepa and Soviet Historiography." Ukrainian Review, Munich. 3: 49-53.
About the hostile attitudes of Soviet historians to Hetman Ivan Mazepa.

399. Krupnycky, Borys. "Trends in Modern Ukrainian Historiography," Ukrainian Quarterly. 6: 337-345. Autumn, 1950.
Characteristics of the most prominent Ukrainian historians, beginning with the middle of the 19th century.

400. Ohloblyn, Alexander. "Ukrainian Historiography, 1917-1953," in Annals of the Ukrainian Academy of Arts and Sciences in the U. S. 5-6: 292-456.
A survey of Ukrainian historiography since 1917.

401. Serbyn, Roman. "Rus in the Soviet Scheme of East Slavic History." <u>The New Review</u>. 8: 4/33-9-3/36, p. 169-182, bibl., p. 180-182.

2. Ukraine - History - Sources.

402. <u>Acta Innocentii pp. III (1198-1216)</u>. A registris Vaticanis, aliisque eruit, introductione auxit, notisque illustravit P. Theodosius Haluscynskyi OSBM. Roma, 1944. Typis poly-glottis Vaticanis, XXXII. 674 p.
    Documents from the archives of the Vatican concerning contacts of the Pope Innocent III with Ukraine, especially its Western part.
    Outlines of the history of all the peoples belonging to the Eastern Christian churches, which had contacts with Pope Innocent III and a bibliography including Ukrainian works, added to this collection of documents.

403. Associated Ukrainian Members of Parliament and Senate in Poland. <u>Under the Yoke of Poland</u>. London, Eyre and Spottiwoods, Ltd., 1930. 18 p.
    Discusses Polish "Pacification" of Ukraine in 1930 (Documents).

404. Buynyak, V. O., ed. <u>The Galician-Volhynian Chronicle</u>. Winnipeg, Ukrainian Free Academy of Sciences, 1964. 23 p. (Ukrainian Free Academy of Sciences. Slavistica no. 50.)
    Translation of the Ukrainian chronicle concerning the West-Ukrainian realm of Halychyna and Volynia.

405. Goodrich, Leland N. and Marie J. Carrol. <u>Documents of American Foreign Relations July, 1944-June, 1945</u>. Princeton, N. J., Princeton University Press for the World Peace Foundation, 1947. 2 v.
    Under the headings "Ukraine," "Curzon Line," "Czechoslovakia," "Poland," etc., many documents concerning Ukrainian problems are found.

406. Great Britain. <u>Documents of Foreign British Policy, 1914-1939</u>. London, H. S. Stationary Office, 1949. v.
    In vol. 3 of the first series on p. 308-827 there are references to the problems of Eastern Ukraine. On p. 828-909 are "Negotiations to the Status and Attribution of Eastern Galicia, June 18-December 22, 1919."

407. Horn, Charles P., ed. <u>Source Records of the Great War</u>. Washington, National Alumni, 1923.
    On pages 18-30 of vol. 6 there are documents concerning the newly created Ukrainian state.

408. Hornykievich, Theophil, comp. and ed. Ereignisse in der Ukraine, 1914-1922, deren Bedeutung und Historische Hintergruende. Philadelphia, Ost-Europaeisches For- schungs-Institut, 1966-1969. 4 v.
   Documents from Austro-Hungarian State Archives con- cerning history of Ukraine in the period 1914-1922.

409. Sheptyckyj, Andrij. Metr. Monumenta Ucrainae Historica. Collegit Metropolita Andreas Sheptycki. Romae, Editiones Universitatis Catolicae Ucrainorum, 1964-1971. 10 v.
   Documents from the Vatican archives concerning the history of Ukraine.

410. SSSR. Akademia Nauk. Vossoiedineniie Ukrainy z Rosiiei; dokumenty i materialy v trekh tomakh Moskva, Izdatelstvo Akademii Nauk SSSR, 1954. 3 v.
   Documents concerning the Pereyaslav Treaty between the Ukraine and Russia.

411. United States, Department of State. Papers Relating to the Foreign Relations of the United States, 1918. Russia.
   References to the Ukraine indexed under the heading "Ukraine," or under other headings keyed to this heading with cross references.

412. United States. Department of State. Papers Relating to the Foreign Relations of the United States, 1918, World War. Washington, D. C., U. S. Government Printing Office, 1933. 4 vols.
   References to the Ukraine indexed under heading "Ukrainian Peace with Central Powers." Also a letter under the heading "Ukrainian Relief."

413. United States. Department of State. Papers Relating to the Foreign Relations of the United States, 1919. Russia. Washington, U. S. Government Printing Office, 1942. 11 vols.
   References to the Ukraine under headings "Ukraine," "South Russia," "Petlyura," a.o.

414. United States. Department of State. Papers Relating to the Foreign Relations of the United States. The Paris Peace Conference. Washington, U. S. Government Printing Office, 1942. 11 vols.
   Many references to the Ukraine under the headings "Ukraine," "Soviet Union," "Russia," "Poland," "Galicia, Eastern," "Bukovina," a.o.

415. United States. Department of State. Foreign Relations of the United States. Diplomatic Papers. The Soviet Union 1933-1939. Washington, U. S. Government Printing Office, 1952.
   References to Ukraine under the heading "Ukrainian

Question." One can also find some references in entries not keyed to this heading.

416. United States. Department of State. Foreign Relations of the United States. Diplomatic Papers. The Conference at Malta and Yalta, 1945.
    Many references to the Ukraine under the headings: "Ukrainian Soviet Republic," "Soviet Union--Ukraine," "Curzon Line," "Poland--Boundary Revision," "Poland-Curzon Line," "Poland-Lvov" a.o. Reference to the "Ruthenian National Committee" on p. 452.

417. United States. Department of State. Text of the Ukrainian Peace. Washington, U. S. Government Printing Office, 1918. 160 p.
    The text of the Ukrainian Declaration of Independence of January 22, 1918. The text of the Treaty of Brest Litovsk and of the secret protocols.

418. Welykyi, Athanasius G. Documenta Pontificum Romanorum Historiam Ucrainae Illustrantia. Collegit, introductione et adnotationibus auxit P. Athanasius G. Welykyi, OSBM. Romae, PP. Basiliani, 1953-54. 2 v. (Sumptibus Ucrainorum apud exteros degentium. Series III; Documenta Romana Ecclesiae Unitae in terris Ucrainae et Belorussiae.)
    A selection of documents from the Vatican archives concerning the history of the Ukraine.

419. Antonovych, Marko. "Comparative Notes on the Earliest Slavic Chronicles." New Review. 5: 44-53, 1965, no. 1.
    Also concerns Ukrainian chronicles.

420. Cross, Samuel H. "The Russian Primary Chronicle." Harvard Studies in Philology and Literature. 12: 17-32.
    An English translation of the oldest Ukrainian chronicle called the Primary or Nestor's Chronicle. A discussion of the authorship, sources, chronology and interpolations.

421. Doroshenko, Dmytro. "Ukrainian Chronicles of the 17th and 18th Centuries." Annals of the Ukrainian Academy of Arts and Sciences in the U. S. 1: 79-87.
    Concerns so-called "Kosak" chronicles.

3. Ukraine - History - General.

422. Allen William Edward David. The Ukraine: a History. 2nd ed. Cambridge, Cambridge University Press, 1963. 404 p., illus.
    A complete course of the history of the Ukraine. Includes the political and economic history of the Ukraine in relation with contemporary European history. In some chapters noticeable influence of Polish or Russian sources is found.

423. Doroshenko, Dmytro. History of Ukraine. Translated from Ukrainian and abridged by Hanna Keller. Edited and introduction by C. W. Simpson. Edmonton, The Institute Press, 1939. 702 p.
 A complete history of the Ukraine from a very early period. Geography of Ukraine included. Genealogical tables, 13 maps, index.

424. Fedenko, Panas. Ukraine--Her Struggle for Freedom. Augsburg, Free Ukraine, 1951. 80 p.
 A brief outline of the history of the Ukraine with stress on more recent times.

425. Florinsky, M. T. Russia: a Short History. New York, MacMillan, 1964. 653 p.
 An objective treatment of the Ukrainian history is included.

426. Gambal, Maria Strutynsky. The Story of Ukraine. Scranton, Pa., Ukrainian Workingmans Association, 1937. 102 p.
 A popular history of the Ukraine.

427. Hrushevsky, Mychailo. A History of Ukraine. Edited by O. J. Frederiksen. Preface by George Vernadsky. Published for the Ukrainian National Association. New Haven, Yale University Press, 1941. 629 p.
 Reprinted: Hamden, Conn., Archon, 1970. c. 1941.
 The history of the Ukraine beginning with pre-historical and classical times; maps and tables. Index and bibliography. The last chapter written by Prof. O. J. Fredericksen.

428. Kuropas, Myron. The Saga of the Ukraine: an Outline of History. Chicago, MUN Enterprizes, 1961. 2 v.
 Contents-- v. 1--The age of royalty (Medieval Period) --v. 2--The age of heroism (Kosak Period). A popular outline of Ukrainian history for youth of Ukrainian extraction. Volume 3 not published as yet but will cover the history of the Ukraine up-to-date. Maps, dynastical and genealogical tables added.

429. Manning, Clarence A. Outline of Ukrainian History. Winnipeg, Ukrainian Canadian Committee, 1949. 59 p.
 A popular outline of Ukrainian history.

430. Manning, Clarence A. The Story of Ukraine. New York, Philosophical Library, 1947. 326 p., maps.
 Recently deceased author was a professor of Columbia University and one of the most prominent American

scholars of Ukrainian and East European problems. He
covers all periods of the history of the Ukraine,
including World War II. He discusses the meaning of
words "Rus" and "Ukraine," geopolitics and economy of
the Ukraine, Ukrainian cultural influence on Russia
and the development of the Western Ukraine.

431. Nahayevsky, Isidore. History of Ukraine. Philadelphia,
America, 1961. 293 p.
    The author gives a full course of the history of the
Ukraine starting from the 10th century. In his course
he stresses the role of the Ukrainian Orthodox and
Catholic churches in the cultural and political life of
the Ukraine. The author states that because of this
influence the Soviet Government destroyed both Ukrainian
churches as enemies of Russian imperialism and communism. He stresses the role of the Ukrainian diaspora
abroad. Bibliographies are added at the end of each
chapter.

432. Prokopiv, Orysia. The Ukrainians: an Outline History.
Published by the Centennial Ukrainian Committee under the
auspices of the Ukrainian Canadian Committee, Calgary
Branch. Calgary, 1967. 40 p.
    A brief popular outline of Ukrainian history.

433. Yaremko, Michael. Galicia-Halychyna (a part of Ukraine)
from Separation to Unity. Toronto, New York-Paris,
Shevchenko Scientific Society, 1967. 292 p. (Shevchenko
Scientific Society. Ukrainian Studies vol. 18. English
Section vol. 3.)
    A comprehensive work covering the history of Halychyna
from the earliest time to the present. First publication
of this kind in English.

434. Korostovets, Volodymyr. "Ukraine: Past and Present
Described by an Ukrainian." Dublin Review. July, 1939,
p. 74-89.
    Survey of Ukrainian history and accound of present
(1939) conditions in the Ukraine.

435. Krupnytsky, Borys. "Ten Centuries of Ukraine: a Brief
Summary of Ukrainian History." Ukrainian Review, London.
2: 67-77, March, 1955.
    A brief outline of the history of the Ukraine from
the very beginnings to the present time.

4. Ukraine - History - Archeology.

436. Artamonov, Mikhail Illarionovich. The Splendor of Scythian Art: Treasures from Scythian Tombs. Introd. by Tamara Talbot Rice. Photos by Werner Forman. Tr. from Russian by V. R. Kyprianova. New York, Praeger, 1969. 296 p. illus., plates (part. col.) maps.
   Translation from a Russian original. An introductory article tells the history of Scythians, a people once living predominantly in the area of Southern Ukraine.
   A description of sites of findings of Scythian art treasures (situated predominantly in Southern Ukraine and adjoining Kuban) over 200 illustrations.

437. Borovko, Gregory, Scythian Art. Translated from the German by Professor V. G. Childs. New York, Frederik and Stiles Co., 1928. 111 p., plates.
   Includes description of Scythian art works pictured on 74 plates.

438. Jettmar, Karl. Art of Steppes. New York, Crown Publishers, 1962. 272 p.
   First 48 pages of the book deal with art of Scythes.

439. Pasternak, Yaroslav. Arkheolohiia Ukrainy. Pervisna, davnia ta serednia istoriia Ukrainy za arkheolohichnymy dzerelamy. Toronto, Naukove Tovarystvo Imeny Shevchenka, 1961. 788 p. illus. Plates, maps, bibl.
   English title: Archeology of Ukraine. English and German resume , biography and selective bibliography of author added. A most complete scholarly course of the archeology of the Ukraine by a prominent Ukrainian archeologist.

440. Rice, Tamara T. The Scythians. London, Thames and Hudson, 1957. 255 p.
   About the Scythians, who lived in Ukraine in antiquity. Ukraine is referred to in the book as "South Russia."

441. Shovkoplas, I. H. Rozvytok Radians'koii Arkheolohii Na Ukraini., 1917-1966. Bibliohrafiia. Kyiv, Naukova Dumka, 1969. 340 p.
   On head of title: Akademiia Nauk Ukrains'koii RSR. Tsentralna Naukova Biblioteka. Bibliography concerning development of the Ukrainian Archeology in the Soviet time. Includes 7,421 items. Arranged by subjects and chronologically in each subject.

442. Smal-Stocki, Roman. Slavs and Teutons: the Oldest German-Slavic Relations. Milwaukee, Wisc., Bruce Publishing Co., 1950. 102 p.

The author traces the influence of the Goths and other German tribes on the early Ukrainians. He gives an explanation of the name "Rus."

443. Sulimirski, Tadeusz. Corded Ware and Globular Amphore North-East of the Carpathians. London, Athlon Press, 1969. 281 p.
Concerns primitive pottery from the mounds of Western Ukraine.

444. Sulimirski, Tadeusz. Prehistoric Russia: an Outline. New York, Humanities, 1970. XXIII, 449 p. 38 plates., illus.
A considerable part of the book concerns Ukraine.

445. Tikhomirov, M. The Towns of Ancient Rus. Moscow, Foreign Languages Publishing House, 1959. 502 p.
Social and economic order of the towns of the medieval Rus being the empire of the Ukrainian people with its center in Kyiv. Official Soviet historiographic approach considers Rus to have been a common state of the pre-Russian people which later divided into the Ukrainian, Russian and Belo-Russian peoples.

446. Chikalenko, Levko. "Origins of the Paleolithic Meander." Annals of the Ukrainian Academy of Arts and Sciences in the U. S. 3?1(7): 518-534.
Paleolithic ornaments found in the North-Ukrainian village Mezina. Description of the individual ornaments. Available in reprints.

447. Chubatyi, Nicholas. "The Beginning of Russian History." Ukrainian Quarterly. 3: 262-273. Spring, 1947.
The author objects to the statement of Russian historians that Ukrainians are only newcomers from the West to present day Ukrainian territory and states that they are aborigines.

448. Chubatyi, Nicholas. "The Ukrainian and Russian Conceptions of the History of Eastern Europe." Shevchenko Scientific Society. Proceedings of the Historical-Philosophical Section. 1: 10-25.
Describes different views of the Ukrainian and Russian historians concerning the history of Eastern Europe. Claims correctness for the Ukrainian views.

449. Cross, Samuel H. "Primitive Civilization of the Eastern Slavs." American Slavic and East European Review. 5: 51-87. September, 1945.
Deals with the material and spiritual culture of the early inhabitants of the Ukraine.

450. Dombrovsky, Alexander. "A Few Examples of Analogy in the Ukrainian and Judaic Cultures." Annals of the Ukrainian

Academy of Arts and Sciences in the U. S." 7(12/23-24): 1531-1541. Bibl., footn.

451. Dombrovsky, Alexander. "Herodotus and Hippocrates on the Anthropology of the Scythians." Annals of the Ukrainian Academy of Arts and Sciences in the U. S." 10(1-2): 85-91.
     Concerns tribes which inhabited the Ukraine in antiquity.

452. Dombrovsky, Alexander. "Prehistory of Ukraine and Russian Historiography." Ukrainian Quarterly. 5: 356-359. Autumn, 1949.
     Explains how Russian historiographers claim that the ancient period of Ukrainian history was the ancient period of Russian history. Claims that in reality Russia was unknown to the ancient.

453. Kordysh, Neonila. "Notes on Weaving in the Trypillyan Culture of the Ukraine." Annals of the Ukrainian Academy of Arts and Sciences in the U. S. 1: 98-112.
     Traces of the weaving craft in the remains of the Trypillyan culture.

454. Kordysh, Neonila. Settlement Plan of the Trypillyan Culture." Annals of the Ukrainian Academy of Arts and Sciences in the U. S. 3: 532-552.
     Plans of Trypillyan settlements in the area of Kyiv.

455. Must, Gustav. "The Inscription on the Spearhead of Kovel." Language. 31: 493-498.
     Discusses a spearhead found in 1858 near Kovel in the Ukraine, probably from the second and third century A.D. The author argues that the inscription on the spearhead is in Illyric characters.

456. Pasternak, Yaroslav. "Lviv at the Dawn of History," in Lviv (see entry no. 135) p. 26-53.
     Archeology of Lviv.

457. Pasternak, Yaroslav. "The Trypillyan Culture in Ukraine." Ukrainian Quarterly. 6: 122-133. Spring, 1950.
     The Trypillian culture, its origin, chronology, settlements, arts and connections with Mediterranean culture.

458. Shcherbakivsky, Vadym. "The Formation of the Ukrainian People." Ukrainian Quarterly. 4: 115-128. Winter, 1948.
     Racial elements among the present Ukrainian people. How waves of invaders left their traces in the Ukrainian people. Differences between Ukrainians and Russians. Claims that only the former Russian upper strata are of

Slavic origin and that the masses are of Finnish origin.

459. Smal-Stocki, Roman. "Vernadsky's Conception of the Origin of the Slavs." Shevchenko Scientific Society. Proceedings of the Historical-Philosophical Section. 1: 56-62.

The author discusses the viewpoint of Professor George Vernadsky (Yale University) on the origin of Eastern Slavs, and presents his own view on this topic.

5. Ukraine - History, Ancient.

460. Boba, Imre. Nomads in the Formation of the Kievan State. Seattle, Wash., University of Washington, 1962.
Unpublished doctoral dissertation.

461. Dombrowsky, Alexander. "The Economic Relations of the Ukraine and the Ancient World." Ukrainian Quarterly. 6: 352-358. Autumn, 1950.
Discusses the trade routes leading from or over the Ukraine beginning with the third millennium B.C. Shows that ancient Ukraine had trade relations with the helenistic and Roman world.

462. Kocevalov, Andrey. "Ukraine's Participation in the Cultural Activities of the Ancient World." Ukrainian Quarterly. 5: 111-121. Spring, 1949.
Cultural contacts of ancient Ukraine with the contemporary civilized world.

463. Mladenovich, M. "War and Society in Eastern Europe before the Kievan Period." New Review. 4: 25-50. 1964, no. 2-3. Bibl., footn.
Deals predominantly with the Ukraine.

464. Polonska-Vasylenko, Natalia. "The Beginnings of the State 'Ukraine-Rus'." Ukrainian Review, London. 10: 33-58, 1963, no. 2. Bibl. footn., p. 54-58.

465. Rich, Vera. "Harald Hardrade, Rognvald Brusason and the "Cities of Cherven." Ukrainian Review, London. 11: 67-72. December, 1964, Concerns Ukrainian-Scandinavian relations.

6. Ukraine - History, Medieval.

466. Billington, James H. The Icon and the Axe: an Interpretative History of Russian Culture. London, Weidenfeld and Nicolson, 1966. 786 p.

A book aiming at presentation of Russian culture.
One chapter deals with culture of the medieval Kyiiv
Rus. Although the author understands the differences in
culture and national characteristics of the inhabitants
of Southern Rus from Northern Moscow he still applies
the name "Russian" to the "Rus."

467. Chadwick, Nora K. The beginning of Russian History. An
Inquiry into Sources. New York, MacMillan, 1946, 180 p.
The early history of the Kyiivan State and Greek and
Oriental influences upon it. Norman and native elements
in the organization of the state.

468. Chyrovsky, Nicholas L. F. An Introduction to Russian History. New York, Philosophical Library, 1967. XIII, 3,
229, 1 p.
The author gives only a brief survey of the history
of medieval Kyiivan state and stresses that according to
the non-Russian historians it does not belong to the
Russian history.
Proper Russian history he starts from the Suzdal and
other Muscovite principalities.

469. Dmytryshyn, Basil. Medieval Russia: a Source Book, 900-
1700. New York, Holt, 1967. 7, 312 p., maps.
On pages 3-117 documents concerning medieval Ukrainian
state--Kyiiv Rus. Excerpts from chronicles, travelo-
gues, the Tale of Ihor's Armament. Also the text of
Pereyaslav Treaty, (1654).

470. Paszkiewich, Henryk. Origin of Russia. New York, Allen,
1954. 556 p.
Presentation of the origins of the medieval Ukrainian
State referred to as Russia. Has a Polish approach to
certain problems, especially to Western Ukraine.

471. Riasanovsky, Alexander Valentinovich. The Norman Theory
of the Origin of the Russian State. A critical analysis.
Stanford, Cal., Stanford University, 1960. 262 p.
Unpublished doctoral dissertation. Concerns the
beginning of the old Ukrainian state called "Rus" and
considered by Russians to have been medieval Russian
state.

472. Seven Hundredth Anniversary of the Coronation of the
Ukrainian King Danylo and the Founding of the City of Lviv.
Winnipeg, Ukrainian Catholic Council of Manitoba, 1953.
12 p.
Deals with the Coronation of the West Ukrainian Prince
Danylo in 1224 and with founding of the city of Lviv in

the same year.

473. Thompson, Wilhelm. The Relations Between Ancient Russia and Scandinavia and the Origin of the Russian State. Oxford, James Parker and Company, 1877. 150 p.
    The author discusses Scandinavian influences on the medieval Ukraine, referred to as Russia, by means of phonetics.

474. Vasiliev, Alexander. The Russian Attack on Constantinople in 860. Cambridge, Mass., The Medieval Academy of America, 1946. 245 p.
    Deals with the attack of the earliest semi-legendary rulers of the Ukraine, Askold and Dyr on Constantinople. Analysis of the available source material.

475. Vernadsky, George and Michael Karpovitch. A History of Russia. New Haven, Yale University Press, 1947-1953. 3 vols.
    Volume 1, Ancient Russia, traces the history of ancient Ukraine from the pre-historical period and includes Trypillian culture. Volume 2, Kievan Russia, concerns the political, cultural, economic and legal history of the Kyiivan state up to the time of its collapse. Volume 3, The Mongols and Russia, deals with the background of the Russian people. In all three volumes the author refers to medieval Ukraine as Russia. He shares the view of other Russian scholars that there was a common Pre-Russian stock which differenciated in the 13th and 14th centuries into Russian, Ukrainian and Belorussian peoples.

476. Andrusiak, Nicholas. "Genesis and Development of East Slavic States," East European Problems. 1: 5-21. Autumn, 1956.

477. Andrusiak, Nicholas. "Lviv from Its Beginnings to 1772." In Lviv (see entry no. 135). Pp. 54-148.

478. Brutzkus, J. "The Khazar Origin of Ancient Kiev." Slavonic and East European Review. 22: 108-124, May, 1944 (American Series, II-IV).
    According to the author Kyiiv was founded and for long time ruled by Khazars.

479. Cheshire, Harold. "The Great Tartar Invasion on Europe." Slavonic and East European Review. 5: 89-105. June, 1926.
    Partially concerns Ukraine.

480. Chubatyi, Nicholas. "The 700th Anniversary of the City of Lviv 1251-1952," Ukrainian Quarterly. 9: 242-254.

History of Lviv--capital of Western Ukraine and its
role in Ukrainian cultural life in Kosak time.

481. Halich, Wasyl. "Ukraine and Medieval Trade." Ukrainian
Quarterly. 3: 377-384. Autumn, 1947.
The foreign trade of medieval Ukraine. Kyiiv and
Lviv as centers of International trade. The influence
of trade on the politics of the Ukrainian rulers.

482. Kaplan, Frederick I. "The Decline of Khazars and the
Rise of the Varangians." American Slavic and East-
European Review. 13: 1-10. 1954.
The author tells about the liquidation of Khazar
influences in Kyiiv in the 9th century along with the
growth of Norman influences.

483. Nazarko, Irenee, OSBM. "Dobroniha Daughter of St. Volodymyr the Great." Slavic and East European Studies.
2: 138-145. Autumn, 1957.

484. Pasternak, Yaroslav. "Peremyshl of the Chronicles and
the Territory of White Croates." Shevchenko Scientific
Society. Proceedings of the Historical-Philosophical
Section. 2: 36-40.
The prominent Ukrainian archeologist tells about
archeological findings in the Western Ukrainian City
Peremyshl (at present in Poland) and about some questions
still unanswered by archeologists.

485. Seniutovich-Berezhny, Viacheslav. "The creation of the
Volynian Nobility and Its Privileges." Shevchenko
Scientific Society. Proceedings of the Historical-
Philosophical Section. 2: 44-47.
The origins of this nobility, having among the fore-
bearers some members of the medieval reigning houses
and its position in the Lithuanian-Ukrainian state.

486. Shevchenko, Ihor. "Sviatoslav in Byzantian and Slavic
Miniatures." Slavic Review. 24: 709-713. Dec., 1965.
Plates.
The author discusses the miniatures of the medieval
ruler of Kyiivan state, Sviatoslav, available in Greek
and Slavic chronicles. These miniatures are reproduced
on plates.

487. Stokes, A. D. The Background and Chronology of the Balkan
Campaigns of Svyatoslav Igorevich." Slavonic and East
European Review. 40/94: 44-57, December, 1961.

488. Stokes, A. D. "The Balkan Campaign of Svyatoslav Igorevich" Slavonic and East European Review. 40/95: 466-496,
June, 1962.

Both articles deal with expansion of the Kyiivan medieval state toward the Balkans in the time of one of the first historical rulers of the Kyiivan Rus, Svyatoslav Ihorevych.

489. Togan, Zeki Velidi. "Timur's Campaign of 1395 in the Ukraine and North Caucasus." Annals of the Ukrainian Academy of Arts and Sciences in the U. S. 6(3-4/21-22): 1358-1371.

   Campaign of the Mongol leader Timur-Lenk against his enemy Tochtemysh involving territory of the Ukraine.

490. Zhdan, Michael. "The Dependence of Halych-Volyn' Rus on the Golden Horde." Slavonic and East European Review. 35: 505-522.

   The author states that the dependence of this state on the Golden Horde was less than the dependence of the other parts of the Ukraine.

7. Ukraine - History - 1340-1648.

491. Cresson, William Penn. The Cossacks: Their History and Country. New York, Brentano, 1919. 239 p.

   On pages 1-43 and 65-144, the author deals with the Ukrainian Kosaks and their prominent leaders Khmelnytsky and Mazepa. The author refers to Ukrainians as little Russians.

492. Gajecky, George and Alexander Baran. The Cossacks in the Thirty Year War. Volume 1: 1619-1624. Rome, PP. Basiliani, 1969. 140 p. (Analecta Ordinis Basilii Magni. Sectio I. Opera vol. XXIX.)

   In this work, (planned as a three-volume publication) the author discusses the participation of the Ukrainian Kosaks in the Thirty Year War. First volume covers the period 1619-1624.

   After a brief history of the Ukrainian Kosaks in general and their activities and history of Kosak mercenaries in different European wars, the authors discuss the participation of Kosak detachment in the war in Hungary, Bohemia, Moravia, on the Rhine and in the lower Palatinate.

   The study is based on source materials from Austrian, Bohemian, Hungarian and Vatican archives.

   It deals with an aspect of the history of the Ukrainian Kosaks almost untouched by historians. A bibliography and selection of original documents with English resume' supplement in this work.

493. Longworth, Philip. <u>The Cossacks</u>. New York, Holt, 1970.
409 p. illus., maps, plates.
Author discusses origin, history and fate of all
Kosak organizations which came into being and existed on
the territory of the present European and Asiatic
Soviet Union.
On pp. 11-47 he discusses the history of the Ukrainian
Kosaks. On pp. 97-124 he tells about prominent Kosak
leader, Hetman of Ukraine Bohdan Khmelnytskyi.
In bibliography author lists many Ukrainian titles.
Author is not sure in matters of terminology. He mixes
terms "Ukraine," "Russia," and "USSR."

494. March, George P. <u>The Cossacks of Zaporozhe</u>. Washington,
D. C., Georgetown University, 1965. 332 p.
Unpublished doctoral dissertation. Deals with
Ukrainian Kosaks and their fortress "Sich" on the
island south of the Dnipro Rapids in the area called
"Zaporozhe"--the area behind the Rapids.

495. Szczesniak, Boleslaw. "The Ostrog Estates and the End of
Knights of Malta in the Commonwealth of Poland," <u>Slavic
and East European Studies</u>. 6/12: 46-55. Spring-Summer,
1961.
Contents: Prince Janusz Ostrogski, polonized son of
the prominent Ukrainian political and church leader
Prince Konstantine Ostrozhskyi, made a trust out of his
estates and decided that after the expiration of his
line, the fortune should go to the Polish branch of the
Knights of Malta.
Author describes unsuccessful legal battle of the
Polish branch and after that of the Central Order of
Knights of Malta for this estate.

<u>8. Ukraine - History - 1648-1654.</u>

496. <u>Bastion of Resistance</u>. Comments on the Treaty of Pereya-
slav between Ukraine and Russia. Winnipeg, Ukrainian
Canadian Committee, 1954. 24 p.
The Treaty of Pereyaslav and its consequences.

497. Moskalenko, Andrij. <u>Khmelnytskyi and the Treaty of
Pereyaslav in Soviet Historiography</u>. New York, Research
Program on the USSR, 1953. 40 p. (Mimeograph Series no.
73.)
Discusses the attitude of Soviet historians to Hetman
Khmelnytskyi and the Pereyaslav Treaty.

498. Ohloblyn, Oleksander. <u>Treaty of Pereyaslav 1654</u>. Toronto-
New York, Canadian League for Ukrainian Liberation Organization for Defense of Four Freedoms for Ukraine, 1954.
103 p.

The author discusses the Pereyaslav Treaty.

499. Chubaty, Nicholas. "The 300th Anniversary of the Second Ukrainian State." Ukrainian Quarterly 4: 144-150. Spring, 1948.
    Discusses restoration of the independent Ukrainian State by Hetman Bohdan Khmelnytsky and the Treaty of Pereyaslav.

500. Czyrowski, Nicholas. "Economic Aspects of the Ukrainian-Muscovite Treaty of 1654." Ukrainian Quarterly 10: 85-92. Winter, 1954.
    The author argues that after the Pereyaslav Treaty, Moskow made a colony of Ukraine, and neglected its development.

501. Ivanytsky, Socrat. "Did the Treaty of Pereyaslav Include a Protectorate." Ukrainian Quarterly 10: 176-182. Spring, 1954.
    Discusses the legal aspects of the Pereyaslav Treaty.

502. Lypynsky, Vyacheslav. The Ukraine on the Turning Point. Annals of the Ukrainian Academy of Arts and Sciences in the U. S. 3: 605-619.
    A translation of the section of the above named work by Lypynsky concerning the Pereyaslav Treaty and the Khmelnytsky's attitude to the Moskow Tsar.

503. Manning, Clarence A. "The Theses of the Treaty of Pereyaslav." Ukrainian Review, London 2: 41-45. June, 1955.
    Concerns the theses published by the Soviet Government on the 300th anniversary of the Treaty of Pereyaslav intended to stress permanent unity of the Ukraine with Russia. Also in Ukrainian Quarterly 10: 22-31. Autumn, 1954.

504. Ohloblyn, Oleksander. "The Pereyaslav Treaty and Eastern Europe." Ukrainian Quarterly 10: 41-50. Winter, 1954.
    A description of conditions of the treaty as presented from the different viewpoints of Ukrainians and Russians.

505. Polonska-Vasylenko, Natalia. "1654." Ukrainian Review, London. 2: 54-64. June, 1955.
    The author presents her view of the Pereyaslav Treaty and claims misinterpretation of its clauses by Moscow.

506. Reshetar, John, Jr. The significance of the Soviet Tercenary of the Pereyaslav Treaty." Annals of the Ukrainian Academy of Arts and Sciences in the U. S." 4(3/13): 981-994. Bibl., footn.

507. Yakovliv, Andrii. "Bohdan Khmelnytsky's Treaty with Tsar

of Muscovy in 1654." Annals of the Ukrainian Academy of Arts and Sciences in the U. S. 4(3/13): 904-916. Bibl., footn.

9. Ukraine - History - 1654-1775.

508. Borshchak, Ilko. Hryhor Orlyk, France's Cossak General. Toronto, Burns and McEachern Company, 1956. 124 p.
    About the son of the last ukrainian Hetman in Exile Pylyp Orlyk, a Marshal of the French King Louis XV.

509. Chevalier, Pierre. A Discourse of the Original Country, Manners, Government and Religion of the Cossacks. Translated by Edward Browne. London, H. Kemp, 1672. 195 p.
    A translation of the French original. About the Ukrainian Kosaks and their military history until the year 1651.

510. O'Brien, C. Bickford. Muscovy and the Ukraine from the Pereyaslav Agreement to the Truce of Andrusovo, 1654-1667. Berkeley, University of California Press, 1963. 138 p.
    The author discusses the period of the "Ruine." He discusses the political, religious and cultural life of the Ukraine during the 17th century and the role of the Kosaks. He points to the disillusionment of Khmelnytsky with Muskovy's attitude toward the Ukraine and describes his efforts to make an alliance with Sweden. He describes the influence of the internal conflicts among the Kosaks on the political situation of the Ukraine. He gives also an analysis of the treaty of Andrusovo.

511. Pauls, John. Pushkin's "Poltava" with a foreword by Prof. Roman Smal Stocki. New York, Shevchenko Scientific Society. Ukrainian Studies English Section, vol. 1. 107 p.
    The aim of the author is to show that Pushkin's glorifying of Peter I's victory at Poltava was intended to discredit Hetman Ivan Mazepa as a leader of the Ukraine.

512. Slowacki, Juliusz. Mazeppa - Polish and American together with a Brief Survey of Mazeppa in the United States, by Marion Moore Coleman. Cheshire, Conn., 1966. 74 p.
    A translation of a poem by a well known Polish poet of the 19th century, Juliusz Slowacki, about Hetman Mazepa, along with the Polish original and a survey of Polish Mazepiana.

513. Three Centuries of Struggle. 300th anniversary of the Treaty of Pereyaslav, 1654-1954. Winnipeg, Ukrainian

Canadian Committee, 1954. 47 p.
Address on the occasion of the 300th anniversary of the Pereyaslav Treaty. Discusses Ukrainian resistance to the Russians, starting after signing of the Pereyaslav Treaty.

514. Chubatyi, Nicholas. "Mazepa's Champion in the 'Secret du Roi' of Louis XVth, King of France." Ukrainian Quarterly 5: 37-51. Winter, 1949.
The story of Hryhor Orlyk, Marshal of Louis XVth.

515. Donzow, Dmytro. "The Campaign of Charles XII in Ukraine," Ukrainian Review, London 2: 6-16, September, 1955.
Discusses Hugo's poem "Mazeppa" written in 1828 and its usefulness toward a true understanding of the Ukraine, its fate and its spirit.

516. Kentrzynskyj, Bohdan. "The Political Struggle of Mazepa and Charles XII for Ukraine's Independence." Ukrainian Quarterly 4: 204-214. Summer, 1948.
About the followers of Hetman Mazepa, who continued to fight for Ukraine's independence after his death.

517. Levitter, L. S. "Poland, Ukraine and Russia in the 17th Century." Slavonic and East European Review 27: 157-171 and 27: 414-429. December, 1948, May, 1949.
Deal with cultural conditions in the Ukraine, Russia and Poland during the 17th century. Pages 167-171 and 414-424 deal with the cultural revival in the Ukraine during the time of Metropolitan Petro Mohyla.

518. Lew Wasyl. "Mazepa in Slavic Literatures." Slavic and East European Studies 5(3-4): 200-208. Fall-Winter, 1966.
A bibliographic review.

519. Mackiw, Theodore. "Mazepa's Election as Hetman in English Press of 1687." Ukrainian Review 14: 65-69. June, 1967.

520. Mackiw, Theodore. "Mazepa in the Light of Contemporary English Press." Ukrainian Review, London. 7: 30-36. March, 1960. Bibl., footn.

521. Mackiw, Theodore. "Ukraine as seen by the 'London Gazette,' 1665-1965." Ukrainian Review, London. 13: 71-77. March, 1966. Bibl., footn.

522. Manning, Clarence A. "The World of Mazepa." Ukrainian Quarterly. 15: 260-270. Sept, 1959.

523. Ohloblyn, Oleksander. "Hetman Orlyk's Manifesto." Ukrainian Review, London 4: 42-47. Autumn, 1957.

About the manifesto to the European rulers issued in 1712 by the Ukrainian Hetman in Exile, Pylyp Orlyk, claiming Ukraine's right to independence.

524. Ohloblyn, Oleksander. "Pylyp Orlyk's Devolution of the Ukraine's Rights." Annals of the Ukrainian Academy of Arts and Sciences in the U. S. 6: 1296-1313.
     The genesis, contents and ideas of the memorandum submitted by the Hetman of Ukraine in Exile, Pylyp Orlyk to the French chancellor, Chauvel, with another argument for the right of the Ukraine to independence. The French text of the memorandum is added.

525. Ohloblyn, Oleksander. "The Year 1709." Ukrainian Review, London, 6: 19-30, December, 1959. Bibl., footn.
     Concerns Poltava battle of 1709.

526. Pauls, John. "Historicity of Pushkin's 'Poltava'." Ukrainian Quarterly 17: 230-246 and 17: 342-361. September and December, 1961.
     Argues Russian bias and distortion of facts in Pushkin's above mentioned poem.

527. Pauls, John P. "Musical Works Based on the Legend of Mazepa." Ukrainian Review, London 11: 57-65. December, 1964. Bibl., footn.

528. Pauls, John P. "Shevchenko on Mazepa." Ukrainian Review. London 15: 59-65. September, 1968. Bibl., footn.

529. Pauls, John P. "The Treatments of Mazepa: Ryleyev's and Pushkin's." Slavic and East European Journal 8/1-2: 17-42. Spring-Summer, 1963.
     Analysis and comparison of poems about Mazepa by the two above mentioned Russian poets.

530. Smal-Stocki, Roman. "Mazepa and Mazepists." Ukrainian Weekly, 1950 no. 32 & 33.
     About the attitudes of the white and red Russians toward Hetman Mazepa and his followers, called by the Russians contemptuously, "Mazepists."

531. Tokarzewski-Karaszewicz, Jan. "The Battle of Poltava." Ukrainian Review, London 6: 13-20, June, 1959 and 6: 49-68, September, 1959. Bibl., footn.

532. Tys-Krokhmaliuk, Yurii. "The Victory at Konotop." Ukrainian Review, London, 6: 34-45. September, 1959.

533. Wasylenko, Mykola. "The Constitution of Pylyp Orlyk."
Annals of the Ukrainian Academy of Arts and Sciences in
the U. S. 6/3-4: 126-129.
     A translation from the Russian language of an article
about the Constitution of the Ukraine submitted and sworn
by Ukrainian Hetman in Exile Pylyp Orlyk after his
election.

10. Ukraine - History - 1775-1914.

534. Bohachevsky-Chomiak, Martha. The Spring of a Nation:
the Ukrainians in Eastern Galicia in 1848. Philadelphia,
Shevchenko Scientific Society, 1967. 80 p. (Shevchenko
Scientific Society. Ukrainian Studies vol. 25. English
section, vol. 6.)
     About the influence of the revolution of 1848 and the
liberalization in Habsburg Austria on Ukrainians.

535. Dushnyk, Walter. In Quest of Freedom. In commemoration
of the fortieth anniversary of the Ukrainian independence.
New York, Ukrainian Congress Committee of America, 1958.
96 p.
     The history of Ukraine beginning from the middle of
the 18th century; the period before and during the first
World War; the period of the Ukrainian independence; the
time before, during and after the second World War.

536. Elwood, Ralph Carter. The RSDRP in the Underground: a
Study of the Russian Social Democratic Labor Party in the
Ukraine 1907-1914. New York, Columbia University, 1969.
496 p.
     An unpublished doctoral dissertation; a study of revo-
lutionary underground in the Ukraine before the first
World War. The author pictures briefly the attitude of
the Russian Social Democrats to the national and agrarian
problems and states that this approach caused this party
to lose its influence in the Ukraine (called by the
author, "South Russia").

537. Hovde, Agnes Louise. Prelude to a Journey. A Story of
the Ukraine. New York, Vantage Press, 1954. 116 p.
     The life of the Ukrainian aristocracy and peasantry
at the time of the liberation of the serfs in the
Ukraine, 1861.

538. Lynch, Donald Francis. The Conquest, Settlement and
Initial Development of New Russia (1780-1837). New Haven,
Yale University, 1965.
     Unpublished doctoral dissertation. Concerns the coloni-
zation of the South Ukrainian steppes.

539. Polonska-Vasylenko, Natalia. The Settlement of the
Southern Ukraine, 1750-1775. New York, Ukrainian Academy
of Arts and Sciences in the U. S., 1955. 350 p. (Annals
of the Ukrainian Academy of Arts and Sciences in the U. S.
IV-V.)
     About the colonization of the sparsely settled Southern
Ukraine by settlers of foreign extraction following the
colonial policy of the Russian Government. Ukrainian
resistance against this colonization.

540. Slosson, Preston, William. Europe Since 1870. Boston,
Houghton Mifflin Company, 1933. 810 p.
     Includes references to the Ukrainians in Russia and
Austro-Hungaria, the war between the Ukraine and Russia
and Poland and the Ukrainians in Poland, the USSR,
Roumania and Czechoslovakia.

541. Taylor, A.J.C. The Habsburg Monarchy, 1809-1918. The
history of the Austrian Empire and Austro-Hungary. London,
Hamish Hamilton, 1966. 279 p.
     Includes many references to the Ukrainians in Austro-
Hungaria. Uses the designation "Little Russians."

542. Andrusiak, Nicholas. "Ukraine in the Twentieth Century:
a Brief Survey." Ukrainian Quarterly. 22: 152-163.
June, 1966. Bibl., footn.

543. Derzhavyn, Volodymyr. "The History of the Rus." Ukrainian
Review, London. 4: 24-31. June, 1957.
     Concerns the anonymous history of the Ukraine from
the end of the 18th century. Several characteristic
passages from this history are included in the article.

544. Doroshenko, Volodymyr. "Lviv in the Era of Modern Ukrainian
Rebirth: History of Relations between Western Ukraine and
Eastern Ukraine in the 19th and 20th Centuries." Lviv
(See entry no. 135.) p. 229-271.
     Discusses Lviv as link between Austrian-dominated
western Ukraine and Russian-dominated eastern Ukraine.

545. Krupnitsky, Borys. "Revolutionary Currents in Modern
Ukrainian History." Ukrainian Quarterly 6: 23-28. Winter,
1950.

546. Luzhnytsky, Gregory. "Ukrainian Cultural Activities in
Lviv, 1848-1918," in Lviv (see entry no. 135). p. 166-190.

547. Manning, Clarence A. "Ukraine and the Year 1848."
Ukrainian Quarterly 3: 205-214. Spring, 1947.
     Repercussions of ideas of 1848 revolution in the

Ukraine. Brotherhood of St. Cyril and Methodius had
the same ideals.

548. Martin, Neil A. "The Brotherhood of St. Cyril and Methodius," Ukrainian Quarterly. 22: 260-271. Fall, 1966.
About organization of young Ukrainian intellectuals
which came into being in 1840's. Its aim was the liberation of the Ukraine from Russian domination and the
organization of a federation of Slavic states.

549. Martin, Neil A. "19th Century Ukrainian National Revival."
Ukrainian Quarterly. 21: 225-267.

550. Odlozilik, Otakar. "Congresses of the Slavic Youth,
1890-1892." Annals of the Ukrainian Academy of Arts and
Sciences in the U. S. 6: 1327-1358.
Discusses the congresses of Slavic students from
various parts of the former Austro-Hungaria in Krakov
1890 and in Vienna 1892. The participation of the
Ukrainian representatives in these congresses and the
influence wielded by them on subsequent relationships
with the leaders of the various other Slavic groups.

551. Ohloblyn, Alexander. "The Ethical and Political Principles
of Istoria Rusov." Annals of the Ukrainian Academy of
Arts and Sciences in the U. S. 2/4: 388-400.
Argues that the principles of "Istoria Rusov" are:
truth, justice, humanity, common good, democracy and
religious tolerance. The anonymous author stands
opposed to an aggressive war but approves a war against
tyranny and oppression.

552. Ohloblyn, Alexander. "Research Studies on Istoria Rusov."
Shevchenko Scientific Society. Proceedings of the Section
of History and Philosophy 2:32-36.
A history of research on this work with the authors
interpretation.

553. Ohloblyn, Alexander. "Ukrainian Autonomists of the 1780's
and 1790's and Count P. A. Rumyantsev-Zadunaysky." Annals
of the Ukrainian Academy of Arts and Sciences in the U. S.
6-3(21-22): 1313-1326.
Concerns Count Rumyantsev-Zadunaysky general-governeur
of the Ukraine in 1770's and 1780's and his favorable
attitude toward Ukrainian needs and problems.

554. Ohloblyn, Alexander. "Where was 'Istoria Rusov' written?"
Annals of the Ukrainian Academy of Arts and Sciences in
the U. S. 3: 670-693.
A description of the place where the author of "Istoria
Rusov" lived and worked.

555. Porsky, Volodymyr. "New Soviet Literature on the December-
ists in Ukraine." Annals of the Ukrainian Academy of
Arts and Sciences in the U. S." 3(1/3): 584-587.

556. Rosciszewska, Pelagia. "Excerpts from the Diary." Annals
of the Ukrainian Academy of Arts and Sciences in the U. S.
1: 29-35. Notes p. 34-35.
    Both articles concern the Decembrist uprising in the
Ukraine.

557. Rudnytsky, Ivan. "Intellectual Origins of the Modern
Ukraine." Annals of the Ukrainian Academy of Arts and
Sciences in the U. S. 6: 1381-1404.
    The author states that the Ukrainian national political
and cultural renaissance in recent times has been tightly
connected with Ukrainian intellectual trends. Discusses
sequence of different intellectual trends in modern
Ukraine.

11. Ukraine - History - European War, 1914-1918.

558. Sands, Beduin. The Russians in Galicia. New York,
Ukrainian National Council, 1916. 43 p.
    A history of Eastern Halychyna before the European
war 1914-1918. Russian rule in Halychyna during their
occupation in years 1914-1916.

559. Shandruk, Pavlo. Arms of Valor. New York, Robert Spellers
and Sons, 1958. 320 p.
    Ukrainian military history beginning with the year 1917.

560. Smal-Stocki, Roman. Beginning of Fight for Rebirth of
Ukrainian Statehood. New York, Shevchenko Scientific
Society, 1967. 15 p., map. (Shevchenko Scientific Society,
Papers, no. 24.)
    Also reprinted in Ukrainian Quarterly. 23: 12-26.
March, 1967. Bibl., footn.

12. Ukraine - History - 1917-1921.

561. Eichenbaum, V. M. The Unknown Revolution - Ukraine, 1918-
1921, Kronstadt, 1921. New York Libertarian Club, 1956.
270 p.
    This is a translation of part of a larger French work
by a well known anarchist, who played an important role
in the civil war in the Ukraine of 1917-1921. He was
adviser to a well known Ukrainian anarchist, Nestor
Machno. In most of the book the author describes the
activities of Machno. The book contains much documentary
material.

562. Kubiyovych, Volodymyr. The Ukrainian Republic of January 22. Chicago, Ukrainian Research and Information Institute, 1963. 23 p.
   Deals with proclamation of Independence of Ukraine of January 22nd, 1918.

563. Lissiuk, Kalenik. For Land and Freedom. Toronto, Ont., the author, 1954. 35 p.
   Memoirs concerning the Ukrainian independence struggle of 1918-1920.

564. Manning, Clarence A. Twentieth Century Ukraine. New York, Bookman Associates, 1951. 243 p.
   About the Ukrainian revival after 1798; short-lived Ukrainian independence. Ukraine between two wars under the rule of four occupants; Carpatho-Ukraine, World War 1939-1945 and the Ukrainian Insurgent Army. Ukrainian Displaced Persons. Ukrainian literature after 1798, economic development and Ukraine between East and West.

565. Margolin, Arnold Davidovitch. From a Political Diary, Russia, the Ukraine and America, 1905-1945. New York, Columbia University Press, 1946. 250 p.
   The author, an Ukrainian lawyer of Jewish origin, tells about his work as a member of the Ukrainian cabinet and a member of the Ukrainian delegation to the Paris Peace Conference and as an Ukrainian representative in London on pages 3-71.

566. Nahayevsky, Isidore. History of the Modern Ukrainian State, 1917-1923. Munich, Ukrainian Free University and Ukrainian Free Academy of Sciences, 1966. 317 p.
   A history of Ukraine beginning with the 18th century. A detailed history of the period of Ukrainian independence, 1917-1923. The role of the Ukrainian churches. A selection of documents concerning this period of Ukrainian history is included.

567. Pap, Michael S. Ukraine's Struggle for Independence, 1917-1918. New York, Shevchenko Scientific Society, 1961. 31 p. Bibl., footn. (Shevchenko Scientific Society. Papers no. 17.)
   A brief survey of the history of the Ukraine during the years 1917-1921.

568. Pidhainy, Oleh Semenovych. The Formation of Ukrainian Republic. Toronto, The New Review Books, 1966. 685 p.
   The author discusses the establishment and working of the Ukrainian Central Rada (Council), its bargaining with the Russian Provisional Government, which was not willing to recognize aspirations toward independence of

the Ukrainians, and the de facto recognition of the
Ukrainian Republic by France and Great Britain. In the
following chapters he discusses recognition of the
Ukrainian Rada by the Bolshevik Russia, the subsequent
Ukrainian-Russian war and the recognition of the
Ukraine by Central Powers in the Brest-Litovsk Treaty.

569. Proceedings of the Brest-Litovsk Peace Conference. The
peace negotiations between Russia and the Central Powers.
Nov. 21, 1917-March 3, 1918. Washington, D. C., Govt.
Printing Office, 1918. 187 p.
   Also concerns peace negotiations with the Ukraine.

570. Seton-Watson, Hugh. The East European Revolution. New
York, Fred A. Praeger, 1951. 406 p.
   Although Ukraine is outside of the scope of this work,
the author makes some references to the Ukraine, to the
situation of the Ukrainians in pre-war Poland and Rumania,
to the Ukrainian church and to the Ukrainian Insurgent
Army. The author shows a good knowledge of the Ukrainian
problems.

571. Smart, Terry Lee. The French Intervention in the Ukraine,
1918-1919. Lawrence, Kansas, University of Kansas, 1969.
186 p.
   An unpublished doctoral dissertation. The author discusses the French intervention in Odessa in mid-Decem-
ber, 1918 in support of the anti-bolshevik forces
(Ukrainian and Denikin).
   He states that the French withdrawal from Odessa was
not due to a French defeat but they did it intentionally
because there was no cooperation between the numerous
anti-bolshevik forces and because there was no one force
of serious military value that was able to organize a
government which could assure order and the safety of
the population.

572. Stakhiv, Mathew and Yaroslav Shtendera. Western Ukraine
at the Turning Point of the Europe's History, 1918-1923.
Scranton, Pa., Ukrainian Scientific Historical Library,
1969-1971. 2 v.
   Authors discuss in this work situation of the Ukrainians
in the Austro-Hungarian Monarchy, Ukrainian-Polish
relations during World War I, Ukrainian claims of right
of national self-determination, political life and
political and social developments in Western Ukraine and
Jewish minority in Western Ukraine. The present con-
flicting interests of Ukrainians and their neighbors
during the World War I and at the Peace Conference in
Paris.
   Bibliography including over 400 titles makes this

unique om English language-work still more valuable for
a student of Ukrainian problems.

573. Woropay, Walentyna. The Hetmanate of P. Skoropadskyi in
Ukraine in 1918. London, University of London, 1959.
Unpublished master's thesis.

574. "Fiftieth Anniversary of Ukrainian National Revolution and
Independence." Ukrainian Quarterly 24: 1-12. Spring,
1968.

575. "Half a Century of Unequal Struggle for Freedom."
Ukrainian Quarterly 23: 5-10. Spring, 1967.

576. Krahl, Wolfgang. "The Ukrainian Revolution Fifty Years
Ago." Ukrainian Review, London 14: 8-19. September,
1967. Bibl., p. 19.

577. Manning, Clarence A. The American and Ukrainian Revolution."
Ukrainian Quarterly 23: 65-74. Spring, 1967.
A comparison of the American and Ukrainian liberation
revolutions.

578. Martos, Borys. "First Universal of the Ukrainian Central
Rada." Ukrainian Quarterly 24: 22-37. Spring, 1968.
Bibl., footn.
A former member of the Ukrainian Cabinet discusses the
first Universal proclamation which proclaimed the autono-
my of the Ukraine.

579. Sheptyckyj, Andrei, Metr. "On the Treaty of Brest Litovsk."
Ukrainian Review, London 15: 73-77. March, 1968. Bibl.,
footn.
The late head of the Ukrainian Catholic church, Metro-
politan of Lviv, discusses the Brest-Litovsk Treaty of
February 9, 1918 between Ukraine and the Central Powers
in his speech in the Upper Chamber of the Austrian
Parliament.

580. Stachiv, Matvij. "The System of the Hetman Government in
Ukraine in 1918, and Its Characteristics as Seen from the
Point of View of the Constitutional Law." Shevchenko
Scientific Society. Proceedings of the Section of Philo-
sophy and History 2: 51-54. 1957.
An abstract. The author claims that in spite of its
monarchistic form, the Hetman regime had all the attri-
butes of a democratic republic.

581. Stakhiv, Matthew. "Thirty-five Years of the Ukrainian
Independence." Ukrainian Quarterly 9: 14-18. Winter, 1953.

Discusses problem of the Ukraine's seat in the U. N. Claims that the expelling of the Ukraine from the United Nations would be a powerful asset to Soviet propaganda. However, representatives of the Soviet Ukraine could be removed from the U. N. together with the representatives of the USSR, but then their seats should be reserved for the representatives of free Ukraine.

582. "The Unfinished Revolution: 50 Years of the National Struggle of Ukraine for Freedom and Independence against Russian Tyranny." Ukrainian Review, London 14: 2-10. March, 1967.

583. Woropay, Valentyna. "The Struggle for Ukrainian Independence in 1917-1918. Ukrainian Review, London, 14: 20-36, September, 1967, 15: 62-73, March, 1968, 15: 61-72, June, 1968, 16: 67-97. March, 1969, 16: 67-87, June, 1969, 16: 65-75, September, 1969, 17: 76-93, June, 1970 (Excerpts from entry no. 573.)

13. Ukraine. German Occupation 1941-1945.

584. Dallin, Alexander. German Policy and the Occupation of the Soviet Union 1941-1944. New York, Columbia University, 1953. 1351 p.
   An unpublished doctoral dissertation concerning German policy in occupied Ukraine. Available in microfilm or Xerox copies from the University Microfilms, Inc., Ann Arbor, Michigan. Abstract in dissertation abstracts 1956.

585. Kamenetsky, Ihor. German Lebensraum Policy in Eastern Europe during World War II. Urbana, Illinois, University of Illinois, 1957. 272 p.
   An unpublished doctoral dissertation dealing chiefly with the role of Ukraine in the German plans to assure sufficient Lebensraum (living space) for Germany in Eastern Europe. Available in Microfilm or Xerox copies from University Microfilms, Inc., Ann Arbor, Michigan. Abstract in Dissertation Abstracts.

586. Kamenetsky, Ihor. Hitler's Occupation of Ukraine. A Study in Totalitarian Imperialism. Milwaukee, Marquette University Press, 1956. 122 p. (Marquette University Slavic Studies.)
   The author discusses the ideological and political background and preparation of this occupation, called "Operation Barbarossa," German policy in occupied Ukraine and Ukrainian anti-German partisan warfare. Bibliography on p. 87-96.

587. Kern, Erich. *Dance of Death*. New York, Charles Scribner's
Sons, 1951. 255 p.
About the German conquest of Greece, Yugoslavia and
the Ukraine and the disillusionment of the Ukrainians
with German occupation.

588. Pabel, Reinhold. *Enemies are Human*. Philadephia, Winston
Publishing Company, 1955. 248 p.
On pages 59-94, the author who participated in the
German campaign against the USSR in 1941-1945, tells
about Eastern and Western Ukraine, about Kyiv and other
Ukrainian cities, about the Ukrainians and their dis-
appointment with German occupation. The author stresses
the differences between the Ukrainians and the Russians.

589. De Weerd, Hans. "Erich Koch and Ukraine," in *Ukrainian
Quarterly*. 11: 29-34. Winter, 1955.
The Reichskommissar of Ukraine, Erich Koch, disregarded
the eastern policy of Alfred Rosenberg and carried on a
policy of extermination in the Ukraine.

590. Dmytryshyn, Basil. "Nazis and the SS Volunteer Division
Galicia." *American Slavic and East European Review*. 15:
1-10, February, 1950.
About how the Germans organized small Ukrainian volunteer units before war with the USSR but later disbanded
them. In 1942 they organized the SS Division Galicia
but guarded against arousing Ukrainian nationalism
through this organization.

591. Joesten, Joachim. "Hitler's Fiasco in Ukraine," *Foreign
Affairs*. 21: 331-339, January, 1943.
About how the Soviet "Scorched Earth Policy" prevented
the Germans from securing a food base; about how Ukrainian
disappointment with German occupation policy also contributed to their failure in this source of supply.

592. Luther, Michael. "Ukrainian National Activities in the
Crimea during the German World War II." *Horizons* 2: 46-
51, 1957 no. 1-2.
About the cultural and political activities of the
Ukrainians in the Crimea during the German occupation
of the Ukraine.

Fiction.

593. Kohanski, Alexander Sissel. *From Kishinev to Babi Yar.*
Cedar Grove, N. J. Alsko Press, 1968. 85 p.
Poems by Yevgenii Yevtushenko, M. Yalan-Stekelis, and
H. N. Bialik concerning mass executions of Kyivan Jews
and Ukrainians by Germans in 1943 in Babi Yar near Kyiv.

594. Kuznetsov, Anatolii Petrovich. Babi Yar; a documental
novel by A. L. transl. by Jakob Guralsky. Illustr. by
S. Brodsky. London, MacGibon and Kea, 1967. 299 p.
Deals with the German occupation of Kyiv.

14. Ukraine - World War 1939-1945.

595. McNeil, William Hardy, ed. America, Britain and Russia;
Their Cooperation and Conflict, 1941-1946. New York,
Oxford University Press, 1953. 505 p. (Survey of Inter-
national Affairs, 1939-1946, published under the auspices
of the Royal Institute of International Affairs, vol. 3.)
The Ukrainian problem discussed under the headings
"Ukraine," "Ruthenia" and "Yalta Conference."

596. Toynbee, Arnold and Veronica Toynbee, ed. The Eve of the
War 1939. New York, Oxford University Press, 1958. (Survey of the International Affairs 1939-1946 published under
the auspices of the Royal Institute of International
Affairs, vol. 10.)

597. Toynbee, Arnold and Veronica Toynbee, ed. The Realignment
of Europe. New York, Oxford University Press, 1955.
(Survey of International Affairs 1939-1946 published under
the auspices of the Royal Institute of the International
Affairs, vol. 6.)
In the last two monographs there is information about
various Ukrainian problems under headings such as
"Ukrainian SSR," "Bukovina," "Curzon Line," "Lvov" and
"Yalta Conference."

598. Toynbee, Arnold and Frank Gwatkin-Ashton, ed. The World
in March, 1939. New York, Oxford University Press, 1952.
(Survey of International Affairs 1939-1945 published under
the auspices of the Royal Institute of International
Affairs, v. 1.)
Contains information about various Ukrainian problems
under the headings "Ukraine," "Carpatho-Ruthenia,"
"Curzon Line," "Eastern Galicia," "Bukovina," "Volynia"
and others with subdivision "Ukraine."

599. Hanch, Joseph. "The Last Mile of Appeasement. A Glance
at Eastern Europe in the Light of Events Leading from
Munich to Prague." Journal of Central European Affairs.
1: 5-17. April, 1941.
Concerns events in Czechoslovakia in the period between
the Munich Conference and Capitulation of Czechoslovakia. A considerable part of the article is devoted to
the Carpatho-Ukraine.

15. Ukraine - History - Biography.

Bandera, Stepan.

600. Bedriy, Anathole W. "An Exemplary Freedom Fighter," in
Ukrainian Review, London, 18: 6-18, January-March, 1970.
    Concerns prominent political leader Stepan Bandera.

601. Chaykovskyi, Danylo. "Stepan Bandera, His Life and
Struggle," Russian Oppression in Ukraine (see entry: 906)
p. 491-504. Plates.

Drahomanov, Mykhaylo

602. Mykhaylo Drahomaniv; a Symposium and Selected Writings.
New York, Ukrainian Academy of Arts and Sciences in the
U. S., 1952. 224 p. (Annals of the Ukrainian Academy of
Arts and Sciences in the U. S. vol. 2.)
    A series of articles by various authors concerning
the various aspects of the scholarly and political work
of Mykhaylo Drahomanov. A selection of his writings is
included.

603. Doroshenko, Dmytro. "Mykhaylo Drahomaniv and the Ukrainian
National Movement." Slavonic and East European Review. 16:
654-666. April, 1938.
    About the influence of the prominent Ukrainian scholar,
professor in the University of Sofia, Bulgaria, on the
Ukrainian national renaissance during the 19th century.

604. Doroshenko, Volodymyr. "The Life of Mykhaylo Drahomaniv,"
Annals of the Ukrainian Academy of Arts and Sciences in
the U. S. 2: 6-22, 1952.
    About the life and activity of Mykaylo Drahomaniv.

605. Drahomaniv, Svitozar. "Drahomaniv and the English-speaking
World," Annals of the Ukrainian Academy of Arts and
Sciences in the U. S. 2: 63-69, 1952.
    Describes how Drahomanov studied and held in
high esteem institutions of the English-speaking
world. How he appreciated American democracy.

606. Drahomaniv, Svitozar and Ivan L. Rudnytsky. "A Bibliography of Drahomaniv's Major Works." Annals of the
Ukrainian Academy of Arts and Sciences in the U. S. 2:
131-140.
    Includes works by Drahomanov and on Drahomanov in dif-
ferent languages.

607. Mosley, Philip. "Drahomanov and the European Conscience."
Annals of the Ukrainian Academy of Arts and Sciences in
the U. S. 2: 1-6, 1952.

608. Rudnytsky, Ivan. "Drahomaniv as a Political Theorist," *Annals of the Ukrainian Academy of Arts and Sciences in the U. S.* 2: 71-130, 1952.
    Describes Drahomanov's views on political and social problems, including the problems of Eastern Europe and of the political union.

609. Stachiv, Matvij. "Drahomaniv's Impact on Ukrainian Politics." *Annals of the Ukrainian Academy of Arts and Sciences in the U. S.* 2: 47-62. 1952.
    About Ukrainian politics before Drahomaniv, the influence on contemporary Ukrainian political leaders and writers, on political activization of the Ukrainian masses and on politics of the Ukrainian state in 1917-1920.

Hrushevskyi, Mykhaylo.

610. Horak, Stephan M. "Mykhaylo Hrushevskyi - Pillar of a Nation." *Ukrainian Review*, London. 14: 37-54. September, 1967. Bibl., footn., illus.

611. Horak, Stephan M. "Portrait of a Historian." *Canadian Slavonic Papers*. 10: 341-356. 1968, no. 3.

612. Kostiuk, Hryhory. "The Last Days of the Academician M. Hrushevsky." *Ukrainian Review*, Munich. 5: 73-83, 1957.
    An account of the last days of the well known Ukrainian historian and political leader, based on Soviet Press accounts, official documents and the memoirs of contemporaries.

613. Ohloblyn, Alexander. "Michael Hrushevsky-Foremost Ukrainian Historian." *Ukrainian Quarterly*, 22: 322-333. Winter, 1965. Bibl., footn.

614. Shulgin, Antin. "Mykhaylo Hrushevsky 1866-1934." *Slavonic and East European Review*, 30: 176-181. 1952.
    An obituary of the prominent Ukrainian historian and first President of the Ukrainian state.

615. Simpson, George. "Hrushevsky, Historian of Ukraine." *Ukrainian Quarterly*, 1: 132-139. February, 1945.
    About the life, scientific and political activity of Hrushevsky.

616. Stakhiv, Matvij. "A Scientist and Social Leader as President of the State." *Ukrainian Quarterly*. 13: 329-336.
    Concerns the scholarly and political work of Hrushevsky.

Khmelnytsky, Bohdan, Hetman of Ukraine.

617. Vernadskij, George Vladimir. Bohdan, Hetman of Ukraine.
New Haven, Yale University Press. Published for Ukrainian
National Association, 1941. VII, 156 p.
   Describes the life of Bohdan Khmelnycky from the up-
rising of 1648 to his death and his political career.
A comparison with other prominent historical figures is
made.

618. Chubatyi, Nicholas. "Bohdan Khmelnycky, Ruler of Ukraine."
Ukrainian Quarterly, 13: 197-204. September, 1957.
   About Khmelnycky and Ukrainian life of his time.

Khmelnytskyi, Yurii.

619. Borshchak, Ilko. "A Little Known Biography of Yuras
Khmelnytsky." Annals of the Ukrainian Academy of Arts
and Sciences in the U. S. 3: 509-517. Spring-Summer,
1953.
   About a rare 17th century French book, containing a
chapter with a biography of the son of Bohdan Khmelnyt-
sky-Yuriy.

Kochubei, Motria.

620. Pauls, John. A Tragedy of Motria Kochubei. London,
Association of Ukrainians in Great Britain, Ltd., 1965.
11 p.
   A reprint from Ukrainian Review, London 11: 73-83.
Sept, 1964. The story of the daughter of a powerful
enemy of Hetman of Ukraine Ivan Mazepa - Colonel Kochubei,
her love with her godfather Hetman Mazepa and her personal tragedy-execution of her father by Mazepa for
treason, fall and death of Hetman Mazepa included.

Konovalets, Euhen, Col.

621. Bandera, Stefan. "The memory of Eugene Konovaletz Lives On."
Ukrainian Review, London, 5: 3-8. June, 1958.
   The speech of a major Ukrainian political leader at
the grave of the late leader of the Ukrainian nationalist
movement, Eugene Konovalets on the 10th anniversary of
his assassination by a Soviet agent. Concerns the
activity of Konovalets and its echo in the present.

Kostomarov, Nicholas, Historian.

622. Papazian, Dennis N. I. Nicholas Ivanovich Kostomarov,

Russian Historian, Ukrainian Nationalist, Slavic Federalist.
Ann Arbor, University of Michigan, 1967.
    An unpublished doctoral dissertation, about a prominent nineteenth century Ukrainian historian who composed a treaty proposing a federation of the Slavic peoples of Europe.

623. Papazian, Dennis N. I. "Kostomarov and the Cyril-Methodian Ideology" Russian Review, 1970 vol. 29: 59-73, no. 1, 1970. Bibl., footn.
    About influence of Kostomarov on ideology of the above mentioned circle of Young Ukrainian intellectuals of middle of the 19th century.

Kotsevalov, Andrii.

624. Dombrovsky, Alexander. "Andrii Kotsevalov." Annals of the Ukrainian Academy of Arts and Sciences in the U. S. 8(1-2/25-26): 219-223. Bibl. footn.
    An obituary of a prominent Ukrainian historian and scholar, who specialized in ancient Ukraine.

Krupnytsky, Borys.

625. Polonska-Vasylenko, Natalia. "Professor B. D. Krupnytsky, 1894-1956." Ukrainian Review, Munich 5: 9-18, 1957.
    About the life and work of a prominent Ukrainian historian.

Livytskyi, Andrii,
President of Ukraine in Exile.

626. Stakhiv, Matthew. "President Andriy Livytsky (1879-1954) A Revolutionary Statesman, President of the Ukrainian Government in Exile," Ukrainian Quarterly. 10: 100-105. Winter, 1954.
    About the life and activity of the late President of the Ukrainian Government in Exile.

Makhno, Nestor.

627. Peters, Victor. Nestor Makhno, the Life of an Anarchist. Winnipeg, Echo Books, 1970. 133 p.
    The life story of the known Ukrainian anarchist Nestor Makhno, who was active in Ukraine in years 1919-1923 and died in Paris in 1935. Bibliography.

Mazepa, Ivan, Hetman of Ukraine.

628. Ivan Mazepa, Hetman of Ukraine: on the 250th Anniversary of His Rising against Russia. New York, Ukrainian Congress Committee of America, 1970. 120 p.
Reprints of articles on Mazepa from issues of the Ukrainian Quarterly. 1959 no. 2, 3 & 4.

629. Mackiw, Theodore. Mazepa, 1632-1709 in Contemporary German Sources. New York, Shevchenko Scientific Society, 1959. 43 p. (Shevchenko Scientific Society. Papers no. 9.)
The author reviews references to Mazepa in German periodicals and in writings of German historians and travellers.

630. Mackiw, Theodore. Prince Mazepa-Hetman of Ukraine in Contemporary English Publications. Chicago, Ukrainian Research and Information Institute, 1967. 126 p.
A review of the References to Ivan Mazepa in contemporary English publications compiled on the basis of research done by the author in the British archives and libraries.

631. Manning, Clarence A. Hetman of Ukraine, Ivan Mazepa. New York, Bookman Associates, 1957. 234 p.
Biography, political and cultural activity of the Hetman, Ivan Mazepa.

632. Manning, Clarence A. The Role of Mazepa in Eastern Europe. Rola Mazepy u Skhidnii Europi. Chicago, Shevchenko Scientific Society. Chicago Study Center, 1960. 16 p. (Shevchenko Scientific Society, Papers no. 12.)
Ukrainian title added. Concerns the political and cultural role of Hetman Ivan Mazepa.

633. Andrusiak, Mykola. "Ivan Mazepa, Hetman of Ukraine." Ukrainian Quarterly. 3: 31-37. Autumn, 1947.
The story of Ivan Mazepa, his cooperation with Charles XII, and his role in the history of the Ukraine.

634. Donzow, Dmytro. "Hugo's Mazeppa'," the Symbol of Ukraine," Ukrainian Review, London. 2: 6-16. September, 1955.

635. Holubnychy, Lydia. "Mazepa in Byron's Poem and History." Ukrainian Quarterly. 15: 336-345. December, 1959. Bibl. footn.
Both these articles deal with the presentation of Mazepa in the works of Western-European authors.

636. Mackiw, Theodore. "A Biographical Sketch of Prince Mazepa, 1639-1709." Ukrainian Review, London. 12: 60-83. December, 1965. Plates. Bibl. p. 79-83.

637. Mackiw, Theodore. "Mazepa in the Light of Contemporary English and American Sources." <u>Ukrainian Quarterly</u>. 15: 346-362. December, 1959. Illus. Bibl. footn.

638. Mackiw, Theodore. "Mazepa in the Light of Contemporary English Press." <u>Ukrainian Review</u>, London. 7: 30-36. March, 1960. Bibl. footn.

639. Mackiw, Theodore. "Reports on Mazepa in Colonial America." <u>New Review</u>. 6: 14-21, 1966. No. 1., Port. Bibl. footn. p. 19-21.

640. Mackiw, Theodore. "Who Was Author of Mazepa's Engravings of 1706." <u>Ukrainian Review</u>, London. 14: 66-67. March, 1967. Bibl. footn.
    There are many anonymous portraits of Hetman Mazepa. The author attempts establish authorship of one of the portraits.

641. Manning, Clarence A. "Mazepa in English Literature." <u>Ukrainian Quarterly</u>. 15: 133-144. June, 1959.

642. Pauls, John P. "Great Maecenas of the Arts Glorified by Painters." <u>Ukrainian Review</u>, London. 13: 17-32. December, 1966. Bibl. footn.
    About the portraits of Hetman Ivan Mazepa.

<u>Mikhnovskyi, Mykola.</u>

643. Bedrii, Anatol W. "Mykola Mikhnovskyi--First Theorician of Modern Ukrainian Nationalism." <u>Ukrainian Review</u>, London. 15: 82-89. June, 1968 and 15: 71-78, December, 1968.
    About the Ukrainian lawyer and political writer who first proposed independent statehood for the Ukraine.

<u>Ohloblyn, Oleksander.</u>

644. Pidhainy, Oleh S. "Oleksander Petrovych Ohloblyn." <u>New Review</u>. 10: 167-174 no. 4/41, 1970.
    Biography of a prominent Ukrainian historian.

<u>Olha, Princess, Saint.</u>

645. Polonska-Vasylenko, Natalia. "The Princess Olha--First Christian Ruler of the Ukraine." c. 945-964. <u>Ukrainian Review</u>, London. 2: 3-11. September, 1955.
    About Princess Olha, wife of Prince Ihor and regent after his death; her activity as a ruler of the Ukraine

and her conversion to Christianity.

Orlyk, Pylyp, Hetman of Ukraine in Exile.

646. Krupnytsky, Borys. "General Characteristics of Pylyp
Orlyk." Annals of the Ukrainian Academy of Arts and
Sciences in the U. S. 6: 1247-1259.
    The author gives a detailed description of this pro-
    minent Ukrainian emigree hetman, including his views
    on political and religious problems and his personal
    background.

Petlura, Symon.

647. Bohdaniuk, Volodymyr. "Symon Petlura-National Hero of
Ukraine." Ukrainian Review, London. 13: 6-12, June,
1966. Port.

648. Donzow, Dmytro. "Why was Petlura Murdered?" Ukrainian
Review, London. 13: 55-61. September, 1966.
    About how the Soviet regime decided to murder Symon
    Petlura, because he was the foremost leader of the
    Ukrainian independence movement and anti-communist
    resistance.

649. France, Attorney General. "Speech at the Trial of Petlura's Assassin in Paris on October . . . 1927." Russian Oppression in Ukraine. (See entry no. 906.) p. 476-
482.

650. "Symon Petlura." Ukrainian Review, London 2: 27-34.
June, 1956.
    About the life and work of Symon Petlura, head of
    the Ukrainian National Republic, killed in Paris in
    1926 by a Soviet agent.

Pidhainyi, Semen.

651. Ohloblyn, Oleksander. "Semen Pidhainy as A Historian."
New Review. 7: 1-7, no. 3/28, 1967. Bibl. footn.

Poletyka, Petro.

652. Huculak, Mychaylo. When Russia Was in America. The
Alaska Boundary Treaty Negotiations 1824-25 and the role
of Pierre de Poletica. Vancouver, Mitchell Press, Ltd.,
1970. 149 p. illus.

Deals with role of an Ukrainian aristocrat Petro de
Poletyka, who was Russian ambassador in Canada in the
first quarter of the 19th century in negotiations concerning establishing Canadian-Alaskan boundaries.

Shcherbakivskyi, Vadym.

653. "Professor Dr. Vadym Shcherbakivskyi." Ukrainian Review,
London. 3: 80-85, March, 1956.
About the life and scholarly work of a prominent
Ukrainian archeologist published on the occasion of his
eightieth birthday.

Shukhevych, Roman.

654. Bedriy, Anatol. "The Year of Chuprynka, vs. the Year of
Lenin." Ukrainian Review, London. 17: 2-12.

655. Stetsko, Slava. "The Supreme Commander of the Insurgent
Army" in Russian Oppression in Ukraine See entry no. 906:
259-266.
About the supreme commander of the Ukrainian Insurgent Army, General Lieutenant Roman Shukhevych, known
under his combat pseudo-Taras Chuprynka.

Volodymyr, the Great, Prince, Saint.

656. Fedorovich, Nicholas. The Great Prince Saint Volodymyr.
New York, Ukrainian Orthodox Church in the United States,
1957. 32 p.
About the life and work of the Grand Duke of Kyiv,
who officially baptised the Ukraine in 988.

Voynarovskyi, Andrii.

657. Wynar, Lubomyr, "Abduction of Andrii Voynarovsky by Tsar
Peter I." (Abridged from a larger work published by the
same author in Ukrainian.) Ukrainian Review, London.
10: 46-59. December, 1963.
About a prominent general of Hetman Mazepa who emigrated
to Western Europe and was kidnapped by agents of the Tsar
Peter the Great after Mazepa's fall.

16. Ukraine - History - Numismatics, Sphragistics, etc.

658. Prokopovich, Vyacheslav. "Sphragistic Studies." Shev-
chenko Scientific Society, Proceedings of the Historical-
Philological Section. 1: 67-76, 1951.
About the earliest Ukrainian state seals.

659. Shuhayevsky, Valentin. "The Derivation of the Term
'Chekh' as the Ukrainian Denomination of the Polish "Piv-
torak" (Poltorak) of King Sigismund III." Shevchenko
Scientific Society. Proceedings of the Historical-Philological Section. 1: 76-79. Bibl. footnotes.
A linguistic analysis of the derivation of the name
of a Polish coin used in Polish occupied Ukraine.

660. Shuhayevsky, Valentin. "Discoveries in Eastern Ukraine
of Venetian Coins of the Thirteenth and Fourteenth Centuries as a Historical Source." Shevchenko Scientific
Society. Proceedings of the Historical-Philological
Section. 1: 80-81.
A report on a lecture concerning finds of coins as
proof of Ukrainian trade with Venice.

VII. UKRAINE - A CONSTITUENT REPUBLIC OF THE USSR.

1. General Publications.

661. Adams, Arthur E. Bolsheviks in the Ukraine. The Second
Campaign, 1918-1919. New Haven, Yale University Press,
1963. 330 p. Map.
The author deals with the Soviet campaign against
The Ukraine in the time between November 1918-June 1919,
which despite heroic defense by the Ukrainians, lasting
until 1921 and guerilla campaigns in certain places
until 1938, led to the final sovietization of the
Ukraine. Besides description of single battles and
campaigns and characterizations of the leaders contending
for political power in the Ukraine, the author describes
national and social forces moving in the Ukraine during
that period.
The author describes the role of the guerilla leader
Marvii Hryhoriiv, who fought Petlura, went over to the
Bolshevik forces, helped them to many victories, but
finally turned against the Bolsheviks and heavily contributed to the failure of this campaign.

662. Bilinsky, Yaroslav. The Second Soviet Republic: the Ukraine
after World War II. New Brunswick, Rutgers University
Press, 1962. 539 p.
Study based on materials from Soviet official sources
on data from the Harvard project of Soviet Social System
and on interviews by the author.
The author presents Soviet policy in the Ukraine after
World War II. He characterizes the Ukrainian nationalism
in general and discusses the Communist Party of the
Ukraine and of the USSR. The integration of Western

Ukraine, Ukrainian armed resistance, the Soviet language policy, Soviet interpretation of the Ukrainian history, and other aspects of the Ukrainian problem are discussed by the author.

663. Carr, Edward Hallet. The Bolshevik Revolution. London, MacMillan, 1951-1952. 3 v. (History of Soviet Russia.)
In the first volume of this work dealing with different aspects of the Bolshevik revolution, the author devotes some space to the role of the Ukraine during the revolution. He describes the independence struggle of the Ukrainian people from the time of the organization of the Central Rada to the period of Ukrainization. He describes the role of the Ukrainian national-communism and emphasizes the economic value of the Ukraine. He shows a very good understanding of the Ukrainian problem.

664. Chamberlin, William Henry. The Russian Revolution, 1917-1921. New York, Grosset and Dunlap, 1965. 2 v.
References to the Brest-Litovsk Treaty, peasant anarchy in the Ukraine, a.o.

665. Communist Takeover and Occupation of Ukraine. Special Report number 4 of the Select Committee on Communist Aggression. House of Representatives, Eighty-Third Congress, Second Session under authority of H.R. Res. 346 and 438. Washington, U. S. Govt. Print. Off., 1955. 36 p.
A short history of the Ukraine with special stress on the occupation of the Ukraine by the Bolsheviks and contemporary conditions in the Ukraine.

666. Fedenko, Panas. Ukraine, Her Struggle for Freedom. Augsburg, Free Ukraine Publishing Company, 1951. 80 p.
A short outline of Ukrainian history. Discusses Ukrainian-Russian war of 1917-1920, Ukrainians in the Ukraine and outside of the Ukraine in USSR, the famine of 1932-1933, Ukrainians in Poland, Roumania and Czechoslavakia, Ukrainians during the Second World War, Ukrainian anti-Soviet resistance and the post-war Ukrainian emigration.

667. Investigation of the Communist Takeover and Occupation of the non-Russian Nations of the USSR. Eighth Interim Report of the Hearing before the Select Committee on Communist Aggression. House of Representatives. Eighty-Third Congress. Second Session. Under authority of H.R. Res. 346 and H.R. Res. 438. Munich, Germany, June 30 and July 1, 1954. New York October 11, 12, 13, 14, 1954. Chicago, Ill., October 18 and 19, 1954. Printed for the Select Committee on Communist Agression. Washington,

Govt. Print. Off., 1954.   370 p.
    About one-half of testimonies concerns the Ukraine.

668.   Luther, Michael Martin.   The Birth of Soviet Ukraine.
New York, Columbia University, 1962.   296 p.
    Unpublished doctoral dissertation.   About how com-
munists tried to seize power in the Ukraine in the year
1917.   About the occupation of the Ukraine by German
and Austro-Hungarian forces after the Brest Litovsk
Treaty of February 9, 1918.   Between the Ukrainian
communists there were differences of opinion concerning
the future fate of the Ukraine.   At conference in
Tahanroh in April, 1918, a proposal of the right-wing
Ukrainian Communists to organize an autonomous Ukrainian
Republic affiliated with the Soviet Russia was made.
This can be considered as the birth of the Ukrainian
Soviet Republic.

669.   Manning, Clarence A.   Ukraine under the Soviets.   New
York Bookman Associates, 1953.   223 p.
    The author discusses the fate of Ukraine under
Soviet rule.   He discusses NEP (New Economic Policy)
and its influence on the fate of the Ukraine.   He discusses the literary and scholarly revival and Soviet
liquidation of the Ukrainian cultural life, Ukraine in
the late thirties, occupation of the Western Ukraine,
the Ukrainian Insurgent Army (UPA) and union of all
Ukraine under Soviet rule and its subsequent religious
and cultural policy.

670.   Report on the Soviet Union in 1956.   A Symposium at the
Institute for the Study of the USSR.   Conference at the
Carnegie International Center, New York, April 28-29,
1956.   Munich, Institute for the Study of the USSR, 1956.
218 p.
    Many references to the different aspects of the life
in Soviet Ukraine.

671.   Studies in History of the Post-Revolutionary Ukraine and
the Soviet Union.   New York, Ukrainian Academy of Arts and
Sciences in the U.S., 1961.   344 p.   (Ukrainian Acad. of
Arts and Sciences in the U.S.   Annals vol. 9, no. 11-12/
27-28.)
    A series of articles written by various specialists
in Soviet nationality policy on different aspects of
the Soviet Ukraine.   A list of post-war doctoral dissertations accepted by American universities on the
Ukrainian topics is included.

672.   Adams, Arthur E.   "The Bolsheviks and the Ukrainian Front
in 1918-1919."   Slavonic and East European Review.   36:
396-417.   1958.
    The author describes the establishment of Soviet
regime in the Ukraine.

673. Dobriansky, Lev. E. "Communist Agression against
     Ukraine and other Non-Russian Nations in USSR." in Exten-
     sion of Remarks of Hon. Michael A. Feighan of Ohio in the
     House of Representatives, Wednesday, January 6, 1955,
     64th Congress, First Session.
          Testimony of Professor Lev E. Dobriansky, Chairman of
     the Ukrainian Congress Committee of America at hearings
     of House Select Committee on Communist Agression,
     United States Courthouse, Chicago, Illinois, Monday,
     October 18, 1954.

674. Jurchenko, Oleksander. "The First Stage in the Bolshevik
     Conquest of the Ukraine." Ukrainian Review, Munich. 6:
     55-67, 1958.
          A review of some Soviet publications on the anniver-
     sary of the Soviet conquest of the Ukraine.

675. Korol, Nestor. "Bolshevik Documents on the Conquest of
     Ukraine." Ukrainian Quarterly. 16: 164-176. Summer,
     1960. Bibl. footn.

676. Mazepa, Isaak. "Ukraine under Bolshevik Rule." Slavonic
     and East European Review. 12: 322-346. June, 1934.
          About the legal ties between the Ukraine and the
     rest of the USSR. The period of armed occupation and
     Ukrainization.

677. Pidhainy, Alexander. "Prelude to the First Soviet Govern-
     ment in Ukraine, Nov.-Dec., 1917." The New Review. 10:
     30-37, no. 1/38, March, 1970. Bibl. footn.

678. Reinisch, Leonard. "Ukraine, a Soviet Republic."
     Ukrainian Review, London. 3: 61-74, Dec., 1956.
          A radio-play depicting the fate of the Ukraine under
     Soviet domination, written by a playwright of the Ba-
     varian Broadcast Company.

679. Teschabai, D. "The Transfer of Crimea to Ukraine."
     Bulletin of the Institute for the Study of the USSR."
     April, 1954. p. 30-33.

680. Teschabai, D. "The Ukraine--a Soviet Problem." Bulletin
     of the Institute for the Study of the USSR. June, 1953,
     p. 14-19.

2. Ukraine - Communist Party.

681. Bilinsky, Jaroslav. Changes in the Central Committee:
     Communist Party of the Soviet Union, 1961-1966. Denver,
     University of Denver Press, 1967. 54 p. (Social Science

Foundation and Graduate School of International Studies.
University of Denver. Monograph Series in World Affairs,
v. 4, no. 4.)
     Concerns also the Ukrainians in top echelons of the
Communist Party of the USSR.

682. Borys, Jurij. The Russian Communist Party and the Sovieti-
      zation of Ukraine. Stockholm, The University of Stockholm.
      1960. IX, 374 p.
           The author states in the preface that "the subject of
      this study is the communist doctrine of the self-deter-
      mination as applied by the Russian Bolsheviks in the
      Ukraine . . ." and "the main part is devoted to Bol-
      shevik policy in the Ukraine as an example of how the
      Communist Doctrine of self-determination of nations has
      been applied." He proves in his study that this type
      of application of the self-determination principle to
      Ukraine led to the subjugation of the Ukraine.

683. Lawrynenko, Jurij. Ukrainian Communism and Soviet Rus-
      sian Policy toward the Ukraine: an annotated biblio-
      graphy, 1917-1953. ed. by David I. Goldstein. New York,
      Praeger, 1953. 454 p. (Research Program on the USSR.)
           A bibliography of publications in Ukrainian, Russian
      and other languages on the development of Communism in
      the Ukraine. Arranged chronologically under each sub-
      ject.

684. Majstrenko, Ivan. Borotbism: a Chapter in the History
      of Ukrainian Communism. New York, Research Program on
      the USSR, 1954. 325 p.
           George Luckyj's translation of a history of left-
      wing Ukrainian political party called Borotbists
      (Friends of Fight) predecessors of Titoism or National
      Communism who demanded that all power in the Ukraine
      be vested in the Ukrainian working class. The group
      was liquidated by the Soviet regime.

685. Pipes, Richard. The Formation of the Soviet Union: Com-
      munism and Nationalism. Cambridge, Harvard University
      Press, 1954. 355 p. (Russian Research Center Studies,
      13.)
           The author describes the development of Communist
      Party in the Ukraine on pages 9-12, 53-73 and 114-150.
      He analyzes the causes of the collapse of the indepen-
      dent Ukrainian state and reveals the percentage of
      Ukrainians and Russians in the Ukrainian Communist Party.

686. Dmytryshyn, Basil. "National and Social Composition of
      the Membership of the Communist Party of the Ukraine,"
      1918-1925." Journal of the Central European Affairs.
      17: 342-358. October, 1958.

This study reveals that the majority of the Communist Party of the Ukraine at that time was Russian. Only in the rural districts was the percentage of Ukrainians in the Communist Party Organization slightly higher than the number of Russians.

687. Holubnychy, Vsevolod. "Outline History of the Communist Party of the Ukraine." Ukrainian Review, Munich. 6: 68-125, 1958.

688. Levytsky, Borys. "The Communist Party in the Ukraine 1955." Ukrainian Review, Munich. 5: 38-55. November, 1957.
The organization and membership of the Communist Party of the Ukraine.

689. Pap, Michael. "Soviet Difficulties in Ukraine." Review of Politics. 14: 204-232, 1952.
A history of the Pereyaslav Treaty. Present problems of the Soviet Regime in the Ukraine, particularly relating to Ukrainian Titoism, a trend toward rising nationalism and the increasingly bad conditions of the collective farms.

690. Pidhainy, Alexander. "The Kiev Bolsheviks and Lenin's April Theses." The New Review. 8-9 (no-4(33)-9(36): 133-138. Bibl. footn. p. 138.

691. Siehs, Karl. "An Example of Warning: Ukrainian National-Communist Writer Mykola Khvylovy." Ukrainian Review, London. 12: 41-52. March, 1965.

692. Smal-Stocki, Roman. "The Origins of National-Communism." Ukrainian Quarterly. 14: 311-326. December, 1958.
Discusses how national-Communism can be traced in literature beginning with the end of the 19th century. Recently it has served as a form of defense for the nations enslaved by Red Russia. The term appeared for the first time in the Ukraine in 1918.

3. Ukraine - Politics and Government.

693. Armstrong, John A. Ideology, Politics and Government in the Soviet Union. New York, Praeger, 1962. 160 p. (Praeger publications in Russian history and world Communism no. 113.)
Many references to the Ukraine and Ukrainians. Discusses the question of Ukrainian anti-Soviet resistance and the role of Ukrainians in the Soviet bureaucratic apparatus.

694. Armstrong, John A. _Soviet Bureaucratic Elite: A Case Study of the Ukrainian Apparatus._ New York, Frederick Praeger, 1959. 174 p. (Praeger Studies in Russian history and world communism.)

On the basis of materials from the Ukraine the author suggests that in the USSR in the time of Khrushchev there came into being a special (partially closed) bureaucratic elite of professional, well-trained and reliable civil servants, and that they were the basis of Khrushchev's strength.

695. Institute for the Study of the USSR. _Key Officials of the Government. Part II. The Union Republics._ Second ed. Munich, 1966. 42 p.

Lists key officials of the Ukrainian Soviet Republic

696. Kostiuk, Hryhory. _The Fall of Postyshev._ New York, Research Program on the USSR, 1954. 75 p. (Mimeograph Series no. 69.)

4. Ukraine. Living Conditions.

697. Chyzh, Marta. _Woman and Child in the Modern System of Slavery--USSR._ Toronto SUZheRO, 1972. 170 p.

The author describes the rights guaranteed by the Soviet Constitution and other laws applying to the women and children and depicts their violations using excerpts and quotations from authoritative works.

All of the author's statements describing the suffering of women and children in the USSR are documented by depositions of people who survived Soviet labor camps and escaped.

698. Gunther, John. _Inside Russia Today._ New York, Harper, 1958. 550 p.

Includes numerous references to the Ukraine; includes illustrations and a bibliography.

699. Kolasky, John. _Two Years in Soviet Ukraine._ Toronto, Peter Martin Associates, 1970. 230 p.

The author who lived for two years in the Soviet Ukraine and who published a book entitled _Education in Soviet Ukraine_ a few years ago, gives a vivid account of Russian political, social and economic imperialism at work within Soviet Ukraine.

He describes a Russian program to destroy the non-Russian languages and culture and growing resistance of the oppressed peoples.

700. Labin, Susanne. _Promise and Reality: 50 Years of Soviet-Russian "Achievements."_ An indictment of Russian communism.

London, European Freedom Council. British Section, 19,
1,932 p.

701. Heiman, Leo. "Goodbye to Odessa." Ukrainian Quarterly.
20: 152-163. Summer, 1964.
A description of life in contemporary Odessa.

702. Heiman, Leo. "Ukraine: 1966." Ukrainian Quarterly. 23:
43-64, Spring, 1967.

703. Plyushch, Vasyl. "Medical Service in the USSR Today, with
Particular Reference to the Ukraine." Ukrainian Review,
Munich 2: 58-69, 1956. Bibl. footn.

704. Plyushch, Vasyl. "Social Insurance and Social Security in
Ukraine." Ukrainian Review, Munich. 4: 15-32, 1957.
Bibl. footn.

705. Psycholoh. "Change in the Psychology of Soviet Ukrainians."
Ukrainian Quarterly. 10: 328-338. Autumn, 1954.

706. "Soviet Legality. Ukraine in the Light of Trials and Deten-
tions of Ukrainians." Ukrainian Quarterly. 24: 206-217,
Autumn, 1968.

707. Ukrainian Constitution. (Constitution Fundamental Law of
January 30, 1937 as Amended through November 21, 1949.)
New York, American Russian Institute, 1950. 17 p.
Text of Constitution of the Ukrainian Soviet Republic.

708. Adams, Arthur E. "Bolshevik Administration in the Ukraine."
Review of Politics. 19: 189-306. June, 1958.
About the system of Soviet administration in the Ukraine.

709. Armstrong, John A. "Administrative Apparatus in Rural
Ukraine." Slavic Review. 15: 17-37. Fall, 1956.
The Soviet administrative apparatus in rural districts
of the Ukraine at the time of the German occupation of
the Ukraine.

710. Armstrong, John A. "The Ukrainian Apparatus as a Key to
the Study of Soviet Politics." Annals of the Ukrainian
Academy of Arts and Sciences in the U. S. 9(1-2/27-28)
225-233.
The author discusses the importance of the Communist
Party of the Ukraine and the Soviet administration of the
Ukraine in life of the U.S.S.R. He considers personal
ties of the Ukrainian party and administration with
Nikita Khrushchev, World War 1939-1945, which was fought
predominantly on Ukraine territory and its consequences
(German occupation, evacuation of the Ukrainian industry,
annexation of the Western Ukraine and the proximity of

the Central European Satellites) as the reasons of this importance.

711. Haliy, Mykola. "Rehabilitation of P. Postyshev." _Ukrainian Quarterly_. 14: 58-62, March, 1958.
     About the crimes against the Ukrainian people committed by the Soviet party boss in the Ukraine, Postyshev, rehabilitated after Stalin's death by the Soviet regime.

712. Lukianenko, Levko. "Letter to D. S. Korotchenko." _Ukrainian Review_, London. 15: 24-36, December, 1958.
     A letter of an Ukrainian lawyer, later imprisoned and condemned as an "Ukrainian nationalist," concerning the constitutional right of the Ukraine to secede from the Soviet Union.

713. Stakhiv, Matthew. "Soviet Statehood of the Ukraine from the Sociological Aspect." _Ukrainian Quarterly_. 16: 38-47, March, 1959.
     Author states that there is practically no independence in Soviet Ukraine because it is ruled from Russian centers with a centralized party and government.
     Letters to the Soviet authorities from Yurii Shukhevych Berezinsky and Michael Horbovy, long-term inmates of Soviet prisons and detention camps, depicting administration of the justice in the Soviet Union.

714. Vinnitsky, R. "Neurological Services in the Ukraine," in _Review of Soviet Medical Sciences_. 2: 41-47. No. 3, 1965.

5. Ukraine - Church.

715. Bociurkiv, Bohdan R. _Soviet Church Policy in the Ukraine, 1919-1939_. Chicago, University of Chicago, 1961.
     Unpublished doctoral dissertation.

716. Bolshakoff, Serg. _Russian Non-Conformity: the Story of Unofficial Religion in Russia_. Philadelphia, Westminster Press, 1950. 192 p.
     Discusses the establishment of the Ukrainian Uniat Church and its liquidation by the Soviet authorities. The author uses the term "the Ruthenians" for Ukrainians.

717. Conquest, Robert. _Religion in the USSR_. New York, Praeger, 1968. 135 p.
     Concerns also the situation of the Ukrainian churches.

718. Curtiss, John Skelton. _Russian Church and the Soviet State, 1917-1950_. Boston, Little, Brown and Company, 1953. 387 p.
     On page 225 the author refers to the League for the Liberation of Ukraine and associates it with the liquidation

of the Ukrainian Orthodox Church. On pages 307-312 he
discusses the liquidation of the Ukrainian Catholic Church
In Western Ukraine.

719. Dushnyck, Walter. Martyrdom in Ukraine. Russia Denies
Religious Freedom. New York, The American Press, 1946. 45 p.
    A history of the Ukrainian Uniat Church and the Polish
attitude toward it. The author discusses the liquidation
of the Uniat Church in Western Ukraine by the Soviet
authorities. Also included are documents giving evidence
about the liquidation of the Ukrainian Orthodox Church.

720. First Victims of Communism: White Book on the Religious
Persecution in Ukraine. Rome, Analecta OSBM, 1953. 114 p.
illus.
    About the persecution and liquidation of the Ukrainian
Catholic Church in Western Ukraine by the Soviet Regime.
One Chapter deals with the liquidation of the Ukrainian
Orthodox Church by the Soviet Regime.

721. Just, Sister Mary. Rome and Russia. A Tragedy of Errors.
Westminter, Maryland, The Newman Press, 1954. 223 p.
    Contains a history of the medieval Ukrainian Church on
p. 1-17 with reference to the Church Union in Berestya
Lytovske, 1956 and to the liquidation of Uniat Church in
Western Ukraine. The author uses the term "Russia"
instead of Ukraine and "Ruthenians" for Western Ukrainians.

722. Kolarz, Walter. Religion in the Soviet Union. New York,
St. Martin's Press, 1961. 518 p.
    The author describes the situation of the Churches in
the USSR. Among other Churches he mentioned the Ukrainian
Authocephalous Orthodox Church, its tendency to independence and its role in the Ukrainian national renaissance,
its liquidation by Soviet authorities. He mentions the
situation of the Ukrainian Orthodox Church in Western
Ukraine under Polish domination. Tells about attempts to
restore Ukrainian Orthodox Church during the German occu-
pation of the Ukraine. Pictures the development of the
Ukrainian Orthodox Church in the U. S. and Canada.
    The author describes the role of the Ukrainian Uniat
Church, mentions its prominent leader Metropolitan Andrew
Sheptyckyi, the destruction of that Church by the Soviet
Government, the imprisonment of the Metropolitan Joseph
Slipyi and the development of that church in the West.
The presentation is good and unbiased.

723. Luzhnycky, Gregory. Persecution and Destruction of the
Ukrainian Church by the Russian Bolsheviks. New York,
Ukrainian Congress Committee of America, 1960. 64 p.
    The author states that hostility to religion is one of
the basic principles of communism, gives the characteristic

traits of the Russian Orthodox Church, corresponding to the Russian mind, describes martyrdom of the Ukrainian Churches under the Czarist regime and the destruction of the Ukrainian Orthodox and Ukrainian Catholic Churches.

724. MacEoin, Gary. Communist War on Religion. New York, Devin Adair, 1951. 264 p.
About the situation of the Ukrainian Catholic and Ukrainian Orthodox Churches in Polish occupied Western Ukraine. The liquidation of the Ukrainian Catholic Church by the Soviet authorities.

725. Mydlovsky, Lev. Bolshevik Persecution of Religion and Church in Ukraine. London, Ukrainian Publishers, Ltd., 1963. 31 p.
About the persecution of the Ukrainian churches by the Soviet authorities in years 1917-1953. Also in Ukrainian Review, London. 4: 12-33. Winter, 1957.

726. Mykula, W. Religion and Church in Ukraine under the Communist Russian Rule. A brief survey. London, Ukrainian Information Service, 1969, 48 p. illus.
Concerns situation of the Ukrainian Orthodox and Catholic Churches in Soviet Ukraine.

727. United States 83rd Congress. First Session. Senate Document no. 69. Tensions within the Soviet Union. Prepared at the request of the Committee of Foreign Relations by the Legislative Reference Service of the Library of Congress.
Contains references to the Ukrainian problems such as the Ukrainian anti-Soviet resistance, members of the Ukrainian Orthodox Church in the penal camps and liquidation of the Ukrainian Catholic Church.

728. Yavdas', Mytrofan. Ukrainian Autocephalous Orthodox Church. Documents for the history of the Ukrainian Autocephalous Orthodox Church. Munich, Council of the Ukrainian Autocephalous Orthodox Church in the West German Federated Republic, 1956. 228 p.
A history of the Ukrainian Orthodox Church with biographies of the bishops and priests who were liquidated by the Bolsheviks. A list of destroyed shrines. In the French, English and German languages.

729. Bociurkiv, Bohdan. "The Renovationist Church in the Soviet Ukraine, 1922-1939." Annals of the Ukrainian Academy of Arts and Sciences in the U. S. 9(1/2/28-29): 41-74.
About a fraction of the Ukrainian Orthodox Church opposed to the Ukrainian Authocephalous Orthodox Church headed by Metropolitan Vasyl Lypkivskyi.

730. Buchak, Lev. "Persecution of the Ukrainian Protestants under the Soviet Rule." Black Deeds of Kremlin I, Toronto, 1953. 1: 528-530.
About the liquidation of the Ukrainian Lutheran and Reformed Church in Western Ukraine during the occupation 1939-1941.

731. Chubaty, Nicholas. "Political Background of the Religious Persecution in the Ukraine by Moscow." Ukrainian Quarterly. 11: 56-65. Winter, 1955.
About how the Czarist and Red Russia pretended to be Third Rome and assumed authority to destroy the autonomy of the Ukrainian Churches, all of which, Orthodox, Uniat and Protestant have been liquidated.

732. Chubaty, Nicholas D. "Russian Church Policy in Ukraine." Ukrainian Quarterly. 2: 43-56. Autumn, 1945.

733. Groschmidt, Geza. "The Kremlin and the Eastern Catholic Church." Ukrainian Quarterly. 9: 324-334. Autumn, 1953.
Deals predominantly with the Ukrainian Catholic Church formerly the largest of Eastern Catholic churches.

734. Manning, Clarence A. "Religion in the USSR and East Europe: A Footnote to the New Catholic Encyclopedia." Ukrainian Quarterly. 23: 344-354. Winter, 1967.
Discusses misinformation about the situation of the Eastern Catholic Churches in communist dominated Eastern Europe.

735. Miller, Michael A. "Bolshevik Persecution of the Orthodox Church in the Ukraine." Ukrainian Review, Munich. 7: 10-21. 1959.

736. "Religious Dissent." Problems of Communism. 17: 96-104, 1968, July-August.
Partially concerns the persecution of the Ukrainian Baptist Church by the Soviet authorities.

737. Teodorovich, Nadiya. "The Catacomb Church in the USSR." Bulletin of the Institute for the Study of the USSR. 12: 13-14. April, 1965.

738. Teodorovich, Nadiya. "The Russian Orthodox Church in the Ukraine: the Exarchate of the Moscow Patriarchate." Ukrainian Review, Munich. 9: 100-111. Bibl. footn.
About how the Ukrainian Orthodox Church in the Ukraine has been liquidated by the Soviet authorities and the present status of the church in the Ukraine.

739. "The Ukrainian Catholic Church and Communism," in Black Deeds of the Kremlin. Toronto, 1953. v. 1: 511-527.

About the persecution of the Ukrainian Catholic Church
in Western Ukraine in 1939-1941 and its liquidation in
1945-1946 by the Soviet regime.

740. "The Ukrainian Orthodox Church." In the Black Deeds of
the Kremlin. Toronto, 1953. v. 1: 484-510.
Deals with the renaissance of the Ukrainian Orthodox
Church after the Revolution and its liquidation by the
Soviet regime. A list of executed or tortured Ukrainian
bishops.

741. Vins, L. (et others). "Another Example of Religious
Persecution in the USSR." (A letter to the Soviet authori-
ties.) Ukrainian Review, London. 17: 67-80, March, 1970.
Partially about Ukraine.

742. Yurchenko, A. "The Ukrainian Autocephalic Orthodox Church,"
in Genocide in the USSR. Munich, Institute for the Study
of the USSR, 1958. p. 172-177.

743. "The Ukrainian Autocephalous Orthodox Church," in Religion
in the USSR. Munich, Institute for the Study of the USSR,
1960. p. 63-69.

6. Ukraine - Education.

744. Bowen, James E. Anton Makarenko and the Development of
Soviet Education. Urbana, Illinois, University of Illinois,
1960.
Unpublished doctoral dissertation. Concerns the prominent Soviet-Ukrainian educator. Partially concerns
education in the Soviet Ukraine.

745. Kolasky, John. Education in Soviet Ukraine. A Study in
Discrimination and Russification. Toronto, Peter Martin
Associates, 1968. 238 p.
The author, a Canadian-Ukrainian teacher and member of
the Canadian Communist Party of the long standing, who
spent two years as a graduate student in the Ukraine,
described the education system in the Ukraine as instrument of Russification. Based on official documents and
exhaustively documented.

746. Polonska-Vasylenko, Natalia. The Ukrainian Academy of
Sciences. Munich, Institute for the Study of the USSR,
1956. 2 vols.
In Ukrainian with an English abstract. A history of
the Ukrainian Academy of Sciences and its forcible russification.

747. Ukraina. Ministerstvo Prosveshcheniia. Rozvytie Narodnoho

Obrazovaniia v Ukrainskoi SSR, 1963-1964 Uchebnyi God.
Doklad Predstavlenyi XVII. Mezhdunarodnoi Konferentsii
po Narodnomu Obrazovaniiu. Geneva, Yuly, 1964. Development of Public Education in the Ukrainian SSR. Kiev, 1964.
107 p.
     In Russian, Ukrainian, English, French and Spanish.
A statistical survey of the Ukrainian educational system
for the academic year 1963-1964. An official report.

748. Bilynsky, Andrew. "Educational and Cultural Institutions
in the Ukrainian SSR." Ukrainian Review, Munich. 7: 67-
82, 1959.

749. Derzhavyn, Volodymyr. "School and Russification."
Ukrainian Review, London. 6: 12-20. September, 1959.
     About the schools in Soviet Ukraine as instruments of
russification.

750. Fedenko, Panas. "The New Trends in Soviet Education and
Its Social Consequences." Ukrainian Review, Munich. 6:
41-55.
     Deals with impact of Khrushchev's education reforms
on the Ukraine.

751. Hordynsky, Sviatoslav. "Three Hundred Years of Moscow
Cultural Policy in the Ukraine." Ukrainian Quarterly.
10: 70-84. Winter, 1954.
     About how Moscow has restricted the freedom of thought
in the Ukraine since the Pereyaslav Treaty and attempted
to liquidate Ukrainian culture because it was essentially
Western. The Soviet regime is continuing this policy.

752. Mishchenko, Michael. "Medical Science in Ukraine under
the Soviets." Ukrainian Quarterly. 5: 310-317. Autumn,
1949.
     About trends in Soviet medicine. Medical Research
Institutes in Ukraine. Contains a list of prominent
Ukrainian scholars in the field of medicine and their
achievement.

753. Ohloblyn, Alexander. "The Ukrainian Humanities and the
Soviets." Ukrainian Quarterly. 5: 10-19. Winter, 1949.
     About the flourishing of Ukrainian humanities during
the NEP period and the subsequent attacks on Ukrainian
culture, the liquidation of Ukrainian universities and
the substitution of Soviet patriotism for Ukrainian
patriotism.

754. Pidhainy, Oleh Semenovych. "Ukrainian Historiography and
the Great East-European Revolution; a Propos of Symonenko's
Polemics." New Review. 7(1-2/30-310: 1-36. Bibl. footn.
p. 22-28.

Also available in reprint: Toronto, New Review Books
1968. 36 p. Also an appendix with list of 218
Ukrainian historians repressed by the Soviet authorities.

755. Prychodko, Nicholas. "Academic and Social Status of a
Student in the USSR." Ukrainian Quarterly. 14: 335-347.
December, 1958.
About discrimination in admission policies to the major
universities; economic conditions and control over the
spiritual life of the Soviet student.

756. Semchyshyn, Myroslav. "The Educational System in the
Soviet Ukraine." Ukrainian Review, Munich. 1: 76-89,
1956.
About the foundation of the Soviet education and types
of schools. Includes a survey of Ukrainian education in
1918 (independence period) and a discussion of the weak-
nesses in the school system of Soviet Ukraine.

757. Weinstein, Harold R. "Language and Education in the Soviet
Ukraine." Slavonic and East European Review. 20: 124-
148 (Slavonic Yearbook, American Series I) 1942.
The author considers Ukrainization during the NEP
period as a transitionary period leading to Russification.

7. Ukraine - Art.

758. Olkhovsky, Andrei V. Music under the Soviets: the Agony
of an Art. New York, F. A. Praeger, 1956. 427 p. (Research
Program on the USSR no. 11.)
Pages 243-261 contain references to Ukrainian music
revealing that in the 18th century the Ukraine had contacts with Western music earlier than Russia did. The
author depicts the history of the Ukrainian Soviet music
and the persecution of Ukrainian composers by the Soviet
authorities.

759. Sichynsky, Volodymyr. Destruction of Ukrainian Monuments
of Art and Culture under the Soviet Russian Administration
1917-1957. New York, Ukrainian Congress Committee of
America, 1958. 22 p.
About the destruction of Ukrainian monuments and
religious shrines by Soviets.

760. Andrievsky, Dmytro. "Soviet Architecture in Ukraine."
Ukrainian Quarterly. 13: 205-212. September, 1957.
About how modern architecture in the Ukraine proves
Russian colonialism in the Ukraine.

761. B. W. Destruction of Ukraine's Monuments." Ukrainian
Review, London. 17: 92-94. September, 1970.

762. Hordynsky, Sviatoslav. "The Stones Cry Out." Ukrainian
     Quarterly. 4: 36-43. Winter, 1948.
          A history and description of St. Michael's Monastery
     in Kyiv, a monument of 11th century destroyed by Soviet
     authorities in 1924.

763. Kulikovich, N. "Music in the Ukrainian RSR in 1958."
     Ukrainian Review, Munich. 9: 70-85. Bibl. footn.
          A survey of new musical works for the year 1958.

764. Kulikovich, N. "Stalin and Post-Stalin Elements in Soviet-
     Ukrainian Music." Ukrainian Review, Munich. 7: 83-92.
     1959.
          About influence of the political situation in the USSR
     on Ukrainian music.

          8. Ukraine-Literature.

765. Hayward, Max and Edward L. Crowly, ed. Soviet Literature
     in the Sixties. Published for the Institute for the
     Study of the USSR. New York, Frederick A. Praeger, 1964.
     222 p.
          Discusses also Ukrainian literature of the sixties.

766. Luckyi, George. Literary Politics in the Soviet Ukraine,
     1917-1934. New York, Columbia University Press, 1956. 323
     p. (Studies of the Russian Institute.)
          Also an unpublished doctoral dissertation by the same
     author: Soviet Ukrainian Literature--a Study in Literary
     Politics (1917-1934). New York, Columbia University, 1954.
     About the Ukrainian literary revival after 1917, organiza-
     tions of writers and literary trends. The information
     is based on the papers of the writer, Arkadii Lubchenko,
     and official Soviet documents. Includes a bibliography.

767. Slavutych, Yar. The Muse in Prison. Eleven sketches of
     Ukrainian poets killed by Russian Communists and twenty-two
          translations of their poems. Jersey City, N. J., Ukrainian
          National Association, 1957. 61 p.
          Sketches and selected poems of eleven Ukrainian poets
     who were victims of Soviet purges.

768. Andreev, M. "The Party and the Literature of the Non-Rus-
     sian Peoples." Studies on the Soviet Union. 3: 109-118, 1963.
     No. 1.
          Also concerns Ukrainian literature.

769. Boyko, Yuri. "The Struggle of the Ukrainian Literature under
     the Soviets against Russian Spiritual Enslavement."

Ukrainian Quarterly. 13: 46-55, March, 1957.
About how Ukrainian authors resisted enslavement by
the Russians and disguised themselves in order to sur-
vive and how in spite of that Moscow liquidated several
hundred Ukrainian writers.

770. Cizevsky, Dmitry. "The Soviet History of Ukrainian Literature." Ukrainian Review, Munich. 1: 19-37, 1957.
About the misrepresentation of the history of Ukrainian
literature by Soviet writers.

771. Fedenko, Panas. "Soviet Exploitation of the Centenary
of the Ukrainian Poet-Laureate Shevchenko" in the Studies
on the Soviet Union. 1: 113-119, no. 3, 1969.

772. Hlobenko, Mykola. "The Official History of the Ukrainian
Soviet Literature." Ukrainian Review, Munich. 5: 19-37,
1957.
A review of an outline of the History of Ukrainian
Literature published in 1954 by the Soviet Academy of
Sciences and the Ukrainian Academy of Sciences.

773. Hlobenko, Mykola. "Thirty-Five Years of Ukrainian Literature in the USSR." Slavonic and East European Review. 33:
1-16 and 33: 19-35.
About how Ukrainian literary activity increased after
the revolution. How Ukrainian writers opposed the Russian chauvinism. About the purges beginning in 1934 and
prohibition of all manifestations of Ukrainian nationalism.

774. Hordynsky, Sviatoslav. "The Fivefold Cluster of the Unvan-
quished Bards." Ukrainian Quarterly. 5: 249-260. Summer,
1949.
The story of five neo-classicist Ukrainian poets.
Three of them were liquidated by the Soviet regime. One
managed to escape abroad and the fifth saved his life by
conforming to regime demands.

775. Koshelivets, Ivan. "A Decade of Ukrainian Literature."
Studies on the Soviet Union. 3: 105-111, no. 2, 1963.

776. Lavrinenko, Jurij A. "Literature of Marginal Situations."
Horizons, 2: 76-91, 1957.
About the status of Ukrainian literature and the behavior
of Ukrainian writers under Soviet domination.

777. Luckyi, George. "Battle for Literature in the Soviet
Ukraine: a Documentary Study of VAPLite, 1925-1928."
Harvard Slavic Studies. 3: 227-246, 1957.
Based on the archives of the late Arkadii Lubchenko,
this article depicts the rise and fall of VAPLite (Free

Academy of Proletarian Literature) an organization of
Ukrainian authors. The author also relates the Russian
opposition to the rebirth of Ukrainian literature.

778. Luckyi, George. "Turmoil in the Ukraine." Problems of
Communism. 17: 14-20. July, August, 1968. Bibl. footn.

779. Manning, Clarence A. "The Attacks on Ukrainian Culture."
Ukrainian Quarterly. 4: 28-35. Winter, 1948.
    About the efforts of the enemies of the Ukrainian people,
past and present, to deprive Ukraine of its intellectual
and political elite.

780. Manning, Clarence A. "Pasternak and Khvylovy." Ukrainian
Quarterly. 14: 348-356, December, 1958.
    Discusses how Pasternak depicted communism as a dis-
integrating force in the book "Doctor Zhivago" thirty
years after Khvylovy expressed this conviction and paid
for it with his life. Manning notes that both authors
prove that anti-communist resistance is essential for
the restoration of freedom for all the world.

781. Nytchenko, D. "Extinction of Ukrainian Literature and
Arts under the Russian Occupation." Ukrainian Review, London. 13: 8-16, December, 1966.

782. "The Trials of Ukrainian Communist Literature." Ukrainian
Quarterly. 6: 203-213, Summer, 1956.
    About how Soviets purge Ukrainian authors for their
nationalism, adherence to Western influence, non-conformism
and non-participation in the campaign for state supremacy. Argues that freedom of Ukrainian literature can
be restored only with the collapse of the Communist regime.

783. Petrov, Victor. "Ukrainian Intellectuals Victims of Bolshevik Terror." Ukrainian Review, London. 2: 46-59.
September, 1956.
    About the liquidation by the Soviet regime of the
Ukrainian intellectual elite, scientists, writers and
artists.

784. Shevelov, George. "A Study of Soviet Ukrainian Literature."
Canadian Slavonic Papers. 1: 102-106.

785. "Trends in Ukrainian Literature under Soviets." Ukrainian
Quarterly. 4: 151-167. Spring, 1948.

786. Slavutych, Yar. "The Ukrainian Literary Renaissance of the
Twenties." Ukrainian Review, London. 4: 9-22, Spring, 1957.
    About the blossoming of Ukrainian literature during the
twenties in Soviet Ukraine and an abrupt liquidation by
the Soviet regime. How Ukrainian literature still exists
in spite of Soviet pressure.

9. Soviet Nationalities Policy - Ukraine.

787. Brezezinski, Zbigniew. "Permanent Purge: Politics in Soviet Totalitarianism. Cambridge, Harvard University Press, 1956. 256 p.
   About the purges as a Soviet technique of ruling from the rise of Stalin till the fall of Malenkov. References to the Ukraine. Bibliography.

788. Chornovil, Viacheslav. The Chornovil Papers. New York, McGraw-Hill, 1968. 246 p.
   The author, a young journalist, in a letter to the First Secretary of the Communist Party of the Ukraine, P. Shelest, criticizes the administration of justice in the Ukraine. There follows a series of biographies of twenty young Ukrainian intellectuals convicted to long terms of imprisonment and forced labor camps for defending the right of Ukrainians to preserve their Ukrainian individuality guaranteed by the Soviet constitution and other laws. Excerpts from their correspondence, essays, poetry, letters a.o. added.

789. Chornovil, Vyacheslav. Voices of Human Courage. Appeals from Two Soviet Ukrainian Intellectuals to Soviet Authorities. By Vyacheslav Chornovil and Valentyn Moroz. New York, Association for Free Ukraine. 1968, 57 p.
   Contents--Chornovil, V. An open letter to the First Secretary of the Communist Party of the Ukraine, Petro Yu. Shelest. Moroz, Valentyn. An Appeal to the Deputies of the Supreme Council of the Ukrainian Soviet Socialist Republic. A description of the administration of justice in the USSR as applied to the non-Russian populations.

790. Dmytryshyn, Basil. "Moscow and the Ukraine, 1918-1953: a Study of Russian Bolshevik Nationality Policy." New York, Bookman Associates, 1956. 310 p.
   A study of Soviet Nationality Policy in which the author states that the slogan "national in form, socialist in contents" means the cultivation of the Russian national heritage.
   Also an unpublished doctoral dissertation under the same title. Berkeley, Cal., University of California, 1955. 310 p.

791. Dobriansky, Lev E. The Vulnerable Russians. Introduction by Edward J. Derwinski. New York, Pageant Press, 1967. 454 p.
   The author discusses the weak points of the USSR as a Russian empire. Very many references to the Ukraine and Ukrainians and the Soviet nationality policy in the Ukraine.

792. Dzyuba, Ivan. <u>Internationalism or Russification</u>. A Study
     in the Soviet Nationalities Problem. Preface by Peter
     Archer. Ed. by M. Davies. London, Weidenfeld and Nicol-
     son, 1968. XIX, 1, 240 p.
          The author, a prominent Soviet Ukrainian journalist
     and literary critic, vehemently attacks present-day
     Soviet nationality policy and demonstrates that it is
     simply camouflaged Russian chauvinism and that violates
     the letter and spirit of Lenin's ideas and the resolutions
     of the early party congresses on the subject by using
     quotations from these sources.

793. Goldhagen, Erich, ed. <u>Ethnic Minorities in the Soviet
     Union</u>. New York, Praeger, 1968. 425 p.
          The proceedings of a symposium concerning non-Russian
     peoples of the USSR. On page 147-185 an article by
     Yaroslav Bilinsky: Assimilation and ethnic assertive-
     ness among Ukrainians of the Soviet Union. The article
     deals with Soviet nationality policy in the Ukraine, and
     its influence on the Ukrainians: assimilation, schools,
     mixed marriages, relocation of the population, Ukrainian
     resistance to the russification.

794. Independent Ukrainian Association for Research of National
     Problems in Soviet Theory and Practice. <u>Russian Bolshe-
     vism</u>. Munchen, Bong and Co., 19 , 334 p.
          Four scholars of Soviet Nationality Problems discuss
     different aspects of Soviet nationality policy. There
     are two articles by Yuriy Boyko. "Russian Historic
     Traditions in the Bolshevist Solution of the Nationality
     Problem" and "Russian Populism (narodnichestvo) and
     Source of the Leninism-Stalinism." By Oleksander Kul-
     chyckyj. "Analysis of the Russian Nature of Bolshe-
     vism in N. A. Berdyaev's writings." O. Sulyma. "The
     Russian Nature of Bolshevism as Seen through Works of
     Russian Writers, Publicists and Scholars."

795. Martovych, Oleh. <u>National Problems of the USSR</u>. Edinburgh,
     Scottish League for European Freedom, 1958. 58 p.
          Among other problems of the USSR, the author deals with
     the Ukrainian problem.

796. Mazlakh, Serhii. <u>On the Current Situation in the Ukraine</u>,
     by Serhii Mazlakh and Vasyl Shakhrai. Ann Arbor, Univer-
     sity of Michigan Press, 1970. 216 p.
          Translation of work of two Ukrainian communists,
     liquidated in time of Stalin's terror regime, dealing
     with chauvinistic policy of the Russian communist party
     in the Ukraine.

797. Moroz, Valentyn. <u>A Chronicle of Resistance in Ukraine</u>.
     Translated by Zirka Hayuk. Baltimore-Paris, Smoloskyp,

1970. 17 p.
   Author pictures Russian cultural genocide in Ukraine
giving as example a backwood village in Carpathian
Mountains-Kosmach. He discusses value of tradition and
national heritage for survival of an oppressed nation.

798. Pankiv, Halyna. Ukrainian Publishing during the Decade
1950-1960. A dissertation submitted to the faculty of
the Graduate Library School in candidacy for the degree of
master of arts. Chicago, Illinois, University of Chicago,
1966. 170 p.
   Brief history of the Ukraine is included in the introductory chapter. A discussion of the Ukrainian publishing
apparatus. An analysis of book and periodicals publishing.
Distribution apparatus, censorship. About how the
increasing percentage of Russian-language publications
released by Ukrainian publishing houses indicates russification trends. The author stresses the insufficient
editions, decreasing editions of periodicals and multi-
volume sets, unsatisfactory distribution apparatus.
Bibliography added. Unpublished master's thesis.

799. Schlessinger, Rudolf. Federalism in Central and Eastern
Europe. London, Paul Trench, Trubner and Co., 1945. 533 p.
   In the chapter on federalism in the USSR, the author
tells about the relation of the central Soviet government to Ukraine and describes Russian methods of surpres-
sing the national cultural and economic life of Ukraine
and the other non-Russian peoples. He also discusses
Ukrainian self-defense against Polish supremacy in Austro-
Hungary and Poland.

800. Smal-Stocki, Roman. The Nationality Problem of the Soviet
Union and Russian Communist Imperialism. Milwaukee, The
Bruce Publishing Company, 1952. 474 p.
   About the conflict of nationalism and communism; the
Soviet attitude towards the non-Russian national groups,
Soviet linguistic theories and attitudes of the present
Soviet regime and non-communist Russians toward the non-
Russian groups.

801. Sullivant, Robert S. Soviet Politics and the Ukraine,
1917-1957. New York, Columbia University Press, 1962.
438 p.
   The author presents the Soviet approach to solve the
Ukrainian problem. Ukraine, the author states, is a
specific political, economic and cultural entity, but is
considered by the Soviet leaders as a part of Russia.
   Also an unpublished doctoral dissertation entitled:
Soviet Politics in the Ukraine, 1917-1957. Chicago,
University of Chicago, 1958. 522 p.

802. Ukraine: Achilles Heel of the Vulnerable Russians. Washington, D. C., Ukrainian Congress Committee of America, 1968. 122 p.
   Reprint of speeches in the U. S. Congress on the occasion of the anniversary of the Independence of Ukraine, on or around January 22, 1968, from the Congressional Record. The speeches stress the importance of the Ukrainian problem in the USSR.

803. "Among the Snows." Ukrainian Review, London. 18: 15-35. Spring, 1971
   Translation of article from an Ukrainian undercover publication circulated in the Ukraine in typescripts and other similar copies. Anonymous author discusses declaration of Ivan Dziuba submitted to the Union of Writers of the Ukrainian Soviet Republic and administration of justice in the Ukraine.

804. Bilinsky, Yaroslav. "Current Soviet Policy Toward the Non-Russian Nations." Ukrainian Quarterly. 24: 63-72. Spring, 1968. Bibl. Footn.

805. Boyko, Yurii. "Mykola Skrypnyk and the Present Situation in Ukraine." Ukrainian Quarterly. 14: 262-273. September, 1958.
   On the occasion of an effort to rehabilitate Mykola Skrypnyk, the author remembers the Skrypnyk's efforts to preserve the Ukrainian cultural independence within the communist system. He tells about Skrypnyk's liquidation by the Soviet rulers.

806. Chaplenko, Vasyl. "The Struggle against the Russification of the Ukrainian Language." Ukrainian Review, London. 14: 2-16. June, 1967. Bibl. footn.

807. Chornovil, Vyacheslav. "Letter to the Attorney General of the Ukrainian S.S.R." Ukrainian Quarterly. 24: 12-21. Spring, 1968 and Ukrainian Review, London. 15: 25-31. September, 1968.
   Excerpts. Concerns the administration of justice in the Ukrainian S.S.R. as an instrument of russification.

808. Derzhavyn, Volodymyr. "The Soviet Language Policy in the Ukraine." Ukrainian Review, London. 6: 29-41. June, 1959.

809. Dobriansky, Lev E. "Lands and Nations in the USSR." Ukrainian Quarterly. 14: 18-40, March, 1958.
   About misconceptions concerning the USSR; the basic features of the Soviet terror regime; two concepts of the Revolution of 1917 (socialist and national liberation revolutions). Many references to Soviet colonialism in the Ukraine. Included maps and charts.

810. Dobriansky, Lev E. "The Spirit of Geneva: Ukraine and the Captive Nations." Ukrainian Quarterly. 11: 349-354, Autumn, 1955.
    A memorandum submitted to the Secretary of State, John Foster Dulles, on the occasion of Geneva Conference. Discusses the freedom of nations, self-determination and evaluates the U.N. membership of the Ukraine and Belorussia, and argues that there can be no trade with the USSR without political concessions.

811. "Examples of Administrative Persecution for Convictions." Ukrainian Review, London. 18: 36-41, I 1971.
    List of Ukrainians fired, expelled from communist party and persecuted for their political or religious convictions.

812. Fedenko, Panas. "Lenin and the Nationality Question." Studies on the Soviet Union. 3: 59-79. No. 3, 1964.

813. Holubnychy, Vsevolod. "The Language of Instruction: an Aspect of the Problem of Nationalities in the Soviet Union." Horizons. 2: 26-29, 1957, no. 1-2.
    Concerning the language used in Soviet Ukrainian schools and its influence on the russianization of the Ukrainians.

814. Hordynsky, Sviatoslav. "Three Hundred Years of Moscow Cultural Policy in Ukraine." Ukrainian Quarterly. 10: 70-84, Winter, 1954.
    About how Moscow restricted freedom of thought in the Ukraine since the Pereyaslav Treaty and attempted to liquidate Ukrainian culture because it was essentially Western. How present Soviet rulers are continuing this policy.

815. Hryshko, Vasyl. "Destruction of the Upper Classes of the Enslaved Nations. Traditional Policy of Moscow." Ukrainian Quarterly. 9: 317-323. Autumn, 1953.
    About how both white and red Russia destroyed the upper classes of the national minorities to break their resistance. How this traditional policy was and is applied to the Ukraine.

816. Kandyba, Ivan. "Letter to P. Yu. Shelest." Ukrainian Review. London, 15: 2-23, December, 1968.
    Letter from an Ukrainian intellectual imprisoned for his criticism of Russian nationality policy in the Ukraine, addressed to Peter Yu. Shelest, who was in this time First Secretary of the Communist Party of the Ukraine, which criticizes Soviet administration of justice in the Ukraine.

817.   aravansky, Svyatoslav Y. "A Petition to the Council of
       Nationalities of the USSR." Ukrainian Quarterly. 24: 108-
       116. Summer, 1968.
          Partially concerns Soviet nationality policy in the
       Ukraine.

818.   Korol, Nestor. "Discrimination against Ukrainians in
       National and Political Relations." Ukrainian Quarterly.
       14: 166-171, June, 1958.
          About how Ukraine is deprived of scientists by luring
       them to the Russian Republic with promise of higher salaries.

819.   Kovalevsky, Mykola. "Mock Trial of Ukrainian Patriots in
       Kharkiv in 1930," in Russian Oppression in Ukraine. (See
       entry no. 906.), p. 49-68.
          Concerns the trial of members of the Union for Liberation
       of Ukraine, a secret organization whose aim was to regain
       the independence of the Ukraine.

820.   Krupnytsky, Borys. "Federalism and the Russian Empire."
       Annals of the Ukrainian Academy of Arts and Sciences in the
       U.S. 2(4): 239-260.
          About how the Russians developed special traits and
       characteristics under the influence of severe conditions
       of their northern country and Mongol domination. They
       were suspicious toward strange peoples, autocratic and in-
       tended increase their empire by force. This argument is
       based on an example of the Novgorod the Great, Pskov,
       Ukraine and especially the Zaporozhe Kosak Republic.

821.   "Letters of the Ukrainian Political Prisoners in Soviet
       Prisons and Detention Camps, Circulating in Ukraine, Con-
       cerning Soviet Nationality Policy and Administration of
       Justice." Ukrainian Review, London. 15: 26-48. March,
       1968.
          Predominantly copies of letters of political prisoners
       sent to judicial or Party authorities.

822.   "A List of 110 Persons Known as Imprisoned for Their Poli-
       tical or Religious Convictions." Ukrainian Review, London.
       15: 11-24, March, 1968.

823.   Ohienko, Ilarion, Metr. "Ukrainian Literary Language in the
       USSR." Ukrainian Quarterly. 6: 229-240. Summer, 1950.
          About the subjection of Ukrainian linguistics to Russian
       dictates.

824.   P. V. "Ukrainian Intellectual Victims of Bolshevik Terror."
       Russian Oppression in Ukraine, (see entry no. 906 p. 85-110).
          About the purges of Ukrainian intellectuals.

825.   Poltava, Leonid. "Destruction of Ukrainian Historical Monu-

ments by Moscow." Ukrainian Quarterly. 24: 346-350.
December, 1968.

826. Reshetar, John, Jr. "Lenin on the Ukraine." Annals of the
Ukrainian Academy of Arts and Sciences in the U. S. 9(1-2/
27-28): 3-11. Bibl. footn.
    A survey of the expressions and declarations of Lenin
favorable to Ukrainian national and cultural aspirations.

827. Reshetar, John, Jr. "National Deviations in the Soviet
Union." American Slavic and East European Review. 12: 162-
174. Spring, 1953.
    About political, economic and cultural national deviations
in the USSR, particularly the Ukraine. The author states
that the existence of the Ukrainian Insurgent Army proves
that Ukrainians are still non-conformists.

828. Roucek, Joseph S. "Revival of Stalinism." Ukrainian Quarterly. 22: 225-236.
    The author discusses the return to Stalinist methods in
national policy in the USSR after Khrushchev's "thau."

829. "Russification of Ukraine." Ukrainian Quarterly. 14: 293-
298. December, 1958.
    About the degradation of the Ukrainian language and efforts
at russification through schools, newspapers and Russian
colonization.

830. Shankovsky, Lev. "The Effects of the Soviet Nationality
Policy in the Light of the 1959 Census and Other Statistical
Data." Prologue. 5: 27-28, 1961.
    Analysis of Soviet census of 1959 and other statistics
demonstrating the consequences of the Soviet policy of
russification in the Ukraine and other non-Russian Republics.

831. Skochok, V. (et al.). ("Letter of Three Ukrainian Intellectuals to the Kiev Satirical Journal 'Perets'") Ukrainian
Review, London. 15: 32-39, September, 1968.
    A criticism of Soviet nationality policy in the Ukraine.

832. Smal-Stocki, Roman. "Reasons for Revocation of the Marr's
Linguistic Theory by Stalin, June, 1950." Shevchenko Scientific Society. Proceedings of the Philologic Section. 2:
5-22, 1953.
    Author considers as reason of revocation of Marr's lin-
guistic theory that all languages will merge in one super-
language in the future, the Panslavism propagated by the
Soviet rulers. How Marr's theory is incompatible with the
ideas of Panslavism.

833. Smal-Stocki, Roman. "The Soviet Drive to World Domination
of Russian Language." Shevchenko Scientific Society. Pro-

ceedings of the Philologic Section. 1: 44-53.
About how Stalin hoped that there would be an international language in the future and that it would be Russian. References to the Marr's theory of the merging of languages.

834. Smal-Stocki, Roman. "Ukraine as Geopolitical Basis of the Russian Imperialism." Ukrainian Quarterly. 8: 116-122. Spring, 1952.
About how the Ukraine is a strategic base for the Soviet Union and therefore the Soviet Government fortifies the Ukraine from all sides.

835. Solchanyk, Roman. "The 'Sophistication' of Soviet Nationality Policy in the Ukraine." Ukrainian Quarterly. 24: 332-347. 1968.
Author describes changes in nationality policy of the USSR, especially in the Ukraine. He states that despite all changes, aim of this policy is russification. Protest of Ukrainian intellectuals, their arrests, writings of Dziuba and Kolasky.

836. Stetsko, Yaroslav. "Cultural Elite Fights Back." Ukrainian Review, London. 14: 11-16. March, 1967.
About resistance of Ukrainian intellectuals to russification.

837. Sullivant, Robert S. "The Agrarian-Industrial Dichotomy in the Ukraine as a Factor in Soviet Nationality Policy." Annals of the Ukrainian Academy of Arts and Sciences in the U.S. 9(1-2/27-28): 110-125.
About how the Soviet government uses the industrialization of the Ukraine for russification purposes.

838. "The Trial of Valentyn Moroz." Ukrainian Review, London. 18: 4-19. Spring, 1971.
Translation from the undercover "Ukrains'kyi Visnyk." (Ukrainian Herald) no. 3, 1970.

839. "Trials and Protests in the Ukraine." Problems of Communism. 17: 73-92. July-August, 1968.
About legal resistance in the Ukraine demanding adapting of constitutions of the USSR and Soviet Ukraine in practice and trials of peoples they raise similar demands.

840. Ukrainian Congress Committee of America. "Memorandum to the International Conference on Human Rights in Teheran." Ukrainian Quarterly. 24: 351-360. Winter, 1968.
Concerns Soviet nationality policy in the Ukraine.

841. Veryha, Vasyl. "Communication Media and Soviet Nationality Policy." Ukrainian Quarterly. 27: 124-149, 1971, and

27: 269-283.
     About status of national languages in Soviet television
     and radio. Based predominantly on materials concerning
     the Ukraine.

842. "The Witches' Sabbath of the Chauvinists." Open letter from
      young creative intellectuals of Dnipropetrovsk. Ukrainian
      Review, London. 16: 46-52, no. 3, 1969.
           Letter signed by representatives of Ukrainian intellectuals
      blaming Russian chauvinism as manifested in the Ukraine.

843. World Conference of Ukrainian Students. "Persecution and
      Destruction of Ukrainian Culture in the Soviet Union."
      Ukrainian Review, London. 16: 33-61, no. 2, 1969.

      10. Soviet Colonialism and Imperialism - Ukraine.

844. Barghorn, Frederick C. Soviet Russian Nationalism. New
      York, Oxford University Press, 1956. 330 p.
           Many references to all aspects of the Ukrainian problem.
      The consequences of the Treaty of Pereyaslav for Ukraine.
      Soviet fight against Ukrainian nationalism. Author uses
      Ukrainian sources.

845. Bohdaniuk, Volodymyr. The Real Face of Russia; Essays and
      Articles, ed. by Volodymyr Bohdaniuk. London, Ukrainian
      Information Service, 1967. 276 p.
           Consists of seven articles written by prominent Ukrainian
      and non-Ukrainian authors, dealing with the philosophical
      and historical elements of Russian imperialism, of bolshe-
      vism and the interrelations between the Russian chauvinism
      and bolshevism, the same being a crossbreed between Russian
      imperialism and international Marxism.

846. Bray, William. Russian Frontier: from Muscovy to Khrush-
      chev. Indianapolis, Indiana, Bobbs-Merril Co., 1963. 173 p.
           Author presents communism as a tool of Russian imperialism.
      He describes Russian conquests since the beginning of Rus-
      sian history and devotes one chapter to the Soviet conquest
      of the Ukraine.

847. Dmytryshyn, Basil. USSR: a Concise History. New York,
      Scribner, 1965. 620 p. Bibl.
           A very objective history of the USSR. Very many references
      to Ukraine, its incorporation into the USSR and the present
      situation of the Ukraine and Ukrainians in the USSR.
      Extensive bibliography.

848. Garelic, Joseph. Soviet City and Its People. New York,
      International Publishers Co., 1950. 96 p.

About life in the Ukrainian industrial city of Dnipro-
petrovsk.

849. Kolarz, Walter. <u>Russia and Her Colonies</u>. London, George
Philip and Sons, Ltd., 1952. 334 p.
      The author discusses at length Ukrainian problem when
discussing Soviet way to subdue other peoples. He stresses
that Ukraine and Georgia led the main opposition against
Stalin's centralism, describes Ukrainian aspirations to
freedom and the fight of the Ukrainian Insurgent Army
against the Soviet regime. He sees the future of the
Ukraine as a member of a non-Communist federation consisting of the present constituents of the USSR.

850. Kononenko, Konstantyn. <u>Colonial Disfranchisement and
Exploitation of Ukraine by Moscow</u>. New York, Ukrainian Congress Committee of America, 1958. 30 p.
      About Soviet Colonialism in the Ukraine.

851. Kononenko, Konstantyn. <u>Ukraine and Russia. A History of
the Economic Relations between the Ukraine and Russia,
1654-1917</u>. Milwaukee, The Marquette University Press, 1958.
257 p. (Marquette Slavic Studies, no. 4.)
      The author analyzes economic relations between the
Ukraine and Russia during the time between the Pereyaslav
Treaty and the Revolution of 1917. He describes the
development of the Ukrainian economy, of the industrialization of the Ukraine and stresses the Russian colonial
exploitation of the Ukraine.

852. Kostiuk, Hryhory. <u>Stalinist Rule in the Ukraine: a Study
of the Decade of Mass Terror</u>. London, Stevens and Sons for
the Institute for the Study of the USSR, 1961. 1-2 p.
      About how the establishment of the Ukrainian Soviet
Republic failed to revive Ukraine as a nation and simply
multiplied the problems of Ukrainization. How Ukraine was
infiltrated by Russians lured by industry and consequently
the Russian language has become more common than the
Ukrainian language. How this mixing of other nationalities
would make it difficult for a possible Ukrainian state to
emerge, especially after a terrific loss of Ukrainians
during Stalin's reign of terror which resulted in the death
of millions and emigration of others.

853. League for the Liberation of the Peoples of the USSR. <u>Cap-
tive Nations in the USSR</u>. Munich, 1963. 191 p.
      In the introduction the authors describe the character-
istic of Russian colonialism and imperialism and stress
the discrepancy between Soviet propaganda of anti-colo-
nialism in Asia, Africa and Latin America and their practice
at home.

Every major nationality has a separate chapter dealing with its history and annexation.

854. League of Ukrainian Social Democratic Youth. Nationalities Question in the Soviet Union. Paris, 1960. 16 p.

855. Revolutionary Voices. Ukrainian Political Prisoners Condemn Russian Colonialism. Munich. Antibolshevik Bloc of Nations. Pressbureau, 1969. 156 p. illus.
    Excerpts from undercover materials written by Soviet political prisoners (predominantly Ukrainians) condemning Russian colonialism in the Ukraine. A list of Ukrainian political prisoners is included.

856. Sciborsky, Mykola. Ukraine and Russia: a Survey of Soviet-Russian Twenty Years Occupation of Ukraine. New York, The Organization for the Rebirth of the Ukraine, 1940. 96 p.
    An illustrated account of the Soviet occupation of the Ukraine between the two world wars.

857. Smal-Stocki, Roman. The Captive Nations: Nationalism of the non-Russian Nations in the Soviet Union. New York, Bookman Associates, 1960. 112 p.
    This work discusses the nationalism of the non-Russian nationalities within the Soviet Union before the First World War, during the First World War and the Revolution of 1917, during and after the Second World War.

858. Adamovich, A. "Soviet Colonialism and the National Republics," in Studies on the Soviet Union. 5: 56-77, no. 1, 1961.

859. Bedrii, Anatole W. "Lenin for the Preservation of the Russian Imperial Rule in Ukraine." Ukrainian Review, London. 18: 61-66. March, 1970.

860. Bedrii, Anatole W. "Russian Imperialism in the Ideas and Policies of Lenin." ABN Correspondence. 17: 41-48, no. 6, 1966, 18: 20-22, no. 1, 1967, 18: 29-35, no. 2, 1967, 18: 20-24, no. 3, 1967, 18: 30-33, no. 5, 1967.

861. Bedrii, Anatole W. "Russian Imperialism toward Ukraine under Brezhnev-Kosygin." ABN Correspondence. 18: 18-22, no. 6, 1967.

862. Broide, Michael. "The Puppets of Soviet Russian Colonialism." Ukrainians and Jews. (See entry no. 238.) p. 97-106.
    Concerns the Academy of Sciences of Soviet Ukraine.

863. Dobriansky, Lev E. "Russia, Ukraine and the World's 50 Years of Conflict." Ukrainian Quarterly. 23: 203-211. Autumn, 1967.

864. Fedenko, Panas. "Liberation Abroad and Colonialism at Home." Studies on the Soviet Union. 5: 5-22, no. 2, 1961.

865. Fedenko, Panas. "Liberalism Abroad and Colonialism at Home." Studies on the Soviet Union. 9: 171-186. no. 4, 1965.

866. Glovinsky, Euhen. "The Ukrainian SSR within the Centralized Soviet System." Ukrainian Review, Munich. 1: 38-52. 1955.
    Discusses the principle of priority of federal interests over these of Ukraine. A comparison of the Ukrainian budget with the Soviet budget is made.

867. Kononenko, Konstantyn. "The Concept of Property and Russian Colonialism in Ukraine." Ukrainian Review, London. 4: 60-68. Summer, 1957.
    The author states that according to its constitution the Ukrainian SSR is the owner of all nationalized property in the Ukraine, but that the Moscow regime considers this property and its income to belong to the USSR.

868. Kosyk, Volodymyr. "Ukraine under Russian Colonial Rule." Ukrainian Review, London. 9: 19-57. September, 1962.

869. Lysenko, Luka. "The Russian Subjugation of Ukraine as Reflected in Soviet Economic Policy and Statistics." Ukrainian Review, London. 4: 53-67.
    Discusses the exploitation of the Ukraine by the Russian Metropoly on the evidence contained in the Soviet statistics.

870. Myronenko, Luka. "Moscow's Annual Income from Ukraine." Ukrainian Quarterly. 11: 46-55. Winter, 1955.
    About exploitation of the Ukraine by czarist and Red Russia. Gives the percentage of Ukrainian economic output in the total Soviet economy and the total income from the Ukraine to Moscow regime.

871. Pap, Michael. "Ukrainian Problem," in Soviet Imperialism, Its Origins and Tactics, a Symposium. Waldemar Gurian, ed., South Bend, Indiana, University of Notre Dame Press, 1953. P. 43-75.
    The contributor discusses the Ukraine as the victim of Soviet imperialism.

872. Pavlyuk, Mykhailo. "The Sixth Soviet Five-Year Plan and the Exploitation of Ukrainian Iron and Fuel." Ukrainian Quarterly. 12: 119-126, 1955.
    About how the Sixth Soviet Five-Year Plan provided for an increase in output of the Ukrainian iron ore and coal. Discusses the Ukrainian contribution to the Soviet output and the provision of the plan for increased exports to the Russian Republic.

873. Prokop, Myroslav. "Current Trends in Moscow's Nationality
Policy." Ukrainian Quarterly. 16: 13-28. March, 1959.
About the policy of the Soviet regime toward Ukraine at
that time.

874. Protsiuk, Stephen. "The Evacuation of Industry in 1941 and
the Postwar Economy of Ukraine." Ukrainian Quarterly. 5:
210-218. Summer, 1949.
About how machinery from over 1,200 Ukrainian plants was
evacuated to east of the Urals and none of it ever returned.

875. Sokolyszyn, Alexander. "References to the Soviet Russian
and Tsarist Russian Imperialism in Ukraine." Ukrainian
Review, London. 12: 89-95. Bibl. footn.

876. Solovey, D. "Exploitation of the Ukraine as Illustrated by
Data on Retail Commodity Turnover." Ukrainian Review,
Munich. 8: 69-77, 1959. Bibl. footn.

877. Solovey, D. "Ukraine's Share in the USSR State Budget for
1962." Ukrainian Quarterly. 21: 342-356. Winter, 1965.

878. "Soviet Reconstruction of the Russian Empire." Problems of
the Peoples of the USSR. 19: 23-46. 1963.

879. Svobodna, Lesya. "In Moscow's Captive Ukraine: Economic
Misery." Ukrainian Quarterly. 20: 205-223. Autumn, 1964.

880. Svobodna, Lesya. "A Look at Ukraine: Russia's Prize Colony."
Ukrainian Quarterly. 17: 131-142. Summer, 1961.

881. "Theses of the 300th Anniversary of the Reunion of Ukraine
with Russia, 1654-1954--Approved by the Central Committee of
the Communist Party of the Soviet Union." New Time Supplement. January, 1954, p. 1-15.
An example of the present approach of the Soviet rulers
to the Ukrainian problem.

882. T. S. "Ukraine and the Budget of the USSR." Ukrainian
Quarterly. 4: 19-27. Winter, 1948.
About how the Moscow regime arbitrarily establishes the
Ukrainian budget. The author claims that only 2.6% of the
income from the Ukraine was returned to the Ukraine.

883. Wynar, Bohdan. "The Establishment of Soviet Economic Colonialism in Ukraine." Ukrainian Quarterly. 13: 23-35,
March, 1957.
About how the Soviet regime pursues policy of economic
centralization in the interest of Russia and how Ukrainian
economists, who opposed this policy, were liquidated.

884. Wynar, Bohdan. "New Economic Regions in Ukraine."
Ukrainian Review, London. 4: 68-73. Fall, 1957.

Discusses the economic districts in the Ukraine
established according to the new plan of the reorganiza-
tion of Soviet economy.

885. Wynar, Bohdan. "Ukrainian Economy--Spoil of Russian Occupation and Victim of War, 1930-1954." Ukrainian Quarterly.
14: 240-252. September, 1958.
About the economic losses of the Ukraine before and
during the war; the centralization of the Ukrainian economy;
how Ukrainian economic research was discontinued; the slow
pace of postwar reconstruction; propaganda on the theme of
Ukrainian-Russian unity. Includes a discussion of the
celebration of the 300th anniversary of the Pereyaslav
Treaty.

11. Ukraine - Arrests, Deportations, Famine, Etc.

886. Black Deeds of the Kremlin. White Book I. Book of Testimonies. Toronto, Ukrainian Association of Victims of Russian Communist Terror, 1953.
A book of the testimonies of former political prisoners,
concerning purges, deportations, the crimes of the NKVD,
collectivisation and the induced famine in the Ukraine.
Also included references to the persecution of the various
Ukrainian churches. Contains photographs.

887. Black Deeds of the Kremlin. White Book Vol. II. The Great
Famine in Ukraine in Years 1932-33. Detroit, The World
Federation of Ukrainian Former Political Prisoners and
Victims of the Soviet Regime--DOBRUS. The Democratic Organi-
zation of Ukrainians Formerly Persecuted by the Soviet
Regime in the United States, 1955. 712 p.
Contains preface by former Representative, Charles Kersten.
A study of Professor Dubynets about this famine, testi-
monies of eye witnesses, illustrations, photos. Photo-
copies of Soviet documents proving that this famine was
pre-arranged by the Soviet government.

888. Chamberlin, William Henry. Russia's Iron Age. Boston,
Little Brown, 1934. 400 p.
In several places author refers to the Ukraine and to
Ukrainian anti-Soviet attitude, to the famine in the
Ukraine in 1932-33, etc.

889. Chamberlin, William Henry. Ukraine, a Submerged Nation.
New York, MacMillan, 1944. 91 p.
History of the Ukraine, description of the country,
Ukrainians in Poland, Carpathian Ukraine, Ukrainians in
the USSR, and hunger in the Ukraine in the years 1932-33.
Ukrainian trend to independence.

890. Ciszek, Walter, S. J. and Daniel L. Fisherty. With God in Russia. New York, McGraw Hill, 1964. 308 p.
    An American Jesuit of Polish extraction, who went for missionary work in the USSR and was imprisoned and sent to the slave labor camp, and tells about life in the Soviet labor camps and his encounters with Ukrainian political prisoners.

891. Conquest, Robert. The Great Terror. London, MacMillan, 1968. 633 p.
    This book is a general history of the great purge period and includes a discussion of Soviet crimes in the Ukraine during that period. Stresses immense scale of the anti-Ukrainian terror, describes methods of extracting confessions and secret trials. Gives figures of the victims of this terror.

892. Fisher, Harold Henry. The Famine in Soviet Russia, 1919-1922. Stanford, Cal., Stanford University Press, 1935. 609 p.
    The author tells about American relief work during the famine in the Ukraine in 1919-1922 and about the discriminatory attitude of the Central Soviet government toward the Ukraine in the relief work and the attitude of the Ukrainian Soviet government to the Central Soviet government.

893. Haliy, Mykola. The Organized Famine in Ukraine, 1932-1933. Chicago, Ukrainian Research and Information Institute, Inc., 1963. 48 p., map.
    Discusses the famine in the Ukraine in 1932-33.

894. Halychyn, Stephanie. Five Hundred Ukrainian Martyred Women. New York, The United Ukrainian Women's Organization of America, 1956. 160 p.
    The story of five hundred women prisoners in the Soviet slave-labor camp in Kingir, crushed to death by the tanks of the Soviet NKVD guards; includes extensive bibliography and illustrations.

895. Institute for the Study of the USSR. Genocide in the USSR. Studies in Group Destruction. New York, Scarecrow Press, 1958. 280 p.
    Deals with Soviet genocide in captive countries. Separate articles describe Soviet genocide in Eastern and Western Ukraine. Two other articles describe the destruction of the Ukrainian Orthodox and Catholic churches.

896. Kalynyk, O. Communism the Enemy of Mankind. Documents about the methods and practice of Russian Bolshevik occupation in the Ukraine. London, Ukrainian Youth Association in Great Britain, 1955. 120 p. plates.
    About Soviet methods of Government applied in Ukraine. Based on documents.

897. Kosyk, Volodymyr. Concentration Camps in the USSR. London, Ukrainian Publishers, 1962. 108 p.
     The book discusses the organization of Soviet concentration camps, their regime and location, and the national composition of inmates.

898. Mykula, W. "Soviet Nationalities Policy in Ukraine, 1920-1930." Ukrainian Review, London XVIII: 3-38, no. 4, 1971. XIX, 21-63, no. 1, 1972. XIX: 37-54, no. 3, 1972, XIX: 56-71, no. 4, 1972, XX: 44-56, no. 1, 1973. 20: 44-55, September, 1973.
     In progress of publication (published in installments) Bachelor's of Litt. thesis. University of Oxford, 1960.

899. Olenko, George, pseud. I Was a Slave and Beggar. New York, Pageant Press, International, 1969. 165 p.
     Recollections of a former inmate of a Soviet prison camp.

900. Pidhainy, Semen. Islands of Death. Toronto, Burns and MacEachern, 1953. 240 p.
     A former inmate of a slave labor camp comments on life in the Solovky camp and on the visits of foreigners; it includes descriptions of the various types of prisoners in this camp.

901. Pigido-Pravoberezhny, Fedir. The Stalin's Famine: Ukraine in the Year 1933. London, Ukrainian Youth Association in Great Britain, 1953. 72 p.
     Concerns the Soviet induced famine in the Ukraine in 1932 which caused the deaths of millions of Ukrainian peasants.

902. Prychodko, Nicholas. One of the Fifteen Millions. Boston, Little, Brown and Co., 1952. 236 p.
     History of an Ukrainian intellectual sent to the prison camp. Discusses life in the camp, characteristics of various groups of prisoners and the fate of the Ukrainians who returned home from Germany and were sent to prisons. Autobiographic.

903. Roeder, Bernard. Katorga. London, William Heinemann, 1958. 271 p.
     The memoirs of a German army officer who spent the years 1949-1954 in a Soviet slave labor camp. Discusses the inmates of these camps and the conditions in the Ukraine during the post-Stalin "thaw."

904. Russian Oppression in the Ukraine. London, Ukrainian Publishers, Ltd., 1962. 576 p.
     A collection of articles written by different authors concerning different aspects of the Soviet regime in the Ukraine.

905. Sandulescu, Jacques. Donbas. New York, McKay, 1968. 217 p.
    Reminiscences of a Rumanian who s an adolescent was
    deported to a Soviet labor camp in Donbas (mining and
    industrial region in the Ukraine on the Donets River).
    Discusses the conditions in the slave labor camps. Tells,
    about compulsory russification.

906. Scottish League for European Freedom. The Crime of Moscow
    in Vinnitsia. Edinburgh, The League, 1952. 32 p.
    About the mass graves of NKVD victims discovered in
    1943 in the Ukrainian town of Vynnytsia.

907. The Shame of the Twentieth Century. Bolshevist methods of
    combatting the Ukrainian national liberation movement. A
    documentary report. London, Ukrainian Publishers, Inc.,
    1962. 79 p.
    A translation of an Ukrainian underground publication of
    the Ukrainian Supreme Liberation Council. Tells about
    Soviet methods of combatting the Ukrainian underground
    with methods contradictory to the principles of warfare and
    humanity.

908. Sholmer, Joseph. Vorkuta. New York, Weidenfeld and Nichol-
    son, 1954, 264 p.
    Memoirs of a German doctor who was formerly an inmate of
    the Soviet labor camp at Vorkuta. Tells about meetings
    with Ukrainian camp inmates.

909. Solovij, Dmytro. The Golgota of Ukraine. Eyewitness account
    of the famine in the Ukraine, instigated and fostered
    by the Kremlin in an attempt to quell Ukrainian resistance
    to Soviet national and social enslavement of the Ukrainian
    people. New York, Ukrainian Congress Committee of America,
    1953. 43 p.
    An illustrated account of the famine in the Ukraine in
    1932-1933.

910. Tuchak, William. Khrushchev and Ukraine: Ukraine in Khrush-
    chev's political biography. Denver (Boulder) University of
    Colorado, 1963. 422 leaves.
    Unpublished doctoral dissertation. Discusses biography
    of Khrushchev, his political career and ability to survive
    Stalin's purges.
    The author states that in 1938-1949 Khrushchev, as Stalin's
    governor in the Ukraine, was a merciless executor of
    Stalin's orders and ruthless Russificator. Ukraine, tells
    the author, was the springboard of Khrushchev's political
    career. The Communist Party of the Ukraine made a core
    of his supporters. He influenced strongly the composition
    of this Communist Party, but vice versa, his long stay in
    the Ukraine influenced Khrushchev's political thinking.
    This dissertation has been microfilmed by the University

Microfilms, Inc. at Ann Arbor, Michigan. Abstract has been published in Dissertation Abstracts.

911. Ukrainian Congress Committee of America. Massacre in Vinnitzia. New York, Corporate author, 1953. 16 p. illus.
Illustrated account of the mass graves of thousands of NKVD victims exhumed in 1943 in the Ukrainian town of Vynnytsia.

912. Ukrainian Congress Committee of America. Violation and Destruction of Human Rights in Ukraine. Memorandum to the International Conference on Human Rights, April 22-May 13, 1968, Teheran, Iran. New York, Corporate author, 1968. 11 p.
A memorandum describing Soviet misrule in the Ukraine and demanding observance of the principles of the Constitution of the USSR, of the Soviet Ukraine and other laws by the rulers of the Ukraine.

913. U. S. Congress 85th. Second Session. Senate. Soviet Empire: The Prison of Nations and Races. A study in genocide, discrimination and abuse of power. Prepared by the Legislative Reference Service of the Library of Congress. Washington, D. C., U. S. Government Printing Office, 1958. 72 p. map. (Senate Document No. 122.)
Also concerns Soviet terror regime in the Ukraine.

914. U. S. Congress. House of Representatives. Committee on the Judiciary. Sub-committee no. 1. Testimony of Dr. Lev Dobriansky, September 23, 1964. Washington, D. C., U. S. Government Printing Office, 1964. 105 p. (Study of Population and Immigration Problems. Special Series No. 17 B)
Prof. Dr. Lev E. Dobriansky, President of the Ukrainian Congress Committee of America, tells in his testimony about the demographic impact of famines of 1921 and 1932-1933 in the Ukraine, about the deportations from the Baltic States, collectivization in Central Asia, slave labor camps and mass executions of political prisoners in the Ukraine and elsewhere in the non-Russian parts of the USSR. He tells about the enforced russification, the fate of churches of all denominations, and states that the policy of the USSR is a continuation of the nationalist policy of the czarist Russia. A large bibliography of works in English language, maps and charts added.

915. Woropay, Olexa. The Ninth Circle: Scenes from the Hunger Tragedy in the Ukraine in 1933. London, Ukrainian Youth Association in Great Britain, 1954. 64 p.
About conditions resulting from the Soviet induced hunger in the Ukraine in 1932 and 1933.

916. "Arrest of Ukrainian Intellectuals." Ukrainian Review,

London. 13: 62-66, September, 1966.
Concerns mass arrests and trials of young Ukrainian intellectuals demanding adherence to the Soviet Constitution and other laws securing national and human rights of Ukrainians.

917. Bahrianyi, Ivan. "Why I Do Not Want to Go Home." Ukrainian Quarterly. 2: 238-251, Spring, 1946.
About Soviet genocide in the Ukraine; the reason why so many Ukrainians lack a desire to go home.

918. Codo, Enrique Martinez. "The USSR in a True Light." Ukrainian Quarterly. 18: 311-322. Winter, 1962.

919. Fedenko, Panas. "Mykola Skrypnyk: His National Policy, Conviction and Rehabilitation." Ukrainian Review, Munich. 5: 56-72, 1957.
About the views, work, fall and posthumous rehabilitation of the prominent Ukrainian National-Communist Mykola Skrypnyk.

920. Gecys, Casimir. "The Post-Stalin Nationality Policy in Ukraine." Ukrainian Quarterly. 11: 153-162, Spring, 1955.
Describes how the Soviet Government changed its policy in the Ukraine after Stalin's death in certain aspects. The author claims that these changes are just changes of tactics and are still against Ukrainians.

921. Gerull, Heinz. "Man Is the Highest." Ukrainian Review, London. 14: 75-90, December, 1967 and 15: 78-91, March, 1968.
Deals predominantly with Ukrainians in Soviet prison camps.

922. Glowinskyi, Euhen. "The Western Ukrainian," in Genocide in the USSR. Munich, Institute for the Study of the USSR, 1958, p. 147-154.

923. Haliy, Mykola. "The 25th Anniversary of the Great Famine in Ukraine." Ukrainian Quarterly. 14: 204-214. September, 1958.
About the collectivization in the Ukraine. References to the famine of 1932-1933 in the reports of foreign correspondents, in the Soviet press and in testimonies of eyewitnesses.

924. Hamaliya, V. "Khrushchev's Purge of Ukraine in 1937-1938." Russian Oppression in Ukraine. (See entry No. 906.) p. 139-146.

925. "International Human Rights Year and Communist Russia."

Ukrainian Quarterly. 24: 101-107. Summer, 1968.
Deals with Soviet enslavement of the Ukraine.

926. Kazdoba, Kuzma. "Deportations to the North: Reminiscences."
Russian Oppression in the Ukraine, (entry no. 906). p. 434-
448.

927. Kokhanovsky, M. "The Examination of a Priest in the Bolshevik Prison: My Memoir of a Bolshevik Prison in 1938."
Ukrainian Quarterly. 10: 168-175. Spring, 1954. Bibl.
footn.

928. Kolymsky, Petro. "How I Became an Enemy of the People and
Was Sent to Kolyma." Ukrainian Quarterly. 8: 165-170.
Spring, 1952.

929. Kolymsky, Petro. "How They Tried to Make Me an Enemy of the
People." Ukrainian Quarterly. 8: 255-266. Summer, 1952.

930. Kolymsky, Petro. "I and Other Enemies of the Soviet People."
Ukrainian Quarterly. 9: 64-75. Winter, 1953.

931. Kolymsky, Petro. "My Journey to Kolyma." Ukrainian Quarterly. 9: 166-174. Spring, 1953.

932. Kolymsky, Petro. "On the Border of Mandzhuria and the
Pacific Shore." Ukrainian Quarterly. 9: 269-273. Summer,
1953.

933. Kolymsky, Petro. "In the Kolyma Gold Mines of the Nizhny
Katynakh." Ukrainian Quarterly. 9: 358-367. Autumn, 1953.

934. Kolymsky, Petro. "Past and Present of the Kolyma Mines."
Ukrainian Quarterly. 10: 380-387. Autumn, 1954.

935. Kolymsky, Petro. "The Return from Kolyma," Ukrainian Quarterly. 11: 163-169, Spring, 1955.

936. Kolymsky, Petro. "Liberation of the Kolyma Prisoners."
Ukrainian Quarterly. 12: 75-81. Winter, 1956.

937. Kolymsky, Petro. "The Kolyma Prisoner after His Release."
Ukrainian Quarterly. 12: 350-359. December, 1957.
A series of memoirs of an inmate of the Soviet slave
labor camps in the Kolyma Peninsula concerned chiefly with
the arrest of an Ukrainian intellectual; the trials, fellow
prisoners, journey to and life in the camps. The account
includes a history of the Kolyma Gold Mines and describes
reviewing of the cases of the prisoners, their subsequent
return and their difficulty in readjusting to normal home
life.

938. Kononenko, Konstantine. "The Dreadful Balance of 39 Years: Ukrainian Population Losses." *Ukrainian Review,* London. 4: 57-63. Spring, 1957.
     About the decrease of Ukrainian population under Soviet rule.

939. Kovalevsky, Mykola. "Collectivization and Starvation of the Farmers." *Russian Oppression in Ukraine.* (See entry no. 906.) p. 69-84.

940. Lyons, Eugene. "Khrushchev" The Killer in the Kremlin." *Readers Digest.* 36: 102-110. September, 1957.
     Discusses bloody Khrushchev's rule in the Ukraine.

941. "The Massacre of Political Prisoners in 1941." *Russian Oppression in Ukraine.* p. 169-197, (see entry no. 906).
     Concerns the murder of thousands of political prisoners during the Soviet retreat before advancing German forces.

942. Mishchenko, Michael. "Hunger as a Method of Terror and Rule in the Soviet Union." *Ukrainian Quarterly.* 5: 219-225. Summer, 1949.
     The author, who is a physician, comments on the physical and social consequences of hunger applied in the Ukraine by the Soviet regime in an effort to break the resistance of the farmers against collectivization.

943. Mishchenko, Michael. "My Testimony on the Genocide in Ukraine." *Ukrainian Quarterly.* 6: 265-274. Summer, 1950.
     About the methods of terror used in the Ukraine by the Soviet rulers: murder, burning alive, and organized famine.

944. Moroz, Valentyn. "A Reportage from Beria Reservation." *Ukrainian Review,* London. 19: 34-42, 1969. No. 1.
     Description of life in Soviet prison camps written (supposedly) by a young Ukrainian scholar now convicted for 9 years of prison and labor camp.

945. "Moscow's Crime in Vynnytsya." *Russian Oppression in the Ukraine.* p. 147-168.
     Concerns the mass graves of NKVD victims discovered in 1943 in Ukrainian town Vynnytia.

946. Mykulyn, Andrii. "The Russian Terrorist Regime and the Artificial Famine in the Ukraine." *Ukrainian Review,* London. 5: 10-25. Summer, 1958.
     About how centuries ago Moscow made use of hunger as torture for subduing other states such as Pskov.

947. Oreletsky, Vasyl. "Starvation of Ukraine by Moscow in 1921

and 1933." <u>Ukrainian Review</u>, London. 10: 18-26. September, 1963.

948. Pavlovych, Petro. "Testimony." <u>Investigation of Communist Takeover and Occupation of the Non-Russian Nations of the USSR.</u>" Washington, D. C., U. S. Government Printing Office, 1954. p. 82-94.
    Concerns the mass graves of the NKVD victims in Vynnytsya.

949. Fidhainy, Alexandra. "The Great Famine in the Ukraine, 1932-1933. A bibliography." <u>New Review</u>. 8: 123-132, no. 3/32, 1968.

950. Prokop, Myroslav. "Current Trends in Moscow's Nationality Policy." <u>Ukrainian Quarterly</u>. 16: 13-28, March, 1959.

951. Seleshko, Mykola. "Vynnytsya, the Katyn of Ukraine." <u>Ukrainian Quarterly</u>. 5: 238-248. Summer, 1948.

952. Serbyn, Roman. "British Public Opinion and the Famine in Ukraine." <u>New Review</u>. 8: 89-101, no. 3/32, 1968.

953. Smal-Stocki, Roman. "The Captive Nations Speak to America from Siberian Slave Labor Camps." <u>Ukrainian Quarterly</u>. 21: 48-56, Spring, 1965.
    A review of a book by the American-born Jesuit Priest Walter J. Ciszek, "With God in Russia," which is an account from his stay in Soviet slave labor camps in Siberia. Many references to encounters with Ukrainian prisoners.

954. Solovey, Dmytro. "On the 30th Anniversary of the Great Man-Made Famine in the Ukraine." <u>Ukrainian Quarterly</u>. 19: 237-246 and 350-363. Autumn and Winter, 1963. Bibl. footn.

955. Stets'ko, Iaroslav. "I Accuse Khrushchev of Mass Murder of the Ukrainian People." <u>Ukrainian Review</u>, London. 7: 3-19. June, 1966.

956. T. S. "Soviet Genocide of the Ukrainian People." <u>Ukrainian Quarterly</u>. 4: 325-338. Autumn, 1948. Bibl. footn.

957. Vashchenko, H. "Bolshevist Terror." <u>Ukrainian Review</u>, London. 4: 32-39. June, 1957.

958. Yurchenko, A. "The Ukrainians," in <u>The Genocide in the USSR</u>. Munich, Institute for the Study of the USSR, 1958. P. 138-147.

Fiction.

959. Bahrianyi, Ivan. <u>The Hunters and the Hunted</u>. New York,

St. Martin Press, 244 p.
>The story in novel form of Ukrainian political prisoner who escaped from a Soviet prison train and met a family of Ukrainian settlers making their living by hunting in the forests and how this family saved his life.

960. Osmachka, Todos. <u>Red Assassins</u>. New York, Dennison, 1959. 375 p.
>A novel depicting the suffering of Ukrainians under the Soviet regime.

961. Prychodko, Nicholas. <u>Stormy Road to Freedom</u>. Foreword by Igor Gouzenko, New York, Vantage Press, 1968. 356 p.
>The author presents in fictional form a story of a typical Ukrainian family of Globa, whose members are caught up, torn apart and scattered in the turmoil of brutal Soviet rule in the Ukraine.

VIII. UKRAINIANS IN POLAND, RUMANIA, CZECHOSLOVAKIA.

1. Ukrainians in Poland, Rumania, Czechoslovakia, 1918-1939.

962. Barr, James. <u>Report on the Polish-Ukrainian Conflict in Eastern Galicia</u> by Rev. James Barr, M. P. and Rhys J. Davies M. P. in House of Commons. Chicago, United Ukrainian Organizations of Chicago and Vicinity, 1931. 23 p.
>A report to the House of Commons of two members who visited Eastern Halychyna in 1930 after Polish "Pacification."

963. Buell, Raymon Leslie. <u>Poland Key to Europe</u>. New York, Alfred A. Knopf, 1939. 364 p.
>Contains references to the Ukrainians in Poland, the history of Ukraine up to partition of Ukraine among four states; Polish policy of assimilation, Ukrainian life in Poland, Polish groups interested in appeasement with Ukrainians and possibilities of such appeasement.

964. Horak, Stepan. <u>Poland and Her National Minorities, 1919-1939</u>. A case study. New York, Vantage Press, 1961. 259 p. tables, maps, appendixes, bibliographies, index.
>The theme of this book is that historical Poland lost its independence through the partitions of Poland because of the vast alien territories which it could not digest, but reborn Poland after 1918 made the same mistake. The aim of the Poles was to reinstate a vast empire with a high percentage of national minorities. The author describes all of the national minorities in Poland, but puts more stress on Ukrainians.

965. The International Committee for Political Prisoners. <u>Political Prisoners in Poland</u>. New York City, 1927. 70 p.

"An exposure of the persecution of political, racial and religious minorities today in Poland. From documentary sources."

On the background of the principles of the Polish constitution, guaranteeing civil liberties, the book describes a real situation. This situation was that all minorities were deprived of all civil liberties. The book includes depositions of former political prisoners, their letters, etc. A considerable part of the material concerns the situation of the Ukrainians in Poland.

966. Kubijovyc, Volodymyr. Western Ukraine within Poland, 1920-1939. Chicago, Ukrainian Research and Information Institute, Inc., 1963. 32 p.
    Concerns situation of Ukrainian in Poland in 1920-1939.

967. Reviuk, Emil, comp. Polish Attrocities in Ukraine. New York, United Ukrainian Organizations of the United States, 1931. 512 p.
    "Pacification" of the Ukrainians in Eastern Halychyna in the summer of 1930 by the Polish police and armed forces.

968. Shepshanks, Mary. Poland and Ukraine: the Danger Spot of Europe. With a foreword by Cecil Malone, MP. London, Ukrainian Bureau, 1931. 74 p.
    A report of an investigation of the situation of the Ukrainians in Poland, by Miss Mary Sheepshanks, with a foreword by a member of the British House of Commons, Cecil Malone.

969. Soborny, V. and V. Bukata. The Truth about Poland. New York, Committee of Protest against Persecution of Ukrainians in Poland, 1938. 15 p. illus.
    Concerns the situation of Ukrainians in Poland. Describes the Polish "pacification" of Ukrainians in 1930 and describes repressions against Ukrainians in 1938 in connection with the proclamation of independence of Carpathian Ukraine.

970. Western Ukraine under Polish Yoke: Polonization, Colonization, Pacification. New York, The Ukrainian Review, 1931. 47 p.

971. Danko, Joseph. "Plebiscite of Carpatho-Ruthenians in the United States Recommending Union of Carpatho-Ruthenia with the Czechoslovak Republic." Annals of the Ukrainian Academy of Arts and Sciences in the U. S. 11(1/2/31-32: 184-207. 184-207. Bibl. footn.
    Author discusses plebiscite organized by organizations of the emigrants from the Carpatho-Ukraine (they called themselves Carpathian Ruthenians and their land Carpatho-Ruthenia) during the Peace Conference in Paris in 1919.

Majority of voters recommended union of the Carpathian Ukraine with Czechoslovakia. This result of plebiscite influenced participants of Peace Conference who approved this union.

972. Hanushchak, Larissa. "The Curzon Line Controversy." Horizons. 5: 26-30, no. 1/8, 1964. Bibl. footn.
    Concerns Polish claims to the Ukrainian and Bielorussian territories east of the Curzon Line.

973. Krofta, Karol. "Ruthenes, Czechs and Slovaks." Slavonic and East European Review. 13: 363-371 and 13: 611-626, January and April, 1935.
    Includes the history of the Carpathian Ukraine from the very beginning and describes cultural development under Czechoslovakian rule.

974. Los, Stanislav. "The Ukrainian Question in Poland," in Slavonic and East European Review. 10: 116-125, June, 1931.
    A Polish answer to the article by Basil Paneyko (see no. 975) which appeared in volume 9 of the same journal.

975. "The Pacification of the Ukrainian Population in West Ukraine in 1930." Ukrainian Review, London. 16: 53-65, no. 3, 1969.

976. Paneyko, Basil. "Galicia and the Polish-Ukrainian Problem." Slavonic and East European Review. 9: 576-587, March, 1941.
    History and geography of Eastern Halychyna, conditions in Halychyna under Polish domination and the prospects for future.

977. Stefan Augustine. "Contacts between Carpatho-Ukraine and Lviv" in Lviv (see entry no. 135) p. 272-279.
    About the cultural and political ties between the Carpatho-Ukraine and Lviv, the cultural, political and religious capital of western Ukraine.

978. W. M. "Ukrainian Political Life under the Polish Rule in the 20's." Ukrainian Review, London. 9: 70-80, September, 1962.

2. Ukrainians in Poland, Rumania and Czechoslovakia, 1945-

979. Dushnyck, Walter. Death and Devastation on the Curzon Line, the Story of Deportations from Ukraine. New York, Committee against Mass Expulsions and Ukrainian Congress Committee of America, 1948. 32 p.
    About the mass resettlement of Ukrainians from the area west of the Curzon Line.

980. Mussakowska, Olha. "Ukrainians in Present-Day Poland."
Ukrainian Review, London. 6: 72-79, December, 1959.
About the deplorable situation of a Ukrainian who remained
in Poland.

981. Yendyk, Rostyslav. "Ukrainians in Present-Day Poland."
Ukrainian Review, London. 4: 64-66, Spring, 1957.
About the Ukrainian minority in Poland.

IX. UKRAINE - FIGHT FOR INDEPENDENCE.

1. Ukraine - Fight for Independence - General.

982. Kyiv Versus Moscow. Munich, Ukrainian Information Service,
1970. 69 p.

983. "Ukraine. A Captive But Unconquerable Nation." Bulletin of
the World Anti-Communist League, 1970.
Ukrainian issue of Bulletin of the World Anti-Communist
League. Collection of articles on Ukrainian topics.

984. Markus, Vasyl. "Ukraine Is Still Largely a Terra Incongnita."
Ukrainian Quarterly. 16: 56-65. March, 1959.
About the results of a survey made by the author among
the participants of the Salzburg Seminar in American
Studies, January, 1958.

985. Smal-Stocki, Roman. "Action of the Union for the Liberation
of Ukraine During World War I." Ukrainian Quarterly. 15:
169-174. June, 1959.
Concerns the activities of an organization of refugees
from the Russian occupied Ukraine.

986. Styranka, Myroslav. "Active Forces of Resistance in the
USSR." Ukrainian Quarterly. 26: 11-24. Bibl. footn.

2. Carpatho-Ukraine.

987. Kozauer, Nicholas John. The Carpatho-Ukraine between the Two
World Wars, with Special Emphasis on the German Population.
New Brunswick, N. J., Rutgers University, 1964.
An unpublished doctoral dissertation dealing with the
German minority in Carpathian Ukraine.

988. Nemec, Frantishek and Vladimir Mudry. Soviet Seizure of
Subcarpathian Ruthenia. Toronto, N. B. Anderson, 1955. 375 p.
Authors, Bohemians, use for Carpatho-Ukraine official
Czechoslovakian name, "Subcarpathian Ruthenia." They
claim Carpatho-Ukraine to be a legitimate part of Czechoslo-
vakia.

989. Stefan, Augustin. From Carpatho-Ruthenia to Carpatho-Ukraine.
      New York, Carpathian Star Publishing Co., 1954. 48 p.
          About the evolution of national consciousness in Car-
      patho-Ukraine.

990. Stercho, Petro George. Carpatho-Ukraine in International
      Affairs, 1938-1939. South Bend, Indiana, Notre Dame Uni-
      versity, 1959.
          An unpublished doctoral dissertation concerning the diplo-
      matic bargaining around Carpatho-Ukraine during the crucial
      years of 1938-1939.

991. Winch, Michael. Republic for a Day: An Eyewitness Account
      of the Carpatho-Ukraine Incident. London, R. Hale, 1939.
      286 p.
          The history of the shortlived independence of Carpatho-
      Ukraine, told by a British press correspondent. Includes
      a description of the country and its inhabitants.

992. Markus, Vasyl. Carpatho-Ukraine under Hungarian Occupation."
      Ukrainian Quarterly. 10: 252-256. Summer, 1956.
          About the policy of the Hungarians in Carpatho-Ukraine
      in 1939-1945.

993. Revay, Julian. "The March to Liberation of Carpatho-Ukraine."
      Ukrainian Quarterly. 10: 227-234. Summer, 1954.
          The author disputes the Hungarian and Czechoslovakian
      claims to Carpatho-Ukraine.

994. Shandor, Vincent. "Annexation of Carpatho-Ukraine to the
      Ukrainian SSR." Ukrainian Quarterly. 13: 243-254, September,
      1957.
          The author disputes claims of Hungary and CSR to Car-
      patho-Ukraine and states that the wish of the Carpatho-
      Ukrainians is to belong to independent Ukrainian state.

995. Shandor, Vincent. "Carpatho-Ukraine in the International
      Bargaining of 1918-1939." Ukrainian Quarterly. 10: 235-
      246. Summer, 1954.

996. Stefan, Augustin. "Myths about Carpatho-Ukraine." Ukrainian
      Quarterly. 10: 218-226. Summer, 1954.
          The author argues that the Carpatho-Ukrainians are con-
      scious of their unity with the other Ukrainians.

997. Voloshin, Augustin. "Carpathian Ruthenia." Slavonic and
      East European Review. 13: 372-378, January, 1935.
          About conditions in Carpatho-Ukraine labeled here
      according to the Official Czechoslovakian nomenclature:
      Carpathian Ruthenia under Hungarian rule and the improve-
      ment under Czechoslovakian rule.

3. Ukrainian Revolutionary Organizations.

998. Martovych, Oleh, pseud. Ukrainian Liberation Movement in Modern Times. Edinburgh, Scottish League for European Freedom, 1951. 176 p.
   The history of the modern Ukrainian liberation movement.

999. Osanka, Franklin Marc, ed. Modern Guerilla Warfare; fighting Communist guerilla movement, 1941-1961. Introduced by Samuel P. Huntington. New York, The Free Press of Glencoe, 1962. XXII, 519 p.
   Includes one article by Enrique Martinez Codo about guerilla warfare in Ukraine. The bibliography includes many books on the Ukrainian resistance.

1000. Piddington, William E. R. Russian Frenzy. London, Elek Books, 1955. 266 p.
   Includes descriptions of encounters with the former Ukrainian guerilla fighters in the Soviet slave labor camp at Vorkuta.

1001. Scottish League for European Freedom. UPA, the Story of the Ukrainian Insurgent Army and the Ukrainian Red Cross. Edinburgh, The League 1951. 24 p.
   The Ukrainian Insurgent Army and Its Red Cross. Reprinted in Ukrainian Weekly, nos. 42, 43, 44, 45, 1952 (Ukrainian Insurgent Army) and in nos. 46, 47, 48 and 49, 1952 (Ukrainian Red Cross).

1002. Ukrainian Congress Committee of America. Ukrainian Resistance: the Story of the Ukrainian National Liberation Movement in the 20th Century. New York, 1949. 192 p.
   In English and Ukrainian. About the Ukrainian independence movement after the First World War; the origin and history of the Ukrainian revolutionary nationalism; disillusionment with German policy and struggle of the UPA (Ukrainian Insurgent Army) against Germany and the USSR. Also discusses the Ukrainian National Council--Ukrainian Government in exile.

1003. Ukrainian Insurgent Army in Fight for Freedom. New York, United Committee of the Ukrainian-American Organizations of New York, 1954. 224 p.
   A collection of reprints of articles. Short stories and drawings from Ukrainian underground publications. Includes addresses delivered by U. S. Senators at the celebration of the 10th anniversary of the UPA.

1004. Bohor, M. "Ukrainian Underground." Ukrainian Review, London. 2: 26-36. March, 1956.
   Describes the political organization and program of the Ukrainian underground.

1005. Chamberlin, William Henry. "Ukrainian Fighters for Freedom." Ukrainian Quarterly. 6: 9-12. Winter, 1950.
     About the Ukrainian Insurgent Army.

1006. Chubatyi, Nicholas. "The National Revolution in Ukraine,
1917-1919." Ukrainian Quarterly. 1: 17-39. October, 1944.
     About the history of the Ukrainian independence struggle
     during 1917-1919.

1007. Chubatyi, Nicholas. "The Ukrainian Underground." Ukrainian
Quarterly. 2: 154-166, Winter, 1946.
     Discusses the history of the Ukrainian underground
     beginning with the units organized in 1941 by Bulba;
     fight of the Ukrainian Insurgent Army (UPA) against the
     Germans and Soviets; the political superstructure of the
     UPA, Ukrainian Supreme Liberation Council (UHVR) and the
     ABN (Anti-Bolshevik Bloc of Nations).

1008. Codo, Enrique Martinez. "Guerillas behind the Iron Curtain--
Past and Future." Ukrainian Quarterly. 22: 130-140.
Summer, 1967.
     About the Ukrainian Insurgent Army.

1009. Krylov, I. "Educational and Pedagogical Aims of the Union
for the Liberation of Ukraine." Ukrainian Review, Munich.
3: 31-38, 1956.
     About a revolutionary organization which existed during
     the 20's and early 30's and its discovery and destruction
     by NKVD.

1010. Lenkavsky, Stepan. "The Organized Resistance Fight for the
Ukrainian State." Ukrainian Review, London. 9: 60-72,
March-June, 1962.
     About the Ukrainian Insurgent Army.

1011. Liron, Yona. "I Was a Soviet Counter-Agency Expert."
Ukrainian Quarterly. 19: 324-334. Winter, 1963.
     The memories of a Soviet defector who worked as an
     expert in the Soviet fight against the Ukrainian Insur-
     gent Army.

1012. Lutarevych, P. "A Resistance Group of the Ukrainian Underground, 1920-1925." Ukrainian Review, Munich. 2: 84-91, 1952.
     A story of a typical Ukrainian resistance group during
     the period between two world wars.

1013. Plyushch, Vasyl. "The Discovery and the Trial of the Union
for Liberation of Ukraine." Ukrainian Quarterly. 12: 63-
69. Winter, 1956.

1014. Plyushch, Vasyl. "The Union for the Liberation of Ukraine,

1924-1930." <u>Ukrainian Review</u>, Munich. 3: 13-30, 1955.

1015. Plyushch, Vasyl. "The Union for the Liberation of Ukraine:
Organization and Ideology." <u>Ukrainian Quarterly</u>. 11: 244-
255. Summer, 1955.
     All these articles by Plyushch concern Spilka Vyzvolennia
Ukrainy (Union for Liberation of Ukraine) an underground
organization of the Ukrainian intellectual elite devoted
to the purpose of liberating Ukraine from Soviet domination.
First article deals with trial and sentencing of members
of this organization in 1930. Second and third articles
discuss organization and aims of this organization.

1016. Rathaus, Alexander. "Underground: USSR." <u>Ukrainian Quar-
terly</u>. 18: 203-224. Autumn, 1962.
     Deals predominantly with the Ukrainian Insurgent Army.

1017. Shankovsky, Lev. "Soviet and Satellite Sources on the
Ukrainian Insurgent Army." <u>Annals of the Ukrainian Academy
of Arts and Sciences in the U. S.</u> 9(1-2/27-28): 234-261.
     A bibliographic survey.

1018. Shankovsky, Lev. "Ukrainian Underground Publications in
USSR in 1945-1951." <u>Ukrainian Quarterly</u>. 8: 225-238.
Summer, 1952.
     Discusses publications issued by the Ukrainian under-
ground during the period 1945-1951.

1019. (Shukhevych, Roman). "Interview with an Underground Leader."
<u>Russian Oppression in Ukraine</u> (see entry no. 906). p. 276-
274.
     A translation from underground publication of the
Ukrainian Insurgent Army of an interview with its Commander in Chief, Roman Shukhevych (combat pseudonym--
Taras Chuprynka) concerning the Ukrainian Insurgent Army
and its aims.

1020. Shukhevych, Roman. "The Origin of the Ukrainian Supreme
Liberation Council." <u>Ukrainian Review</u>, London. 17: 19-28.
No. 1, 1970.
     Author tells about organization of the Ukrainian Supreme
Liberation Council (UHVR), a political superstructure of
the Ukrainian Insurgent Army.

1021. Smal-Stocki, Roman. "The Struggle of the Subjugated Nations
in the Soviet Union for Freedom: Sketch of History of the
Promethean Movement." <u>Ukrainian Quarterly</u>. 3: 324-344.
Autumn, 1947.
     The story of the Promethean Movement, an organization
of the nationalities enslaved by the Soviet Union, aimed

at their liberation which was initiated after the First
World War by the Ukrainians and its activities as told by
its organizer.

1022. "The Unfinished Revolutions." Ukrainian Quarterly. 22: 1-
14. March, 1957.
   About the social revolution beginning in Russia in 1917
and the revolutions national in Ukraine and other countries
enslaved by Russia. The author claims that these remained
unfinished because of neutral attitudes of neutral powers.

1023. Vaskovych, H. "The Struggle of the O.U.N. after the War."
Russian Oppression in Ukraine (see entry no. 906). P. 505-
514. Bibl. footn. p. 514.

4. Ukrainian Anti-German Resistance.

1024. Chamberlin, William Henry. "The Ukrainian Struggle for
Freedom." Ukrainian Quarterly. 2: 111-119. Winter, 1945.
   About the Ukrainian disappointment with the German
occupation; also about the Soviet occupation of the Ukraine
and the Ukrainian anti-Soviet resistance.

1025. Shankovsky, Lev. "German Security Policy Reprisals against
the Revolutionary OUN." Ukrainian Review, London. 15: 60-
66, no. 2, 1968.
   OUN is the acronym for the Organization of Ukrainian
Nationalists.

5. Publications in Defense of the Ukrainian Freedom.
Issued Before 1939.

1026. Case for the Independence of Eastern Galicia. Published
under the authority of the President of the Ukrainian
National Council. London, 1922. 71 p.
   An official publication of the Western Ukrainian Govern-
ment in exile which rejects Polish claims to Eastern
Galicia.

1027. Central Executive Committee of the Representatives of
Ukrainian Refugee Organizations in Czechoslovakia. Extir-
pation of Ukrainians in Poland. Prague, 1930. 26 p.

1028. Fedortchouk, Yaroslav. Memorandum on the Ukrainian Question
in Its National Aspect. London, Griffith, 1914. 44 p.
   A publication sponsored by the emigre' Union for
Liberation of Ukraine.

1029. Swystun, Vasyl. Ukraine--the Sorest Spot of Europe. Winnipeg, The Ukrainian Information Bureau, 1931. 67 p.
   Concerns situation of Ukrainians in Poland and especially
the "pacification" of 1930.

1030. Ukraine Claims to Freedom. An Appeal for Justice on Behalf of Thirty-Five Millions. New York, Ukrainian National Association and Ruthenian National Association, 1915. 125 p.
   A collection of articles by prominent Ukrainian and non-Ukrainian writers which demand freedom for Ukraine; includes a bibliography, charts and a map.

1031. Ukrainian National Committee of the United States. Ukraine on the Road to Freedom. Selection of Articles, Reprints and Communications concerning Ukrainian people in Europe. New York, 1919. 80 p.
   A selection of materials concerning Ukraine published in a year that was crucial for Ukraine in arousing the American public opinion.

1032. Pidhainy, Oleh S. "Documents of the Brothers Zaliznyak in Stockholm, 1917." The New Review. 8(4/33): 9(3/36): 227-251, 1968-1969.
   Memoranda of the brothers Mykola and Volodymyr Zalizn-yak to the German Foreign Ministry on Ukrainian matters.

   6. Publications in Defense of the Ukrainian Freedom
                Issued After 1939.

1033. Ukrainian Congress Committee of America. Communist Russia Tramples Human Rights in Ukraine. Crass violations of U. N. Universal Declaration of Human Rights by Moscow--a Challenge to the Civilized World. New York, 1968. 15 p.
   Published on the occasion of the Teheran Conference on Human Rights.

1034. Ukrainian Information Bureau. Ukrainian Policy of Liberation. Augsburg, Ukrainian Information Bureau, 1951. 15 p.
   A declaration of the Executive Committee of the Ukrainian National Council criticizing policy of the Russian emigrants desiring to preserve the unity of the Russian-dominated Soviet Union.

1035. World Congress of Free Ukrainians. Captive Ukraine--Challenge to the World Conscience. New York, 1967. 31 p.
   A declaration of the World Congress of Free Ukrainians in the matter of the Ukrainian independence claims.

1036. World Congress of Free Ukrainians. First Manifesto to the Ukrainian People in Ukraine and beyond its Borders, in the USSR and in the Lands of the Russian Communist Bloc. New York, N. Y., U.S.A. November 16-19, 1967. 7 p.

1037. World Congress of Free Ukrainians. Memorandum Submitted to the Secretary General of the United Nations. New York,

November 16-19, 1967. 8 p.
    Also published in the Ukrainian Review, London. 15:
    48-55. March, 1968.

1038. World Congress of Free Ukrainians. Human Rights Commission.
       Ukrainian Press and Information Service. Documents. Win-
       nipeg, 1970. 67 p.
           About the violation of human rights in the Ukraine.

1039. Association of Ukrainians in Great Britain. "Appeal to
       International Conference on Human Rights." Ukrainian
       Review, London. 15: 90-96. June, 1968.
           A memorandum to the Teheran Conference on Human Rights.

1040. Dobriansky, Lev E. "The Making of a Mission." Ukrainian
       Quarterly. 8: 328-338, 1952.
           Ukrainians can take part in a common anti-Communist
       front when its ideology will be based on the principle
       of equality of all national groups.

1041. Dobriansky, Lev E. "The Success of a Mission and Its
       Eclipse." Ukrainian Quarterly. 9: 48-62, Winter, 1953.
           Author explains the reasons why the emigree Ukrainians
       in Europe do not want to cooperate with the Coordinating
       Center for the Anti-Bolshevik action.

1042. Dushnyck, Walter. "The Publications of the UCCA; a Weapon
       of Truth and Education." In IX Konhres Amerykans'kykh
       Ukraintsiv 7. 8 i 9. Zhovtnia 1966. New York, Hilton
       Hotel. New York City, Ukrains'kyi Konhresovyi Komitet
       Ameryky, 1966. P. 94-99.
           An article evaluating the publications of the Ukrainian
       Congress Committee of America.

1043. "Historic Event for Ukraine: First World Congress of Free
       Ukrainians." Ukrainian Quarterly. 23: 197-202. Autumn,
       1967. Bibl. footn.

1044. Nakashidze, George. "Professor Roman Smal-Stocki and the
       Promethean Movement." Ukrainian Quarterly. 25: 252-261, no.
       3, 1969.

1045. Ukrainian Congress Committee of America. "Memorandum of
       the Ukrainian Situation to the Paris Peace Conference."
       Ukrainian Quarterly. 3: 56-65, 1946.
           Situation of the Ukraine under Soviet domination.
       Ukrainian struggle for freedom, Ukrainian underground and
       Ukrainian displaced persons.

X. UKRAINE AND OTHER COUNTRIES AND STATES.

1. Ukraine - Geopolitics.

1046. Gustloff, Stephen W. Russia, Poland and Ukraine. Jersey City, N. J., Ukrainian National Council, 1915. 32 p.
    The author discusses the attitudes of Poland and Russia to the Ukraine during the First World War. He states that Russian Panslavism does not appeal to the Ukrainians and that they demand complete freedom.

1047. Budurovych, Bohdan B. "The Ukrainian Problem in International Politics October, 1938 to March 1939." Canadian Slavonic Papers. 3: 59-75, 1958. Bibl. footn.
    About how because of Czechoslovakian crisis and emerging problem of Carpatho-Ukraine with its repercussions for Poland, Hungaria and USSR, the Ukrainian problem was in focus of the international politics at this time.

1048. Chubatyi, Nicholas. "Ukraine between Poland and Russia." Review of Politics. 8: 331-353. July, 1946.
    About relations of the Ukraine to Poland and Russia and the problem of the Polish-Ukrainian border. The conditions in the Ukraine under Soviet rule.

1049. Dolnytsky, Myron. "A Geographer Looks at East Europe." Ukrainian Quarterly. 7: 32-42, Winter, 1951. Map.
    About the influence of the geographic situation of the Ukraine on her history.

1050. Dombrowsky, Alexander. "The Struggle with the East European Space." Ukrainian Quarterly. 8: 73-79. Winter, 1952.
    About how the wide open spaces of Eastern Europe, and especially Ukraine, were dangerous for invaders from early times to the time of Hitler.

1051. Giannini, Amadeo. "Ukraine as a Mediterranean Power." Ukrainian Quarterly. 8: 303-306. Autumn, 1952.
    The author argues that the Ukraine is a Mediterranean power and must have access to the sea because when it regains its independence sea transport is the best for the products of the Ukrainian farming and mining.

1052. Goldman, Ilya. "West-East Antagonism in Pereyaslav." Ukrainian Quarterly. 9: 13-21. Winter, 1953.
    The author argues that the Ukraine is a part of the Western World and that the Treaty of Pereyaslav was a victory of the East over the West.

1053. Hayuk, Hlib. "The Impact of Georgraphy on Ukrainian History." Horizons. 5: 20-25, no. 1(8), 1964. Bibl. footn.

1054. Heiman, Leo. "Warsau, Prague and the Ukrainian Question."

Ukrainian Quarterly. 21: 299-326. Winter, 1965.
A travelogue. The author visited Czechoslovakia and
Poland including Lemkoland, a territory ceded to Poland
in Yalta. Many references to the Ukrainian Insurgent
Army met in Czechoslovakia and Poland.

1055. Krupnytsky, Borys. "Ukraine between West and East."
Ukrainian Review, London. 5: 9-25. Spring, 1958.
About the Western orientation of the Ukraine as expressed
by Ukrainian history and Ukrainian spirituality.

1056. Manning, Clarence A. "Ukraine and the Straits." Ukrainian
Quarterly. 3: 313-323. Autumn, 1947.
About how the Ukraine has been an European granary
since ancient times and wars were fought for access to
the Ukrainian grain. Therefore, the straits are important for the Ukraine.

1057. Roucek, Joseph S. "Geopolitics of the Ukraine." Ukrainian
Quarterly. 7: 303-311. Autumn, 1951.
The author argues that the Ukraine, because of its
location, has always been a defense base of Eurasia and
that it can be a key point in a Soviet attack on Europe,
or an ally of the Western World.

2. Ukraine and the U.S. and Canada.

1058. Celebration of 41st Anniversary of the Ukrainian Independence in United States Congress. New York, Ukrainian Congress Committee of America, 1959. 40 p.
Reprint of speeches of the members of both chambers of
the U. S. Congress on occasion of the anniversary of the
Ukrainian Independence.

1059. Chapman, Oscar L. The Spirit of Independence: America and
Ukraine. Extension of Remarks of Hon. Blair Moody of
Michigan in the Senate of the United States, Saturday, July
5, 1952. Washington, D. C. U. S. Government Printing
Office, 1952. 7 p.
A comparison of the Ukrainian and American struggles
for Independence and demand to acknowledge the errors of
the past in matters of independence of other peoples
and of the recognition of the fact that freedom and
peace go together.

1060. Dobriansky, Lev E. The non-Russian Nations in the USSR,
Focal Points in American Policy of National Liberation.
Extension of Remarks of Hon. Brien McMahon of Connecticut
in the Senate of the United States, Thursday, May 15, 1952.
Washington, D. C. U. S. Government Printing Office, 1952.
8 p.

About the subjugation of the non-Russian peoples of the USSR by the Russians with special stress on the history of the subjugation of the Ukrainians and the role of the subjugated peoples in American cold-war policy.

1061. Dobriansky, Lev E. <u>Tactic Not a Strategy of Freedom</u>. Extension of Remarks of the Hon. H. Alexander Smith of New Jersey in the Senate of the United States, Wednesday, January 17, 1951. Washington, D. C., U. S. Government Printing Office, 1951. 7 p.
    The author argues that a positive strategy of freedom is essential for an alliance with the established anti-Communist forces. It includes support of the fighting Ukrainian underground.

1062. Dobriansky, Lev E. <u>U.S.A. and the Soviet Myth</u>. Old Greenwich, Devin Adair, 1971. 274 p.
    Author, a scholar of the Soviet problems, president of the Ukrainian Congress Committee of America, discusses in the first part of his study nations held subjugated by the USSR, with emphasis on the Ukraine.
    In the second part of his book the author discusses the attitude of the U. S. to the USSR and to the problem of the captive nations. He argues that the Ukrainian Congress Committee of America makes a valuable contribution to the cause of self-determination of the captive nations throughout the world.

1063. Dobriansky, Lev E. <u>A U.S. Policy of Unfinished Liberation</u>. New York, Ukrainian Congress Committee of America, 1965. 24 p.
    About the undecided U.S. policy toward the Soviet-subjugated peoples. Also in <u>Ukrainian Quarterly</u>. 22: 300-321. Winter, 1966.

1064. Evach, Honore. <u>Ukraine's Call to America</u>. Detroit, the Ukrainian Cultural Society of Detroit, 1947. 173 p.
    A contrast is made of Ukrainian democracy and Russian autocracy. Also discusses the history of the Ukraine and of the Ukrainian fight for independence.

1065. <u>Favoring Extension of Diplomatic Relations with the Republic of Ukraine and Byelorussia</u>. Hearing before Committee on Foreign Affairs House of Representatives. Eighty-Third Congress, Third Session before the Special Subcommittee on H. Con. Res. 58, July 15, 1953. Printed for the use of the Committee on Foreign Affairs. Washington, U. S. Government Printing Office, 1953. 112 p.
    The protocols of hearings held by the above mentioned Subcommittee and exhibits submitted by witnesses.

1066. Hlynka, Anthony. <u>The Struggle of Freemen</u>. Detroit, Ukrainian Cultural Society, 1942. 25 p.

A speech by the author in the Canadian Parliament, asking that Canada support Ukrainian cause for independence.

1067. Myshuga, Luke. Ukraine and American Democracy. Jersey City, Ukrainian Press and Book Company, 1939. 32 p.
Calls upon the United States to aid the Ukrainian National Movement.

1068. Ukraine: Achille's Heel of the Vulnerable Russians. 50th anniversary of Ukraine's independence. Proceedings and Debates of the 90th Congress, Second Session. Washington, Ukrainian Congress Committee of America, 1968. 122 p.
Reprints from the Congressional Record. Speeches in the U.S. Congress on the occasion of the 50th anniversary of Ukraine's independence. The speakers stress the importance of the Ukrainian problem in the USSR.

1069. Ukrainian Congress Committee of America. Ukrainian Independence Day. Anniversary of January 22, 1918. New York, 1955. 96 p.
Declarations of United States Congressman and Senators; proclamations of Governors and Mayors on the occasion of this anniversary.

1070. Balavyder, A. "Canada and the Famine in Soviet Russia and the Ukraine, 1921-1923." New Review. 4: 1-10. Bibl. footn. on end of article.

1071. Chamberlin, William Henry. "Ukraine: Ally behind the Iron Curtain." Ukrainian Quarterly. 4: 10-18. Winter, 1948.
Author claims that in case of war with the USSR the United States would have allies among the people of the countries behind the Iron Curtain.

1072. Dobriansky, Lev E. "H. Con. Resolution 58; a Solid Test of American Initiative." Ukrainian Quarterly. 10: 158-165. Spring, 1954. Bibl. footn.
Concerns the possibility of establishing diplomatic relations with Soviet Ukraine and Soviet Belorussia.

1073. Dobriansky, Lev E. "The Voice of America and Ukraine." Ukrainian Quarterly. 11: 35-45. Winter, 1955.
The author claims that "Voice of America" disregards the longing for freedom of the Ukrainian people and argues that effective communication will be brought about only through a change of attitude.

1074. Halajchuk, Bohdan. "Has the United States Recognized Ukraine." Ukrainian Quarterly. 11: 24-28. Winter, 1955.
The author states that according to the experts in international law, the admission of Ukraine to the United

Nations includes implicit acknowledgement of Ukrainian
statehood.

1075. Kulchycky, George. "The Foreign Policy of Presidents
Wilson and Collidge in Eastern Europe." Horizons. 7: 7-2,
1966, 1, Bibl. footn. p. 25.
    Also concerns Ukraine.

1076. Manning, Clarence A. "Ukraine and American Diplomacy."
Ukrainian Quarterly. 4: 129-137. Spring, 1948.
    The author argues that support of the Ukrainian cause
would assure the United States friends inside the USSR.

1077. Manning, Clarence A. "The Ukrainians and the United States
in World War I" Ukrainian Quarterly. 13: 346-354. December, 1957.
    Deals with the activities of the American Ukrainian
during World War I on behalf of the Ukrainian cause.

1078. Olesnicki, Roman. "The Problem of Ukraine in Recent American Peace Planning Literature." Ukrainian Quarterly. 1:
72-78. October, 1944.

1079. Shumeyko, Stephen. "American Interest in Ukraine during
World War I." Ukrainian Quarterly. 2: 66-79. Autumn,
1945.
    A review of articles in American newspapers during the
World War I concerning Ukraine.

1080. Smal-Stocki, Roman. "George Washington Traditions in
Ukraine." Ukrainian Quarterly. 24: 250-252. Autumn, 1968.
    Discusses the references to George Washington in the
Diary of Pelagia Rosciszewski and in the poetry of Taras
Shevchenko.

1081. Stoyko, Volodymyr. "The Principles of Self-Determination
In Eastern Europe, and Our Foreign Policy." Horizons.
2: 9-20, no. 1-2, 1957.
    The author claims that the Soviets use Ukrainian
national self-determination for propaganda purposes and
argues that the United States should have a more clear
self-determination policy for Eastern Europe.

1082. "United States and the 40th Anniversary of the Ukraine's
Independence." Ukrainian Quarterly. 13: 293-296. December, 1957.
    The author argues that the above anniversary is signi-
ficant not only for Ukrainians but also for the whole
world.

3. Ukraine and Russia.

1083. Bowder, Robert Paul and Alexander Kerensky. Russian Provisional Government: Documents. Stanford, Cal., Stanford University Press, 1961. 3 v.
    In volume 1 a few documents are included concerning the formation of the Ukrainian Central Rada and the relations between the Russian Provisional Government and the Ukraine.

1084. Choulguine, Alexander. Ukraine against Moscow. New York, Spellers and Sons, 1959.
    The memoirs of the first Prime Minister of independent Ukraine.
    Includes a history of Ukraine and discusses the relations of Ukraine with the Western Powers, Central Powers and Russia and activity of the Ukrainian emigration.

1085. Hryshko, Vasyl. Experience with Russia. New York, Ukrainian Congress Committee of America, 1956. 180 p.
    A short review of Ukrainian-Russian relations before 1917. The story of the years 1917-1920. The author tells about Soviet imperialism between two World Wars, the Ukrainian struggle for freedom during and after the Second World War and present relations. The attitude of non-Communist Russians to Ukraine and the U.S. Bibliography in footnotes.

1086. Prychodko, Nicholas. Ukraine and Russia. Winnipeg, Ukrainian-Canadian Committee, 1953. 22 p.
    About the relationship of Ukraine to Russia.

1087. Stakhiv, Matthew. Ukraine and Russia. An Outline of History of the Political and Military Relations (December, 1917-April, 1918). Translated from Ukrainian by Walter Dushnyck. Preface by Clarence A. Manning. New York, Ukrainian Congress Committee of America, 1967. 215 p. (Shevchenko Scientific Society. Ukrainian Studies Series 20. English Section 4.)
    The author deals with the first phase of the Russian trend toward the conquest of the Ukraine. He describes the efforts to produce a Communist coup d'etat, when that did not succeed, an effort to overthrow the legitimate Ukrainian regime was made with the help of the red regiments brought from the German front, which eventually resulted in the forming of a puppet regime in Kharkiv. After the signing of the Brest Litovsk Treaty, this government dissolved itself. This book is the first scholarly publication in the English language about this phase of Ukrainian-Russian relations.
    A bibliography and a list of the author's publications are included.

1088. Stepankovsky V. <u>The Russian Plot to Seize Galicia.</u>
       (Austrian Ruthenia). London, Henry James Hall Co., 1914.
       30 p.
            A publication of the Union for the Liberation of the
       Ukraine issued during the period when the Russians occupied
       Halychyna (Galicia) and claimed it as belonging to the
       Russian empire.

1089. De Weerd, Hans. "An Anglo-Dutch Voice on Ukraine and the
       Russians." <u>Ukrainian Quarterly.</u> 11: 239-243. Summer,
       1955.
            About the references to Ukrainian-Russian relations in
       a work of an English historian translated into the Dutch
       language in 1734-35.

1090. LaVerne, R. and John P. Pauls. "Ryleyev and Ukraine."
       <u>Ukrainian Review</u>, London. 17: 49-60. March, 1970. Bibl.
       footn.
            Authors discuss Ukrainian sympathies of the Russian
       Decembrist Kindrati Ryleyev.

1091. Manning, Clarence A. "Kerensky and Ukraine Liberation."
       <u>Ukrainian Quarterly.</u> 26: 251-257. No. 3-4, 1970.
            The author tells about the chauvinist attitude of the
       Russian Provisional Government headed by the Alexander
       Kerensky to the question of the independence of Ukraine.

1092. Pidhaini, Oleg S. "Stalin's Negotiations on Behalf of the
       Soviet Government with the Ukraine, November 30, 1917 and
       Conversation with Bakinsky: Surpressed Text." <u>New Review.</u>
       3: 4-12. No. 6, 1963.
            Concerns telephone conversation between the Secretary
       of Labor of the Ukrainian Republic and Stalin and his
       plenipotentiary for Ukraine Sergei Bakinskii in the matter
       of the Ukrainian-Russian relations held on November 30,
       1917. This conversation is not included in official
       editions of Stalin's works and other similar publications.

1093. Prychodko, Nicholas. "Three Hundred Years of Russian Dealing
       with the Ukraine." <u>Ukrainian Quarterly.</u> 10: 92-99. Win-
       ter, 1954.
            About how Russia subjugated Ukraine beginning with the
       Pereyaslav Treaty. Also deals with the destruction of
       Sitch in 1775, the famine in 1932-33, the murder of
       prisoners during the retreat of 1941, and the liquidation
       of the Ukrainian Orthodox and Catholic churches.

1094. Shankovsky, Lev. "Disintegration of the Imperial Russian
       Army in 1917." <u>Ukrainian Quarterly.</u> 13: 305-328. Decem-
       ber, 1957.
            Cause of disintegration: negative attitude of the Rus-

sian Provisional Government to the problem of the national liberation of the non-Russian peoples and their growing nationalism.

1095. Stakhiv, Matthew. "The Ukrainian Revolution and Russian Democracy." Ukrainian Quarterly. 23: 212-225. Winter, 1967.

Hostile attitude of the Russian Democrats, represented by the Russian Provisional Government to the independence of Ukraine.

4. Ukraine and Poland.

1096. Budurovych, Bohdan. Polish-Soviet Relations, 1932-1939. New York, Columbia University Press, 1963. 229 p.

Also unpublished doctoral dissertation under the same title. Columbia University, 1958. 314 p. Concerns partially Polish-Ukrainian relations.

1097. Dziewanowski, M. K. Joseph Pilsudski: a European Federalist, 1918-1922. Stanford, Cal., Hoover Institution Press, 1970. 380 p.

Book discusses the life and activity of a Polish political leader, commander-in-chief of the Polish armed forces and head of the Polish state, especially his project to organize a mid-east European federation including also Ukraine.

In a separate section of the book the author discusses Polish-Ukrainian relations, Polish-Ukrainian Warsau Pact of 1920, the role of the Ukrainian armed forces in the battle of Warsau in 1920, the problem of Eastern Halychyna. Bibliography includes many Ukrainian titles.

1098. Konowalow, Serge, ed. Russo-Polish Relations--A Historical Survey. Princeton, N. J., Princeton University Press, 1945. 110 p.

Deals with the problems of Polish-Russian relations in which the author includes the Polish-Ukrainian border dispute. On pages 62-102, there is a survey of historical sources relating to this border dispute from the close of World War I to the Yalta Conference.

1099. Kubijovych, Volodymyr. Western Ukraine within Poland, 1920-1939. Chicago, Ukrainian Research and Information Institute, Inc., 1963. 32 p.

The situation of the Western Ukraine including Eastern Halychyna, Volynia, Polissia, Kholmland and Pidlashsha under Polish domination.

1100. Luciw, Wasyl. Ukrainians and the Polish Revolt of 1963.

New Haven, Slavia, 1961. 66 p.
Also an article by the same author entitled: "Ukrainians and the Polish Revolt of 1863; a Contribution to the History of Polish-Ukrainian Relations," in East-European Problems. 1: 22-24, Autumn, 1956.
Author stresses that Polish intellectual circles insisted that the Ukraine should be some kind of "Lebensraum" for Poland. Therefore, during the Polish revolution of 1863, the attitude of the Ukrainians was passive. This neutrality caused the failure of the uprising which largely occurred on Ukrainian territory.

1101. Pidhaini, Oleg S. The Ukrainian-Polish Problem in the Dissolution of the Russian Empire 1914-1917. Toronto, New Review Books, 1962. 125 p.
In this book which is practically an introduction to the author's work" Formation of the Ukrainian Republic the author inquires into the problem of the Polish-Ukrainian border dispute which arouse when the Ukraine and Poland, in consequence of the World War 1914-1918, became an object of international interest. Not digging into the development of Polish-Ukrainian relations, the author depicts the attitude of the belligerent countries to the East-European affairs.

1102. Ripetzkyj, Stepan. Ukrainian-Polish Diplomatic Struggle, 1918-1923. Chicago, Ukrainian Research and Information Institute, Inc., 1963. 39 p.
Concerning Eastern Halychyna, which was in 1919 occupied by Poland, and with the decision of the Council of Ambassadors of March, 1923 incorporated in Poland.

1103. Ukrainian Information Bureau. Ukraine and Poland: A Memorandum of the Ukrainian National Council to Mr. Dean Acheson. Augsburg, 1951. 14 p.
Explains the Ukraine's claim to Western Ukraine, which belonged to Poland up to 1939.

1104. United States Congress. House. Appendix to Committee Report on Communist Takeover and Occupation of Poland. Polish Documents, Reports of the Select Committee of Communist Aggression. House of Representatives Eighty-Third Congress. Second Sess. H. R. Res. 346 and 348. December 31, 1954. Washington, Government Printing Office. 1955. 175 p.
Includes many documents from Poland and other countries concerning the Polish-Ukrainian border.

1105. Van Valkenburg, Samuel. Peace Atlas of Europe. New York, Duell, Pearce and Sloan, 1946. 176 p.
Author discusses establishment of Curzon Line. He considers this borderline justified. He considers Curzon

Line not Polish-Ukrainian but Polish-Russian borderline.

1106. Wandycz, Piotr Stefan. <u>Soviet-Polish Relations, 1917-1921.</u>
Cambridge, Harvard University Press, 1969. 403 p. Maps,
Bibl. p. 293-309.
Book has many references to Ukrainian problem and to
Ukrainian-Polish relations during the period mentioned in
title. Author discusses the Warsau Pact (Polish-Ukrainian
pact of 1920).

1107. Chubatyi, Mykola. "The Ukrainians and the Polish-Russian
Border Dispute." <u>Ukrainian Quarterly.</u> 1: 57-71, October,
1944.

1108. Horak, Stefan. "Why Western Ukrainian Territories were
Annexed to Poland 1918-1923." <u>East European Problems.</u> 1:
51-68, no .1/1956.

1109. Hordynsky, Sviatoslav. "Stubborn Polish Claims to Western
Ukraine." <u>Ukrainian Quarterly.</u> 6: 265-269, Summer, 1950.
Author reviews the book of a Polish writer, Stanislaw
Skrzypek, "The Problem of Eastern Galicia," and repudiates
Polish claims to the Western Ukrainian territories.

1110. Manning, Clarence A. "The Yalta Conference." <u>Ukrainian
Quarterly.</u> 11: 145-152, Spring, 1955.
Among the other problems settled by the Yalta Conference,
the author mentions the Ukrainian-Polish border situation
and admission of the Ukraine to the United Nations.

1111. Schechtman, J. B. "Polish-Soviet Exchange of Population."
<u>Journal of Central European Affairs.</u> 9: 289-314, 1949.
Concerns exchange of population between Ukraine and
Poland. Published also in <u>Review of Politics</u>, April,
1953.

1112. Varvariv, Konstantine. "Polish-Ukrainian Relations, November, 1916-November, 1918." <u>East European Problems.</u> 1: 35-
51, 1956.
Author deals with Polish-Ukrainian relations during the
period before the Russian revolution and before the
Polish-Ukrainian war of 1918-1919.

1113. Vess, John S. "Yalta Agreement and America." <u>Ukrainian
Quarterly.</u> 8: 293-302, Autumn, 1952.
Author states that rejecting by the United States of
the Yalta Agreement would not liberate the satellite
countries but would only offend the feelings of the
Ukrainian people.

1114. Volacic, M. "The Curzon Line and Territorial Changes in
Eastern Europe." <u>Byelorussian Review.</u> 2: 37-97, 1956.

Also concerns the problem of the Polish-Ukrainian border.

1115. Wynot, Edward D. "The Ukrainians and the Polish Regime."
Ukrainskyi Istoryk. 7: 44-60. 4/28/70. Bibl. footn.
A study of the situation of Ukrainians in Poland from
1919 to 1939.

5. Ukraine and Germany.

1116. Blunden, Godfrey. Time of the Assassins. Philadelphia,
Lippincott, 1953. 375 p.
Pictures of the situation of Kharkiv during the German
occupation. Comparison of the Nazi and NKVD methods.
Author mistakenly states that all guerilla activity in
Ukraine was Communist.

1117. Fedyshyn, Oleh Sylvester. German Plans and Policies in the
Ukraine and the Crimea, 1917-1918. New York, Columbia
University, 1962.
Unpublished doctoral dissertation, dealing with eastern
policy of Imperial Germany.

1118. Fedyshyn, Oleh Sylvester. Germany's Drive to the East and
the Ukrainian Revolution, 1917-1918. New Brunswick, N. J.,
Rutgers University Press, 1971. 401 p. maps.
Author gives a comprehensive review of the Ukrainian
national movement prior to the outbreak of World War I.
He mentions the Union for the Liberation of Ukraine. He
indicates that Germans in their "Drang nach Osten" did
not have any Ukrainian program. They were ready to cede to
the Russians Eastern Halychyna in exchange for the Baltic
States and the Russian part of Poland. There were,
according to the author, not too many German experts of
the Ukrainian problem.
Even after signing of the Brest Litovsk Treaty, Germany
still did not have a clear Ukrainian policy.
He discusses the time of Hetman Skoropadsky, when Germany
reduced the Ukrainian state to the role of a German
satellite.
He stresses shortsightedness of the German Ukrainian
policy. Germany was interested only in Ukrainian bread.

1119. Kamenetsky, Ihor. Secret Nazi Plans for Eastern Europe.
A Study of Lebensraum Policies. New York, Bookman Associates,
1961. 263 p.
Published also in the year 1964 by College and Universities Press at New York. The author discusses the
plans of Nazi Germany to exterminate, enslave, or deport
east of Ural, the populations of East European countries,
including the Ukraine, to have living territory (Lebensraum)
for surplus of German population.

1120. Toynbee, Arnold and Veronica Toynbee, editors. Hitler's
Europe. New York, Oxford University Press, 1954. (Survey
of International Affairs, 1939-1946 v. 4.) Published under
the auspices of the Royal Institute of International
Affairs.
Numerous references to the Ukrainian problems are
indexed under headings "Ukraine," "Ukrainians in Poland,"
"Appended Territories (Nebenlaender)," "Ruthenia,"
"Galicia," and under subheadings "Ukraine" with different
subjectheadings; also under names of different Nazi dig-
nitaries.

1121. Dmytryshyn, Basil. "German Occupation of Ukraine, 1918.
Some New Evidence." Slavic and East European Studies. 10:
79-92. Autumn-Winter, 1965-66.
Concerns German policy in the Ukraine during World War I.

1122. Dushnyck, Walter. "New Germany and Eastern Europe."
Ukrainian Quarterly. 17: 301-310. 1961, Bibl. footn.

1123. Epstein, Julius. "German-Ukrainian Relations During World
War I." Ukrainian Quarterly. 15: 162-168. June, 1959.

1124. Horak, Stefan. "Ukraine and Germany in Both World Wars."
Ukrainian Quarterly. 13: 36-45. March, 1957.
Between the two world wars the Germans favored the
Ukrainian independence movement, but during the occupa-
tion they applied "ausrotten" (to exterminate) to the
Ukrainians. However, they again played on Ukrainian
national sentiments as late as 1944.

1125. Meyer, Henry Cord. "Germans in the Ukraine 1918: Excerpts
from Unpublished Letters." American Slavic and East
European Review. 9: 105-115, April, 1950.
German duplicity was revealed in the correspondence of
the high officials who outwardly favored a strong
Ukrainian state, but in reality, sought raw materials and
grain.

1126. Paneyko, Basil. "Germany, Poland and the Ukraine." Nineteenth Century and After. 125: 34-43.
The attitude of Poland and Germany towards the Ukraine.

1127. Prokop, Myroslav. "Ukraine in Germany's World War Plans."
Ukrainian Quarterly. 11: 134-144. Spring, 1952.
The author states that on the basis of discovered German documents, Alfred Rosenberg planned the organization
of a strong Ukrainian-Byelorussian-Caucasian federation
as an ally of Germany.

1128. Shankovsky, Lev. "Nazi Occupation of Ukraine." Ukrainian
Review, London. 2: 8-118, June, 1955.

The German occupation policy in the Ukraine in 1941-1944, and the Ukrainian anti-German resistance.

5. Ukraine and Other States.

1129. The Ukrainian Question and Its Importance to Great Britain. London, The Serjeants Press, Ltd. for the Anglo-Ukrainian Committee, 1935. 36 p.
  Contains an address given by a member of Parliament, Lancelot Lawton, in the House of Commons on May 29, 1935. In appendices extracts from international treaties and agreements defining juridical position of Ukraine.

1130. Kulchyckyi, George. "Ukraine--A Vasal State of Turkey." Phoenix. 12: 48-61, no. 3-4, 1966. Bibl. footn. p. 60-61.
  Discusses Ukrainian-Turkish relations during the time of Hetman Petro Doroshenko when Ukraine was a vasal state of the Ottoman Empire.

1131. Oreletsky, Vasyl. "Ukraine and Turkey." Ukrainian Review, London. 4: 17-23, Summer, 1957.
  Deals with Ukrainian-Turkish relations in the 16th and 17th centuries and at present time. Includes a discussion of the Brest-Litovsk Treaty.

XI. UKRAINE - STATEHOOD.

1. Ukraine - Statehood - General.

1132. Lawton, Lancelot. Ukraine: Europe's Greatest Problem. 1950. 32 p.
  Reprint from East Europe and Contemporary Russia, volume 3. Spring, 1939. Second reprint.
  History of the Ukraine. Ukraine under four nations between the two world wars, Carpatho-Ukraine, the attitude of Poland, Germany and Russia to the Ukraine, differences between the Ukraine and Russia, and the resources of the Ukraine.

1133. Sawchak, Volodymyr. The Status of the Ukrainian SSR in View of State and International Law. London, Ukrainian Information Service, 1971. 32 p.
  Reprint from the Ukrainian Review, London, Volume 17, no. 4. Author discusses problem of the Ukrainian Soviet Socialist Republic in the time before the forming of the USSR in 1923 and after as a constituent of the USSR. He stresses differences between western and Soviet blocs in understanding of independence and federation.

1134. Simpson, George W. Ukraine: the Pressing Problem in

European Politics. Edmonton, Ukrainian Self-reliance
League, 1931.
Ukraine as one of the unsettled European problems.

1135. Halajczuk, Bohdan T. "The Soviet Ukraine as A Subject of
International Law." Annals of the Ukrainian Academy of
Arts and Sciences in the U. S. 9(1-2/27-28): 167-188.
Bibl. footn.
Author discusses opinions of scholars of international
law and states that the statehood of the Soviet Ukraine
according to international law is based on establishment
of the independent Ukrainian state in 1917 by the will of
the Ukrainian people and is a continuation of that state.

1136. Halajczuk, Bohdan T. "The Ukrainian State A Legal Con-
stituted Entity." Ukrainian Quarterly. 14: 357-362.
Winter, 1958.
The author traces Ukrainian statehood according to
international law from the medieval Kyiv State to the
Soviet Ukrainian Republic and membership in the U. N.

1137. Shandor, Vincent. "Ukraine and the 'Status Quo' in Central
and Eastern Europe." Ukrainian Quarterly. 16: 330-341.
Winter, 1960. Bibl. footn.

1138. Shulgin, Alexander. "Ukraine and Its Political Aspirations."
Slavonic and East European Review. 13: 350-362. January,
1935.
Ukrainian history, present aspirations and its government in exile.

2. Ukrainian Nationalism.

1139. Armstrong, John A. Ukrainian Nationalism. 2nd ed. New
York, Columbia University Press, 1963. 361 p.
Also unpublished doctoral dissertation by same author
entitled: Ukrainian Nationalism, 1939-1945. New York,
Columbia University, 1953. Growth of the Ukrainian
Nationalist movement after beginning of the Second World
War; nationalist activity in 1930-1941; nationalism and
Ukrainian Churches; territorial varieties of Ukrainian
nationalism and attitude of the Ukrainian masses to the
nationalist movement. The author uses term nationalistic
to describe the revolutionary groups.

1140. Bilinsky, Yaroslav. Ukrainian Nationalism and Soviet
Nationality Policy After World War II. Jersey City,
Princeton University, 1958.
Unpublished doctoral dissertation deals with Soviet
nationality policy after World War 1939-1945 and Ukrainian
nationalism as a reaction to this policy.

1141. Birch, J. The Ukrainian Nationalist Movement in the U.S.S.R. Since 1956. London, Ukrainian Information Service, 1971. 48 p.
    Reprint from the Ukrainian Review, London. 17: 2-47. Author in this footnoted essay discusses nationalist groups emerging in the late fifties and in the sixties, protests of Ukrainian lawyers and political trials of Ukrainian intellectuals in 1966. Also mentions later developments in the Ukraine in connection with publishing of novel of Oles Honchar "Sobor" and its later surpression by Soviet authorities.

1142. Hodnett, Grey and Peter Potichnyi. The Ukraine and the Czechoslovak Crisis. Canberra, Australian University. Research School of Social Science. Department of Political Science, 1970. 154 p. (Occasional papers, no. 6.)
    Authors discuss the role of the Soviet Ukraine in Soviet intervention in Czechoslovakia. They discuss the development of the political situation in the Ukraine in the last decade, before CSR crisis, and the situation of the Ukrainians in Slovakia (Priashiv region).
    Their conclusion is that Soviet and among them, Soviet-Ukrainian leaders, pressed for Soviet intervention in CSR not only because they feared that liberalization in CSR might cause the same trends in the Ukraine, but that it might reinforce these trends toward liberalization, which came into being in the Ukraine earlier than in CSR.

1143. Reshetar, John, Jr. Ukrainian Revolution 1917-1920: A Study in Nationalism. Princeton, N. J., Princeton University Press, 1952. 363 p.
    History of Ukrainian nationalism beginning with the 19th century through 1920; reasons for the Ukrainian defeat; Ukrainian nationalism as a positive force in Eastern Europe.
    Also an unpublished doctoral dissertation by the same author under the title: Ukraine and Revolution (1917-1920) submitted to the Harvard University in 1950.

1144. Smal-Stocki, Roman. Captive Nations: the Nationalism of the non-Russian Nations in the Soviet Union. With the preface by Lev E. Dobriansky. New York, Bookman Associates, 1960. 118 p.
    Author discusses nationalism of the non-Russian nations of the USSR prior to, between, and after the two world wars. Attitude of Communist Russians to the non-Russian nations of the USSR. Nationalism of the non-Russian nations as a problem of the USSR and an international problem.

1145. Chubatyj, Nicholas. "Modern Ukrainian Nationalist Movement."

Journal of Central European Affairs. 6: 281-305, October, 1944.
   History of Ukrainian nationalism from the 18th century to the Second World War.

1146. Stetsko, Yaroslav. "Strategy and Tactics of the Ukrainian National Revolution." Ukrainian Review, London. 18: 52-78. Spring, 1971.

1147. "Ukraine in Modern World," a discussion. Slavic Review. 22: 199-262. Included: Rudnycky, Ivan L. Role of the Ukraine in Modern History." P. 199-217. Adams, Arthur J. "The Awakening of the Ukraine," p. 217-223. (Author tells of the forces which led to awakening of the Ukrainian national consciousness. Stresses the role of anarchy.)
   Pritcak, Omeljan and John Reshetar, Jr. "The Ukraine and the Dialectics of Nation Building," p. 224-255. Author discusses western tendencies in the Ukrainian culture, the role of the Ukrainian Church, Pereyaslav Treaty, the name of the Ukraine and Ukrainian national renaissance. Rudnycky, Ivan "Reply," p. 256-262.

3. Ukrainian Independence Claims.

1148. Hrushevsky, Michael. The Historical Evolution of the Ukrainian Problem. Translated by G. Raffalovich. London, Association for the Liberation of Ukraine, 1915. 58 p.
   History of the Ukrainian liberation movement by a prominent Ukrainian historian and statesman.

1149. Kyiv Versus Moscow. Political guidelines of the Organization of Ukrainian Nationalists. Munich, Ukrainian Information Service, 1970. 69 p.
   A collection of articles dealing with the platform of an Ukrainian political party known as the Organization of Ukrainian Nationalists (OUN) and its 40th anniversary. Articles also deal with the situation in the Ukraine and include an appeal by the Fourth Congress of Ukrainian Nationalists, held in 1968, to the Free World concerning the menace of Communism.

1150. Lukash, Elena. The Ukraine at the Paris Peace Conference, 1919. Chicago, University of Chicago, 1962. 75 p.
   Unpublished master's thesis. Concerns the Ukrainian problem and the participation of the Ukrainian Government in the Paris Peace Conference.

1151. Scott, W. L. The Ukrainians Our Most Pressing Problem. Toronto, The Catholic Truth Society, 1930. 64 p.
   Author stresses the necessity of solving the Ukrainian problem.

1152. Shelukhin, S. <u>Ukraine, Poland and Russia and the Right of</u> <u>Free Disposition of Peoples</u>. Washington, D. C., Friends of Ukraine, 1919. 15 p. map.
    The author formerly Secretary of Justice of the Ukrainian Republic, presents the history of relations of the Ukraine with Russia and Poland, going back to the Kosak period. He claims the right of the Ukraine to self-determination.

1153. <u>Ukrainian Problems</u>. 1st-   1919-   London, Ukrainian Press Bureau, 1919-
    An irregular Bulletin of the Ukrainian Press Bureau in London, including articles and in some cases, large treatises on aspects of the Ukrainian problem. Published first in 1919 because of the Paris Peace Conference.

1154. Chamberlin, William Henry. "The Issue of Ukrainian Nation-hood." <u>Ukrainian Quarterly</u>. 1: 228-235, June, 1945.

1155. Chubatyi, Nicholas. "The Conceptions of the Ukrainian Nationality in Their Historical Development," in <u>Shevchenko</u> <u>Scientific Society. Historical-Philosophical Section.</u> Proceedings. 2: 10-16, 1957.
    History of the development of the name of the Ukraine. Different conceptions of the Ukrainian nationality, from the conception of an ethnographic entity to the conception of an emotional entity (V. Lypynsky).

1156. Chubatyi, Nicholas. "Dumbarton Oaks and Ukraine." <u>Ukrainian Quarterly</u>. 1: 140-151. February, 1945.

1157. Chubatyi, Nicholas D. "Ukraine and the Western World." <u>Ukrainian Quarterly</u>. 3: 145-158. Winter, 1947.

1158. Granovsky, Alexander. "Free Ukraine is Vital to Lasting Peace." <u>Ukrainian Quarterly</u>. 1: 117-131. February, 1945.
    Multi-national states are not stable. For the sake of world peace the Ukrainian problem must be settled.

1159. Granowsky, Alexander. "Ukraine's Case for Independence." <u>World Affairs</u>. 6: 25-40, March, 1940.
    Pleads for independence of the Ukraine.

1160. Jurchenko, Oleksander. "The Bolshevik Conquest of Ukraine." <u>Ukrainian Review</u>, Munich. 1: 5-28, 1951.
    Soviet historians try to belittle the importance of the Ukrainian state consciousness. They try to present Ukrainian anti-Soviet guerilla warfare as the uprising of wealthy landowners. However, great majority of the Ukrainians are opposed to Soviet rule which was imposed only by the use of force.

1161. Nielsen, Jens. "Ukraine Will Triumph." <u>Ukrainian Review</u>,

London. 14: 10-17, December, 1967.

1162. Shulgin, Alexander. "The Doctrine of Wilson and the Building of the Ukrainian National Republic." Ukrainian Quarterly. 12: 326-331, December, 1956.
Ukraine was defeated at Versailles but the Ukrainian Declaration of Independence of January 22, 1918 was issued by a democratic selected body. The Union with the USSR is illegal.

1163. Stakhiv, Matthew. "U. N. Membership of Nations Dominated by Communists." Ukrainian Quarterly. 11: 14-23. Winter, 1955.
Countries enslaved by red Russia: Ukraine and Byelo-russia should retain their U. N. Membership. Ukraine should be recognized as an independent nation because it proclaimed its independence and still fights for it. Recognition of Ukrainian statehood would be a powerful asset in an anti-Communist fight.

1164. Stetzko, Jaroslav. "Principles of Ukrainian Foreign Policy: the Present International Situation and Its Assessment." Ukrainian Review, London. 12: 25-43, June, 1965.
Ukrainian liberation tactics in connection with inter-national situation.

1165. Stetzko, Jaroslav. "The Status and Role of Ukraine in the World." Ukrainian Review, London. 9:49-69. December, 1962 and 10: 30-37. September, 1963.
Problem of independence of the Ukraine is a world political problem.

1166. Studynsky, Yurii. "The Idea of Independence and Unity of Ukraine in History." Ukrainian Review, London. 6: 13-18. Spring, 1959.
The author traces the ideas of Ukrainian independence and unity from the beginning of the 19th century.

4. Ukraine - Diplomatic History.

1167. Dnistrianskyj, Stanislaus. Ukraine and the Peace Conference. n.p. 117 p., 1919. (The Ukrainian Problems, no. 6.)
Author, a noted Ukrainian scholar, gives in his book a description of the Ukrainian territory, discusses the economy of Ukraine, necessary statistics, history of the Ukraine, history of Ukrainian literature and culture. Stresses differences between the Ukrainians and Russians and the right of self-determination for Ukrainians. A special issue of Bulletin listed as entry no. 1050.

1168. Great Britain. Treaty of Peace Signed in Brest Litovsk between the Central Powers and the Ukrainian Peoples Republic

together with the Supplementary Treaties Hereto. London,
H. M. Stantionary Office, 1918.
  Text of the Brest Litovsk Peace Treaty of February 9,
1918 between the Central Powers and the Ukraine.

1169. Polonska-Vasylenko, Natalia. Dmytrivna. Ukraine-Rus' and
Western Europe in 10th-13th Centuries. London, Association
of Ukrainians in Great Britain, 1964. 47 p. illus.
  About diplomatic, economic and cultural ties of
medieval Ukraine with Western countries.

1170. Sawchuk, Konstantyn. The Ukraine in the United Nations
Organization: A Study in Soviet Foreign Policy, 1944-1950.
New York, Columbia University, 1969. 271 p.
  Unpublished doctoral dissertation. Author states that
Western Allies agreed to Stalin's demand to grant U. N.
membership to Soviet Ukraine and Soviet Byelorussia. Due
to that Ukraine became a charter member of the U. N.
U. N. delegation of Ukraine was headed by good diplomat
Dmitri Manuilski. This delegation was, during this period
of time, very active and helped to establish USSR foreign
policy.
  But there were, the author states, no independent
activities of the Ukrainian delegation. Its activities
were identical with those of the USSR delegation.
  Author discusses international status of Soviet Ukraine.
He concludes that the Ukraine has limited sovereignty,
but, as a member of the U. N. has equality to all other
U. N. members.

1171. Stercho, Petro George. Carpatho-Ukraine in International
Affairs, 1938-1939. South Bend, Indiana, University of
Notre Dame, 1959. 475 p.
  Unpublished doctoral dissertation concerning diplomatic
bargaining about the Carpatho-Ukraine during the German
aggression on Czechoslovakia.

1172. Ukrainian League of Nations Union. Application of the
Ukrainian Republic for the Admission to the League of
Nations. Paris, 1930. 32 p.
  Application of the Ukrainian Government in exile. Pre-
face by Prof. Dr. Roman Smal-Stocki, former minister of
the Ukraine to Berlin.

1173. Bilinsky, Yaroslav. "The Ukrainian SSR in International
Affairs after World War II." Annals of the Ukrainian
Academy of Arts and Sciences in the U. S. 9(1-2/27-28):
147-166. Bibl. footn.
  Deals with reasons for the establishment of the Ministry
of Foreign Affairs in the Ukraine and the Soviet bid for
Ukrainian U. N. membership and participation in interna-
tional conferences.

1174. Borshchak, Ilko. "Early Relations between England and Ukraine." _Slavonic and East European Review_. 10: 138-160, June, 1931.
    About the Ukrainian-English relations in the era of the Kosaks.

1175. Harvey, Elizabeth Anne. "The Norman Conquest of England and Its Connections with Old Ukraine." _Ukrainian Review_, London. 13: 33-53. December, 1966. Bibl. footn.
    Repercussions of the Norman occupation of England in medieval Ukraine.

1176. Horak, Stephan M. "The Peace Treaty with Ukraine in the German Parliament. _Ukrainian Review_, London. 15: 74-81. June, 1968. Bibl. footn.
    Discussions in German Parliament concerning ratification of the Brest-Litovsk Treaty with the Ukraine.

1177. Krupnytsky, Borys. "The Swedish-Ukrainian Treaties of Alliance, 1708-1709." _Ukrainian Quarterly_. 12: 47-57. Winter, 1956.
    The author discusses the Ukrainian-Swedish Treaty of 1708-1709, the original of which disappeared from the Swedish archives after the Poltava defeat. The author uses references available in contemporary Ukrainian and Swedish sources.

1178. Krupnytsky, Borys. "Treaty of Pereyaslav and the Political Orientation of Bohdan Khmelnytsky." _Ukrainian Quarterly_. 10: 32-40. Winter, 1954.
    Hetman Bohdan Khmelnycky considered the Pereyaslav Treaty only a temporary move. He worked after that on a Baltic Treaty but his sudden death prevented completion of this plan.

1179. Mackiw, Theodore. "Peace Treaty of Brest Litovsk." _Ukrainian Review_, London. 15: 56-61. March, 1968. Bibl. footn.

1180. Oreletsky, Wasyl. "Ukraine's International Treaties and Conventions." _Ukrainian Review_. 3: 66-61. June, 1956.
    Treaties and conventions signed by the Ukrainian National Republic and Ukrainian Soviet Republic and the consequences of these acts in the area of international law.

1181. Orlykovsky, O. "Ukraine's Diplomatic Relations with the Byzantine Patriarchate." _Ukrainian Review_, London. 8: 60-64. March, 1961.

1182. Pidhainy, Oleg S. "Establishment of Relations between the Ukrainian Republic and the Central Powers." _New Review_. 5: 7-29, no. 4, 1965.

1183. Pidhainy, Oleg S. "The International Status of the Ukrainian Republic in the East European Peace." (March, 1918) New Review. 6: 8-21, no. 2-3/23-24, 1966.
Deals with the recognition of the Ukrainian Republic by the states signing Brest Litovsk Treaty with the Ukraine.

1184. Sonevytsky, Leonid C. "The Ukrainian Question in the R. H. Lord's Writings on the Paris Peace Conference of 1919." Annals of the Ukrainian Academy of Arts and Sciences in the U. S. 10: 65-84. Bibl. footn.
Traces references to the Ukrainian problem in writings of a historian of the Paris Peace Conference.

1185. Sydorenko, Alexander. "A Case of Incipient Nationhood." Ukrainian Quarterly. 24: 117-128. Summer, 1968. Bibl. footn.
Concerns Brest Litovsk Treaty.

1186. Trembicky, Walter. "Greek-Ukrainian Diplomatic Relations, 1918-1920." Ukrainian Quarterly. 19: 342-349. Winter, 1963.

1187. Wynar, Lubomyr. "The Question of Anglo-Ukrainian Relations during the Rule of the Great Ukrainian Hetman Bohdan Khmelnytsky." Ukrainian Review, London. 10: 28-52. March, 1963. Bibl. footn. p. 49-52.

1188. Wynar, Lubomyr. "The Question of the Anglo-Ukrainian Relations in the Middle of the 17th Century." Annals of the Ukrainian Academy of Arts and Sciences in the U. S. 6(3-4): 1411-1418.
In Khmelnytsky's time England was interested in Ukrainian problems but there is no evidence that there were any direct Ukrainian-English relations.

1189. Wynar, Lubomyr. "Ukrainian Kosaks and the Vatican in 1594." Ukrainian Quarterly. 21: 65-78, 1965.
Vatican tried to win support of Ukrainian Kosaks against Turkey.

XII. LAW AND POLITICAL SCIENCE.

1. Ukrainian Law.

1190. Okinshevych, Leo. The Law of the Grand Duchy of Lithuania. Background and Bibliography. New York, Research Program of the USSR, 1953. 53 p. (Mimeo series no. 32.)
Law of the Grand Lithuanian Duchy which is a continuation of Ukrainian Medieval Law.

1191. Vernadsky, George, Tr. Medieval Russian Laws. New York, Norton, 1969. 106 p. (Records of civilization. Sources and Studies.)
   Translation of law codes of the medieval Rus' (old name of empire with centre in present capital of Ukraine Kyiv) called "Russka Pravda."

1192. Fedynskyj, Jurij. Sovietization of the Occupied Area through the Medium of the Court." American Slavic and East European Review. 12: 44-56, 1953.
   Application of the Soviet law by the Courts of the Bukovyna occupied in 1940 by the Soviet Union.

1193. Krugovoy, George. "A Norman Legal Formula in Russian Chronicles and in 'Slovo o Polku Igoreve'." Canadian Slavonic Papers, XI: 497-514, IV, 1969.
   Author traces influences of Normanic law on medieval chronicles of the "Rus" and on "Slovo o Polku Igoreve."

1194. Laskovsky, Nicholas. "Practicing Law in the Occupied Ukraine." American Slavonic and East European Review. 11: 123-137. Spring, 1952.
   The legal system in the Reichskommisariat Ukraine under German occupation.

1195. Okinshevich, Leo. "Direct Popular Rule in the Central Government of Ukraine of the 17th Century." Ukrainian Quarterly. 6: 151-157. Spring, 1950.
   Account of the General Council consisting of all Kosaks sitting as a legislative body in the Kosak state.

1196. Oreletsky, Vasyl. "The Leading Feature of Ukrainian Law." Ukrainian Review, London. 4: 48-62. Autumn, 1957.
   Moral principles of the Ukrainian civil, penal and political law traced from the medieval period to the present.

1197. Yakovliv, Andrii. "Ukrainian Common Law Procedure." Annals of the Ukrainian Academy of Laws and Sciences in the U. S. 2/4: 365-387. Autumn, 1952.
   Common law procedure in medieval Ukrainian law, in the Lithuanian Statute which was continuation of the medieval law of "Rus" (name of medieval empire with capital in Kyiv) and in the law of the Kosak state.

2. Political Science.

1198. Drahomaniv, Mykhaylo. "Selected Writings." Annals of the Ukrainian Academy of Arts and Sciences in the U. S. II: 141-244, 1952.
   Selection from writings of a prominent Ukrainian scholar,

ethnographer, political writer and one of the first
(in modern times) political emigrants from the Ukraine
who later became a professor of the University at Sofia,
Bulgaria.

1199. Hryhoriiv, Nykfor. The War and Ukrainian Democracy: A
Compilation of Documents of Past and Present. Toronto,
Industrial and Educational Publishing Company, 1945. 206 p.
    Author states that Ukrainians were always democratic
and supported democratic countries during the Second World
War.

1200. Kostomariv, Nikola Ivanovich. Books of Genesis of the
Ukrainian People, with a commentary by B. Yaniwskyj. New
York, Research Program on the USSR, 1954. 45 p.
    A political treatise. Author presents plan of a Slavic
federation with all Slavic nations as independent members.
It was the political program of the Brotherhood of St.
Cyril and Methody. Discovery of this clandestine organization of young enthusiastic Ukrainian intellectuals led
to a trial and convictions. Most affected by this trial
was Taras Shevhenko.

1201. Koval, Lubomyr. Economic Doctrines of M. I. Tugan-Baranov-
sky. Urbana, University of Illinois, 1965.
    Unpublished doctoral dissertation concerning prominent
Ukrainian economist Mychailo Tuhan-Baranovskyi.

1202. Ragosin, Boris Ivan. The Politics of Michail P. Drahomanov:
Ukrainian Federalism and the Question of Political Freedom
of Russia. Cambridge, Mass., Harvard University, 1967. 2 v.
    Unpublished doctoral dissertation. (See entry no. 1195.)

1203. Chyz, Yaroslav and J. C. Roucek. "Ukrainian Sociology: Its
Development to 1914." Journal of Central European Affairs.
1: 74-87. October, 1944.
    An account of the Ukrainian Academy of Arts and Sciences
in Kyiv prior to the Soviet and German occupation.

1204. Chyz, Yaroslav. "Ukrainian Scholarly Research and the War."
Ukrainian Quarterly. 3: 22-30. Autumn, 1946.
    Ukrainian scholarly research before, during, and after
the Second World War and also in the DP camps.

1205. Koval, Lubomyr M. "Mykhaylo Ivanovych Tuhan Baranovsky:
His Political, Teaching, Scientific and Cooperative Activity
in Ukraine, 1917-1919." Ukrains'kyi Tekhnichno-Hospodarskyi
Instytut. Naukovi Zapysky, vol. 18. 1868/69, p. 52-68.
Bibl. footn. Ukrainian resume' p. 66-68.
    Two chapters from an unpublished doctoral dissertation
by the same author: Economic Doctrines of M. I. Tuhan

Baranovsky. Urbana, University of Illinois, 1965.

1206. Ohloblyn, Alexander. "American Revolution and Ukrainian Liberation Ideas during the Late 18th Century." Ukrainian Quarterly. 11: 203-212, Summer, 1955.
At the time of the American Revolution, the Ukrainian nobility tried to regain freedom analogous to that proclaimed by the Declaration of Independence. This idea was expressed in the writings of contemporary Ukrainian authors.

XIII. UKRAINIAN CULTURE.

1. Religion.

a. Religion - General.

1207. Barclay, Clayton. The Role of the Ukrainian Catholic Church in the World Today. Winnipeg, Ukrainian Catholic Youth Organization of Manitoba, 1966(?).
Reprint from Les Cloches de Saint Boniface. October, 1966, volume 5, no. 6

1208. Fedorow, George. Russian Religious Mind: v.1. Kievan Christianity. Cambridge, Mass., Harvard University Press, 1947. 438 p.
Deals with religious mind of the medieval Ukrainians, their idea of God as a merciful father and with religion as expressed in the story of Ihor's Campaign.

1209. Khoroshyi, Michael, Archbp. The Spiritual World, the Human Soul and the Parapsychology. Toronto, Author, 1966. 180 p.
Author, an Ukrainian orthodox clergyman, discusses parapsychology from the point of view of the Orthodox Church.

1210. Senyshyn, Ambrose. OSBM, Metr. Catholics of the Byzantine-Slavonic Rite, and Their Divine Liturgy. Stamford, Conn., Ukrainian Catholic Seminary, 1946. 44 p. illus.
Information on the Catholics of Eastern Rite and translation from the Church Slavic of the Mass of Eastern Rite.

1211. Slipyi-Kobernyckyi-Dychkovskyi, Iosyf, Card. Tvory (Opera Omnia Josephi Slipyi Kobernyckyj-Dychkovskyj) Archiepiscopi Maioris. Zibraly Ivan Khoma i Ivan Iatskiv. Rym. Ukrains'kyi Katolyts'kyi Universytet im. Sv. Klymenta Papy, 1966-1971. 5 v.
Collected works of the Archbishop Major of the Ukrainian Catholic Church Cardinal, Joseph Slipyi-Kobernyckyj-Dychkovskyj. Single works in Ukrainian, English, German or Polish.

1212. Stets'ko, Yaroslav. For the Ukrainian Catholic Patriarchate. London, Ukrainian Information Service, 1971. 10 p.
Includes a petition to the Pope, Paul VI and memorandum to the Head of Congregation for the Eastern Church Cardinal Gustavo Testa by the Chairman of the Organization of the Ukrainian Nationalists Abroad, demanding establishment of the Patriarchate of the Ukrainian Catholic Church.

b. Ukrainian Church - History.

1213. Bilon, Petro. Ukrainians and Their Church. Translated from the Ukrainian by Reverend S. P. Symchych. Johnstown, Pa., Western Pennsylvania Regional Branch of the U.O.L., 1953. 22 p.
Brief account of the Ukrainian Orthodox Church.

1214. Boysak, B(asil). Eucumenism and Manuel Michael Olshavsky, Bishop of Mukachevo 1743-1767. Montreal, University of Montreal Press, 1967. 233 p. illus. Theologiae Montis Regii. Publications of the Faculty of Theology of the University of Montreal, 49 p.
Analysis of an unionistic work of Bishop Olshavsky, entitled "Sermo de Unione."

1215. Boysak, Vasyl. "The Fate of the Holy Union in the Carpatho-Ukraine." New York-Toronto. No publisher, 1963.
This book deals with the Church Union with Rome of the Ukrainian Church in Carpatho-Ukraine and connections with Church-Union movement in other parts of Ukraine. The author stresses obstacles put to the Church union by the Hungarian Church hierarchy, who considered the Union as an obstacle to the magyarization of Ukrainians inhabiting Carpatho-Ukraine. This led to revival of the Ukrainian Orthodox Church in Carpatho-Ukraine. Rich historical background.
There is also an unpublished doctoral dissertation by the same author: The Struggle of Church Union in Carpatho-Ukraine. Montreal, University of Montreal, 1961.

1216. Coughlin, G. F. Ukrainians, Their Rite, History and Religious Destiny. Toronto, Lundy and Company, 1945. 32 p.
An account of the Ukrainian Catholic Church.

1217. Drahomaniv, Mykhaylo Petrovych. Notes on the Slavic Religio-ethical legends: The Dualistic Creation of the World. Translated by Earl W. Count. Bloomington, Indiana University, 1961. 153 p. (Indiana University Publications. Russian and East European Series, v. 23.)
Concerns also Ukrainian legends.

1218. Halecki, Oskar. From Florence to Brest (1439-1596). Second ed. Hamden, Conn., Archon, 1968. 456 p.

Discusses attempts to unite Eastern Orthodox and Catholic Churches in the period between the Florence Council and Brest Union.

1219. Heppel, M. The Paterikon of the Kievan Monastery of Caves as a Source for Monastic Life in Pre-Mongolian Russia. London, University of London, 1964.
    Unpublished doctoral dissertation. Discusses the influence of Paterikon (lives of the prominent monks) of the oldest Ukrainian monastery, Pecherska Lavra (Monastery of Caves) in Kyiv on spiritual life of the Ukrainian monasteries.

1220. Hominiuke, J. A Centenary of Ukrainian Baptists, 1852-1952: A Century of Struggle and Martyrdom for the "Faith Once Delivered to the Saints." Winnipeg, published under the auspices of the Ukrainian Evangelical Baptist Alliance. 32 p. illus., ports, maps.
    History of the Ukrainian Baptist movement in the Ukraine and abroad.

1221. Kortschmaryk, Frank B. Christianization of the European East and Messianic Aspirations of Moscow as the "Third Rome." Toronto, Studium, 1971. 44 p. (S.S. no. 10.)
    Author discusses role of Ukraine-Rus in the Christianization of Eastern Europe and efforts of Moscow's rulers to get a leading role in the Eastern Christian world as the third religious center after Byzantium and Rome.

1222. Lencyk, Wasyl. The Eastern Catholic Church and Czar Nicholas I. Rome-New York, Ukrainian Catholic St. Clemens University, 1965. XIII, 148 p. (Centro di Studi Universitari Ukraini a Roma. Obras de Faculta di Filosofia a Filologia v. 2.)
    Also unpublished doctoral dissertation by the same author under the same title submitted to the Fordham University at New York in 1961. Both deal with liquidation of the Uniate Church in Ukraine and Belorussia during the rule of Czar Nicholas I.

1223. Perejda, George J. Apostle of Church Unity: The Life of the Servant of God, Metropolitan Andrew Sheptytsky. Yorkton, Sask., Redeemers Voice Press, 1960. 40 p.
    A biography of prominent leader of the Ukrainian Catholic Church.

1224. Pospishil, Victor J. and Hryhor M. Luzhnycky. The Quest for an Ukrainian Patriarchate. A foreword by Bishop Basil H. Losten. Philadelphia, Ukrainian Publication, 1971. 76 p.
    Concerns efforts of Ukrainian Catholics to organize their Church as an authonomic Patriarchate in affiliation with the Roman Catholic Church. Authors discuss historical and legal aspects of the problem.

1225.   Redemptorists. Eastern Rite Branch. Jubilee Book of Redemp-
        torist Fathers of the Eastern Rite. Yorkton, Saskatchewan,
        Redemptorist Fathers, 1956.   444 p.
            Collection of articles and personal reminiscences in
        Ukrainian and English language concerning history of the
        Eastern Branch of the Redemptorist Order in Ukraine and
        elsewhere.

1226.   Shchudlo, Mykola, RNI. Ukrainian Catholics. Yorkton,
        Saskatchewan, Redeemers Voice Press, 1951. 174 p.
            An account of the Ukrainian Catholic Church.

1227.   Solovii, Meletii M., OSMB. The Byzantine Divine Liturgy.
        History and commentary by Meletius Michael Solovey. Trans-
        lated by Demetrius Emil Wysochansky. Washington, Catholic
        University of America Press, 1970. 346 p. Bibliographical
        references.
            Text of Mass used in churches of Byzantine Rite with
        commentaries by a professor of the University at Ottawa.

1228.   The Tragedy of Greek-Catholic Church in Czechoslovakia.
        New York, Carpathian Alliance, Inc., 1971. 70 p.
            Concerns situation of the Ukrainian-Catholic Church in
        Eastern Slovakia.

1229.   Wilbur, Morse Earl. History of Unitarianism, Socinianism
        and Its Antecedents. Cambridge, Harvard University Press,
        1947. 617 p.
            Author discusses the spread of Socinianism in the Ukraine
        during the 17th century on pages 456-459 and 467-468.
        Refers to the prominent Ukrainian Socinian Simon Budny,
        who translated parts of the Bible in contemporary
        Ukrainian language to him.

1230.   Wlasowsky, Iwan. Outline History of the Ukrainian Orthodox
        Church. New York, Ukrainian Orthodox Church of the United
        States, 1956. v. 1. 312 p.
            Translation from the original Ukrainian of a history of
        the Ukrainian Orthodox Church by the same author. Only
        volume 1 of the 4 volume work has been translated into the
        English language. A bibliography added.

1231.   Zernov, Nicholas. The Ukrainians and Their Church. London,
        Society for Promoting of Christian Knowledge, 1945. 193 p.
            Author discusses the history of the Ukrainian Church,
        Christianity in medieval Ukraine and the Union of the
        Ukrainian Church with Rome (1596), which caused religious
        wars in the Ukraine.

1232.   Botsiurkiv, Bohdan R. "The Autocephalous Church Movement
        in Ukraine: The Formative Stage, 1917-1921." Ukrainian

Quarterly. 16: 211-223. Autumn, 1960. Bibl. footn.
    History of the Ukrainian Autocephalous Church, inde-
pendent from both Constantinople and Moscow Patriarchs.

1233. Chubatyi, Nicholas. "Moscow and the Ukrainian Church after
the Year 1654." Ukrainian Quarterly. 10: 60-70, Winter,
1954.
    After the Pereyaslav Treaty, Moscow destroyed the
autonomy of the Ukrainian Church and liquidated the
Metropolitan See in Kyiv. Moscow introduced censorship
of the church books. In 1945-1946 the Soviet Government
destroyed the Ukrainian Catholic Church in Western Ukraine
after destroying the Ukrainian Orthodox Church in the
thirties.

1234. Doroshenko, Dmytro. "The Uniate Church in Galicia, 1914-
1917." Slavonic and East European Review. 12: 622-627.
April, 1934.

1235. Ericsson, V. "The Earliest Conversion of the Rus' to
Christianity." Slavonic and East European Review. 44:
98-122, January, 1961.
    Tells about conversions in medieval Ukraine, then called
"Rus."

1236. Levytsky, Orest. "Socinianism in Poland and Southwest
Rus'." Annals of the Ukrainian Academy of Arts and
Sciences in the U. S. 3: 485-508, Spring-Summer, 1953.
    The author describes the spread of Socinianism among
the Ukrainian nobility in the 17th century and the fate
of the Ukrainian Socinians during the Ukrainian Revolution of 1648 (Bohdan Khmelnyckyi) and the subsequent
emigration of the Socinians to the Western Europe.

1237. Mirchuk, Ivan. "The Ukrainian Uniate Church." Slavonic
and East European Review. 10: 377-385, 1932.
    History of the Ukrainian Uniate Church in Western
Ukraine and its conditions under Polish domination between
the two world wars.

1238. "Mission of St. Cyril and Methodius: A Discussion."
Slavic Review. Volume XXIII, no. 2, January, 1964.
    Articles included: Dvornik, Francis. "The Signifi-
cance of the Mission of Cyril and Methodius." p. 185-211.
Lunt, Horace G. "The Beginning of Written Slavic." p.
212-219. Shevchenko, Ihor. "The Paradoxes of the
Cyrillo-Methodian Mission," p. 220-226. Dvornik, Francis,
"Reply."
    Authors discuss mission of the St. Cyril and Methodius
called, "Apostles of the Slave" and the beginning of the
Slavic writing, which was used for centuries in Ukraine

and which is basis for the contemporary Ukrainian alphabet.

1239. Polonska-Vasylenko, Natalia. "Was There a Ukrainian Ortho-
      dox Church." Ukrainian Review. 15: 57-62. December, 1968.
         Author proves that Ukrainian Orthodox Church was dif-
      ferent from the Russian Orthodox Church.

1240. Reshetar, John. "Ukrainian Nationalism and the Orthodox
      Church." American Slavic and East European Review. 10:
      38-49. February, 1951.
         Struggle of the Ukrainian Orthodox Church during the
      czarist period of Russian rule and the organization of the
      Ukrainian Autocephalous Church after the Revolution of
      1917; liquidation of this Church by the Soviet Govern-
      ment and its restoration under the German occupation.

1241. Veliky, Athanasy, OSBM. "One Thousand Years of Christianity
      in Ukraine." Pamphlet: One Thousand Years Christianity in
      Ukraine. Women's International Exposition. Ukrainian Sec-
      tion. November 3-13, 1955. New York, Ukrainian Women's
      Exposition Committee of New York City, 1955. p. 4-8.
         In this article author explains the significance of
      baptism of Princes Olha, grandmother of the Prince Volo-
      dymyr the Great who made Christianity the official
      religion of the medieval Ukraine.

1242. Vernadsky, George. "The Status of the Russian Church
      During the First Half-century Following Vladimir's Conver-
      sion." Slavonic Year Book. Slavonic and East European
      Review 20. American Series I. 1941: 294-314.
         Discusses the earliest period of Christianity in the
      Ukraine beginning with the bishopric established before
      the official conversion of the Ukraine; includes the first
      statute of the Ukrainian Church independent of the
      Patriarch in Constantinople.

1243. Zernov, Nicholas. "Vladimir and the Origin of the Russian
      Church." Slavonic and East European Review. 28: 123-138.
      November, 1949.
         The author selects passages from early Ukrainian
      chronicles in which he refers to the Kievan Principality
      as Russia, and proves that Prince Volodymyr (Vladimir)
      the Great established autocephaly of the Ukrainian
      Church. He reveals also that his son Yaroslav the Wise
      submitted the Ukrainian Church to the authority of the
      Patriarchs of Constantinople.

c. Ukrainian Church - Biography.
Kuntsevych, Josaphat, Saint.

1244. Boresky, Theodosia. Life of St. Josaphat, Martyr of the
Union, Archbishop of Polock, Member Order of St. Basil the
Great. New York, Comet Books, 1955. 381 p.
   Biography of Josaphat Kuntsevych, Archbishop of Polock
(at present in Byelorussia) killed by the enemies of
union of the Ukrainian and Byelorussian Orthodox Church
with Rome and canonized by the Roman Catholic Church.

Mohyla, Petro, Metropolitan.

1245. Graham, Hugo F. "Peter Mogila, Metropolitan of Kiev."
Russian Review. 14: 343-365. October, 1955.
   Concerns prominent Ukrainian churchman and educator
of the 17th century, Metropolitan of the Ukrainian
Orthodox Church.

1246. Simpson, George. "Petro Mohyla, Ecclesiastic and Educator."
Ukrainian Quarterly. 3: 242-248. Spring, 1948.
   His life, educational and cultural activity.

Sas-Kuilovsky, Julian, Metropolitan.

1247. Nazarko, Ireneus OSBM. Metropolitan Julian Sas-Kuilovsky,
1826-1900. New York, Shevchenko Scientific Society,
1959. 9 p. (Shevchenko Scientific Society. Papers no.
7.) Bibl. footn. p. 7-9.
   Biography of an Ukrainian Catholic Metropolitan of
Lviv--religious and cultural center of the Western Ukraine.

Sheptytskyi Andrii, Metropolitan.

1248. Kazymyra, Bohdan. Achievement of Metropolitan A. Sheptytskyi. Toronto, Basilian Press, 1958. 32 p.
   About the role played in the life of the Ukrainian
people by Andrii Sheptytskyi, Metropolitan of the
Ukrainian Catholic Church.

Sikorsky, Polikarp, Metropolitan.

1249. Chubatyi, Nicholas. "Polikarp Sikorski, Metropolitan of
the Ukrainian Autocephalous Orthodox Church." Ukrainian
Quarterly. 9: 313-316. Autumn, 1953.
   Obituary of a prominent churchman of the Ukrainian
Orthodox Church who refused during the first occupation
of the Western Ukraine by the Red Army (1939-41) to sub-
mit Ukrainian Orthodox Church of the Western Ukraine to
the Moscow Patriarch.

d. Ukrainian Church - Miscellaneous.

1250. Dushnyck, Walter. **The Ukrainian Rite Catholic Church at the Eucumenical Council, 1963-1965.** A collection of articles, book reviews, editorials, reports, and commentaries with special emphasis on Ukrainian Rite and other Eastern Churches. New York, Shevchenko Scientific Society, 1967. 191 p. plates. Pictorial section p. 161-186. (Shevchenko Scientific Society. Ukrainian Studies volume 23. English section volume 5.)
  Compiler was an Ukrainian press correspondent to the Vatican Council II.

1251. Fedorovich, N. **My Church and My Faith.** South Bound Brook, N. J., Ukrainian Orthodox Church in U. S., 1969. 40 p.
  A catechism.

1252. Luhovy, Anton. **Bible History: The Old and New Testament.** Winnipeg, n. p., 1944. 136 p.
  Bible history with parallel Ukrainian-English texts for Ukrainian children of Eastern Rite.

1253. Luhovy, Anton. **Our Religion. Cathechism for Ukrainian Catholic Youth.** Yorkton, Saskatchewan, Redeemers Voice Press, 1953. 128 p.
  Cathechism for Ukrainian Youth of Eastern Rite.

1254. **The Pathway to Heaven: A Prayer Book for Youth.** Yorkton, Saskatchewan, Redeemers Voice Press, 1954. 128 p.
  A prayer book for English-speaking Ukrainian Catholic youth.

1255. Piddubcheshen, Eva. **And Bless Thine Inheritance.** Introduction by G. A. Maloney, S. J. Published by Friends of the Ukrainian Catholic University in Rome. New York, Eric Hugo Printing Co., (Shenectady, N. Y.), 1970. 64 p.
  Author discusses the problem of the autonomy of the Ukrainian Catholic Church and efforts of the Ukrainian laymen to obtain Ukrainian Catholic Church autonomy under the Patriarch. She pictures the attitude of the Congregation for Eastern Churches toward the Ukrainian Catholic Church and the damages done to the eucumenic idea by this attitude.
  Author discusses the attitude of certain Ukrainian bishops to the Archbishop Major, Cardinal Slipyi. Author quotes father Maloney, S. J. as saying that according to the II Vatican Council's Decree on Eastern Churches, Cardinal Slipyi has power equal to the power of eastern Patriarchs.

1256. Theodorovich, John. Metropolitan. American-Ukrainian
       Orthodox Cathechism. South Bound Prook, N. J., Ukrainian
       Orthodox Church of the United States, n.d. 142 p.
           In English and Ukrainian.

1257. Ukrainian-English Orthodox Prayer Book. South Bound Brook,
       N. J. Ukrainian Orthodox Church of the United States,
       n. d., 140 p.

                2. Ukrainian Philosophy.

1258. Edie, James M. Russian Philosophy. Chicago, Quadrangle
       Books, 1965. 3 volumes.
           Discusses philosophy of the prominent Ukrainian philo-
       sopher of the 18th century, Hryhorii Skovoroda.

1259. Janiw, Wolodymyr and Ludwig Zeise. East-West Tension in
       the Light of Psychology. Proceedings of the scientific
       conference in Munich held on March 7 and 8, 1953. Munich,
       Molode Zhyttia, 1954. 32 p.
           Lectures dealing predominantly with Ukrainian national
       character, making a bridge between East and West.
           The lectures were presented at a conference arranged
       by the Bavarian Branch of the Professional Association
       of German Psychologists and the Institute of Psychology
       of the Ukrainian Free University.

1260. Andrusyshen, Constantine H. "Skovoroda the Seeker of the
       Genuine Man." Ukrainian Quarterly. 2: 316-330, Summer,
       1946.
           Life and teachings of this philosopher.

1261. Chizhevsky, Dmitry. "The Influence of the Philosophy of
       Schelling (1775-1854) in the Ukraine." Annals of the
       Ukrainian Academy of Arts and Sciences in the U. S. 6:
       1128-1139, 1958.
           Schelling's influence on Ukrainian philosophy.

1262. Chubatyi, Nicholas. "Ukraine and the Western World."
       Ukrainian Quarterly. 3: 145-158, Winter, 1947.

1263. Mirtschuk, Ivan. "The Basic Traits of the Ukrainian People."
       Ukrainian Quarterly. 3: 231-241. Spring, 1947.
           Ukrainians are idealists, individualists in life and
       philosophy, love the soil and have respect for Western
       culture. Russians are collectivistically minded.

1264. Mirtschuk, Ivan. "Evil in the Mirror of the Ukrainian
       and Russian Mind." Ukrainian Quarterly. 3: 368-376.
       Autumn, 1947.

For the optimistic Ukrainian, the devil is not the
equal counterpart of God as for Russian. In Russian
literature this dualism is reflected.

1265. Mirtschuk, Ivan. "Western Tendencies in Ukrainian Culture."
Ukrainian Quarterly. 4: 263-268. Autumn, 1948.
Ukrainians are individualists, Russians collectivists.
Ukrainians have Western tendencies, Russians are orientally
minded. The Ukraine is at present an East-West counter-
balance to Communism.

1266. Psycholoh W., pseud. "Change in the Psychology of the
Soviet Ukrainians." Ukrainian Quarterly. 10: 328-338.
Autumn, 1954.
Soviet efforts to change psychology of the Ukrainian
farmer and intelligencia have proved futile.

1267. Yaniv, Volodymyr. "A Psychological Interpretation of
Ukrainian Occidentalism." Ukrainian Quarterly. 6: 65-79,
Winter, 1950.
A study of Ukrainian occidentalism from the viewpoint
of psychology.

3. Ukraine - Education and Scholarship.

1268. Collection of Papers Presented at the Conference Honoring
Prof. Clarence A. Manning on His 70th Birth Anniversary.
New York, Shevchenko Scientific Society, 1964. 29 p. port.
(Shevchenko Scientific Society. Papers, 23.)
Proceedings of a conference honoring the 70th birth
anniversary of a well-known scholar of Ukrainian language,
history and literature, author of several books on
Ukrainian topics, professor emeritus of Columbia Univer-
sity.

1269. Dushnyck, Walter, ed. Professor Roman Smal-Stocki and His
Contributions to the Ukrainian Nation. Collected Papers.
New York, Shevchenko Scientific Society, 1970. 67 p.
(Shevchenko Scientific Society. Ukrainian Studies volume
17. English Section volume 8.)

1270. Grekov, B. D. Culture of Kiev Rus. Moscow, Foreign Languages Publishing House, 1947. 133 p.
Outline of the culture of Kyiv (Kiev) Rus especially
the archeological discoveries. Referred to as Russian
culture.

1271. Holiat, Roman S. Short History of the Ukrainian Free
University. New York, Shevchenko Scientific Society,
1964, 32 p. ports. Bibl. p. 31-32.
Also in Ukrainian Quarterly. 19: 204-226, Autumn, 1963.

Illus. Bibl. p. 225-226. History of the Ukrainian Free
University founded by the political emigrants from the
Ukraine in Vienna in the year 1921, later transferred
to Prague, Czechoslovakia. After World War II moved to
Munich, Germany.

1272. Mandryka, Mykyta Ivan. Bio-Bibliography of J. B. Rudnycky.
Winnipeg, Ukrainian Free Academy of Sciences, 1969. 72 p.
(Ukrainian Free Academy of Sciences. Ukrainian Scholars,
10.)
    Bio-bibliography of a prominent Ukrainian scholar,
bibliographer, chairman of the Slavic Department at the
University of Manitoba.

1273. O'Neil, John. Prodigal Genius. The Life of Nikola Tesla.
New York, Ives-Washburn, Inc., 1962. 326 p.
    Life story of a well-known American physicist and
inventor, originating from the present day Yugoslavia,
probably of Ukrainian origin.

1274. Shimoniak, Wasyl. Reforms of Peter Mohyla. Milwaukee,
Marquette University Press, 1965. 24 p. (Marquette
University. Slavic Institute Papers, no. 20.)
    About the activity of Petro Mohyla, head of the
Ukrainian Orthodox Church in ecclesiastic and educational
areas.

1275. Snovyd, Dmytro. Spirit of Ukraine: Ukrainian Contribution
to the World Culture. Jersey City, N. J., Jersey City
Press and Book Company, 1935. 152 p.
    History of Ukrainian culture and its influence on
world culture.

1276. Bedriy, Anathole W. "The Age of Grand Duchess Olha."
Ukrainian Review, London. 19: 83-86.
    About the culture and economics of Kyiv Rus' in the
time of St. Olha.

1277. Bojko, Jurij. "Shevchenko's 150th Anniversary and the
Task of Ukrainian Scholarship." Ukrainian Review, London.
11: 6-13, March, 1964.
    Written to counteract Russian falsifications and mis-
interpretations of Shevchenko.

1278. Chernivchanyn. "40th Anniversary of a Ukrainian College
in Exile." Ukrainian Review, London. 10: 63-67. June,
1963.
    Anniversary of the Ukrainian Husbandry Academy, an
economic college organized by Ukrainian emigree scholars
originally in Podiebrady, Czechoslovakia and presently
in Munich.

1279.   Chubaty, Mykola. "The Ukrainian Catholic University,
        Its Conception and Realization," in Archbishop Major
        Joseph Cardinal Slipy. Cardinal Slipy Jubilee Committee,
        1967. p. 33-39.
            Concerns the Ukrainian Catholic St. Clemens University
        in Rome.

1280.   Danko, Joseph. "West European and American Doctoral Dis-
        sertations on the Ukraine, 1945-1946." Annals of the
        Ukrainian Academy of Arts and Sciences in the U. S. 9(1-
        2/27-28): 313-333.
            List of doctoral dissertations on Ukrainian topics in
        different languages.

1281.   Dobriansky, Lev E. "A Man and Patriot." Ukrainian Quar-
        terly. 25: 204-218, 1969. Bibl. footn.
            Concerns Professor Roman Smal-Stocki, former President
        of the Shevchenko Scientific Society in America.

1282.   Holiat, Roman S. "Fiftieth Anniversary of Ukrainian Free
        University." Ukrainian Quarterly. 27: 252-268, 1971. Illus.

1283.   Horak, Stepan. "The Kiev Academy: a Bridge to Europe in
        the 17th Century." East European Quarterly. 3: 117-137,
        1969, no. 2.
            Concerns Kyiv Academy reorganized on West European pat-
        tern by prominent churchman and educator, Metropolitan
        Petro Mohyla, and its cultural influence on Eastern and
        Southeastern Europe.

1284.   Jasinchuk, Lev. "Education in Lviv," in Lviv: 280-303,
        (see entry no. 135).
            History of educational institutions in Lviv, capital
        of Western Ukraine.

1285.   Kedryn-Rudnytsky, Ivan. "Roman Smal-Stocki, a Statesman
        and Diplomat." Ukrainian Quarterly. 25: 230-245, 1969.
        Bibl. footn.

1286.   Kocevalov, Andrey. "Ukraine's Participation in the Cul-
        tural Activities of the Ancient World." Ukrainian Quar-
        terly. 5: 111-121. Spring, 1949.
            Cultural contacts of the ancient Ukraine with the
        ancient civilized world.

1287.   Korol, Nestor. "An Outline of the University Education
        in the Russian Empire." Ukrainian Quarterly. 25: 376-
        398, 1969.
            Also in reprint. Concerns also the university educa-
        tion in Ukraine which was a part of the Russian Czarist
        empire.

1288. Manning, Clarence A. "The Jubileum of the Shevchenko
       Scientific Society, 1873-1948." Ukrainian Quarterly. 5:
       26-28, Winter, 1949.
            About 75-year anniversary of a learned society being
       Academy of Sciences of the Western Ukraine.

1289. Manning, Clarence A. "Roman Smal-Stocki in Service of
       Ukraine." Ukrainian Quarterly. 25: 246-251, 1969.

1290. Mirchuk, Ivan. "The 40th Anniversary of the Ukrainian
       Free University." Ukrainian Review, London. 8: 72-86,
       September, 1961.

1291. Mirchuk, Ivan. "(Ukraine) Cultural Life," in Ukraine and
       Its People." (See entry no. 136.) p. 217-267.
            Ukrainian culture and Ukrainian cultural and educa-
       tional institutions.

1292. "The New Ukrainian University of St. Clemens in Rome."
       Interview with the Head of the Ukrainian University, Dr.
       Ihor Monciak. Ukrainian Review, London. 16: 80-85, no.
       2, 1969.
            About Ukrainian Catholic University at Rome.

1293. Pidhainy, Oleh S. "East European History at Youngstown
       State University." New Review. 7: 67-73, no. 1-2 (30-
       31).
            Program in East European History including a program
       in history of Ukraine at this Ohio University.

1294. "Prof. Roman Smal-Stocki, Ukrainian Scholar, Educator and
       Statesman." Ukrainian Review, London. 16: 87-90, no. 3,
       1969.

1295. Radzykevych, Volodymyr. "Lviv--a Center of Ukrainian Cul-
       ture between Two World Wars," in Lviv (see entry no. 135).
       p. 203-228.
            Development of scholarly and other cultural institu-
       tions in Lviv between 1919 and 1939.

1296. Sichynsky, Volodymyr. "Ukrainian Culture in the Age of
       Princess Olha." Women's International Exposition,
       Ukrainian Section, November 13, 1955. 1000th Anniversary
       of Christianity in the Ukraine, Princess St. Olha. New
       York City, 1955. p. 14-21. Illus.
            With the Ukrainian medieval state as a background,
       the author depicts the development of all branches of
       Ukrainian culture.

1297. Stakhiv, Matthew. "Roman Smal-Stocki, Organizer of Uk-
       rainian Scholarship." Ukrainian Quarterly. 25: 219-225,
       1969.

1298. Vaskovych, George. "The Activity of Ukrainian Communities and Self-Government in the Field of Public Education." Ukrainian Review, London. 17: 46-52, 1970, no. 2.
    Discusses educational activities of the communities and higher self-government units in the Ukraine in czarist time.

1299. Vernadsky, Vladimir. "The First Year of the Ukrainian Academy of Sciences, 1918-1919." Annals of the Ukrainian Academy of Arts and Sciences in the U. S. 11(1-2/31-32): 3-31.
    Memories of the first president of the Ukrainian Academy of Sciences.

1300. Vetukhiv, Michael. "A Hundred and Fifty Years of Kharkiv University." Annals of the Ukrainian Academy of Arts and Sciences in the U. S. 5: 1140-1159. 1955.
    The role of the university at Kharkiv as a bastion of academic freedom, its contribution to academic progress and its stress on cultural values.

4. Ukrainian Books, Libraries, Printing.

1301. Bosnjak, Mladen. A Study of Slavic Incunabula. Munchen, Kubon and Sagner, 1968. XXXII, 195 p.
    An analysis of incunabula of Bohemians, Croatians, Montenegrins and Ukrainians. Author discusses role of the "father of Ukrainian printing" Schwaipoldt Fiol. Bibliography included.

1302. Goy, Peter A., ed. A Biographical Directory of Librarians in the Field of Slavic Studies. Ed. Peter Goy with the editorial assistance of Laurence H. Miller for the Slavic and East European Subsection of the Assn. of College and Research Libraries. Chicago, American Library Association, 1967. 88 p.
    Includes the names of many Ukrainian professional librarians and subject specialists in the U. S. and Canada with information on family, education, work history, membership in organizations and publications.

1303. Horecky, Paul. Libraries and Bibliographic Centers in the Soviet Union. Bloomington, Indiana, University of Indiana Press, 1959. 217 p.
    Subject arrangement. Includes information on library network, collections, bibliographies, library schools, a.o. Many references to the Ukraine.

1304. Muchin, John. Slavic Collection of the University of Manitoba Libraries. Winnipeg, The University of Manitoba

Libraries and UVAN, 1970. 70 p.
   UVAN in imprint stands for Ukrainians'ka Vilna Akademia
Nauk (Ukrainian Free Academy of Sciences in Canada).
Publication includes among collections in other Slavic
languages also detailed description of the Ukrainian
collection in the University of Manitoba libraries.

1305. Rudnyckyj, Jaroslav B. Ukrainica in Library of Congress:
A Preliminary Survey. Washington, D. C. Library of Congress. Reference Department. Central and Central European Division, 1965. 94 p. Mimeo.
   An operational document for administrative use only;
review of Ukrainica in the Library of Congress based on
a survey carried out by the author.

1306. Wynar, Lubomyr B. History of Early Ukrainian Printing,
1491-1600. Denver, University of Denver. Graduate School
of Librarianship, 1962. 96 p. (University of Denver.
Graduate School of Librarianship. Studies in Librarianship v. 1. no. 2.)
   Discusses early period of Ukrainian printing which can
be considered as incunabula period because Eastern
Europe, including the Ukraine, switched from hand-
writing to printing later than Western and Middle Europe.
Early Ukrainian printers, printing shops and publications.

1307. AWB. "Problems of Acquisitions of Materials on Ukraine in
Humanities and Social Sciences." Ukrainian Review, London.
13: 75-78. September, 1966.

1308. Bedriy, Anatol W. "Survey of Holdings by the Columbia
Libraries on Ukraine (in the field of Social Sciences)."
Ukrainian Review, London. 13: 94-96. December, 1966.

1309. Holubec, Myroslava. "Printing in the Pecherska Lavra
(Monastery of Caves)." Horizons. 8: 17-30. 167. Bibl.
footn. p. 29-30.
   History of printing shop and bibliography of publica-
tions of the oldest Ukrainian monastery--Pechers'ka
Lavra in Kyiv.

1310. Rudnyckyj, Jaroslav B. "History of the Ukrainian Holdings
in the Library of Congress." Annals of the Ukrainian
Academy of Arts and Sciences in the U. S. 6: 1406-1410.
1958.
   Short history of the development of the Ukrainian collection in the Library of Congress.

1311. Rudnyckyj, Jaroslav B. "Psalterium Winnipegense Cyrillicum;
A Note on Hitherto Unknown Manuscript in Canada." Annals
of the Ukrainian Academy of Arts and Sciences in the U. S.

11(1-2/31-32): 105-108. Facsim.
Description of a recently discovered medieval Ukrainian
manuscript in Canada.

1312.   Rudnyckyj, Jaroslav B. "Ukrainian Libraries in Canada
and Ukrainica Canadiana, 1952." Svoboda-Ukrainian Weekly.
1953, nos. 159, 163, 173, and 178.
Lists collections of Ukrainica in Canadian university
libraries and other libraries in Canada. Also includes
a list of Ukrainian libraries in Canada.

1313.   Sokolyszyn, Aleksander. "Sveipolt Fiol; the First Slavic
Printer in Cyrillic Characters." Slavonic and East Euro-
pean Review. 37: 88-94. February, 1959.
History of the printer of the first religious books
for Ukraine, his works, and his significance in the
Ukrainian and Slavic world.

1314.   Tarnavsky, Marta. "Bookburning a la Soviet." Ukrainian
Quarterly. 22: 53-62. Spring, 1966.
Libraries in the USSR and still more in Soviet-ruled
Ukraine are an instrument of the state and party policy.
Systematic weedings of books are done because of
political reasons.

1315.   Tarnavsky, Marta. "The Founding Fathers of Ukrainian
Printing: Shvaipolt Fiol and Ivan Fedorov." Ukrainian
Quarterly. 21: 206-218. Autumn, 1965. Bibl. footn.
Deals with Shvaipolt Fiol who in his printing shop in
Cracow was printing books for Ukrainian churches at the
end of the 15th century and Ivan Fedorov or Fedorovych.
(This form of the name he used in colophons of his
books.) The latter was the founder of two earliest
Ukrainian printing shops at Ostrih, where he printed,
among other church books, famous Ostrih Bible, the first
translation of the complete Bible in Church Slavic language and at Lviv, where among other things he printed
a speller.

1316.   Tarnavsky, Ostap. "The Libraries in Ukraine." Ukrainian
Quarterly. 18: 323-333. Winter, 1962. Bibl. footn.
p. 332-333.

1317.   Wynar, Lubomyr R. "Early Ukrainian Printing in Lviv (16th
Century)." New Review. 7: 57-66, 1957 no. 1-2(30-31).
Bibl. footn. p. 63-66.

XIV. UKRAINIAN LANGUAGE AND LITERATURE.

1. Ukrainian Language - General.

1318. Foster, James Maurice. Slavic in North America. Winnipeg, Ukrainian Free Academy of Arts and Sciences, 1965. 24 p. (Ukrainian Free Academy of Arts and Sciences. Slavistica, 53.)
    Concerns Slavic languages spoken in North America. For the most part study concerns Ukrainian language.

1319. Foster, James Maurice. Some Phonological Rules of Modern Standard Ukrainian. Urbana, Illinois, University of Illinois, 1966. 260 p.
    Unpublished doctoral dissertation. Author discusses development of present phonological system of the modern standard Ukrainian and its peculiarities.

1320. Gerus-Tarnavetska, Iraida. Anthroponymy in the Pomianyk of Horodysce of 1484. Winnipeg, Ukrainian Free Academy of Sciences, 1965. 80 p. (Ukrainian Academy of Arts and Sciences. Onomastica, 30.) Bibl. p. 75-80.
    Discusses forms of personal names found in "Pomianyk," a list of names of deceased persons which used a parish priest to recite these names in church memorial services on certain occasions. Compiled in 1484 in Western Ukrainian village Horodyshche.

1321. Hursky, Jakob. Patronymic Surnames in Ukrainian. Philadelphia, University of Pennsylvania, 1957. 141 p.
    Unpublished doctoral dissertation giving derivations of patronymic surnames used in Ukraine. Available in microfilm or Xerox copies by the University Microfilms, Inc., Ann Arbor, Michigan. Abstract in Dissertation Abstracts 1957, no. 20.793.

1322. Jashchun, W. Phonetic, Morphological and Lexical Peculiarities of the Shnyriv Dialect. Winnipeg, Ukrainian Free Academy of Sciences, in the U. S., 1964, 32 p. (Ukrainian Free Academy of Arts and Sciences, Slavistica, 49.)
    Discusses peculiarities of the dialect spoken in a Western Ukrainian village.

1323. Kirkonnel, Watson. Common English Loan Words in East European Languages. Winnipeg, Ukrainian Free Academy of Sciences, 1952. 16 p. (Ukrainian Free Academy of Sciences. Slavistica, no. 14.)
    Includes English loan words in the Ukrainian language.

1324. Kovaliv, Panteleymon. Participal Adjectives in the Slavic Languages. Winnipeg, Ukrainian Free Academy of Sciences.

Slavistica, no. 29.)
Includes participal adjectives in Ukrainian language.

1325. Kovaliv, Panteleymon K. Systems of Phonemes in Slavic
Languages. New York, Shevchenko Scientific Society, 1969.
29 p. (Shevchenko Scientific Society. Papers, no. 33.)
Includes Ukrainian language.

1326. Lunt, Horace G. The Orthography of Eleventh Century Russian Manuscripts. New York, Columbia University, 1950.
Unpublished doctoral dissertation. Concerns 11th
century manuscripts of the Kyiv Rus'.

1327. Novovirsky, Nestor P. Introduction to the Study of the
Ukrainian Language and Culture. New York, 1949. 2 v.
Handbook for the study of Ukrainian language with
section on Ukrainian culture.

1328. Pazuniak-Ishchuk, Natalia. The Vocative Case in Ukrainian.
Philadelphia, University of Pennsylvania, 1956. 198 p.
Unpublished doctoral dissertation. Reveals the
vocative case as a distinctive feature of Ukrainian in
contrast to Russian, in which it is not used. Available
in microfilm or Xerox copy from University Microfilms,
Inc., Ann Arbor, Michigan. Abstract in Dissertation
Abstracts.

1329. Rudnyckyi, Iaroslav. Ethymological Formula with Special
Reference to Slavic. Winnipeg, Ukrainian Free Academy of
Sciences, 1962. 64 p. (Ukrainian Free Academy of
Sciences, Slavistica, 44.)
Author discusses methodology of working on ethymological
dictionaries of Slavic languages, and includes history
of work on his cthymological dictionary of the Ukrainian
language and the method used. Illustrated by selected
entries from this dictionary.

1330. Shevelov, George. A Prehistory of Slavic. The Historical
Phonology of Common Slavic. New York, Columbia University
Press, 1955. 622 p. fold. col. map. (Columbia Slavic
Studies.)
Author discusses grammar of pre-Slavic language, com-
mon to all Slavic tongues. Important to history of
Ukrainian language.

1331. Shevelov, George Yury and Fred Holling, ed. Reader in the
History of Eastern Slavic Languages: Russian, Belorussian,
Ukrainian. New York, Columbia University Press, 1958. 81 p.
(Columbia University. Department of Slavic Languages.
Columbia Slavic Studies.)
Includes material concerning Ukrainian language.

1332. Simovych, Vasyl. <u>Contributions to Onomastics</u>. Winnipeg, Ukrainian Free Academy of Sciences, 1967. 24 p. (Ukrainian Free Academy of Sciences. Onomastica, no. 34.)
Selection of author's articles on problem of the Ukrainian onomastics.

1333. Stankiewicz, Edward. <u>A Selected Bibliography of Slavic Linguistics</u>. The Hague, Mouton, 1966. 2 v. (Slavic Printings and Reprintings, no. 49.)
Bibliography of Ukrainian linguistics in v. 2, p. 295-344. For some other Ukrainian entries see author index.

1334. Starchuk, Orest. <u>The Ukrainian Language Questionnaire</u>. Edmonton, University of Alberta, Department of Slavonic Languages, 1969. 262 p.

1335. Svoboda, Victor. <u>Ukrainian Studies</u>. Reprinted from <u>The Year's Work in Modern Language Studies</u>, vol. 24, p. 622-663. London, 1963.
Bibliographies of studies on Ukrainian language.

1336. Zaharychuk, Andrew. <u>The Ukrainian Alphabet</u>. Winnipeg, n.p., 1961. 32 p.
Concerns Cyrillic alphabet used by Ukrainians.

1337. Altbauer, Mosche. "Phonetic Loan-Words of Hebrew Language in Ukrainian." <u>Annals of the Ukrainian Academy of Arts and Sciences in the U. S.</u> 8(1-2/24-25): 115-120. Bibl. footn.

1338. Bida, Constantine. "Dialect Vocabulary in the Old Kievan Literature." <u>Slavic and East European Studies</u>. 3: 133-142. Autumn, 1958. Bibl.
Author traces influence of the Ukrainian dialects on the monuments of medieval literature of the Kyiv Rus'."

1339. Chaplenko, Vasyl. "Adyghe Languages As the Key to the Ethnogenesis of Slav and Other Nationalities." <u>Ukrainian Quarterly</u>. XXVI: 277-283, 1970.
Abstracts and discussion of two of the author's books in the Ukrainian language. He stresses importance of the Adyghe language (a small people living in Caucasus) for study of history of Slavic, including Ukrainian, languages.

1340. Chorney, Stephen. "350 Years Since M. Smotrytsky's Fundamental Work on Languages." <u>Ukrainian Quarterly</u>. XXVI: 301-303.
About known Ukrainian author and religious polemist of 16th and 17th centuries, Meletii Smotryts'kyi, as linguist.

1341. Hursky, Jacob P. "Linguistic Studies of Prof. G. Y. Shevelov." <u>Ukrainian Quarterly</u>. XXV: 159-164. 1969.
   Discusses works of prominent Ukrainian linguist, professor of Columbia University, George Shevelov.

1342. Hursky, Jacob P. "The Origin of Patronymic Surnames in Ukrainian." <u>Annals of the Ukrainian Academy of Arts and Sciences in the U. S.</u> 8(1-2/25-26): 169-190. Bibl. footn.
   Ethymology of patronymic surnames in Ukrainian language.

1343. Jacobson, Gunnar. "Some Remarks on the Origin of the Gerund in Ukrainian." <u>Annals of the Ukrainian Academy of Arts and Sciences in the U. S.</u> 8(1-2/25-26): 45-54. Bibl. footn.
   Discusses history of Gerund form in Ukrainian language.

1344. Kolessa, Alexander. "Bibliography of the Ukrainian Language." <u>Slavonic and East European Review</u>. 5: 169-172. 1926.
   List of works concerning Ukrainian linguistics up to 1928.

1345. Kovaliv, Panteleymon. "The Original Inhabitants of the Kievan State and the Formation of the Literary Language." <u>Shevchenko Scientific Society. Proceedings of the Philological Section</u>. 1: 39-43, 1951.
   The author discusses different theories concerning the origin of the Slavs and states that various peoples referred to in history as inhabitants of the Ukraine left their traces in the current Ukrainian language.

1346. Kovaliv, Panteleymon. "The Problem of the Formation of the Ukrainian Language." <u>Shevchenko Scientific Society. Proceedings of the Philological Section</u>. 2: 23-30, 1952.
   An abstract of new studies revealing that the distinctions between the Ukrainian and Russian languages existed from the beginning.

1347. Kovaliv, Panteleymon. "Problems of the Ukrainian Literary Language." <u>Annals of the Ukrainian Academy of Arts and Sciences in the U. S.</u> 3(1/7): 571-583. Bibl. footn.
   This is a review of work of the Metropolitan Ilarion Ohienko (in civic life Prof. Ivan Ohienko) "Ukrains'ka Literaturna Mova," (Ukrainian literary Language), 1951 Author stresses value of this work for Ukrainian linguistics.

1348. Kovaliv, Panteleymon. "The Vocabulary Fund of the Ukrainian Literary Language between the Tenth and Fourteenth Centuries." <u>Shevchenko Scientific Society. Proceedings of the Philological Section</u>. 2: 10-13, 1952.
   Abstract of a study discussing the vocabulary of the

medieval Ukrainian literary masterpieces.

1349. Kysilevskyi, Konstantine. "An Attempt At a New Classification of Ukrainian Dialects." Shevchenko Scientific
Society. Proceedings of the Philological Section. 1: 14-
19, 1952.
New scheme for classification of Ukrainian dialects.

1350. Kysilevskyi, Konstantine. "The Most Important Achievements
of Ukrainian Philology in the Last 60 Years." Shevchenko
Scientific Society. Proceedings of the Philological Section. 2: 31-38, 1952.
Discusses well-known Ukrainian linguists and their works.

1351. Manning, Clarence A. "The Linguistic Question in Carpatho-
Ukraine." Ukrainian Quarterly. 10: 247-251, Summer, 1954.
In the Carpatho-Ukraine many archaic dialects existed
until recently. Strong Rusophile tendencies existed but
the national renaissance eventually pushed the people
toward unity with other Ukrainians.

1352. Mathews, W. K. "The Phonetic Basis of Pleophony in East
Slavonic." Slavic and East European Review. 36: 94-99,
1958.
Concerned chiefly with Ukrainian language.

1353. Mathews, W. K. "The Ukrainian System of Declension." Languages. 28: 60-71, 1949.

1354. Pauls, John P. "The Russian Academy on the Ukrainian Language." Ukrainian Quarterly. 18: 70-74, 1962.
In 1905 Russian Academy of Sciences asked Russian government to repeal restrictions imposed on the use of the
Ukrainian language and stated that from pre-Tatar times
Ukrainian language was not a dialect of Russian language but was a separate language.

1355. Samilov, Mikhael. "The Treatment of a Common Slavic o in
Ukrainian." Annals of the Ukrainian Academy of Arts and
Sciences in the U. S. 8(1-2/25-26): 15-31. Bibl. footn.

1356. Stankiewicz, Edward. "Stress Alternations in the Ukrainian
Substantive Declension." Annals of the Ukrainian Academy
of Arts and Sciences in the U. S. 8(1-2/25-26): 141-151.
Bibl. footn.

1357. Zhyla, Volodymyr T. "Adjectival Surnames in the Kharkov
Register of 1660." Names. 18: 89-96. June, 1970.
Available also in separate reprint.

1358. Zhyla, Volodymyr T. "The Name Dnieper and the Name of
Some of Its Tributaries." Proceedings of the Ninth Inter-

national Congress of Onomastic Sciences, University College, London, July 3-8, 1966. Louvain, International Centre of Onomastics, 1966(?), p. 487-494.

1359. Zhyla, Volodymyr T. "The Origin and Meaning of the Name Karpaty," in Disputationes Montium Vocabula Allorumque Nominum Significationen Pertinantia. Tom 1. Proceedings of 10th International Congress of Onomastic Sciences, Vienna, Wiener Medizinische Akademie, 1969(?), p. 517-523.

1360. Zhyla, Volodymyr T. "Ukrainian Anthroponymy in the Kharkov Register of 1660." In Proceedings of the Eighth International Congress of Onomastic Sciences. The Hague Mouton & Co., 1966, p 596-604.
  Available also in reprint.

2. Ukrainian Language - Dictionaries, Grammars, Readers.

1361. Andrusyshen, Constantine N. and James Krett. A Complete Ukrainian-English Dictionary. Saskatoon, University of Saskatchewan Press, 1955. 1,163 p.

1362. Bilash, Berislav N. Ukrainian with Ease. Part one. Winnipeg, Curatorium of Ukrainian Schools, 1966. 148 p.
  Used by the Department of Education in Manitoba for classes in Ukrainian.

1363. Dojacek, F. New Ukrainian Interpreter and Ukrainian-English and English-Ukrainian Dictionary. Winnipeg, Dojacek Publishing House, 1930. 378 p.
  A textbook of English language for Ukrainian immigrants with dictionary.

1364. Evach, Honore and Paulo Yuzyk. Ukrainian Reader with Vocabulary and Notes. Winnipeg, Ukrainian-Canadian Committee, 1960. 240 p.

1365. Evach, Honore. Ukrainian Self-educator for the Beginners. Winnipeg, Kalyna Ukrainian Cooperative, Ltd. 1953. 96 p.
  Principles of Ukrainian grammar, idioms and reading. Intended to develop skill in conversation and in reading Ukrainian with help of a dictionary.

1366. Krett, James. A Pocket Dictionary of the English and Ukrainian Languages. Giving the Pronunciation of English Words in Ukrainian Characters and Sounds. Winnipeg, Ukrainian Booksellers and Publishers, 1931. 446 p.

1367. Lew, Wasylj and Iwan Werbianyj. An English-Ukrainian and Ukrainian-English Dictionary. Nuremberg - Bayreuth. Newspaper "Czas"--(The Time)--Cooperative "Pracia" and "Plast,"

1947. 3 v.
　　Ukrainian t.p. added. English-Ukrainian part 147 p.
Ukrainian-English part 2 volumes. Outline of English
grammar, international table of pronunciation, etc.,
added.

1368.　Luckyj, George Stephen Nestor and Jaroslav Bohdan Rudny-
　　　　ckyj. A Modern Ukrainian Grammar. 4th Printing. Winni-
　　　　peg, Ukrainian Free Academy of Sciences, 1961. 186 p.
　　　　Processed.
　　　　　Ukrainian grammar for English-speaking students.

1369.　Lunt, Horace G. Old Church-Slavonic Grammar. S'Gravenhage,
　　　　Mouton, 1955. 143 p. (Slavistic printings and reprintings,
　　　　3.)

1370.　Medushevskyi, Andrii Petrovych. Ukrainian Grammar. Kiev,
　　　　Radyans'ka Shkola, 1963. 211 p.
　　　　　On t.p. added: A. Medushevsky and R. Zlotkovska.
　　　　English t.p. added. Grammar of Ukrainian language for
　　　　English-speaking students. Text in English.

1371.　Podwesko, M. L. English-Ukrainian Dictionary. New York,
　　　　1954. 792 p.
　　　　　A reprint of an edition published in Kyiv by the
　　　　Radianska Shkola Publishing House. Available also in a
　　　　thumb indexed edition.

1372.　Podwesko, M. L. Ukrains'ko-Anhliys'kyi Slovar. New York,
　　　　1954. 1007 p.
　　　　　English t.p. added. Reprint of an edition by the
　　　　Radians'ka Shkola Publishing House in Kyiv. Available
　　　　also in a thumb indexed edition. This dictionary and
　　　　dictionary listed in no. 1371 put stress on technical
　　　　language.

1373.　Popovich, J. Damascenus, OSBM and Cornelius J. Pasichny.
　　　　Church-Slavonic-Ukrainian-English Dictionary. Mundare,
　　　　Alberta, Basilian Publishing House, 1962. 114 p.
　　　　　Dictionary of Church-Slavic language which used to be
　　　　the literary language of the medieval Ukraine and until
　　　　recently was used as cultus language in the Ukrainian
　　　　Catholic Church.

1374.　Poznansky, Mykhaylo, comp. List of Ukrainian Terminologic
　　　　Dictionaries Available in the United States and Canada.
　　　　New York, 1955. 66 p.
　　　　　A Union list of such dictionaries available in the
　　　　libraries of the United States and Canada and in private
　　　　possession.

1375. Readings in Ukrainian Literature. Saskatoon, University
       of Saskatchewan. Department of Slavic Studies, 1966, IV,
       104 p.

1376. Rudnyckyj, Jaroslav Bohdan. An Ethymological Dictionary
       of the Ukrainian Language. Winnipeg, Ukrainian Free
       Academy of Sciences, v.
           Publishing still in progress. Only existing ethymo-
       logical dictionary of Ukrainian language.

1377. Salastin, John. English-Ukrainian Dictionary. Richmond
       Hill, N. Y., 1956. 893 p.
           Added t.p. in Ukrainian: "Anhliis'ko-Ukrains'kyi
       Slovnyk."

1378. Shevelov, George Ioury. "The Syntax of Modern Literary
       Ukrainian: The Simple Sentence." The Hague, Mouton,
       1963. 319 p. (Slavistic printings and reprintings, 38.)
           A scholarly study concerning one aspect of Ukrainian
       grammar.

1379. Slavutych, Yar. Conversational Ukrainian. Preface by
       Orest Starchuk. 2d ed. Edmonton, Gateway Publishing Co.,
       1961. 609 p.

1380. Slavutych, Yar. Introduction to Ukrainian. Edmonton,
       Slavuta, 1962. 22 p.

1381. Slavutych, Yar. Ukrainian by the Audio-visual Method.
       Part one. Montreal-Paris-Brussels, Didier, 1968. 65 p.
       (#2106).

1382. Slavutych, Yar. Ukrainian by the Audio-visual Method.
       Student's copybook. Montreal-Paris-Brussels, Didier,
       1968. 110 p. (#2105).

1383. Slavutych, Yar. Ukrainian for Beginners. 3rd rev. ed.
       Edmonton, Slavuta. 1968. 60 p.

1384. Slavutych, Yar. Ukrainian in Pictures. Edmonton, Gateway
       Publishing Co., 1965. 90 p.
           Series of Ukrainian textbooks and readers of different
       grades for English-speaking students. Methods presented
       differ. Author of these textbooks is chairman of the
       Department of Slavic Studies at the University of Alberta,
       Canada.

1385. Speak Ukrainian with Us. Book 1. Aut. Coll. Makarkova,
       H., Palamar, L., Prisyaznyuk, N. Kiev, Ukraina Society,
       1970. 63 p.
           A textbook of Ukrainian for English-speaking students.

1386. Stechyshyn, Julius William. Ukrainian Grammar. Winnipeg, Ukrainian Canadian Committee, 1951 502 p. and Winnipeg, Trident, 1966. Illus. maps, portraits.
   Ukrainian-English and English-Ukrainian vocabulary added.

1387. Surmach, Myron. Ukrainian-English and English-Ukrainian Pocket Dictionary. New York, Surma, 1931. 286 p.

1388. Svoboda, Victor. The "Slavonica" Part of the Oxford Heptaglot Dictionary. A Ukrainian-Latin Vocabulary of the first half of the 17th century. (In Ukrainian, English and Latin). Winnipeg, Ukrainian Free Academy of Sciences, 1956. 64 p. (Ukrainian Free Academy of Sciences. Slavistica no. 25.)
   Description of this dictionary which contained 2,722 Latin words with their equivalent in seven other languages, among other also contemporary literary Ukrainian. List of these Ukrainian words.

1389. United States Army Languages School, Presidio, California. Ukrainian Basic Courses. Presidio de Monterey, Cal., 1955.
   Textbook, grammar and reader for soldiers studying Ukrainian language.

1390. Wexler, Paul Natan. Purism in the Development of a Standard Language with Special Reference to Modern Standard Belorussian and Ukrainian. New York, Columbia University, 1967. 643 p.
   Unpublished doctoral dissertation. Purism, states the author, shows in languages which have been denied an independent existence. It can last indefinitely. In other languages it is only temporary. In Ukrainian and Belorussian languages, directed against Polish and Russian influences, this purism enabled survival of these languages.
   Available in microfilm or Xerox copy from University Microfilms, Inc., Ann Arbor, Michigan. Abstract in Dissertation Abstracts.

1391. Whitman, Robert H. The Morphology of the Svjatoslav Izbornik of 1073. Cambridge, Mass., Harvard University, 1964.
   Unpublished doctoral dissertation. Concerns language of the oldest monument of the literature of medieval Ukraine.

1392. Yasenitsky, M.P.B. A Pocket Dictionary of the Ukrainian-English and English-Ukrainian Languages. Winnipeg, Ruthenian Bookstore, 1914. 1,577 p.

1393. Zernovsky, Serge A. Medieval Russian Epics, Chronicles and Sagas. A superb anthology containing much material translated into English for the first time. New York, Dutton, 1963. 436 p.

Most of the material is monuments of medieval Ukrainian literature referred to as Russian. Excerpts from Ukrainian chronicles, legends, lives of saints, Tale of Ihor's Armament. On p. 43-167 article "Literature of Medieval Russia," concerns medieval literature of Kyiv Rus.

3. Ukrainian Literature - General.

1394. Gudzii, Nikolai K. History of Early Russian Literature. Translated from the 2d Russian edition by Susan Wilbur Jones. New York, The MacMillan Company, 1949. 545 p. (Reprint: Octagon, 1970.)

Contains a history of medieval Ukrainian literature. The author assumes the theory that the common pre-Russian nation was Russian rather than Ukrainian. He reveals slight pro-Communist and anti-religious bias but gives a good description and analysis of the Tale of Ihor's Campaign and of Ukrainian folk poetry.

1395. Lewanski, Richard Casimir. The Slavic Literatures. Compiled by Richard C. Lewanski. Assisted by Lucia G. Lewanski and Maya Deriugin. New York Public Library and F. G. Ungar Pub. Co., 1967. XII, 630 p.

Includes also section on Ukrainian literature.

1396. Lewitter, Lucian Ryszard. A Study of the Academic Drama in Russia and the Ukraine in the Seventeenth and Eighteenth Centuries, with Special References to Its Polish Origins. Cambridge, Cambridge University, 1950.

Academic drama was cultivated in the Ukrainian colleges of the 17th and 18th centuries. These colleges had common traits with the Jesuit colleges of the contemporary Poland, therefore, the author tries to prove that this kind of drama emerged in Ukrainian colleges under Polish influence. Unpublished doctoral dissertation.

1397. Luzhnycky, George. Ukrainian Literature within the Framework of World Literature. A short outline of Ukrainian literature from Renaissance to Romanticism. Philadelphia, America, 1961. 86 p.

In Ukrainian literature, one can notice the same trends that dominated Western literatures.

1398. Manning, Clarence A. Ukrainian Literature: Studies of the Leading Authors. Jersey City, N. J., Ukrainian National Association, 1944. 126 p.

Introduction to Ukrainian literature: biographies of
Ukrainian prominent poets, novelists and philosophers.
Bibliography.

1399. Olynyk, Roman. <u>Literary and Ideological Trends in the
Literature of Western Ukraine, 1919-1939</u>. Montreal, University of Montreal, 1962.
        Unpublished doctoral dissertation. Author proves that
political situation of the Polish domination in the
Western Ukraine influenced West Ukrainian literature of
that time period.

1400. Pohorilyi, Semen. <u>The Unpublished Novels of Volodymyr
Vynnychenko</u>. New York, New York University, 1971, IX,
244 p.
        Doctoral dissertation. Concerns novels of the promi-
nent Ukrainian writer Volodymyr Vynnychenko, still in
manuscripts. Added t.p. in Ukrainian: Neopublikovani
romany Volodymyra Vynnychenka.

1401. Romanenchuk, Bohdan. <u>Modernistic Trends in Ukrainian
Literature, 1900-1923</u>. Philadelphia, University of Pennsylvania, 1958. 178 p.
        Study of trends in Ukrainian literature in the first
quarter of the twentieth century. Doctoral dissertation.

1402. Shabliovsky, Yevhen. <u>Ukrainian Literature through the
Ages</u>. Translated from the Ukrainian by Abraham Mostetsky,
Andrew Marko and Anatole Bilenky. Versus (translated) by
John Weir. Kiev, Mystetstvo, 1970. 241 p.
        Translation of an Ukrainian textbook of history of
Ukrainian literature. Expresses official Soviet views
on this history.

1403. Slavutych, Yar. <u>Modern Ukrainian Poetry</u>. Philadelphia,
Pennsylvania, 1950. 71 p.
        In Ukrainian with an English abstract on p. 59-71.
Concerns modern Ukrainian poetry beginning with 1918.
The author considers Ivan Franko and Lesya Ukrainka
(pseudonym of poetess: Laryssa Kosach-Kvitka) as the
predecessors of modern Ukrainian poetry.

1404. Andrusyshen, Constantine H. "Ukrainian Literature a Mirror
of the Common Man." <u>Ukrainian Quarterly</u>. 4: 44-54.
Winter, 1948.
        Ukrainian literature reflects problems of everyday
life.

1405. Andrusyshen, Constantine H. "Ukrainian Theatre as a Political Factor." <u>Ukrainian Quarterly</u>. 3: 249-261. Spring,
1947.

The Ukrainian theatre played a steady political role
in Ukrainian life.

1406. Cizevsky, Dmitry. "On the Question of Genres in Old Rus-
       sian Literature." Harvard Slavic Studies. 1954: 105-
       115, issue 2.

1407. Coleman, Arthur Prudden. "A New Golden Age for Ukraine
       (Three Phases of Ukrainian Cultural Life)." Ukrainian
       Quarterly. 26: 36-47, 1970.
           Concerns ups of the Ukrainian literature; last one in
       60's in Ukraine.

1408. Derzhavyn, Volodymyr. "Postwar Ukrainian Literature in
       Exile." Ukrainian Review, London. 4: 13-24, September,
       1957, 4: 56-66, December, 1957, 5: 30-40, September, 1958,
       and 5: 50-61, December, 1958, 7: 17-29, March, 1960.
           Discusses the work of the Ukrainian writers--political
       emigrants.

1409. Fedenko, Bohdan. "Recent Development in Ukrainian Litera-
       ture." Studies on the Soviet Union. 3: 136-139, 1963,
       no. 2.

1410. Horbatch, Anna Halya. "The Young Generation of Ukrainian
       Poets." Ukrainian Review, London. 12: 23-34. December,
       1965.
           Discusses appearance of a group of young poets in the
       Ukraine called "shestydesiatnyky" (poets of the sixties).

1411. Jefremov, Serhii. "Historiography of Ukrainian Literature."
       Annals of the Ukrainian Academy of Arts and Sciences in
       the U. S. 1: 4-20, Winter, 1951.
           Translation of an Ukrainian article by a prominent
       Ukrainian historian of literature who discusses his-
       toriography of Ukrainian literature beginning with the
       19th century.

1412. Kuchar, Roman. "The Traditional and the Contemporary in
       Ukrainian Literature." Ukrainian Review, London. 19:
       66-81, March, 1972.
           Discusses topics of works of the Ukrainian emigree
       authors.

1413. Luciw, Luka. "Literature," in Ukrainian Arts. Compiled
       by Olya Dmytriw. New York, Ukrainian Youth League of North
       America, p. 183-212.
           Survey of Ukrainian literature beginning with 968 A.D.
       to the mass liquidation of Ukrainian writers by the
       Soviet authorities and the German occupation forces.
       Includes discussion of the Ukrainian folk poetry (byliny
       and dumy).

1414. Pelenski, Yaroslav. "Recent Ukrainian Writing." <u>Survey</u>. 59: 102-112, April, 1966.
    Available also in reprint. Discusses literature of the young Ukrainian writers "shestydesiatnyky."

1415. Segel, H. B. "Censorship and Literature: Russia, Poland and the Ukraine." <u>Slavic and East European Journal</u>. 16: 222-235. Fall, 1958.
    Because of censorship in Czarist Russia, Russian, Ukrainian and Polish writers tried to evade censorship in different ways. For example, Lesya Ukrainka (Laryssa Kosach-Kvitka) and Taras Shevchenko, chose topics of their work from ancient history. Author discusses plays of Lessya Ukrainka with classical topics.

1416. Simovych, Vasyl. "A Brief Survey of Ukrainian Literature." <u>Ukrainian Review</u>, London. 11: 76-80, June, 1964.

1417. Vincenz, A. de. "Recent Ukrainian Writing." <u>Survey</u>. 46: 143-150, January, 1963.
    Discusses Ukrainian literature in the "thau" period in Khrushchev's era.

4. Monographs and Articles
<u>Concerning Single Authors.</u>

<u>Burevii, Kost'.</u>

1418. Shevelov, George. "Eduard Strikha, the History of a Literary Mystification." <u>American Slavic and East European Review</u>. XIV: 93-107, February, 1955.
    Story of an Ukrainian poet, Kost' Burevii, Born in 1888 and executed during Stalin's purges in 1934. After assuming a penname, Eduard Strikha, he convinced his contemporaries that Strikha was a different person than Burevii.

<u>Dray-Khmara, Mykhaylo.</u>

1419. Asher, Oksana. <u>A Ukrainian Poet in the Soviet Union</u>. New York, Svoboda, 1959. 49 p.

1420. Asher, Oksana. "Dray-Khmara's Poetical Creativeness." <u>Ukrainian Quarterly</u>. 13: 355-365, December, 1957 and 14: 77-83, March, 1958.
    Concerns poetry of Mykhaylo Dray-Khmara, a well-known Ukrainian poet, a neo-classicist, who died in slave labor camp. Written by the poet's daughter.

1421. Asher, Oksana. "Ukrainian Poet Dray-Khmara on the Ukrainian Literary Life under the Soviets." Ukrainian Quarterly.
13: 255-264, September, 1957.
    Excerpts from the diary of Mykhaylo Dray-Khmara, com-
piled by his daughter, in which he tells of Ukrainian
literary life in the Ukraine from 1924-1934.
    Concerns life story and poetry of Mykhaylo Dray-Khmara.

1422. Asher, Oksana. "A Ukrainian Poet's Fate in the Soviet
Union." Ukrainian Quarterly. 13: 127-137, June, 1957.
    Life and death of Mykhaylo Dray-Khmara.

Franko, Ivan.

    Ivan Franko, born in 1856, died in 1916. Prominent
Ukrainian poet, novelist, playwright, scholar (history,
history of Ukrainian literature, economic and social
history of Ukraine) and political leader.

1423. Manning, Clarence A. Ivan Franko. New York, Ukrainian
Society, 1938. 32 p.
    Life and works of Ivan Franko.

1424. Rudnycka-Antonovych, Maryna. Frankiana in American and
Canadian Libraries. Winnipeg, Shevchenko Foundation for
Ukrainian Free Academy of Sciences, 1955. 32 p.
    A union list of works on and by Ivan Franko in American
and Canadian libraries. In Ukrainian with English title.
Regular symbols of concerned libraries used.

1425. Berlstein, Alfred. "The Figure of Adam Mickiewicz in Ivan
Franko's Life." Annals of the Ukrainian Academy of Arts
and Sciences in the U. S. 6: 1372-1380. 1958.
    The role played by the life and works of the prominent
Polish poet, Adam Michiewicz, in the life of Ivan Franko.

1426. Bida, Constantine. "Religious Motives in the Scholarly
Works of Ivan Franko." Etudes Slaves et East Europeans.
1: 104-116 and 1: 139-145, 1956.
    Concerns Franko's works from the area of literature
and folklore and also includes other fields.

1427. Chizhevsky, Dmitry. "Ivan Vyshenskyi." Annals of the
Ukrainian Academy of Arts and Sciences in the U. S. 1:
113-126, 1951.
    About one of the most famous works of Ivan Franko,
"Ivan Vyshenskyi."

1428. Derzhavyn, Volodymyr. "The Corypheus of Ukrainian Literature." Ukrainian Review, London. 3: 35-40. September,
1956.

Ivan Franko and his influence on Ukrainian literature.

1429. Doroshenko, Volodymyr. "Ivan Franko as a Scholar."
Ukrainian Quarterly. 12: 144-151, June, 1956.
      Contributions of Ivan Franko in the area of Ukrainian
poetry, history and history of Ukrainian literature.

1430. Gaboda, Mary. "Ivan Franko's First Love." Ukrainian
Review, London. 14: 54-65. December, 1967.
      Ivan Franko's love for Miss Olha Roshkevych.

1431. Hordynsky, Sviatoslav. "Moses, the Conscience of the
People." Ukrainian Quarterly. 12: 152-157. June, 1956.
      "Moses," a poem by Ivan Franko on a biblical theme
was a powerful factor in the national renaissance of the
Ukrainian people.

1432. Manning, Clarence A. "The Literary Work of Ivan Franko."
Ukrainian Quarterly. 12: 118-125. June, 1956.
      Deals with the literary works of Ivan Franko from the
beginning, and with his translations from foreign
literatures.

1433. Manning, Clarence A. "Sculptor of the Modern Ukrainian
Nation." Ukrainian Quarterly. 12: 101-109, June, 1956.
      Franko influenced growth of Ukrainian nationalism
resulting in the Ukrainian anti-Russian resistance.

1434. Masiutko, Mykhaylo. "Ivan Franko, the Fighter for Freedom
and Unity of the Ukrainian People." Ukrainian Review,
London. 18: 70-76, December, 1971.
      Translation of an article from the undercover Ukrains'-
kyi Visnyk (Ukrainian Herald) no. 4.

1435. Ovcharenko, Maria. "Stress in Ivan Franko's Poetry."
Annals of the Ukrainian Academy of Arts and Sciences in
the U. S. 8: (1-2/25-26) 121-140. Bibl. footn.

1436. Rich, Vera. "Ivan Franko and the English Poets." Ukrainian Quarterly. 22: 122-128. 1966. Bibl. footn.
      About influence of English poets on Ivan Franko and
Franko's translations of English poetry.

1437. Siehs, Karl. "A Great European Mind: Ivan Yakovych
Franko." Ukrainian Review, London. 13: 3-15. September,
1966.

1438. Stakhiv, Matthew. "Social and Economic Ideas of Ivan
Franko." Ukrainian Quarterly. 12: 134-143. June, 1956.
      Exposition of the political and economic views of Ivan
Franko, who although a socialist, opposed Marxism and

based his views on Christian morality.

1439. Starchuk, Orest. "Ivan Franko: A Ukrainian Interpreter of Shakespeare." Canadian Slavic Papers. 2: 106-110, 1957.
     About Franko's translations of Shakespeare's plays into Ukrainian language.

1440. Sydoruk, Ivan. "Moses of Ivan Franko." Ukrainian Quarterly. 13: 159-167, June, 1957.
     An analysis of the poem. Author discusses importance of the poem in the Ukraine and its universal influence.

1441. Ukrains'ke Tovarystvo Druzhby i Kulturnoho Zv'yazku z Zarubizhnymu Krainamy. Ivan Franko, 1856-1916. On the Occasion of His 110th Birth Anniversary. Translated by N. Demidenko. Kiev, 1966. 18 p.
     Translation of a publication of a Soviet Society for contacts with foreign countries.

1442. Vytanovych, Ilya. "Political Views of Ivan Franko." Ukrainian Quarterly. 12: 126-133, June, 1956.
     Political views of Ivan Franko were based on a demand for freedom for all nations.

1443. Yendyk, Rostyslav. "Ivan Franko against Communism." Ukrainian Review, London. 3: 14-16. December, 1956.
     Soviet propaganda presents Ivan Franko as a Communist and partisan of the idea of Ukrainian-Russian unity. Views expressed in his works show the opposite.

Franko, Ivan. Works.

1444. Franko, Ivan. Boa Constrictor and Other Stories. Translated from the Russian by Fainna Solasko. Moscow, Foreign Languages Publishing House, 1957. 293 p. illus.
     Added t.p. in Russian. A Novel and selection of short stories. Translation done not from Ukrainian originals but from Russian translation.

1445. Franko, Ivan. Ivan Franko, the Poet of Western Ukraine. Selected poems. Translated with a biographical introduction by Percival Cundy. Edited by Clarence A. Manning. New York, Greenwood Press, 1968 (c1948). 265 p. port.
     Re-publication of selected poems of Ivan Franko with biographical sketch by translator.

1446. Franko, Ivan. Moses. New York, United Ukrainian Organizations of the U. S., 1938. 93 p.

Translation of one of the most prominent poems of
Ivan Franko.

1447. Franko, Ivan. <u>Poems and Stories</u>. Translated by John Weir.
Toronto, Ukrains'ka Knyha, 1956.   341 p.
   Selection of poems and introduction.

1448. Franko, Ivan. <u>A Voice from Ukraine</u>. Biographical sketch
and translation from the works of Ivan Franko, by Percival
Cundy. Roland, Man., B.E. Buffy and Co.,   74 p.
   Selection of the works of Ivan Franko translated by
Percival Cundy. Includes a biographical sketch.

1449. Franko, Ivan. <u>Zachar Berkut</u>. Translated by Theodosia
Boretsky. New York, published by translator, 1944. 230 p.
   First English translation of this historical novel
set in the 13th century.

Hohol, Mykola.

   An Ukrainian-born writer. Born 1813-died 1852. Major
part of his adult life was lived in Petersburg (Lenin-
grad) or abroad. Part of his writings (a novel, short
stories, and plays) have Ukrainian topics. Other novels
and plays -- predominantly Russian satyrical. Therefore,
both Ukrainians and Russians claim him as their national
writer. In Ukrainian and Russian writing the name is
Hohol and is spelled the same way (like Ukrainian).
When we transliterate it into English from the original
Ukrainian it will be Hohol, and from Russian it will be
Gogol because of the different pronunciation of the
Cyrillic "H" in both languages.

1450. Bogojavlensky, Marianna. <u>On the Development and Concept</u>
<u>of Religious Thought in Gogol</u>. Philadelphia, University
of Pennsylvania, 1959. 137 p.
   Unpublished doctoral dissertation concerning religious
views of Hohol.

1451. Debreczeny, P. A. <u>A Study of Gogol's Style</u>. London,
University of London, 1960.
   Unpublished doctoral dissertation.

1452. Ehrlich, Victor. <u>Gogol</u>. New Haven, Yale University Press,
1969. 230 p.
   A biography of Hohol and analysis of his works.

1453. Luckyj, George S. N. <u>Between Gogol and Sevcenko: Polarity</u>
in the Literary Ukraine, 1798-1847. Cambridge, Mass., Harvard University Press, 1971. 211 p. (Harvard series in
Ukrainian Studies.)

Consists of seven chapters. In separate chapters the
author discusses Ukrainian historians and folklorists,
classicists and romanticists. He discusses Hohol, a
writer claimed by historians of both literatures--
Ukrainian and Russian. Mentions the prominent Ukrainian
poet of the 19th century, Taras Shevchenko. He also
discusses Brotherhood of St. Cyril and Methodius. Final
chapter gives authors conclusions and a comparison of
both authors and their lives, works and their relations
to Ukraine and Ukrainians.

1454. Magarshack, David. Gogol: A Life. London, Faber & Faber,
       1957. 329 p.

1455. Ovcharenko, Maria M. Gogol (Hohol) and Osmachka. Charles-
       ton, Va., Winnipeg, Ukrainian Free Academy of Sciences,
       1969. 48 p. (Ukrainian Free Academy of Sciences. Sla-
       vistica, no. 64.)
           Comparison of Mykola Hohol with the prominent Ukrainian
       author of 20th century Todos (Theodore) Os'machka.

1456. Pfeffer, Carl R. "The Comparisons in Gogol's 'Dead Souls'."
       State College, Pa., University of Pennsylvania, 1958.
           Unpublished doctoral dissertation dealing with rich-
       ness of comparisons peculiar to works of Mykola Hohol.

1457. Stilman, Leon. Nikolai Gogol. Historical and Biographical
       Elements in His Creative Personality. New York, Columbia
       University, 1952.
           Unpublished doctoral dissertation discussing elements
       of Hohol's works.

1458. Yurieff, Zoya. Gogol as Interpreted by Russian Symbolists.
       Cambridge, Mass., Radcliffe College, 1956.
           Unpublished doctoral dissertation discussing interpre-
       tation of Hohol by Russians.

1459. Besushko, Volodymyr. "Nicholas Gogol and Ukrainian Litera-
       ture." Ukrainian Quarterly. 16: 263-268, 1960.
           Author states that Hohol, being of Ukrainian origin
       was interested in Ukrainian culture, folklore and songs,
       and that trends in Ukrainian literature contemporary to
       Hohol influenced his works.
           He wrote some works on Ukrainian topics. His Russian
       language was rich in Ukrainian components. Hohol
       influenced Ukrainian literature. Some of his works were
       dramatized and were material for Ukrainian operas.

1460. Chizhevsky, Dmitry. "Gogol Artist and Thinker." Annals
       of the Ukrainian Academy of Arts and Sciences in the U. S.
       2: 261-278. Summer, 1952.

Artistry and philosophy of Hohol.

1461. Malaniuk, Euhen. "Hohol-Gogol." Ukrainian Review, London.
14: 55-69. September, 1967. Bibl. footn.
    Ukrainians and Russians both claim that Hohol belongs
    to them.

1462. Manning, Clarence A. "Gogol and Ukraine." Ukrainian
Quarterly. 6: 323-330. Autumn, 1950.
    Mykola Hohol had no political concern for Ukraine's
    independence but in his writings he was an Ukrainian.
    All of his positive characters were Ukrainians and the
    negative ones Russians.

1463. Stromecky, Ostap. "Ukrainian Elements in Mykola Hohol's
'Taras Bulba'." Ukrainian Quarterly. 25: 350-361, 1969.
Bibl. p. 360-361.

Hohol, Mykola - Works.

1464. Gogol, Nikolai. Evenings Near the Village of Dikanka.
Moscow, Foreign Language Publications, n.d. 277 p.

1465. Gogol, Nikolai. Evenings Near the Village of Dikanka.
Stories ed. by beekeeper Rudi Panko (Tr. by Ovid Gorchakov,
il. by A. Kanevsky.) New York, Ungar Publishing Co., 1960.
276 p.
    The same: Atlantic Paperbacks, 1966. 277 p.

1466. Gogol, Nikolai. Evenings on a Farm Near Dikanka. New
York, Alfred A. Knopf, 126. 306 p.
    A collection of short stories on various Ukrainian
    themes.

1467. Gogol, Nikolai Vasilevich. Mirgorod. Included also:
The Old World Landowners, Taras Bulba, Wii, Ivan Ivanovich
and Ivan Nikiforovich. Translation with an introduction
by David Magarshack. New York, Farrar, Straus, 1962. 275 p.
    Most of the included works have Ukrainian themes.

1468. Gogol, Nikolai Vasilevich. Taras Bulba and Other Tales
with the Inspector General. Introd. by Nikolai Andreyev.
New York, Dutton, 1962. 410 p.
    Inspector General, a play criticizing corruption of
    Czarist administration.

1469. Gogol (Hohol), Nikolai Vasilevich. Taras Bulba: the
Classic Epic of the Ukrainian Cossacks. Ed. by Andrew
Gregorovich. Toronto, Acropolis Press, 1962. 171 p.

1470. Gogol, Mykola. Taras Bulba: Tale of the Cossacks. Translated by Isabel F. Hapgood, illustrated by Zenya Gaye. New York, Alfred A. Knopf, 1931. 284 p.
Taras Bulba, a historical novel with fictitious characters, depicts the struggle of Ukrainian Kosaks against Polish domination.

1471. Ray, Deborah. The Fair at Sorochintsi. A Nikolai Gogol story, retold and illustrated by Deborah Ray. Philadelphia, Macrae Smith, 1969, 31 p.
Hohol's fantastic tale with character from Ukrainian folklore retold for children.

Honchar, Oles.

1472. Sverstiuk, Yevhen. "Cathedral in Scaffoldings." Reflections on O. Honchar's novel "Sobor," (Cathedral). Ukrainian Review, London. 17: 23-48, September. 1960.
Translation of excerpts from author's larger work, "Sobor u ryshtovanni" (Cathedral in Scaffolds), circulated as an underground publication in the Ukraine, smuggled abroad and published here without the knowledge or permission of the author. Appears both in Ukrainian original and in excerpts in English translation. Deals with russification of the Ukraine and with Russian fellow-travellers among Ukrainians.

Kosach-Kvitka, Laryssa.

A prominent Ukrainian poetess born 1872 and died 1913. Known better under penname Lesya Ukrainka.

1473. Skrypnyk, Mary. Lesya Ukrainka: A Heritage for Today and Tomorrow. Toronto, Kobzar Publishing Co., 1971. 35(11) p. illus. ports.
On p. 37-46 article of V. I. Kassian; Lesya Ukrainka in etchings.

1474. Ukrains'ke Tovarystvo Druzhby i Kulturnoho Zv'yazku z Zarubizhnymy Krainamy. Glorious Daughter of the Ukrainian People: In Commemoration of the 50th Death Anniversary of Lesya Ukrainka. Kiev, 1963. 15 leaves and portfolio (25 plates including illus., facsims, and portraits).
A commemorative publication of an official Soviet Ukrainian agency for contacts with foreign countries.

1475. Cundy, Percival. "Lesya Ukrainka." Ukrainian Quarterly. 2: 252-264.
Biography and discussion of works.

1476. Derzhavyn, Volodymyr. "The Dramatic Works of Lesya Ukrain-

ka." Ukrainian Review, London. 3: 34-42, June, 1956.
   Author discusses dramatic works of Laryssa Kosach-
Kvitka.

1477. Kuchar, Roman. "'Orgy' the Tragedy of Individual and
   National Dignity." Ukrainian Review, London. 17: 17-24.
   June, 1970.
      Author discusses one of the plays of Lesya Ukrainka
   and deciphers its idea.

1478. Manning, Clarence A. "Lesya Ukrainka and Don Juan."
   Modern Language Quarterly. 15: 42-48, 1955.

      Author discusses the play "Kaminnyi Hospodar" (A Stone
   Host), an Ukrainian version of Don Juan.

1479. Manning, Clarence A. "New England in Lesya Ukrainka 'In
   the Wilderness'." Comparative Literature. 8: 136-141,
   1956.
      Author discusses description of New England in play
   "W Pushchi" (In the Wilderness) by Laryssa Kosach-Kvitka
   depicting life of American pioneers.

1480. Pazuniak, Natalia. "Lesya Ukrainka--Ukraine's Greatest
   Poetess." Ukrainian Quarterly. 27: 237-252, 1971.

1481. Rudnyckyj, Jaroslav B. "Afrika in Life and Work of Lesya
   Ukrainka." Ukrainian Review, London. 17: 49-57, 1970.
   Bibl. footn.
      Discusses visits of Laryssa Kosach-Kvitka to North
   African resorts and African plots in her works.

1482. Svitlychnyi, Ivan. "Steel Does Not Rust." Ukrainian
   Review, London. 18: 38-44, June, 1971.
      Translation of an article by a prominent Ukrainian
   literary critic, published in monthly "Dnipro," concerning Laryssa Kosach-Kvitka and her works.

                Kosach-Kvitka, Laryssa - Works.

1483. Kosach-Kvitka, Laryssa. Lesya Ukrainka: Life and Works.
   Selected works translated by Vera Rich. Editor Konstantine Bida. Toronto, published for the Women's Council of
   the Ukrainian Canadian Committee by the University of
   Toronto Press, 1968. 259 p.
      This volume includes a large essay on the life and
   works of Laryssa Kosach-Kvitka and a selection of her
   poetry and plays. Selected for translation are her
   plays with well-known international themes: The Orgy,
   Kassandra and Kaminnyi Hospodar (The Stone Host).

1484. Kosach-Kvitka, Laryssa. The Spirit of Flame. Translated by Percival Cundy. New York, Bookman Associates, 1950. 320 p.

    A selection of poetry and plays by Laryssa Kosach-Kvitka with a large introductory section on the poetess and her works by the translator.

1485. Kosach-Kvitka, Laryssa. V. Katakombakh. Dramatychna Poema. In the Catacombs. Dramatic Poem. Kyiv, Mystetstvo, 1971. 86 p. plates.

    Parallel Ukrainian text and English translation. Article on the author and her play in Ukrainian and English by Babyshkin. Dramatic poem on life of the first Christians in Rome. It is a camouflaged denunciation of the official Russian Orthodox Church.

Kotlyarevs'kyi, Ivan.

1486. Manning, Clarence A. "Ivan Kotlyarevsky." Ukrainian Quarterly. 26: 164-170, 1970.

1487. Rich, Vera. "Ivan Kotlyarevsky: an Appreciation." Ukrainian Quarterly. 25: 331-334, 1969.

Kotsiubynskyi, Mykhailo.

1488. Ukrains'ke Tovarystvo Druzhby i Kulturnoho Zv'yazku z Zarubizhnymy Krainamy. "Mikhailo Kotziubinskyi: Lecture Notes." 14 p. n.p., n.d.

    Publication of a Soviet Ukrainian Agency for Cultural contacts with foreign countries.

Kulish, Mykola.

1489. Dyky, Luba M. "Some Aspects of the 'Sonate Patetique' by Mykola Kulish." Annals of the Ukrainian Academy of Arts and Sciences in the U. S. 11(1-2/31-32): 109-128. Bibl. footn.

    Concerns the "Sonate Patetique," a play by Ukrainian playwright, liquidated during Stalin's purges. The play depicts the beginning of the revolution in the Ukraine and the struggle of the three concurrent forces: Ukrainian nationalism, Russian nationalism and Communism.

1490. Manning, Clarence A. "Mykola Kulish and the Ukrainian Communists." Ukrainian Quarterly. 11: 256-263, 1955.

    Life and works of Mykola Kulish.

1491. Revutsky, Valerian. "The Prophetic Madman: the Peoples
       Malakhii, a Play by Mykola Kulish." Canadian Slavonic
       Papers. 1: 45-56, 1961.
            Discusses a play "Narodnyi Malakhii" by Mykola Kulish
       depicting, like "Sonate Patetique," the struggle of
       Ukrainian and Russian nationalism and Communism in the
       Ukraine in the time of the revolution of 1917.

                    Malaniuk, Euhen.

1492. Derzhavyn, Volodymyr. "A Poet of His Epoch: to Mark the
       60th Birth Anniversary of Yevhen Malaniuk." Ukrainian
       Review, London, 4: 25-32, Autumn, 1957.
            About the prominent Ukrainian poet and essayist who
       worked between two wars and after the second World War
       died in the U. S.

1493. Halaichuk, Maia. "The History of Ukraine as Seen by Yevhen
       Malaniuk." Ukrainian Review, London. 4: 33-42. Autumn,
       1957.
            Concerns political views of Yevhen Malaniuk.

          Orest, Mykhailo, Pseud. See Zerov, Mykhailo.

                  Potebnia, Alexander.

1494. Fizer, John. Psychologism in Russian Literary Scholar-
       ship. Alexander Potebnia and His School. New York,
       Columbia University, 1960.
            Unpublished doctoral dissertation. Concerns prominent
       Ukrainian linguist of 19th century.

1495. Shevelov, George. "Alexander Potebnia as a Linguist."
       Annals of the Ukrainian Academy of Arts and Sciences in
       the U. S. 5: 1079-1111, 1956.

1496. Vetukhiv, Oleksa. "Towards an Understanding of Potebnia:
       Critical and Bibliographical Observation." Annals of the
       Ukrainian Academy of Arts and Sciences in the U. S. 5:
       1112-1116, 1956.

               Prokopovych, Teophan.

1497. Shevelov, George. "On Teophan Prokopovich as Writer and
       Preacher in Kiev Period." Cambridge, Harvard Slavic
       Studies. 2: 211-223, 1956.
            Discussion of the Ukrainian churchman and writer of the
       17th century.

1498. Yendyk, Rostyslav. "Markian Shashkevych-Poet and Cultural
Pioneer of West Ukraine." Ukrainian Review, London. 9:
18-24, March-June, 1962. Port.
About an Ukrainian clergyman living in the first-half
of the nineteenth century, poet and civic leader. He
was the first in the Western Ukraine to start writing
in the Ukrainian language used by the people instead of
the out-of-dated macaronism used by his contemporaries
in writing.

Shevchenko, Taras.

1499. Andrusyshen, Constantine N. Ukrainian Literature and Its
Leading Light, Shevchenko. Winnipeg, Ukrainian Canadian
Committee, n.d. 32 p.
Shevchenko's important role in Ukrainian literature.

1500. Budynok-Musei T. H. Shevchenka. T. G. Shevchenko House-
Museum in Kiev. Autor-uporiadchyk V. H. Kasian. Redaktor
V. I. Kostiuk. Kyiv, Mystetstvo, 1964. 24 p. illus.
ports.
In Ukrainian and English. Description of Taras Shev-
chenko memorial museum.

1501. Centennial of Taras Shevchenko, 1861-1961. U 100-littia
Tarasa Shevchenka. Winnipeg, Ukrainian Canadian Committee,
1961. 32 p. illus.
English and Ukrainian.

1502. Doroshenko, Dmytro. Shevchenko, Bard of Ukraine. Jersey
City, N. J., Ukrainian Press and Book Company, 1936. 39 p.
Biographical sketch and evaluation of Shevchenko's
poetry.

1503. Doroshenko, Dmytro. Taras Shevchenko, the National Poet
of Ukraine, by D. Doroshenko, Professor at the University
of Prague with preface by Professor R. W. Seton Watson.
Prague, E. Wyrowyj, 1936. 58 p.
Life and works of Taras Shevchenko. His meaning to a
national renaissance of the Ukrainian people.

1504. Gregorovich, Andrew Svyatoslav. Ukrainian Youth Federation of Canada Presents the Life of the Poet. A tribute
to Shevchenko, O. Keefe Centre, October 11, 1964. Edited
by Andrew Gregorovich. Toronto, Ukrainian National Youth
Federation of Canada, 1964. 64 p. illus.
Transcript of speeches on an anniversary celebration
of Shevchenko's birth. Single speeches in English or
Ukrainian.

1505. Kovaliuk, Jeannete Yaroslava. Shevchenko and Pan-Slavic
       Ideas. New York, Shevchenko Scientific Society, 1962. 12 p.
       (Shevchenko Scientific Society. Papers, no. 20.)
            Taras Shevchenko, a member of the Brotherhood of St.
       Cyril and Methodius, expressed in his works panslavist
       ideas. His slogan was "let all Slavs become brothers."

1506. Lindal, W. J. Taras Shevchenko, His Message to Humanity.
       Winnipeg, Ukrainian Free Academy of Sciences, 1964. 14 p.
       (Ukrainian Free Academy of Sciences. Literature 9.)
            Political, social and ethical views of Taras Shevchenko.

1507. Lysiak, Julian. Archaisms in Poetical Works of Taras
       Shevchenko. Ottawa, University of Ottawa, 1952.
            Unpublished doctoral dissertation. Concerns language
       used by Taras Shevchenko.

1508. Mathews, W. Taras Shevchenko the Man and the Symbol. 2nd
       ed. Winnipeg, Ukrainian Free Academy of Sciences, 1961.
       24 p. (Ukrainian Free Academy of Sciences. Slavistica
       #41.)
            The importance of Shevchenko's ideas.

1509. Myshuga, Luke. Shevchenko and Women. Jersey City, N. J.,
       Ukrainian National Association, 1946. 94 p.
            Role of certain women in Shevchenko's life.

1510. Panchuk, Ivan. Shevchenko's "Testament." Annotated Com-
       mentary. Jersey City, N. J., Svoboda Press, 1965. 154,
       6 p.
            Series of essays discussing single parts and phrases
       of Shevchenko's "Testament."

1511. Polovy, Hannah. The World Is My Village: A Story of the
       Great Kobzar Taras Shevchenko, by Hannah Polovy and Mitch
       Sago. Toronto, the authors, 1964. 197 p.
            "Published on the occasion of the 150th anniversary
       of Taras Shevchenko's birth." Text in Ukrainian and
       English.

1512. Rylskyi, Maksym. Taras Shevchenko: a biographical sketch.
       Translated from the Russian by John Weir. Moscow, Progress
       Publishers, n.d. 78 p. illus. ports.
            Author a prominent Ukrainian poet.

1513. Shevchenko Jubilee Commemorative Committee. Taras Shev-
       chenko the Bard of People's Freedom. Collection of essays.
       New York, 1962. 144 p.
            Essays discussing the life and work of Shevchenko,
       especially his political and social views.

1514. Slavutych, Yar. Greatness of Taras Shevchenko. Edmonton, Slavuta Publishers, 1962. 11 p. illus.
An Eulogy.

1515. Smal-Stocki, Roman. Shevchenko Meets America. Milwaukee, Marquette University. Slavic Institute, 1964. 71 p.
Political and philosophical views of Shevchenko.

1516. Sokolyszyn, Aleksander. "Shevchenkology in English." Selected chronological bibliography of Taras Shevchenko's works, including works about him. New York. Shevchenko Memorial Committee. New York Branch, 1964. 58 p.
A bibliography compiled for the occasion of the unveiling of the Shevchenko monument in Washington, D. C.

1517. Taras Sevcenko, 1814-1861. A symposium edited by Volodymyr Mijakovs'kyi and George V. Shevelov on behalf of the Ukrainian Academy of Arts and Sciences in the United States. S'Gravenhage, Mouton, 1962. 302 p. (Slavic printings and reprintings, no. 31.)

1518. Ukrains'ke Tovarystvo Druzhby i Kulturnoho Zv'yazku z Zarubizhnymy Krainamy. The Ukraine Honours the Memory of Taras Shevchenko, n.p., n. d. 6 leaves and portfolio (42 illustrations).
A publication of an official Soviet Ukrainian Agency for cultural contacts with foreign countries.

1519. U. S. Congress. House of Representatives. 86th Congress. 2d Session. Document no. 445. Europe's Freedom Fighter, Taras Shevchenko, 1814-1861. A documentary biography of Ukraine's poet laureate and national hero. Washington, D. C., Government Printing Office, 1960. 45 p.
A collection of brief articles and excerpts from articles by Ukrainian and non-Ukrainian authors, concerning the life, works, political and social ideas of Taras Shevchenko.

1520. U. S. Congress 88th. Second Session. The Shevchenko Statue of Liberty in the Nation's Capital. Speeches of Hon. Edward J. Derwinski of Illinois (et al.) in the House of Representatives and Senate of the United States. Washington, D. C., Government Printing Office, 1964. 149 p.
Speeches, documents and articles concerning the erection of the Shevchenko monument in Washington, D. C.

1521. Boyko, Yurii. "Taras Shevchenko and West European Literature." Slavonic and East European Review. 34: 77-98, 1956.
The author gives evidence of Shevchenko's familiarity with West European literature through the analysis of his works, diary and correspondence.

1522.   Buyniak, Victor O.   "Shevchenko the Artist."   Slavonic
        Papers.   7: 143-158, 1965.
            Concerns Shevchenko as painter.   Available also in
        reprint.

1523.   Dickens, Charles.   "A South Russian Poet."   Ukrainian
        Quarterly.   3: 159-167.   Winter, 1947.   Bibl. footn.
            First reference to Shevchenko in American newspapers,
        published by Charles Dickens in May 5, 1877th issue of
        the weekly, "All the Year Around."

1524.   Dobriansky, Lev E.   "The Shevchenko Affair."   Ukrainian
        Quarterly.   20: 108-117.   Summer, 1964.   Bibl. footn.
            Concerns the Shevchenko monument in Washington, D. C.

1525.   Doroshenko, Dmytro.   "Bard of Ukraine," in Europe's Free-
        dom Fighter, Taras Shevchenko, 1814-1861.   (See entry 1519)
        p. 9-17.

1526.   Dziuba, Ivan.   "The Cleansing and Living Fire."   Ukrainian
        Review, London.   14: 24-32.   June, 1967.
            Role of Shevchenko for Ukrainians as viewed by a young
        prominent Ukrainian literary critic.

1527.   Franko, Ivan.   "On the Anniversary of T. Shevchenko:
        Speech Delivered in 1903."   Ukrainian Review, London.   12:
        32-40.   March, 1965.
            Eulogy of Shevchenko by Ivan Franko.

1528.   Giergelewicz, Mieczyslaw.   "Shevchenko and World Literature,"
        in U Stolittia Smerty Shevchenka. Dopovidi . . . Philadel-
        phia, 1962.   p. 19-32.
            An article on familiarity and influence of Shevchenko
        with and on world literature in proceedings of scholarly
        session of the Philadelphia Branch of the Shevchenko
        Scientific Society in memory of death anniversary of
        Shevchenko.

1529.   Horniatkevyc, Damian.   "Problems in the Evaluation of
        Sevcenko's Art as a Painter," in Taras Sevcenko, 1814-1861
        . . . (See entry no. 1517) p. 127-135.

1530.   Kirkonnell, Watson.   "The Shevchenko Centennary."   Ukrainian
        Quarterly.   17: 50-60, Spring, 1961.

1531.   Kravtsiv, Bohdan.   "Taras Shevchenko's Poetry in Foreign
        Translations," in Taras Shevchenko. Povne Vydannia Tvoriv
        Chicago, M. Denysiuk 1959-1964 v. 12, p. 9-26.
            Preface to volume of translations of Shevchenko's poetry
        in foreign languages.

1532.   Lenza, Anthony.   "Taras Shevchenko--a Knight of Freedom."

Horizons. 8: 43-48, 1967, no. 2.

1533. Maksymovych, Volodymyr. "The Shevchenko Centennial."
Ukrainian Review, London. 8: 43-52, September, 1961.

1534. Malaniuk, Euhen. "Shevchenko and Ukrainian National Idea."
Ukrainian Review, London. 11: 38-55, June, 1955.
        Political and social views of Shevchenko.

1535. Malaniuk, Euhen. "The Way to the True Shevchenko."
Ukrainian Review, London. 11: 27-38. Port. December, 1964.
        Philosophical views of Shevchenko.

1536. Manning, Clarence A. "Education of Shevchenko." Shevchenko
Scientific Society. Proceedings of the Historical-Philosophical Section. 1: 55-61, 1951.
        Shevchenko completed his formal education in Vilna and
in St. Petersburg at the Academy of Arts. He continued
to educate himself through reading widely in foreign
languages and through association with the contemporary
Russian intelligencia.

1537. Manning, Clarence A. "English Translations of Shevchenko,"
Souvenir Book of the Unveiling and Dedication of the Taras
Shevchenko Monument at the Ukrainian National Association
Estate, Kerkhonson, New York, Sunday, June 16, 1957. Jersey
City, N. J. The Ukrainian National Association, 1957, p.
14-15.
        List of translations in English of Shevchenko's poetry
and list of his English, American and Ukrainian transla-
tors.

1538. Manning, Clarence A. "Taras Shevchenko, the Poet of Ukraine."
Ukrainian Quarterly. 9: 118-126. Spring, 1953.
        Political views of Shevchenko.

1539. Mijakovskyj, Volodymyr. "Shevchenko in the Brotherhood of
Saint Cyril and Methodius." In Taras Sevcenko, 1814-1861.
Symposium. (See entry no. 1517.)
        About relations of Shevchenko to the Brotherhood, its
effect on his poetry and Shevchenko's influence on
Brotherhoods ideology.

1540. Naidko, I. "Shevchenko in Slovakia, 1861-1917." Ukrainian
Review, London. 17: 68-75, June, 1970.
        Translation from the periodical Slovenska Literatura,
(Bratislava). 11: 101-116, 1962, no. 2. About transla-
tions of poetry of Shevchenko and writings on him in
Slovakian.

1541. Odarcenko, Petro. "Sevcenko in Soviet Literary Criticism."

In Taras Sevcenko, 1814-1861. A Symposium. (See entry no.
1517, p. 252-302. Bibl. footn.
Misrepresentations of Shevchenko's works and ideas by
Soviet literary critics.

1542. Odarcenko, Petro. "The Struggle for Sevcenko," in Annals
of the Ukrainian Academy of Arts and Sciences in the U. S.
3: 824-827.
Soviet authorities changed attitude toward Shevchenko
according to their political needs. At one time they
considered him a bourgoise nationalist and later as a
supporter of Ukrainian-Russian amity. At present he is
considered as an enemy of the Ukrainian nationalists.

1543. Shevelov, George. "The Year 1860 in Sevcenko's Work," in
Taras Sevcenko, 1814-1861. A Symposium. (See entry no.
1517. p. 37-61.
Analysis of Shevchenko's poetry in the last year before
his death.

1544. Shlemkevych, Mykola. "The Substratum of Sevcenko's View
on Life," in Taras Sevcenko, 1814-1861. A Symposium. (See
entry no. 1517) p. 37-61.
Shevchenko's philosophy.

1545. Simpson, George M. "The Political Significance of Taras
Shevchenko," in Kanads'ke Naukove Tovarystvo imeny Shevchenka. Zbirnyk Materialiv Naukovykh Konferentsii ch. 6.
Toronto, 1962, p. 112-123.
Political and social views of Taras Shevchenko and
their influence on development of the Ukrainian national
consciousness.

1546. Smal-Stocki, Roman. "The Stature of Shevchenko in the
Past and Present," in U Stolittia Smerty Shevchenka;
Dopovidi. Philadelphia, Oseredok Pratsi Naukovoho Tovary-
stva imeny Shevchenka, 1962. p. 91-97. Bibl. footn.
Transcript of a lecture held on a conference honoring
Shevchenko.

1547. Smal-Stocki, Stepan. "Shevchenko's Mind and Thought," in
Annals of the Ukrainian Academy of Arts and Sciences in
the U. S. 2: 227-238.
Translation of an Ukrainian article by a student of
Shevchenko in which he points out Shevchenko's ideas on
honesty, truth, ethics, religion and liberty.

1548. Svoboda, Victor. "Shevchenko and Belinsky." Slavonic and
East European Review. 40: 168-183. December, 1961, no. 94.
Attitude of Russian critic Belinsky to Shevchenko.

1549. Svoboda, Victor. "Shevchenko and Censorship." <u>Ukrainian</u>
<u>Review</u>, London. 8: 13-22. March, 1961 and 9: 25-32,
March-June, 1962.
Russian censorship and the works of Shevchenko.

1550. Svoboda, Victor. "Some Recent Shevchenkiana from the
American Continent." <u>Slavonic and East European Review</u>.
43: 179-188, December, 1964.
Bibliographical survey.

1551. Welyhorsky, Ivan. "English Echoes in the Stories of Taras
Shevchenko." <u>Ukrainian Quarterly</u>. 12: 360-364. December,
1956.
Shevchenko's works reveal wide acquaintance with the
leading English authors and their literature.

1552. Zajcew, Pavlo. "Sevcenko's Creative Process." <u>Taras</u>
<u>Sevcenko, 1814-1861. A Symposium</u>. (See entry no. 1517)
p. 107-126. Bibl. footn.

Shevchenko, Taras - Editions of Works.

1553. Shevchenko, Taras. <u>The Kobzar of Ukraine</u>. Translated by
A. J. Hunter. Winnipeg, 1922. 144 p.
Selection of the poetry of Shevchenko with illustrations.

1554. Shevchenko, Taras. <u>Poems-Poesies - Gedichte</u>. Munich,
Molode Zhyttia, 1961. 116 p.
Selection of Shevchenko's poetry in English, French and
German translations.

1555. Shevchenko, Taras. <u>The Poetical Works of Taras Shevchenko--</u>
<u>the Kobzar</u>. Translated from Ukrainian by C. H. Andrusyshen
and Watson Kirkonnell. Published for the Ukrainian Canadian
Committee. Toronto, University of Toronto Press, 1964.
563 p.
It is the first complete translation of poetical works
of Taras Shevchenko, done by an Ukrainian and a non-
Ukrainian, both students of Shevchenko. Introduction and
footnotes by C. Andrusyshen.

1556. Shevchenko, Taras. <u>Selected Works, Poetry and Prose</u>. Moscow, Progress Publishers, 1964. 469 p.

1557. Shevchenko, Taras Hryhorovych. <u>Selections</u>. Translated by
John Weir. Toronto, The Ukrainian Canadian, 142 p. illus.
facsim. ports.

1558. Shevchenko, Taras Hryhorovych. <u>Song of Darkness. Selected</u>
<u>Poems</u>. Translated from the Ukrainian by Vera Rich. With

preface by Paul Selder. A critic essay by W. R. Matthews. Introduction and notes by Victor Svoboda. London, Mitre Press, 1961. 128 p.
   A young English poetess and student of Ukrainian problems, translated thirty-eight poems of Taras Shevchenko.

1559. Shevchenko, Taras. Taras Shevchenko: Selected Poems. Translated with an introduction by Clarence A. Manning. Jersey City, N. J., Ukrainian National Association, 1945. 217 p.
   Biographical and critical introduction by Prof. Clarence A. Manning with selection of poems translated by C. A. Manning.

1560. Shevchenko, Taras. Zapovit, English Translations in John Panchuk. Shevchenko's Testament. (See entry no. 1510.) Supplement p. 9-18.
   On pages 9-10 of supplement list of published English translations of Shevchenko's "Zapovit" (Testament) on p. 11-18 selected English translations.

Shevelov, George - Bibliography.

George Shevelov, an outstanding Ukrainian linguist, professor of Columbia University.

1561. Hursky, Jacob P. "Linguistic Studies of Prof. George Y. Shevelov." Ukrainian Quarterly. 25: 159-164. 1969.

Stefanyk, Vasyl.

1562. Klynovyi, Iurii, pseud. "Vasyl Stefanyk's Heroes in Reality." Ukrainian Quarterly. 28: 28036, 1972.
   Account written by scholar of Stefanyk who knew him intimately for decades.

Symonenko, Vasyl.

1563. Bedrii, Anathole W. "The Concept of Man in the Works of Vasyl Symonenko." Ukrainian Review, London. 17: 61-67.

1564. Bedrii, Anathole. "Vasyl Symonenko--1935-1963, Troubadur of Ukraine's Freedom" ABN Correspondence. 17: 18-21, 1966, no. 2.
   About an Ukrainian poet of the younger generation. In his poetry and diary he vehemently attacked Soviet colonialism and imperialism.

1565. Dziuba, Ivan. "Speech Commemorating the 30th Birthday of

Vasyl Symonenko." <u>ABN Correspondence</u>.   17: 3-9, 1966, no. 1.

1566. Dziuba, Ivan. "Vasyl Symonenko." <u>Ukrainian Review</u>, London.
14: 43-49, March, 1967.

1567. Shankovsky, Ihor. "He Had No Time to Waste." <u>ABN Corres-
pondence</u>. 17: 16-21, 1966, no. 6.
        About the brief but very active life of Symonenko who
died at the age of 28.

1568. Shankovsky, Ihor. "Thirteen Short Stories by V. Symonenko."
<u>Ukrainian Review</u>. 17: 33-42, 1970. March. Bibl. footn.

1569. Shankovsky, Ihor Peter. "Vasyl Symonenko and His Background." <u>Ukrainian Review</u>, London. 14: 20-38, March,
1967. 14: 33-43, June, 1967, and 14: 44-55, December, 1967.
        Circumstances and undercurrent trends in Ukraine
which helped to form the political and social philosophy
of Vasyl Symonenko.

Svitlychny, Ivan.

1570. Zinkevych, Osyp. <u>Svitlychny and Dziuba, Ukrainian Writers
Under Fire</u>." Baltimore-Toronto, Smoloskyp, 1966. 52 p.
        About two literary critics of the younger Ukrainian
generation who mercilessly attacked Soviet imperialism
and colonialism in Ukraine. Dziuba's book <u>Internationalism
or Russification</u> has been smuggled abroad and published
here both in Ukrainian and in English.

Vilinska-Markovych, Maria.

1571. Cundy, Percival. "Marko Vovchok." <u>Ukrainian Quarterly</u>.
3: 116-125, Winter, 1947.
        Story of the life and works of the Ukrainian short-
story writer, Maria nee Vilinska Markovych who used penname Marko Vovchok.

1572. Slavutych, Yar. "Marko Vovchok: An Ukrainian Scourge of
Russian Serfdom." <u>Ukrainian Quarterly</u>. 14: 363-367, 1958.
        On the centenary of the publication by Maria Markovych
(Marko Vovchok)((pseud.)) under her pseudonym "Tales of
the Common People," the author cites the importance of
this collection as a protest against Russian imperialism
and serfdom.

Yavorsky, Stefan.

1573. Shevelov, George. "Stefan Yavorsky and the Conflict of Ideologies in the Age of Peter I." Slavonic and East European Review. 30: 40-62, no. 74. December, 1971.
     Yavorsky, a writer and a churchman, accepted the call of Czar Peter the Great to reorganize the Russian Orthodox Church, even though he disagreed with the official Russian Church policy.

Zerov, Mykhaylo.

1574. Slavutych, Yar. The Poetry of Mykhaylo Orest and Its Background. Philadelphia, University of Pennsylvania, 1955. 128 p.
     Unpublished doctoral dissertation concerning the life, works and philosophy of the Ukrainian poet, Mykhaylo Zerov who used pen-name of Mykhaylo Orest.
     Available in microfilm of Xerox copy at the University Microfilms, Inc., Ann Arbor, Michigan. Abstract in Dissertation Abstracts. (Publication no. 13.433.)

1575. Slavutych, Yar. "Mykhaylo Orest a Thinker in Poetry." Canadian Slavonic Papers. 12: 97-107, no. 2, Summer, 1970.
     Also available in reprint.

Zilinskyi, Ivan.

1576. "In Memory of Ivan Zilinskyi, Professor and Researcher of Ukrainian Language." Shevchenko Scientific Society. Proceedings of the Philological Section. II: 59-63. Photo.
     Deals with the prominent Ukrainian linguist Professor Ivan Zilinskyi.

5. Monographs or Articles Concerning Single Works, Types of Works, or Literary Forms.

The Aeneid.

1577. Manning, Clarence A. "The Aeneid of Kotlyarevsky." Classical Weekly. 36: 182-185. December 7, 1942.
     Discusses a parody of Virgil's Aeneid written and published in 1798 by Ukrainian poet and playwright Ivan Kotlyarevskyi. It was the first literary work published in the contemporary Ukrainian language. Dialect of Poltava District used by Kotlyarevskyi emerged as the standard Ukrainian language.

Alliteration in the Old Ukrainian Epic Literature.

1578. Chizhevsky, Dmitry. "On Alliteration in Ancient Russian Epic Literature." Russian Epic Studies, edited by R. Jacobson and E. J. Simmons. Philadelphia, American Folklore Society, 1949. P. 125-130.
     Alliteration was a distinctive feature of early Ukrainian literary works. To medieval Ukrainian literature author refers as Russian.

Apocrypha.

1579. "The Homily of Adam in Hades to Lazarus." Slavonic and East European Review. 10: 244-252. December, 1931.
     An early Ukrainian apocrypha translated from old Church Slavic into Ukrainian by Mykhailo Hrushevsky, a prominent Ukrainian historian and literary critic.

Byliny.

1580. Hapgood, Isabel Florence. The Epic Songs of Russia, New York, Charles Scribner Sons, 1886. 358 p.
     Prose translation of early Ukrainian historical songs called "byliny"--"the songs of the past," preserved in oral form in Northern Russia, but they are of Ukrainian origin. Characters of byliny are predominantly Ukrainian.

1581. Magnus, Leonard. The Heroic Ballads of Russia. Reprint of 1921 edition. Fort Wilmington, N. Y., Kennikut, 1967. 210 pages.
     Prose translation of byliny.

Dumy.

1582. Andrusyshen, Constantine H. "The Dumy: Lyrical Chronicle of Ukraine." Ukrainian Quarterly. 3: 134-144. Winter, 1947.
     Deals with "Dumy" epic Ukrainian ballads with historical and social settings, popular in Ukraine in the 16th and 17th centuries.

Epic Poetry.

1583. Jacobson, Roman and Ernest J. Simmons. Russian Epic Studies. Philadelphia, American Folklore Society, 1949. 223 p. Also: New York, Kraus reprints, 1970.
     A collection of articles in English as well as one in French on old Ukrainian literature (referred to as Rus-

sian). Concerned chiefly with "Tale of Ihor's Armament," and other Ukrainian epics.

Tale of Ihor's Armament.

1584. Besharov, Justinia. "Imagery of the Igor's Tale in the Light of Byzantine-Slavic Poetic Theory. Leiden, E. J. Brill, 1956. 115 p.
    Deals with imagery of the 12th century masterpiece of Ukrainian literature "Tale of the Ihor's Armament," and traces influences of contemporary Byzantine Rhetoric on the unknown author.
    Also an unpublished doctoral dissertation: Besharov, Justinia. The Imagery of the Igor Tale in the Light of a Byzantine Text on Rhetoric.

1585. Chaplenko, Vasyl. The Language of the Slovo o Polku Ihoreve. Winnipeg, Ukrainian Free Academy of Sciences, 1950. 28 p. (Ukrainian Free Academy of Sciences, Slavistica, no. 7.)
    Concerns the problem of language in the "Tale of Ihor's Armament," a very important problem in the controversy over whether "Tale" is an old Ukrainian or old-Russian literary masterpiece. In Ukrainian in English resume'.

1586. Cizevska, Tatjana. Glossary of the Igor's Tale. The Hague, Mouton, 1966. 405 p. (Slavic printings and reprintings, 53.)
    Latin bibliography, p. 17-28. Kyryllovskaya byblyohrafyia, p. 27-63.

1587. Cizevska, Tanja. The Vocabulary of the Igor Tale Compared with Other Old Russian Texts. Cambridge, Mass., Radcliffe College, 1955.
    Unpublished doctoral dissertation. Compares vocabulary of "Tale" with other contemporary literary monuments of Kyiv Rus' referred here as "Russia."

1588. Menger, Karl Heinrich. The Oriental Elements in the Vocabulary of the Oldest Russian Epos "The Igor's Tale"-- "Slovo o Polku Igoreve." New York, Linguistic Circle of New York, 1951. VI, 98 p. (Supplement to Word v. 7. Monograph no. 1.) Bibl. footn.

1589. Shajkovich, Vladimir. The Tale of Ihor: Studies on the Question of Its Authenticity. Trends in the History of Its Criticism. Philadelphia, University of Pennsylvania, 1953. 141 p.
    Unpublished doctoral dissertation revealing different

schools of criticism and suggesting new methods of appraisal.

Available in microfilm or Xerox copies from University Microfilms, Inc., Ann Arbor, Michigan. (Publication no. 5616.) Abstract in Dissertation Abstracts.

1590. Bida, Constantine. "Linguistic Aspects of the Controversy Over the Authenticity of the Tale of Ihor's Campaign." Canadian Slavonic Papers. 1: 76-88, 1956.
Role of the linguistic research in the controversy over the authenticity of the "Tale of Ihor's Campaign."

1591. Gronicki, Andrew von. "Rainer Maria Rilke's Translation of the Ihor Song." Russian Epic Studies. (See entry no. 1583.) p. 179-202.
Translation of the "Tale of Ihor's Campaign" by prominent German poet with introduction and notes by the author of the article.

1592. Hordynsky, Sviatoslav. "The Poetic and Political Aspects of the "Tale of Ihor's Campaign." Ukrainian Quarterly. 5: 20-28, 1949.
Poem depicts the struggle of early Ukrainians with Asiatic invaders.

1593. Hordynsky, Sviatoslav. "The Problem of Rhytm in the 'Tale of Ihor's Campaign'." Shevchenko, Scientific Society. Proceedings of the Philological Section. I: 28-31.
An abstract of lecture held on one of the sessions of the above mentioned Section.

1594. Kriedl, Manfred. "The First Polish Translation of the 'Slovo'." Russian Epic Studies. (See entry no. 1583.) p. 171-178.
Discusses a translation of the "Tale of Ihor's Campaign" in the Polish language.

1595. Manning, Clarence A. "Classical Influences on the 'Slovo'." Russian Epic Studies. (See entry no. 1583.) p. 87-97.
In this article passages of the "Slovo" are cited which prove the author's familiarity with classical Greek and Latin literature.

1596. Sharleman, M. "The Song of Ihor," from the Aspect of Natural Science. Ukrainian Review, London. 10: 39-61. September, 1963. Bibl. p. 60-61-
References to nature (trees, animals, sun, etc.) in "Slovo."

1597. Schlauch, Margarett. "Scandinavian Influence on the 'Slovo'." Russian Epic Studies. (See entry no. 1583.) p. 99-124.

1598. Solov'yev, Aleksander. "New Traces of the 'Igor Tale' on the Russian Literature." Harvard Slavic Studies. 1: 73-83, 1953.
Influence of the "Slovo" on the 16th century Russian literary epic "Slovo o Pogibeli Russkyia Zemli."

1599. Ward, Dennis. "On Translating 'Slovo o Polku Igoreve'." Slavonic and East European Review. 36: 502-512, 1958.
Account of the problems of translating the Tale of Ihor's Armament into modern languages.

1600. Yarmolinsky, Avram. "The 'Slovo' in English." Russian Epic Studies. (See entry no. 1583.) p. 203-233.
An appraisal of the various English translations of "Slovo."

Editions of Text of "Slovo o Polku Ihoreve."

1601. Prince Ihor's Raid against the Polovtsi. Translated by Paul C. Crath, versified by Watson Kirkonnell. Saskatoon, P. Mohyla Ukrainian Institute, 1947. 14 p.
Translation in verse.

1602. Slovo o Polku Igoreve. The Song of Igor's Campaign. A epos of the twelfth century. Translated from old Russian by Vladimir Nabokov. New York, Vintage Books, 1960. 134 p.

Translations from Other Languages in Ukrainian.

1603. Zujewskyj, Oleh. The Problem of Ukrainian Artistic Translation. Philadelphia, University of Pennsylvania, 1962. 156 p.
Unpublished doctoral dissertation. Author considers translation as an artistic activity. After Kotlarevsky's parody of "Aeneis" there was an opinion that the Ukrainian language was good only for burlesque translation. Artemovskyi Hulak proved that one can make also good translations in the Ukrainian language. Author discusses the Kharkiv School of translators, mentions so prominent translators from foreign literatures as Panteleimon Kulish and Ivan Franko and the first translation of Shakespeare's sonets in Ukrainian language by Ihor Kostetsky.
Dissertation has been microfilmed by the University Microfilms, Inc. and abstracted in the Dissertation Abstracts no. 62-4357.

Vseslav Epos.

1604. Jacobson, Roman and Marc Sheftel. "The Vseslav Epos."
Russian Epic Studies (See entry no. 1583.) p. 13-86.
A discussion of an Ukrainian "bylina" (a medieval historical song) on legendary prince Vseslav who was also
mentioned in the "Tale of Ihor's Campaign."

6. Linguistic and Literary Relations
of Ukraine with Neighboring Peoples.

1605. Borovskyi, Mykhailo. Ukrainian Topo-and Anthroponymy in
the International Botanical Terminology. Winnipeg, Ukrainian
Free Academy of Sciences, 1955. 64 p. (Ukrainian Free
Academy of Sciences. Onomastica, no. 9.)
Study of Ukrainian terms in the international termino-
logy of botany. In Ukrainian with English abstract.

1606. Coleman, Marion Moore. Klonowicz and Ukraine: Introduction
to the Poem Roxolania. Milwaukee, Wisconsin, Marquette
University. Slavic Institute, 1963. 18 p.
About so called Ukrainian school in Polish literature,
a group of Polish writers living or born in Ukraine and
their interest in Ukraine and its problems. Klonowicz,
author of the above mentioned poem "Roxolania" belonged
to this group.

1607. Czizhevsky, Dmitry. "Mickiewicz and Ukrainian Literature,"
in Laurence, S. Thomas. Adam Mickiewicz in World Literature, Berkeley, California, University of California Press,
1956. p. 409-435.
On influence of Adam Mickiewicz a prominent Polish poet
on Ukrainian literature.

1608. Doroshenko, Dmytro. "Shakespeare in Ukrainian." Slavonic
and East European Review. 9: 708-713, March, 1931.
A bibliography of known translations of Shakespeare's
works in Ukrainian up to 1928.

1609. Leeming, N. "Polonisms in a 17th Century Ruthenian Text,"
in Slavonic and East European Review. volume 46, July,
1968, p. 282-314.
Author discusses polonisms in an Ukrainian manuscript
biography from 17th century.

1610. Mandryka, Mykyta. "The Influence of Shevchenko on Bulgarian
Poetry." Ukrainian Review, London. 11: 22-31, March,
1964.

1611. Rich, Vera. "Ivan Franko and the English Poets," in
Ukrainian Quarterly. 22: 122-128. Summer, 1966. Bibl. footn

Discusses Franko's knowledge of English literature and its role as a source of inspiration and ideas. Samples of Franko's translations of English poetry.

1612. Shevelov, George. "On Slavic Linguistic Interrelations." Ukrainian influences on the Polish language in the 16th and 17th centuries. Annals of the Ukrainian Academy of Arts and Sciences in the U. S. 3: 696-730, 1953.
   Review of a book by a Polish linguist about foreign influences on the Polish language in the 16th and 17th centuries.

1613. Shevelov, George. "The Problem of the Polish-Ukrainian Linguistic Relations from the Tenth to the Fourteenth Century." Word. 8: 329-349, 1952.

1614. Sydorenko, Alexander. "Kievan Scholars in Muscovy." Horizons. 8: 31-42, 1967. Bibl. footn. p. 39-42.
   The brain drain from Ukraine to Moscow.

7. Ukrainian Fiction.

(See also subdivision: Works on some authors in chapter 4. Ukrainian Literature-Single Authors.)

1615. Almedingen, E. M. Young Mark. New York, Farrar, Straus and Giroux, 1967. XLI, 178 p.
   Based on the life story of the prominent Ukrainian opera singer Marko Poltorats'kyi (1729-1795).

1616. Bloch-Halun, Maria. Aunt America. New York, Atheneum, 1963. 148 p.
   Grade school level story. Encounter of two worlds: An Ukrainian girl and her aunt who came to visit her family in the old country.

1617. Bloch-Halun, Marie. Bern, Son of Mikula. Illustrated by Edward Kozak. New York, Atheneum, 1972. 10, 177, 1 p. illus.
   Story for children based on Ukrainian history.

1618. Bloch-Halun, Marie. The Two Worlds of Damyan. New York, Atheneum, 1966. 169 p.
   For grade-school children. The author, a known American children's writer of Ukrainian origin, describes conflict between the education   a Soviet-Ukrainian child gets at home and in school, pioneer organization, etc.

1619. De, Alexander. Without Tears. Poems. London, The Mitre Press, 1967. 67 p.

1620. Domazar, Serhij. _Castle on the Voday_. Sydney, Australia, Zeta Press, 1971. 225 p.
   Translation from Ukrainian original.

1621. Ewach, Honore. _Ukrainian Songs and Lyrics_. Winnipeg, Ukrainian Publishing Company, 1933. 77 p.
   Translations of the Ukrainian poetry of the 19th and 20th centuries with brief biographies of the authors.

1622. Honchar, Oleksander Terentiovych. _Short Stories, by Oles Gonchar_. Translated from Russian by V. Shneerson, edited by J. Gibbins. Moscow. Foreign Languages Publishing House, 194?. 266 p. illus. (Library of Selected Soviet Literature.)

1623. Khvylovy, Mykola. _Stories from the Ukraine_. Translated by G.S.N. Luckyj. New York, Philosophical Library, 1960. 234 p.

1624. Korniichuk, Oleksander. _Wings: a Play in Four Acts_. Translated from the Russian by John Gibbons. Moscow, Foreign Languages Publishing House, 195?. 131 p. port. (Library of Selected Soviet Literature.)
   Play by the Soviet-Ukrainian playwright, written after Stalin's death. Critized by Soviet reviewers for its denouncement of Soviet bureaucracy. Published also in _News from the Iron Curtain_. December issue, 1955. p. 28-53 (Different translation).

1625. Kotsiubinsky, Mykhaylo. _Chrysalis and Other Stories_. Moscow, Foreign Languages Publishing House, 1958. 257 p.
   Translation of selected short stories by a prominent Ukrainian writer who died before the first World War.

1626. Kvitka, Hryhory. _Marusia_. Translated by F. R. Livesay. New York, E. P. Dutton, and Company, 1940. 219 p.
   Life and customs of the Ukrainian peasants is depicted in this novel with a setting in first half of the 19th century.

1627. Lamb, Harold. _The Curved Saber: the Adventures of Klith the Cossack_. Garden City, New York, Doubleday and Co., 1964. 568 p.
   Short stories depicting adventures of old Ukrainian Kosak Khlit in many countries of Assia. His Ukrainian identity and his ties with the Ukrainian Kosak Host-Zaporozhska Sich are stressed throughout the book.

1628. Luckyj, George Stepan Nestor. _Four Ukrainian Poets: Drach, Korotych, Kostenko, Symonenko_. Translated by Marta Bohachev-

sky-Chomiak and Danylo S. Struk. With an introduction by
George S. N. Luckyj. New York, Quicote, 1969. 83 p.
   Selection of poetry of four prominent Ukrainian poets
of younger generation with introduction on the poets.

1629. MacMillan, Anne. Levko. Toronto, Longman, Green, 1956.
159 p.
   A novel with the hero an Ukrainian boy living in Canada.

1630. Slavutych, Yar. Oasis, Selected Poems. New York, Vantage
Press, 1959. 63 p.
   Translation of selected poems by author.

1631. Songs of Ukraine with Ruthenian Poems. Translated by
Florence Randall Livesay. London, New York, Dent & Sons,
1916. 175 p.
   Translation of a selection of Ukrainian poetry. Terms
"Ruthenian" refers to the West Ukrainian authors where
the term "Ruthenian" ("Rusyn") was used before the first
World War to designate Ukrainians.

1632. Stefanyk, Wasyl. The Stone Cross and Other Stories. Toronto,
McCleland and Stewart, 1970. 164 p. port.
   Selection of short stories of a known West Ukrainian
author.

1633. Stelmakh, Mykhailo P. Let the Blood of Man Not Flow. Mos-
cow, Foreign Languages Publishing House, n.d. 325 p.
   Translation of a novel by an author from the Soviet
Ukraine.

1634. Stories of the Soviet Ukraine. Moscow, Progress Printers,
1970. 303 p.
   Selection of short stories by contemporary Ukrainian
writers translated from Ukrainian.

1635. Their Land. An anthology of Ukrainian short stories.
M. Luchkovich, ed. New York, Svoboda, 1964. 325 p.
   Preface by Clarence A. Manning. Introduction by Luke
Luciw. Biographical sketches by Bohdan Krawciw.

1636. Turiansky, Osyp. Lost Shadows. Translated from Ukrainian
by Andrew Mykytiuk. New York, Empire Books, 1935. 246 p.

1637. The Ukrainian Poets. Selected and translated into English
verse by C. H. Andrusyshen and Watson Kirkonnell. Toronto,
University of Toronto Press, for Ukrainian Canadian Committee, 1965. 500 p.
   Representative selection of Ukrainian poetry starting
with the Tale of Ihor's Campaign, through Dumy to
selection of 100 Ukrainian poets starting from philosopher

Skovoroda to the late Canadian poet Honore Evach. The selection reflects trends in Ukrainian poetry.

1638. West, Morris L. _The Shoes of the Fisherman_. New York, William Morrow and Co., 1963. 374 p.

A novel based on the life story of Cardinal Joseph Slipyj, Archbishop Major of the Ukrainian Catholic Church, who was for 18 years imprisoned by Soviet authorities for refusal to renounce his ties to the Holy See.

Good novel. But there are many distortions. For the author is not clear enough that Cardinal Joseph Slipyj or author's Gregory Lakota is not Russian but Ukrainian and does not consider Russian language his native language and Russia his home country.

1639. Khvylovyi, Mykola. "Puss in Boots." _Slavonic and East European Review_. 9: 187-197. June, 1930.

A translation of a political satire on the conditions in Soviet occupied Ukraine by a disappointed Ukrainian Communist who committed suicide to avoid arrest by the Russians.

1640. Kotsiubinsky, Michael. "Shadows of Forgotten Ancestors." Translated by Stephen Shumeyko. _Ukrainian Weekly_. January 27-March 16, 1940 (serial).

A novelette in which the author depicts the life and pre-Christian customs and beliefs of the Huzuls, the Ukrainian inhabitants of the Carpathian Mountains.

1641. Kulish, Panteleymon. "Black Council: Historic Novel of the 17th Century." Translated by Stephen Shumeyko. _Ukrainian Weekly_. August 8-September 18, 1943.

A historical novel depicting life of the Ukrainian Kosaks.

1642. Lutsiv, Luka. "Ukrainian Short Stories," in _Their Land, An Anthology of Ukrainian Short Stories_. (See entry no. 1635.) p. 7-14.

An introduction to a collection of Ukrainian short stories.

1643. Lyman, Leonid. "The Tale of Kharkiv." _Ukrainian Review_, London. 5: 50-73, March, 1958, 5: 38-50, June, 1958, 5: 41-50, September, 1958, 6: 63-72, March, 1959.

A novelette depicting the life of an Ukrainian student in Kharkiv before the outbreak of the Soviet-German war.

1644. "Volodymyr's Way." _Ukrainian Weekly_, 1957, nos. 192, 198, 202, 212, 217.

Translation (by Volodymyr Lukachyk) of the well-known medieval masterpiece concerning the education of future ruler--"Testament of the Volodymyr Monomach"--in which are found the precepts and instructions of an old Ukrainian ruler to his children.

XV. Ukrainian Art.

1. Ukrainian Art - General.

1645. Dmytriv, Olya, Comp. Ukrainian Arts. 2d edition. New York, Ukrainian Youth League of North America, 1955. 212 p. illus, plates.
   Articles by various authors on different types of Ukrainian art with an introduction by Professor Clarence A. Manning. Article on Ukrainian literature included.

1646. Nahai, V. Ukrainian Decorative Design. Kiev, The State Publishing Co., n.d. 10 p. 26 colored plates.
   Collection of illustrations with an explanatory article.

1647. Hordynsky, Sviatoslav. "Fine Art," in Ukrainian Arts (See entry 1645.) p. 125-139.
   History of Ukrainian fine arts from pre-historic time to the present. Includes history of Ukrainian fine arts in Ukraine and abroad.

1648. Hordynsky, Sviatoslav. "Ukrainian Art Past and Present." 33rd Annual of the Women's International Exposition, Ukrainian Section. New York, Ukrainian Women's Exposition Committee, 1956. 4 p.
   A pamphlet including an illustrated history of Ukrainian art from the pre-historic to the modern period, written by a painter and art critic.

1649. Hordynsky, Sviatoslav. "Ukrainian Underground Art," in the Ukrainian Insurgent Army in Fight for Freedom. New York, United Committee of the Ukrainian-American Organizations of New York, 1954. p. 91-94.
   Concerns illustrators of the underground publications of the Ukrainian Insurgent Army, especially noted graphic Nil-Khasevych.

2. Ukrainian Architecture.

1650. Povstenko, Oleksa. The Cathedral of St. Sophia in Kiev. New York, Ukrainian Academy of Arts and Sciences in the U.S., 1956. 446 p. (Its Annals v. VI.)
   Work written by a prominent scholar of Ukrainian archi-tecture. It describes a monument of Ukrainian architecture built in the 11th century. Numerous illustrations and

charts complete the work.

1651. Povstenko, Oleksa. Zolotoverkhyi Kyiv. (Kyiv with golden domes.) Washington, D. C., Author, 1957, 400 p.
      Monograph on Kyiv, its history and architecture with over 400 pictures. Text in Ukrainian with an English summary. English captions under pictures.

1652. Coleman, Arthur Prudden. "The Wooden Churches of Ruthenia." Art and Archeology. 34: 137-145, 1933.
      The author states that the wooden churches of Carpatho-Ukraine (referred to as Ruthenia) are not a product of oriental influences but a blending of the Byzantine and Ukrainian architecture.

1653. Conant, Kenneth John. "Novgorod, Konstantinople and Kiev in the Old Russian Church Architecture." Slavonic and East European Review. 22: 75-92. August, 1944.
      Influence of Byzantine architecture on the early Ukraine and Moscowia and the influence of Kievan architecture on neighboring countries.

1654. Kaye, Volodymyr J. "A Great Byzantine Slav Cathedral." Ukrainian Quarterly. 7: 256-258. Summer, 1951.
      Concerns the medieval cathedral in the old capital of the West Ukrainian principality, Halych, whose fundaments were discovered by the known Ukrainian and archeologist, Professor Yaroslav Pasternak.

1655. Ohloblyn, Alexander. "Western Europe and the Ukrainian Baroque: An Aspect of Cultural Influences at the Time of Hetman Mazepa." Annals of the Ukrainian Academy of Arts and Sciences in the U. S. 1: 127-137, 1951.
      Cultural influences from the West during Mazepa's time in relation to Ukrainian architecture.

1656. Sichynsky, Volodymyr. "Architecture," in Ukrainian Arts. (See entry no. 1653.) p. 143-152.
      History of the Ukrainian architecture beginning with the monumental structures in Greek settlements in the Southern Ukraine dating from the 8th century. The author shows that modern Ukrainian architects have made use of earlier styles.

1657. Sichynsky, Volodymyr. "Architecture and Art of the City of Lviv." Lviv. (See entry no. 135.) p. 149-165.
      An article by a noted Ukrainian art historian for a symposium on the capital of Western Ukraine, Lviv, published on the 700th anniversary of Lviv's founding.

1658. Sichynsky, Volodymyr. "Early Christian Architecture in Ukraine." Shevchenko Scientific Society. Proceedings of

the Historical-Philosophical Section. 1: 63-66, 1951.
A report of a lecture on early churches and cloisters in the Ukraine.

1659. Sichynsky, Volodymyr. "Ukrainian Architecture during the 17th and 18th Centuries." Ukrainian Quarterly. 7: 45-51, 1951.
Concerning the brilliant period of Ukrainian architecture called the "Kosak Baroque."

3. Ukrainian Painting and Graphic.

1660. Shramchenko, Mykola. In the Beginning. A Interpretation of the Old Testament. Biblical editing by John M. Paul. New York, Obolensky, 1962. 95 p.
Illustrations to Old Testament.

1661. Ukrainian Underground Art. Album of the Woodcuts made in the Ukraine in 1950, by the artist of the Ukrainian Underground, Nil Khasevych (Bey-Zot) and his disciples. Philadelphia, Prolog, 1952. 69 p.
Reprints from woodcuts made in underground publishing plants in the Ukraine and smuggled into the Western World.

1662. Cross, Samuel H. "The Mosaic Eucharist of St. Michael's (Kiev). American Slavic and East European Review. 6: 56-61, 1946.
Description of the medieval mosaics of an Ukrainian monastery called, "St. Michael with Golden Domes." It was built around 1069 and destroyed by Soviet authorities in 1936-37. Referred to by author as a Russian monument.

1663. Donzow, Dmytro. "Maria Bashkirzeva, a Crippled Glory." Ukrainian Review, London. 4: 27-30, March, 1957.
About a girl from an Ukrainian aristocratic family who in her short life won in Paris fame as a painter and socialite.

1664. Hordynsky, Sviatoslav. "Ukrainian Graphic Art." Ukrainian Quarterly. 4: 224-226, Summer, 1948.
History of Ukrainian graphic art with a list of contemporary Ukrainian graphics.

1665. Horniatkevych, Damian. "Shevchenko the Painter." Ukrainian Review, London. 8: 8-12, March, 1961 and 8: 41-52, June, 1961.
About the painting of Shevchenko who was a graduate of the Petersburgh Academy of Arts and Professor of Art in the University of Kyiv.

1666. Horniatkevych, Damian. "The Ukrainian Medieval Paintings on Polish Soil." Ukrainian Quarterly. 7: 162-169, 1951.
Paintings in the castles and churches in the different parts of Poland reveal the cultural influence of the Ukraine on Poland in the 14th and 15th centuries.

1667. "Maria Bashkirtseva, the Famous Ukrainian Paintress, 1860-1884." Ukrainian Review, London. 10: 75-80, June, 1963.

1668. Osinchuk, Mykhaylo. "Contemporary Ukrainian Paintings." Ukrainian Quarterly. 3: 345-354. 1947.
Twentieth century painting in Eastern and Western Ukraine.

1669. Osinchuk, Mykhaylo. "Icon." In Mykhaylo Osinchuk. Mystets'-Malar. New York, Nakladom autora, 1967. p. 24-29.
An English article in an Ukrainian autobiography. Concerns Ukrainian religious paintings (i.e. Icons) typical to the Eastern Christian rites.

1670. Sichynskyi, Volodymyr. "Shevchenko as Etcher and Painter." Ukrainian Quarterly. 5: 347-355, 1949.
Views of Shevchenko on art and his superiority over his Russian contemporaries. Discusses his work as a sculptor and etcher and his inventions of new etching methods.

1671. Stebelsky, Bohdan. "Mykola Burachok a Master of Ukrainian Impressionism." Ukrainian Review, London. 4: 44-49. June, 1957.
Life and interpretation of the work of a prominent Ukrainian painter.

1672. Tys, Jurij. "Victor Tsymbal." Ukrainian Review, London. 4: 44-49.

4. Ukrainian Sculpture.

1673. Alexander Archipenko. The World Ritchie Press, 1957. 80 p. plates.
Published on the occasion of an exhibition of Archipenko's works in the University of California at Los Angeles Art Galleries. Articles on Archipenko's life and works. Bibliography.

1674. Archipenko Exposition of Sculpture and Paintings in Ukrainian Pavillion at a Century of Progress, Chicago, 1933. Plates, lists of exhibits, press comments.

1675. Archipenko: Fifty Creative Years. By Alexander Archipenko and fifty art historians. New York, Techne, 1960. 109 p. 281 p. (30 in color).

Life and works of Alexander Archipenko.

1676. Archipenko, Alexander. Portrait of the Artist and Sixty-
six Illustrations. Berlin, Ukrainian Slovo, 1923. 28 p.
66 plates.
An Articles in Ukrainian and English about Alexander
Archipenko and his works.

1677. Karshan, Donald H. Archipenko: Content and Continuity,
1908-1963. Exhibition Kovler Gallery, Chicago. Pref. by
Marjorie B. Covler. Chicago, Covler Gallery, 1968. 64 p.
plates.
An exhibition catalog consisting predominantly of
reproductions of Archipenko's works. Chronology of
works. Description of exhibits. Preface and index.

1678. Karshan, Donald, ed. Archipenko: International Visionary.
Published for the National Collection of Fine Arts. Washington, Smithsonian Institution, 1969. 116 p. illus.
(part. col.) bibl.
Consists of excerpts from writings of Archipenko,
translations of two catalogs (from French) of Archipenko's
exhibitions in years 1912 and 1914 by Appolinaire, and of
article by Guy Habasque on the place of Archipenko in
the birth and evolution of contemporary sculpture. Photos
of Archipenko, his family and friends, his art works and
documents.

1679. Hordynsky, Sviatoslav. Kruk, Pavlos, Muchyn, Three
Ukrainian Sculptors. Munich, Association of Ukrainian
Plastic Artists, 1947. 39 p. 47 black and white plates.
Ukrainian with English abstract.

1680. Bauer, Isa. "Gregory Kruk, the Sculptor." Ukrainian
Review, London. 14: 68-72. March, 1967. Plates.

1681. Hordynsky, Sviatoslav. "The Art World of Archipenko."
Ukrainian Quarterly. 1: 219-226, 1955.

1682. Kruk, Gregory. "My Life Story." Ukrainian Review, London.
14: 72-77. March, 1967.

5. Ukrainian Music.

1683. Dziobko, J. My Songs: A Selection of Ukrainian Folksongs
in English Translation. Winnipeg, Ukrainian Canadian
Pioneer Library, 1958. 102 p.
Eighty-six Ukrainian folk-songs translated by Honore
Evach.

1684. Fomenko, Mykola. Ukrain'ki Molodi Pisni (Ukrainian Juvenile

Songs). New York, Ukrainian Institute of America, Inc., 1958 96 p.
  Sixteen Ukrainian songs, words by Ivanna Savyts'ka, with music for solo singer and piano by Mykola Fomenko. Text in both Ukrainian and English.

1685. Koshets, Alexander. Genetic Relationship and Classification of Ukrainian Ritual Songs. Winnipeg, Ukrainian Cultural and Educational Center, 1943. 13 p. illus.
  Discusses ritual songs which were very important in the lives of the Ukrainian people. Some of these songs are very old.

1686. Kovalsky, Humphrey. Ukrainian Folk Songs: A Historical Treatise. Boston, Stratford Company, 1925. 76 p.
  Excerpts of some songs are translated and included as illustrations.

1687. Simpson, George W. Alexander Koshetz in Ukrainian Music. Winnipeg, Ukrainian Cultural and Educational Center, 1945. 32 p.
  Concerns the prominent Ukrainian composer and conductor of the Ukrainian State Choir which toured Europe and America starting from 1919, Alexander Koshetz.

1688. 201 Ukrainian Folk Songs. Paris-New York, Ukrainian Music Publishing Co., 1943. 136 p.
  Songs have English texts.

1689. Wytwyckyj, Wasyl. Ukrainian Bandurist Chorus under the Direction of Volodymyr Bozhyk. 1951 p. Quarto, unpaged.
  History of Ukrainian folkmusic and folk instruments with special stress on Bandura. Five pages in a program of the Ukrainian Bandurist Chorus.

1690. Lasovskyj, Jaropolk. "Music in Ukraine under Soviet Rule." Ukrainian Review, London. 14: 94-95. Septemb 1967.

1691. Lutsiv, Volodymyr. "Kobza-Bandura" and "Dumy" and their significance in the "History of the Ukrainian People." Ukrainian Review, London. 13: 53-70. March, 1966. Bibl. P. 70.
  Article written by known bandurist and singer dealing with historical songs "dumy" performed usually to the accompaniment of the folk instrument kobza or bandura.

1692. Wytwyckyj, Wasyl. "Music" in Ukrainian Arts (See entry no. 1645, p. 155-180.)
  The influence of geography on Ukrainian music. Includes history of Ukrainian music from the earliest period, folk music and instruments, and contemporary Ukrainian composers and performers.

1693. Wytwyckyj, Wasyl. "Mykhaylo Hayvoronsky, the Bard of the Ukrainian Army." Ukrainian Quarterly. 6: 170-174, 1950.
    Concerns composer who lived in the United States from 1923 to his death in 1949.

6. Ukrainian Dance.

1694. Association of United Ukrainian Canadians. Ukrainian Folk-Dances and Others. Toronto, issued by National Executive Committee. Association of United Ukrainian Canadians, 196? 108 p. illus., plates, music.
    Textbook for study Ukrainian folk-dances.

1695. An Aid in Reading Choreography. Toronto? n.p. 196? 43 p. diags., music.

1696. Klymash, Bohdan, comp. Ukrainian Folk Dance. A Symposium. Toronto, Ukrainian National Youth Federation of Canada, 1961. 58 p.
    Eight essays on Ukrainian dances. One of them in Ukrainian.

1697. Shambough, Marie Effie. Folk Dances for Boys and Girls. New York, Barnes and Co., 1929. 143 p. music.
    Twelve Ukrainian folk dances with descriptions of the steps and costumes.

7. Ukrainian Moving Pictures and Theatre.

1698. Nemirovich-Danchenko, Vladimir Ivanovich. My Life in Russian Theatre. Translated from the Russian. New ed. London, Bless, 1968. 365 p. ports., illus., 12 plates.
    Reminiscences of an actor of Ukrainian origin who used to play in Russian theatre.

1699. Andrusyshen, Constantine H. "The Ukrainian Theater as a Political Factor." Ukrainian Quarterly. 3: 249-261, 1947.
    Role of the Ukrainian theatre in building up of an Ukrainian national consciousness.

1700. "Contemporary Drama in the Ukrainian SSR." Ukrainian Review, Munich. 2: 70-83, 1956.
    Ukrainian playwrights who live and work under Soviet regime are forced to falsify Ukraine's history.

1701. Halchenko, I. "The Soviet Film Industry in the Ukrainian SSR." Ukrainian Review, Munich. 8: 57-68. Bibl. footn.

1702. Heiman, Leo. "Ukrainian Nationalists in Soviet Film." Ukrainian Quarterly. 21: 142-147. Summer, 1965.

A former actor of Ukrainian Theatre "Berezil" closed
during Stalin's purges, describes the history and liquidation of this theatre.

1704. K-l, F. "The Great Ukrainian Film Producer." Ukrainian
Review, London. 3: 83-85. September, 1956.
    About prominent Ukrainian film regisseur, producer and
writer of film scripts, Alexander Dovzhenko.

1705. Poltava, Leonid. "The Ukrainian Film Industry in 1958."
Ukrainian Review, Munich. 9: 86-99.
    Concerns film industry in the Ukrainian-Soviet Socialist
Republic.

1706. Revutsky, Valerian. "Shevchenko and the Theatre." Taras
Shevchenko, Symposium. (See entry no. 1522.) p. 136-152.
    About interest of Taras Shevchenko in theatre, his
writing of plays, friendship with authors, etc.

8. Ukrainian Folk-art.

1707. Ostapchuk, Emilie, ed. Folk-art of Carpatho-Ukraine.
Toronto, Philip Ostapchuk, 1957. 152 p. illus. plates.
    Discussion of all types of folk-art of the Carpatho-
Ukraine, i.e., ceramics, woodcarvings, etc.

1708. Ruryk, Nancy R., ed. Ukrainian Embroidery, Designs and
Stitches. Winnipeg, Ukrainian Women Association of Canada,
1958. 130 p.
    Color plates and explanation of them.

1709. Burachynska, Lydia. "Folk Dress." Ukrainian Arts. (See
entry no. 1645.) p. 31-47, plates.
    History and description of Ukrainian costume from the
earliest period. Arranged by districts and periods.

1710. Hocij, Mychaylo. "Ukrainian Folk Art." Ukrainian Review,
London. 4: 34-55. December, 1957.
    Author discusses different types of Ukrainian folk-
art such as glass and metal-craft, etc., and also architecture. Discusses also the continuation of folk art
among Ukrainian exiles.

1711. Horniatkevych, Damian. "Ceramics." Ukrainian Arts. (See
entry no. 1645.) p. 73-79.
    History of the Ukrainian ceramics beginning with the
Trypillyan culture. Ukrainian china factories and
schools for study of ceramic art and the Soviet policy of
suppressing the Ukrainian style of pottery.

1712. Horniatkevych, Damian. "Kilim." Ukrainian Arts (See
    entry no. 1645, p. 83-91.)
        History of Ukrainian carpets from 977 A.D. through the
    workshops of the 18th century and a description of con-
    temporary Ukrainian carpets from the various geographic
    areas.

1713. Horniatkevych, Damian. "Wood Carving." Ukrainian Arts.
    (See entry no. 1645.) p. 63-70.
        Earliest preserved examples of Ukrainian wood carving,
    history of wood carving in the Ukraine, and a discussion
    of pyrography (carving with flames).

1714. Nenadkevych, Lydia. "Embroidery." Ukrainian Arts (See
    entry no. 1645.) p. 51-70.
        Types of embroidery, stitches and patterns identified
    with the various geographic areas. Includes church
    embroidery.

1715. Surmach, Gloria. "Easter Eggs." Ukrainian Arts. (See
    entry no. 1645.) p. 95-121.
        History of Ukrainian hand-painted Easter eggs (Pysanky).
    The ornament and technique of making "pysanky."
    Including Ukrainian Easter customs and their significance.

Miscellaneous.

1. Ukrainian Women.

1716. Povroznyk, Lubov. Ukrainian Women in the Modern Age. Lon-
    don, Association of Ukrainian Women in Great Britain, 1963.
    36 p.
        Facts on Ukraine. The role of Ukrainian women in
    Ukrainian life. The work also includes information on
    Ukrainian women authors.

1717. Women of Ukraine, Her Part on the Scene of History. Phila-
    delphia, Ukrainian Women's League of America, 1956. 48 p.
        Account of well-known Ukrainian women of the past and
    the present.

1718. Chyzh, Yaroslav. "Ukrainian Women and Their Organization,"
    in Jubilee Book of the Ukrainian Women's League of America,
    Commemorating the Fiftieth Anniversary of Its Founding.
    New York, Ukrainian Women's League of America, 1949. p.
    220-250.
        Role of Ukrainian women in the history of Ukrainian
    arts, literature, sciences and politics and the history
    of Ukrainian women's organizations in the old and new
    worlds.

1719. Mosichuk, Zenovia. "The Role of Women in the Liberation Struggle of the Ukrainian Nation." Ukrainian Review, London. 6: 54-62. Spring, 1959.

The author traces the struggle for liberation of the Ukraine beginning with the 19th century and the part played by Ukrainian women in this struggle.

2. Ukrainian Folklore.

1720. Bloch-Halun, Maria, editor and translator. Ukrainian Folk Tales translated from original collection of Ivan Rudchenko and Maria Lukianenko. Illus. by M. Hnizdovsky. New York, Coward McCann, 1964. 76 p.

Published also by M. Davis in 1965. Translation of selected Ukrainian folk tales with illustrations by Ukrainian painter M. Hnizdovsky.

1721. Ivanko and the Dragon. An old Ukrainian folk tale from the original collection of Ivan Rudchenko. Translated by Marie Halun Bloch. Illustrations by Yaroslava. New York, Atheneum, 1969. 48 p.

1722. Klymash, Robert Bohdan. The Ukrainian Winter Folksongs Cycle in Canada. Ottawa, National Museum of Canada, 1971. 156 p.

Ukrainian carols and other ritual folksongs of winter cycle collected among Ukrainian in Canada.

1723. Orlov, Damon D. Red Wedding. Chicago, Regnery and Company, 1952. 244 p.

Life and customs of the Ukrainian farmers in the Eastern Ukraine in the early 20th century.

1724. Osadcha-Janata, Natalia. Herbs Used in the Ukrainian Folk Medicine. New York, Research Program on the USSR and the New York Botanical Garden, 1952. 114 p. (East European Foundation, Mimeo series, no. 21.)

1725. Rudnyckyj, Jaroslav B., editor and translator. Ukrainian Canadian Folklore. Test in English translation. Winnipeg, Ukrainian Free Academy of Sciences, 1960. 232 p. (Ukrainian Free Academy of Sciences. Ukrainica Occidentalia, no. VII ((5)).)

Selection of samples of Ukrainian folk literature (tales, ritual songs, proverbs, etc.) collected among Ukrainian immigrants in Canada.

1726. Sechrist, Elizabeth Hoyt. Red Letter Days. Philadelphia, Macrae, 1940. 252 p.

About holidays of different religious and ethnic groups, and customs connected with these days. Information about Ukrainian Christmas and Easter customs is given under the heading "Ukraine."

1727. Vincenz, Stanislav. On the High Uplands: Sagas, Songs, Tales and Legends of Carpathians. Translated by N. C. Stevens. New York, Roy Publishers, 1956. 344 p.
      Folklore of the Huzuls, Ukrainian inhabitants of the Carpathian Mountains.

1728. Weiser, Francis X. The Easter Book. New York, Harcourt, Brace and Company, 1954. 214 p.
      Includes Ukrainian Easter customs and beliefs.

1729. Weiser, Francis X. Handbook of Christian Feasts and Customs: The Year of the Lord in Liturgy and Folklore. New York, Harcourt, Brace and Company, 1958. 366 p.
      Ukrainian customs with religious significance are referred to under the heading "Ukrainian." Includes further information under specific holidays with subheading, "Eastern Church."

1730. Zheleznova, Irina Lvovna, Comp. Folks Tales from Russian Lands. New York, Dover, 1969. 278 p.
      Second edition of 1963 publication by the same compiler under title: A Mountain of Gems. Fairy tales of the peoples of the Soviet lands. Also includes Ukrainian fairy tales.

1731. Jopson, Norman B. "Early Slavonic Funeral Ceremonies." Slavonic and East European Review. 6: 59-67. June, 1947.
      Discusses an account by an Arab traveller, Ibn Fadlan, who in the 6th century A.D. travelled in the area of the present Ukraine. Contains an account of the funeral of a wealthy merchant.

1732. Nandris, G. "The Relations between Moldavia and Ukraine according to Ukrainian Folklore." Ukrainian Review, London. 5: 26-48, Spring, 1958.
      Refers to Ukrainian-Moldavian relations in Ukrainian folklore from the medieval period to the present.

1733. Odarchenko, Petro. "Drahomanov as Folklorist." Annals of the Ukrainian Academy of Arts and Sciences in the U. S. 2: 36-46, 1952.

1734. Odarchenko, Petro. "A Survey of Publications on Ukrainian Ethnography and Folklore in the Years 1957-1962." Annals of the Ukrainian Academy of Arts and Sciences in the U. S. 10(1-3): 92-110.
      A bibliographical survey.

1735. Senkiv, Ivan. "Yearning for Another Life in Ukrainian Folklore." Ukrainian Review, London. 12: 50-55. December, 1965.

1736. Smal-Stocki, Roman. "Taboos on Animals' Names in Ukrainian." Language. 26: 489-493, 1950.
    Magic associated with taboos on the names of certain animals such as the wolf or the bear, among the backwood people of the Ukraine.

1737. Stechishin, Savella (et al.). "Ukrainian Christmas Customs and Their Origins." Ukrainian Yearbook 1953-1954. p. 27-34.

1738. Woropay, Olexa. "Customs of Our People." Ukrainian Review, London. 16: 41-48. December, 1969, 17: 43-48, March, 1970, 17: 53-61, June, 1970, 17: 58-64. September, 1970, 17: 80-87, December, 1970, 18: 79-96, March, 1971.

1739. Woropay, Olexa. "Traditions of Harvest Time." Ukrainian Review, London. 2: 67-70, September, 1955.
    Description of harvest time customs practiced in the Ukraine.

1740. Woropay, Olexa. "Ukrainian Fairy Tales." Ukrainian Review, London. 2: 31-37. June, 1955.
    Discussion of Ukrainian fairy tales. Including translation of a typical Ukrainian fairy tale.

3. Biography.

Dzus, William.

1741. Bern, Donald Lawrence. An American in the Making, the Biography of William Dzus, Inventor. New York, William Barton Marsh Co., 1961. 140 p.
    The life story of an Ukrainian immigrant to the U. S. who became an inventor, made a fortune, and became a prominent Ukrainian philanthropist.

Gouzenko, Ihor.

1742. Gouzenko, Ihor. This Was My Choice. Gouzenko--A Story. Toronto, J. M. Dent., 1948. 324 p.
    Story of a cipher clerk at the Soviet Embassy in Ottawa, Canada, Ukrainian Ihor Gouzenko, who defected in 1945, furnished Western intelligence agencies information concerning Soviet espionage in Western States and helped them to counteract this espionage.

Kapytsia, Petro.

1743. Kapitsa, Petro Leonidovich. Peter Kapitsa on Life and

Science. Addresses and essays collected, translated and
annotated by Albert Parry. New York, MacMillan, 1968.
271 p.
    Selection of addresses and essays by prominent Soviet
atomic scientist of Ukrainian origin, Petro Kapytsia.

Makarenko, Anton, Educator.

1744. Makarenko, His Life and Work. Articles, talks and reminiscences. Moscow, Foreign Languages Publishing House, 1963.
279 p., illus., ports.
    Collection of essays, reminiscences, etc. of and by
    prominent Ukrainian educator, Anton Semenovych Makarenko
    (1888-1939).

Markievich, Constance, Countess.

1745. Marecco, Anne. The Rebel Countess: The Life and Times of
Constance Markievich. Philadelphia, Chilton, 1967. 330 p.
    Life story of Ukrainian Count Stanislav Markievich.
Plenty of information on the Ukraine and Ukrainians of
19th century.

Sas-Yavorsky, Alexander.

1746. Choate, Joe. The Best Answer is America: A Biography of
Dr. Alexander Sas-Yavorsky. New York, Vantage Press, 1959.
200 p., illus.
    This is a biography of a Louisiana veterinarian who
came as displaced person from the Ukraine. He won
$128,000 in 1958 in the $64,000 quiz.
    Many references to the conditions in Western Ukraine,
the closer home country of the biographee, during the
first and second world wars and in the displaced persons
camps.

Symyrenko, Volodymyr.

1747. Rozhin, Ivan. "Volodymyr Symyrenko." Ukrainian Review,
Munich. 8: 95-102. Bibl. p. 100-102.
    About known Ukrainian pomologist Volodymyr Symyrenko.

Tymoshenko, Stepan.

1748. Timoshenko, Stephen. As I Remember the Autobiography.

Translated from Russian by Robert Addis. Princeton, N. J.,
Van Nostrand, 1968. 430 p. port. illus.
   Autobiography of a prominent American scholar of
Ukrainian origin.

4. Miscellaneous

1749. The Art of Cooking Ukrainian Style. Vancouver. Ukrainian
Women's Association of Canada, 1966. 106 p.
   Traditional Ukrainian cookery as well as modern recipes.

1750. Gauk, Roma. Ukrainian Christian Names: A Dictionary.
Edmonton, Orma, 1961. 31 p.
   An alphabetically arranged list of Ukrainian names with
their ethymology.

1751. Greaves, A. V. and C. W. Roberts. The Trident Issues of the
Ukraine. Part 1. Kiev. Chesterfield, England, 1950. 24 p.

1752. Greaves, A. W. and C. W. Roberts. The Trident Issues of the
Ukraine. Part 2. Odessa. Chesterfield, England, 1950.
22 p.

1753. Roberts, C. W. The Trident Issues of the Ukraine. Part 3.
Kharkov, Yekaterinoslav and Poltava. Winchombe, West By-
fleet, England, 1953. 33 p.

1754. Roberts, C. W. The Trident Issues of the Ukraine. Part 4.
Podolia and the Postal Stationery. Ilminster, England, 1955.
39 p.

1755. Roberts, C. W. The Trident Issues of the Ukraine. Part 5.
Special Issues. Ilminster, England, 1956. 27 p.
   A series of monographs privately printed by the authors,
concerning the Ukrainian overprints on Russian and other
non-Ukrainian postage stamps called "Trident Issues"
because they were overprinted with the Trident--the state
emblem of the Ukraine.

1756. Setiroff, G. Slavonic Names in Greek and Roman Antiquities.
Winnipeg, Ukrainian Free Academy of Sciences, 1969. 23 p.
(Ukrainian Free Academy of Sciences. Onomastica, 37.)

1757. Stechishen, Savella. Traditional Ukrainian Cookery. 2d ed.
Winnipeg, Trident Press, Ltd., 1967. 497 p.
   Concerned chiefly with Ukrainian recipes for desserts,
appetizers, preserves and pickles.

1758. Ukraine and the 16th Olympic Games. Washington, D. C.,
Ukrainian World Committee for Sport Affairs, 1956. 28 p.
   Claim of the Ukrainian Soviet Socialist Republic's right
to participate in Olympic games as an independent country.

1759. Zinkevych, Osyp. _Ukrainian Olympic Champions_. New York, Ukrainian Information Service "Smoloskyp," 1968. 43 p. illus.
     Sketches of Ukrainians who earned medals of the Olympics as members of the Soviet Olympic Team.

1760. Trembicky, Walter. "The National Anthem of Ukraine." _Ukrainian Quarterly_. 27: 169-174, no. 2/1972. Bibl. p. 173-174.

1761. Trembicky, Walter. "The Taras Shevchenko Stamp." _Ukrainian Quarterly_. 25: 164-170. Bibl. footn.
     Taras Shevchenko in stamp issues.

Supplement.

In this Supplement we included items published since the basic part of this bibliography was completed or items which have been for various reasons either omitted or overlooked.

The arrangement of this Supplement is identical with the arrangement of the basic part of the bibliography. All entries of the Supplement have been included in the author's and subject indexes.

Selected Bibliography of Ukrainian Bibliography.

1762. Sokolyszyn, Aleksander. _Ukrainian Selected and Classified Bibliography in English_. New York-Munich-Chicago. Ukrainian Bibliographical and Reference Center. New York-Chicago, Ukrainica in English Series, 1.
     This is a master's thesis completed still in 1960 with recent references appended. It consists of two sections. Both are arranged by subjects and alphabetically arranged in single subjects. In the first section the entries are not annotated. In the second section the entries are annotated and numbered in each section. It includes books, pamphlets, parts of books and articles. It includes a large selection of small pamphlet publications issued in defense of Ukrainian freedom. Some entries which will fit in several subject areas are listed simultaneously in a few subject sections and tied up by see references.

1763. Gregorovich, Andrew. _Canadian Ethnic Groups Bibliography_. A selected bibliography of ethno-cultural groups in Canada and the Province of Ontario. Toronto. Department of the Provincial Secretary and Citizenship of Ontario, 1972. 208 p.

This bibliography includes over 2,100 entries and covers 50 ethnic groups. There are 46 general bibliographies covering all 50 ethnic groups in Canada. Special publications concerning single ethnic groups of Canada arranged by subjects.

Bibliographies of publications concerning single ethnic groups in Canada, including Ukrainians, are included. These are arranged alphabetically by the name of ethnic group. Entries in single bibliographies are arranged alphabetically by authors.

1764. Wynar, Lubomyr. Encyclopedic Directory of Ethnic Newspapers and Periodicals in the United States. Littleton, Colorado, Libraries Unlimited, Inc., 1972. 260 p.

This directory lists 943 periodicals issued in the U. S. by 43 ethnic groups either in their native language, in English, or in both.

Arrangement: Ethnic groups arranged alphabetically by name, in each group periodicals arranged alphabetically by title in two groups: in native language or in native language and in English and solely in English. All necessary information on each title is supplied, including price circulation, frequency, number of issues per year and language of publication.

A brief annotation characterizing each publication is added. Added are statistical tables analyzing publications of all ethnic groups and of single ethnic groups by name, frequency, circulation, number of issues per year and language of publication. An alphabetical index of listed periodicals is added.

There are included 72 Ukrainian periodical publications. Besides that there are listed 13 publications issued by the Carpatho-Ruthenians (a group of Ukrainians from Carpatho-Ukraine using an archaic dialect of Ukrainian language in their writings and calling themselves Ruthenians or Rusnaks) and one Kosak publication published in Russian, Ukrainian, and English languages.

Ukrainian Reference Books.

Libraries.

1765. Biblioteky Ukrains'koi RSR. Dovidnyk. Kharkiv, Knyzhkova Palata URSR, 1969. 186 p.

A directoгy of the most important libraries of the Ukrainian Soviet Socialist Republic. Geographically subdivided by Kyiv and "Oblast" (Districts). Subject, name and geographical index added.

<u>Professionals.</u>

1766. <u>Directory of Ukrainian Professionals in the United States</u>.
Chicago, Ukrainian Professional Organization of the United
States, 1939. 54 p.
    Alphabetically arranged list of the Ukrainian profes-
sionals. Each entry includes information about education,
profession, family, position, membership in professional
and Ukrainian organizations, office and home address.
Added index arranged by professions and alphabetically
in every profession.

<u>Part B.</u>

I. <u>Ukraine: Name.</u>

1767. Gregorovich, Andrew. <u>Ukraine, Rus' and Muscovy: A Selected
Bibliography of the Names</u>. Toronto, The New Review Books,
1971. 23 p.
    A bibliography of onomastics of the above mentioned
terms. Published also in <u>New Review</u>. 10: 193-213.

II. <u>UKRAINE - GEOGRAPHY.</u>

1. <u>Geography - General.</u>

1768. Boiko, Maksym. <u>Bibliographical Abstracts of Volhynian
Settlements XIX Century</u>. Bloomington, Indiana, Volhynian
Bibliographical Center, 1972. 199 p.

1769. Simpson, George Wilfred. <u>Ukraine</u>: A series of seven radio-
addresses given by George W. Simpson over the network
of the Canadian Broadcasting Corporation and one address
given by W. Swystun. Saskatoon, Sask., Ukrainian National
Federation of Canada, 1939. 3-15, 5-14, 3-19 p. port.

1770. Veryha, Vasyl and Bohdan Stebelsky. <u>Ukraine: A Synopsis</u>,
by Vasyl Veryha and Bohdan Stebelsky. Toronto, University
of Toronto, Ukrainian Students' Club, 1964. 30 p. illus.,
map.
    First author discusses the meaning of the terms
"Rus'," "Russia," and "Ukraine." Contains a discussion
(by the second author) of the Ukrainian folk-art.

2. <u>Ukraine - Description and Travel.</u>

1771. Daen, Leonid Abramovich. <u>Kiev, A Guide and Directory</u>.
Compiled by Leonid, Daen, Pavlo Poznyak and Mark Cherp.

Translated from Ukrainian by A. S. Mostetsky. 2d rev. and supplemented ed. Kyiv, Publishing House for Political Literature of the Ukraine, 1965. 187 p. illus. map. (fold. col. in pocket).

1772. **Kiev: Travel Guide**. Kiev, Novosti Publishing House, 1970. 224 p.

1773. Kohl, Johann George. **Russia:** St. Petersburg, Moskow, Kharkoff, Riga, Odessa, the German provinces of the Steppes and the Interior of the Empire. New York, Praeger, 1970. 530 p. (Praeger, scholarly reprints. Source books and studies in Russian history.)
  Reprint of a 1944 condensation of a travelogue which also includes some places in the Ukraine. Foreword by Harry Schwartz.

1774. Seymour, Henry Danby. **Russia on the Black Sea and Sea of Asof**. A narrative of travels in the Crimea and bordering provinces with notices of the naval, military and commercial resources of these countries. London, J. Murray, 1955. XXIV, 361 p. illus. 4 folded maps.
  Concerns Crimea and Sourthern Ukraine.

IV. UKRAINE - POPULATION.

1. Ukrainians.

1775. French, R. A. **The Settlement of Poles'ye, USSR**. London, University College, 1953.
  Unpublished doctoral dissertation.

1776. Nowosiwsky, Ivan N. **Bukovinian Ukrainians: a Historical Background and Their Self-determination**. Foreword by Matthew Stakhiw. Translated from Ukrainian by Walter Dushnyck. New York, Association of Bukovinian Ukrainians, 1970. 200 p. illus, maps, port. coat of arms, facsim.
  The author describes the development of the national consciousness of Bukovynian Ukrainians. The relations between the Ukrainian peasants and Rumanian boyars (big landowners). The cultural growth of the Bukovynian Ukrainians. Ukrainian and rusophile trends among the Bukovynian Ukrainians and the victory of the Ukrainian. The problem of the political self-determination of Bukovynian Ukrainians. National minorities in Bukovyna and their attitude to the Ukrainian problem. Bukovyna in Soviet historiography. Appendix: Documents.

2. Ukraine - National Minorities.

1777. Mendelson, Ezra. "From Assimilation to Zionism in Lvov:

The Case of Alfred Nossing." <u>Slavonic and East European Review</u>. 49: 521-534, no. 117, October, 1971.

1778. Mendelson, Ezra. "Jewish Assimilation in Lvov: the Case of Wilhelm Feldman." <u>Slavic Studies</u>. 28: 577-590, no. 4, December, 1969.

V. UKRAINIANS - ABROAD.

2. Ukrainians outside the USSR
(Except in the U.S. and Canada).

1779. Dushnyck, Walter. <u>Ukrainians in the Free World</u>. Jersey City, Ukrainian National Association, 1967. 23 p. illus.
Discusses various Ukrainian immigrant communities. Published on the occasion of the First Congress of Free Ukrainians.

3. Ukrainians in the U.S. and Canada.

a. History.

1780. Bociurkiv, Bohdan R. "Ethnic Identification and Attitudes of University Students of Ukrainian Descent: The University of Alberta Case Study," in <u>Inter-University Committee on Canadian Slavs</u>. Slavs in Canada. 3: 15-110, 1971.

1781. Foster, Mathew James. <u>Ethnic Settlement in the Barton Street Region of Hamilton</u>," 1921-1961. M.A. Thesis. Hamilton, Ontario, McMaster University, 1965.

1782. Fromson, Ronald David. <u>Acculturation or Assimilation: A Geographic Analysis of Residential Segregation of Selected Ethnic Groups</u>. Metropolitan Winnipeg, 1951-1961. M.A. Thesis. Winnipeg, Manitoba, The University of Manitoba, 1965.

1783. Hobart, C. B. <u>Persistence and Change: A Study of Ukrainians in Alberta</u> by C. W. Hobart, W. E. Kalbach, J. T. Borhek and A. P. Jacoby. Edmonton, Alta, University of Alberta Press for the Department of Sociology, 1966. 605 p. Maps. (Ukrainian Canadian Research Foundation. Canadian Centennial Series, 3.) Bibl.
A sociological study.

1784. Kuropas, Myron. <u>Ukrainians in America</u>. Minneapolis, Minnesota, Lerner Publications Company, 1972. 86 p. (The in America Series.) Illus.

Published in a series of publications for high school students dealing with single ethnic groups of the United States. In the first part the author discusses the history of the Ukraine from the pre-historic times until most recent.

In the following chapters the author presents the history of the Ukrainian community in the U.S., its organized life and contributions to the culture, science and economics of the U. S. The book is very richly illustrated. An index concludes the book.

1785. Makers of America. Editor: Wayne Moquin. General editor: Mortimer J. Adler and Charles Van Doren. Chicago, Encyclopedia Britannica. Educational Corporation, 1971. 10 v.

Some information about Ukrainian immigrants in the U.S. (farmers and miners) is based on out-of-date sources published in the 1940's.

1786. Porter, Richard P. R. Vancouver: The Role of Ethnic Origin in Population Distribution. B. A. Essay. Vancouver, B. C., The University of British Columbia, 1965. 40 p. illus.

1787. Ukrainian Canadian Research Foundation, Toronto. Reviews and Letters of Early Ukrainian Settlements in Canada, 1895-1900. Dr. Oleskiv's Role in the settlement of the Canadian Northwest, by Vladimir J. Kaye. Toronto, Published by the University of Toronto Press for the Ukrainian Canadian Research Foundation, 1965. 14 p. port. (Canadian Centennial Series.)

1788. Zadrozhny, John Thomas. The Development of Nationality Movement. Chicago, University of Chicago, 1963. 576 p.

An unpublished doctoral dissertation. The history of Ukraine with stress on the development of Ukrainian national consciousness. Attitude of the neighbors (Polish, Russians, a.o.) toward this development.

1789. Pohorecky, Zenon and Alexander Royick. "Anglicization of Ukrainians in Canada between 1895 and 1970. A case study of linguistic crystallization." Canadian Ethnic Studies, University of Calgary, volume I., no. 2. December, 1969.

1790. Sharan, Renata Maria. "Type of Ethnic Identification and Generational Position. A Study of the Ukrainian Immigrant Group in the U.S.A." Ukrainian Review, London. 18: 46-78, no. 3, 1971 and 18: 77-106, no. 4, 1971.

A Master's thesis.

1791. "Ukrainian Ethnic Community in America: A Symbol of Freedom." Ukrainian Quarterly. 28: 229-235, no. 3, 1972. Bibl. footn.

b. Culture and Education.

1792. Burstynsky, E. N. "Languages in Contact: Ukrainian and English." _Slavs in Canada_. 3: 149-255.
Describes English influences on Canadian Ukrainian.

1793. Cipyvnyk, Sonia Violet. _Educational Implications of Ukrainian-English Bi-lingualism in Saskatchewan_. M. Ed. thesis. Saskatoon, Saskatchewan, University of Saskatchewan, 1968.

1794. Duravetz, George N. _The Importance of Ukrainian Language Study_. A recommendation for the introduction of Ukrainian language instruction in Ontario secondary schools. The Educational Committee of the Ukrainian Canadian Committee in Toronto. Toronto, Ministry of Community and Social Services, (Government of Ontario), 1972. 52 p.

1795. Harasym, Carolyn Rose. _Cultural Orientation of Rural Ukrainian High School Students_. M. Ed. thesis. Calgary, Alta, The University of Calgary, 1969. XI, 128 p.
Unpublished Master's thesis.

1796. Harasymiv, Elaine Verchomin and Alexander Malycky. "Ukrainian Canadian Creative Literature--A Preliminary Check List of Imprints," in _Bulletin of the Research Centre for Canadian Ethnic Studies at the University of Calgary_. Volume 2, 1970, p. 205-225.
A bibliography of titles published in Canada by Canadian authors or concerning Canadian Ukrainians. 252 entries.

1797. Canadian Association of Slavists. _A Bibliography of Publications of Canadian Slavists_, by Daniel Dorotich, ed. Vancouver, B. C., University of British Columbia, 1967. 551 p.
Also includes Ukrainistic publications by Canadian Slavists.

1798. Jaenen, Cornelius J. "Ruthenian Schools in Western Canada, 1897-1919," in _Paedagogica Historica-International Journal of the History of Education_. 10: 517-541, no. 3, 1970. Bibl.

1799. Malycky, Alexander. "Ukrainian Canadian Periodical Publications. First Supplement." _Bulletin of the Research Centre for Canadian Ethnic Studies at the Calgary University_. Volume 2, 1970. p. 195-203.
Consists of a supplementary list of Canadian-Ukrainian periodicals and a separate list of Ukrainian periodicals in languages other than Ukrainian. Also a supplement concerning geographical distribution of these periodicals.

1800. Malycky, Alexander and Elaine Verchomin Harasymiv. "A
Preliminary Checklist of Studies on Ukrainian Creative
Literature." Part 2. Specific Studies." In Bulletin
of the Centre for Canadian Ethnic Studies at University
of Calgary. Volume 2, 1970. p. 229-244.
    A bibliography of monographic publications and articles
about Ukrainian Canadian literature. Some bibliographies
included. Includes 141 entries. Index of mentioned
authors is included.

1801. Malycky, Alexander. "University Research on Ukrainian
Canadians. First Supplement." Bulletin of the Research
Centre for Canadian Ethnic Studies at the University of
Calgary. Volume 2, 1970. p. 193-194.
    A list of doctoral dissertations and Master's and
Bachelor's theses on Canadian-Ukrainian topics. No
pagination of theses is given. Most theses listed are
in English, and some in French or Ukrainian. Sources
used in compiling of list appended.

1802. Pritsak, Omelyan. "The Present Status of Ukrainian Studies."
Canadian Slavic Studies. 14: 139-152, no. 2, 1972.
    French resume' p. 152.

1803. Ukrainian Canadian Committee. Brief to the Royal Commission on Education in Manitoba Requesting the Introduction
of Ukrainian Language as an Elective Subject in Grades
IX-XII in the Secondary School of Manitoba. Winnipeg,
1957, 4, 6 p.

1804. Ukrainian Canadian Committee. Implementing Ukrainian by
the Audio-Visual Method in American Schools and Colleges.
Part I. Preliminary edition. Montreal, Didier for
Ukrainian Canadian Committee, 1969. 159 p.

1805. Walhouse, Freda. "The Influence of Minority Ethnic Groups
on the Cultural Geography of Vancouver, B. C. Vancouver,
B. C., The University of British Columbia, 1961. 379 p.
    Unpublished Master's of Education thesis.

1806. Woolatt, Lorne Hedley. A Study to Discover Any Characteristic Differences in Sentence Structure in the Written
English of Saskatchewan Elementary School Pupils Belonging
to Different National Groups. Saskatoon, Sask., University
of Saskatchewan, 1944. VI. 89 p.
    Unpublished Master's thesis.

d. Organizations.

1807. Ukrainian National Association. To Our Youth. Jersey
City, N. J., 1939. 46 p.
    Concerns the role of the Ukrainian National Association
in the life of the Ukrainian Community of North America
and the role of Ukrainian youth in the Ukrainian community.

e. Their Role in the Political
Life of Their Countries.

1808. Boudreau, Joseph Amadee. The Enemy Alien Problem in Canada,
1914-1921. Los Angeles, University of California, 1965.
213 p. illus.
    Unpublished doctoral dissertation.

1809. David, Jerome. The Russians and Ruthenians in America;
Bolsheviks or Brothers. With an introduction by Charles
Hatch Sears. New York, G. H. Doran, 1922. 155 p. illus.,
maps. Bibl. p. 139-147.
    "One of the studies of racial groups in the New Ameri-
can Series produced under the auspices of the Inter-
church World Movement," (from introduction) concerns
American Ukrainians and their loyalties. Discusses the
problem of the Americanization of the Ukrainian group.
A section concerns Russian emigrants.

1810. Veryha, Vasyl. The Ukrainian Canadian Committee, Its Origin
and War Activities. Ottawa, University of Ottawa, 1967.
160 p. bibl.
    Unpublished master of arts thesis.

VI. UKRAINE - HISTORY.

1. Ukraine - History - Historiography.

1811. Dyadichenko, V. Development of Historical Science in the
Ukrainian SSR by V. Dyadichenko, F. Los and V. Sabrey.
Kiev, Naukova Dumka, 1970. 80 p.
    On head of title page: Academy of Sciences of Ukrainian
S.S.R. Institute of History.

6. Ukraine - History, Medieval.

1812. Curtin, Jeremiah. The Mongols in Russia. Boston, Little,
Brown, 1908. 481 p.
    Deals in part with Mongol attacks and occupation of
Kyiv Rus.

1813. Grekov, Boris Dmitrievich. Kiev Rus. Translated from the
       Russian by Y. Sdobnikov. Edited by Dennis Ogden. Moscow,
       Foreign Languages Publishing House, 1959. Bibl. footn.
       685 p.
            Discusses the history of Kyivan Rus. A special emphasis
       is put on the economic and social relations in that state
       and on the development of the feudalism there.

1814. Minns, Ellis Hovell. Scythians and Greeks: a survey of
       Ancient historiography and archeology on the north coast
       of the Euxine from the Danube to the Caucasus. Cambridge,
       England, Cambridge University Press, 1913. XI, 720. illus.,
       maps (part. fold).

1815. Paszkiewicz, Henryk. The Making of the Russian Nation.
       London, Darton, Longman and Todd, 1963. 509 p. fold. maps.
       Bibl. p. 416-485.
            Concerns in part the medieval history of the Kyivan
       Rus.

1816. Rybakov, Boris Aleksandrovich. Early Centuries of Rus-
       sian History. Translated from Russian by John Weir.
       Moscow, Progress Publishers, 1965. 230 p. illus. col.
       map.

1817. Stender-Peterson, Adolf. Varangica. Aaarhus Universitets
       Slaviske Institut, 1953. 262 p.
            Articles in English, French, German and Russian.
       Edited by A. Stender-Peterson. Discusses the history of
       the Ukraine to 1340 and the influence of Varangians in
       the Ukraine.

1818. Thompson, Michael Welman. Novgorod the Great. Excavations
       at the medieval city directed by A. V. Artsikovsky and
       B. A. Kolchin. Compiled and written by M. W. Thompson.
       New York, Praeger, 1967. XVII, 104. illus., map. plan.
       Bibl. footn.
            About the excavations in the Hanseatic city of Novgorod
       the Great which was part of the Kyivan Rus Empire in
       medieval times.

1819. Thomsen, Wilhelm Ludwig Peter. The Relations between
       Ancient Russia and Scandinavia and the Origin of the Rus-
       State. New York, B. Franklin, 1964? 150 p. (Burt Frank-
       lin Research and Source Work Series, 77.)
            A reprint of a book published at Oxford in 1877 by
       J. Parker which includes "three lectures delivered at
       the Taylor Institution of Oxford in May, 1876." Deals
       with the relations of the Kyivan Rus with Scandinavia.

1820. Vernadsky, George. The Origins of Russia. Oxford, Cla-
       rendon Press, 1959. X, 354 p. illus. Bibl. p. 323-333.
       Includes the history of Kyivan Rus.

Ukraine - History - 1654-1775.

1821. Kentrschynskyj, Bohdan. _Mazepa_. Stockholm, Wahlstrom and
Widstrand, 1962. 538 p. illus., ports., maps., facsims.

1822. Krasinski, Henryk, Hrabia. _The Cossacks of Ukraine_.
Comprising biographical notices of the most celebrated
Cossack chiefs, with a memoir of Princess Tarakanof, and
some particulars respecting Catherine II of Russia and her
favorites. By Count Henry Krasinski. London, Partridge
and Oakey, 1848. XIV, I, 312 p.

1823. LaVerne, R. & John P. Pauls. "Mazepa in World Literature."
Ukrainian Review, London. 18: 60-69, no. 4, 1971. Bibl.
footn. p. 69.

1824. Waugh, Daniel Clarke. "On the Origins of the 'Correspondence' between the Sultan and the Cossacks." _Recensia_.
2: 3-461 Illus. plates. Bibl. footn.
    The author argues that legendary letter of the Zapo-
rogian Kosaks to the Turkish Sultan, the wording of
which has been pictured in the well-known picture of the
Ukrainian painter Illa Repin, had its inspiration in
various publications on the same topic published in
Central and Western Europe.

Ukraine - History - 1775-1914.

1825. Kisilevskyj, Vladimir J. _Ukrainian National Revival in
Austria_, 1772-1848. London, University of London, 1936.
145 p.
    Unpublished doctoral dissertation.

1826. Manning, Clarence A. "Changing Conditions," in _Manning_,
C. A. Ukrainian Literature. (See entry no. 1398, p. 71-75.)

1827. Serbyn, Roman. "Ukrainian Participation in the War of
1812." _New Review_. 11: 59-72, 2/43-4/45, 1971. (Pruves.
War and _Society_ in Nineteenth Century Russian Empire.)

Ukraine - History - 1917-1921.

1828. Kossak-Szczucka, Zofia. _The Blaze: Reminiscences of
Volhynia_, 1917-1919. Translated from the original Polish.
New York, Polish Book Importing co., 1927. 324 p.
    The memories of a Polish author who lived in Volhynia
during the years of Ukrainian independence and the
struggle between the Ukrainian government and the Bolsheviks. Editor, Francis Bauer Czarnomski.

1829. Kulchycky, Peter George. The Ukrainian Insurgent Movement, 1919-1926. Washington, Georgetown University, 1970.
308 p.
    Unpublished doctoral dissertation. A history of the
Ukraine. The changes in and the collapse of the Ukrainian
Government. The organized partisan raids. (1st and 2d
Winter Campaigns.) The massacre of Ukrainian war prisoners
at Bazar. The development of the Ukrainian insurgent
movement which was overpowered by Soviet forces around
1926.

1830. Nomad, Max, pseud. Apostles of Revolution. Rev. ed. New
York, Collier, c. 1964. 413 p. (Collier books. Political
history.)
    The author discusses the Ukrainian anarchist Nestor
Machno along with other revolutionaries.

1831. Paliy, Michael. The Peasant Partisan Movement of the
Anarchist Nestor Machno, 1918-1921: An Aspect of Ukrainian
Revolution. Lawrence, Kansas, University of Kansas, 1971.
469 p.
    The history of the Ukrainian anarchist Nestor Makhno
who fought against the conservative government of Hetman
Pavlo Skoropadskyi, against the anti-Communist Russians
and finally against the Soviet army. Unpublished doctoral
dissertation

1832. Pidhainy, Oleh S. and Alexandra I. Pidhainy. The Ukraine
in the Great East-European Revolution. A Bibliography.
Toronto. The New Review Books, 1970-   v.
    In process of publication. Planned for three volumes.
Includes over 20,000 entries of titles published in
1917-1920 in languages Ukrainian, Russian, German,
English, French, a.o. Divided chronologically and geographically.

VII. UKRAINE - A CONSTITUENT REPUBLIC OF THE USSR.

1. General Publications.

1833. Petrov, S. S. ed. Meet Ukraine. Kyiv, Mystetstvo, 1965.
108 p. illus. (part. col.)
    A richly illustrated description of the Ukraine.

1834. Ukraine: A Short Sketch of Economic, Cultural and Social
Constructive Work of the Ukrainian Socialist Soviet Republic.
Charkiv, All Ukrainian Society for Cultural Relations with
Foreign Countries, 1929. 2, 7. 100 p. illus. plates., diags.
    A handbook about Ukraine published during the period
of Ukrainization.

1835. <u>Ukrainian Soviet Socialist Republic</u>. Moscow, Novosti
Press Agency Publishing House, 1968. 85 p. illus.
    Concise information on Ukrainian Soviet Socialist
Republic.

1836. <u>Ukrainian SSR in Figures. Statistical Reference Book</u>.
Kiev, 1967. 190 p. illus.

1837. Vasyliev, Oleh Oleksandrovych. <u>Soviet Ukraine</u>. Kiev,
Vydavnytstvo Politychnoi Literatury Ukrainy, 1970. 74 p.
illus. (part. col.).
    Information on various aspects of the Ukrainian Soviet
Socialist Republic.

<u>Ukrainian Soviet Socialist Republic - History</u>.

1838. Pigido, F. <u>The Ukraine under the Bolshevik Occupation</u>.
Munich, Institute for the Study of the USSR, 1956. 140 p.

1839. Rudnytsky, Ivan. "The Ukraine in Historical Perspectives."
<u>Canadian Slavonic Papers</u>. 14: 234-250, no. 2/1972. French
resume' p. 250. Bibl. footn.

<u>Ukrainian Soviet Socialist Republic - Economics</u>.

1840. Koropeckyi, Ivan S. <u>Location Problems in Soviet Industry</u>
<u>before World War II; the Case of Ukraine</u>. Chapel Hill,
North Carolina. The University of North Carolina Press,
1971. 220 p. Bibliography. Indexes.
    The author argues that before World War II Soviet
Union neglected development of Ukrainian industry in
favor of building up several industrial regions on both
sides of Ural Mountains. This saved Soviet industry
from heavy war damages but the author thinks that if they
had built up industry of the Ukraine they would have been
better prepared for war.

2. Ukraine - Communist Party.

1841. Solchanyk, Roman. "The Foundation of the Communist Movement in Eastern Galicia, 1919-1921." <u>Slavic Review</u>. 30:
774-794, 1971, no. 4. (December issue.)

3. Ukraine - Politics and Government.

1842. Borys, Jurij. "Who Ruled the Soviet Ukraine in Stalin's
Time." <u>Canadian Slavonic Papers</u>. 14: 212-234. French

resume' p. 234. Bibl. footn.

4. Ukraine - Living Conditions.

1843. Bociurkiv, Bohdan. "Social Stratification and Mobility in
the Soviet Ukraine." Aspects of Contemporary Ukraine.
New Haven, Human Relations Files, 1955, p. 60-78.

5. Ukraine - Church.

1844. Bociurkiv, Bohdan. "The Church and the Ukrainian Revolu-
tion," in John Van der Heide and Taras Hunchak. A Study in
Revolution. Munich, Wilhelm Fink Verlag,
(Harvard Series in Ukrainian Studies, 13.) (Forthcoming.)

1845. Bociurkiv, Bohdan R. "Church in Ukraine." Aspects of
Contemporary Ukraine, New Haven, Human Relations Files,
1955, p. 243-261.

1846. Bociurkiv, Bohdan R. "The Closing and Liquidation of
Churches in the Soviet Ukraine, 1919-1924." In Nationali-
taetenpolitic Moskau's 5-6: 13-21, no. 1, 1961.

1847. Bociurkiv, Bohdan R. "The Orthodox Church and the Soviet
Regime in the Ukraine, 1953-1971." Canadian Slavonic
Papers. 13: 190-212. French resume' p. 212. Bibl. footn.
no. 2/1971.

1848. Bociurkiv, Bohdan R. "The Uniate Church in the Soviet
Ukraine: a Case Study in Soviet Church Policy." Canadian
Slavonic Papers. 7: 89-113, 1965.

1849. Dunn, Dennis J. "The Disappearance of the Ukrainian Uniate
Church--How and Why," in Ukrains'kyi Istoryk. 9: 59-65,
no. 1-2/33-34, 1972. Bibl. footn.

1850   Marshall, Richard H., ed. Aspects of Religion in the
Soviet Union. Chicago, University of Chicago Press, 1971.
489 p.
     Also discusses the Ukrainian Church, especially the
Ukrainian Catholic Church. Some articles written by
Ukrainian Sovietologists.

6. Ukraine - Education.

1851. Pennan, John, Ivan Bakalo and Z. P. Faraday. Modernization
and Diversity in Soviet Education, with Special References
to National Groups. New York, Praeger, 1971. 394 p.
     One of the authors, Ivan Bakalo, is an Ukrainian
scholar. The book deals partially with education in the
Ukraine.

1852. Shimoniak, Vasyl. Communist Education: Its History, Philosophy and Politics. Chicago, Rand McNally, 1969. (c1970). 506 p. maps.
Also concerns education in the Ukraine.

9. Soviet Nationalities Policy - Ukraine.

1853. Allworth, Edward. Soviet Nationality Problems. New York, Columbia University Press, 1971. 440 p.
Also concerns Ukraine.

1854. Horak, Stefan. "From Internationalism to Nationalism, or the Soviet Version of Valuyevshchina." Ukrainian Quarterly. 266-285, no. 3/1972. Bibl. footn.

1855. Horak, Stephen M. "Non-Russian Nationalities of the USSR in American Studies." Ukrainian Review, London. 19: 81-91, no. 2/1972.

1856. Postyshev, Pavel Petrovich. Soviet Ukraine Today. The Results of the Agricultural Year 1933 and the Immediate Tasks of the Communist Party of the Ukraine, by P. P. Postyshev and The Results and Immediate Tasks of the National Policy in the Ukraine, by S. V. Kosior. New York, International Publishers, 1933. 116 p.

10. Soviet Colonialism and Imperialism - Ukraine.

1857. Sawczuk, Konstantyn. "The Ukrainian SSR: A Sovereign and Independent State." Ukrainian Review, London. 19: 36-54, no. 2/1972. Bibl. footn.

1858. Stetsko, Jaroslav. An Imperialist Russia or Free National States? Is a compromise of the enslaved peoples of the U.S.S.R. with the concept of one and indivisible Russia possible? Foreword by John F. Steward. Edinburgh, Scottish League for European Freedom, 1953. 16 p. (Foreign Information Series, no. 16.)
The author argues that only the dismemberment of the USSR into its ethnic components can solve the problem of the non-Russian peoples of the USSR.

11. Ukraine - Arrests, Deportations, Famine, Etc.

1859. Among the Snows. Protest writings from the Ukraine. London, Ukrainian Information Service, 1971. 65 p.
A collection of materials smuggled from Ukraine. Includes the trial of V. Moroz. How the trial of V. Moroz

was prepared. Letter to the KGB from Raisa Moroz.
Among the Snows (an essay depicting life in the Soviet
concentration camps). An article about the death of
the painter Raisa Moroz, list of Ukrainian political
prisoners known to be in Soviet prisons and concentration camps and other materials.

1860. Levytsky, Boris. The Use of Terror. The Soviet Secret
Service, 1917-1970. Translated by H.A.P. Priehler. London, Sedgwick and Jackson, 1971. 344 p.
    The author, an authority on the USSR, discusses the
Soviet Secret Service and its organizational changes
during 1917-1970. Tables of changes, bibliographies
and indexes added.

1861. Pidhainy, Oleh Semenovych. Mr. Khrushchev Goes Slave
Hunting. Introduction by Igor Gouzenko. New York, World
Federation of Ukrainian Former Political Prisoners and
Victims of Soviet Regime, 1956. 36 p.

1862. Vovchuk, Ivan. In Defense of Humanism: The Case against
Myt-Creation in the U.N. Buffalo, N. Y., American Friends
of ABN. Ukrainian Division. Information Bureau, 1970.
27 p.
    The author argues that the U. N. was wrong in obser-
ving the centenary of birth of Lenin as a prominent
humanist.

1863. Moroz, Valentyn. "Instead of Last Plea." Ukrainian Quarterly. 28: 126-130. no. 2/1972.

1864. Osadchyi, Mykhailo. "Cataract." Ukrainian Review, London.
19: 55-67, no. 2/1972, 19: 25-43, no. 4, 1972, 20: 30-43,
no. 1, 1973, 20: 56-69, no. 3, 1973.

12. Ukraine - Anti-Russian Resistance.

1865. Bociurkiv, Bohdan R. "Political Dissent in the Soviet
Union." In Studies in Comparative Communism. 3: 74-148.
April, 1970.
    Partially about the dissent of the young generation in
the Ukraine.

1866. Browne, Michael, ed. Ferments in the Ukraine. Foreword
by Max Hayward. New York, MacMillan, 1971. 257 p.
    Contents: Chapter 1. The jurists case of 1961. Chap-
ter 2. 1965 arrests. Voices from the labor camps.
Appeals of the M. Masyutko and M. Horyn. Chapter 3.
Writings of Valentyn Moroz. Chapter 4. Case of Vyacheslav Chornovil. Chapter 5. Memoranda, petitions and

letters smuggled from the Ukraine which cast light on conditions in the Ukraine. Simul aneous edition by MacMillan in London.

1867. Brumberg, Abraham, comp. In Quest of Justice: Protest and Dissent in the Soviet Union Today. New York, Praeger, 1970. 476 p.
Includes chapters by Ukrainian authors on Ukrainian topics. George Luckyj, "Turmoil in Ukraine," p. 52-61, an essay by Viacheslav Chornovil on p. 183-200, and by Ivan Dzyuba. "Address on Anniversary of Babyn Yar."

1868. Canadian Union of Students. Report of Intellectual Dissent in Ukrainian SSR. Guelph, Ontario, University of Guelph, 1969. 40 p.
Excerpts from undercover publications smuggled west and published here.

1869. Lakehead University. Port Arthur, Ontario. Report on Intellectual Dissent in the Ukraine. Port Arthur, Ontario, 1969? 40 p. map.
Discusses trends against Russification and in defense of human liberties among the young Ukrainian intellectuals and the Russian influence on these trends.

1870. Luckyj, George S. N. "Polarity in Ukrainian Intellectual Dissent." Canadian Slavonic Papers. 14: 268-279, no. 2/1972. Bibl. footn. French resume' p. 279.

1871. Potichnyi, Peter J., ed. Dissent in the Soviet Union. Papers and Proceedings of the Fifth Annual Conference Organized by the Inter-departmental Committee on Communist and East-European Affairs. MacMaster University, held at Hamilton, Ontario on October 22 and 23, 1971. Sponsors: McMaster University and the Canada Council. Winter, 1972.
Concerns intellectual dissent in the Ukraine.

1872. Pritsak, Omelyan and John S. Reshetar, Jr. "Ukraine and the Dialectic of Nation Building." Ukrainian Review, London. 119: 3-35, no. 2/1972. Bibl. footn.

IX. UKRAINE - FIGHT FOR INDEPENDENCE.

2. Carpatho-Ukraine.

1873. Shandor, Vincent. "Carpatho-Ukraine: Important Part of the Ukrainian State." Ukrainian Quarterly. 25: 337-349, no. 4/1969. Bibl. footn.

1874. Stercho, Peter. Diplomacy of Double Morality. Europe's

Crossroads in Carpatho-Ukraine, 1919-1939. Introduction
by Michael S. Pap. New York, Carpathian Research Center,
1971. 495 p.
   About the more recent history of the Carpathian
Ukraine including Carpathian Ukraine as the object of
diplomatic bargaining.

1875. Tarjan, Odon. Hungarians, Slovaks and Ruthenians in the
Danube Valley, by Odon Tarjan and Dr. A. Fals. Budapest,
Hornyanszky, Ltd., 1938. 59 p. fold. map.
   Published at the time of the Munich Agreement of 1938.
The authors try to convince Slovak and Sub-Carpathian
Ukrainians (referred to as Ruthenians) that in their
interest is to rejoin Hungary.

1876. Velychenko, S. "Carpathian Ukraine in Eastern European
Politics." Ukrainian Review, London. 18: 34-45, no. 3/
1971.
   Carpathian Ukraine as the object of diplomatic bargaining
during the crucial years 1938-1939.

3. Ukrainian Revolutionary Organizations.

1877. Honcharuk, O. If War Comes Tomorrow: The Ukrainian Insurgent Army (UPA) the Standardbearer of the Ideas of Liberation and Friendship of Peoples. Toronto, Society of Veterans of Ukrainian Insurgent Army in Canada, 1953. 63 p.
illus. port.
   Translated from the Magazine of the Ukrainian Supreme
Liberation Council (UHVR), "Samostiynist," published by
the Ukrainian underground movement in the Ukraine.

1878. Tys-Krokhmaliuk, Yuriy. UPA Warfare in Ukraine. Strategi-
cal, Tactical and Organizational Problems of Ukrainian
Resistance in World War II. Preface by Prof. Ivan Wowchuk.
Translated from Ukrainian by Walter Dushnyck. Yonkers,
N. Y., Society of Veterans of Ukrainian Insurgent Army, 1972
XIII, 449 p. illus.
   A complete story of the Ukrainian Insurgent Army (UPA).
Twenty-four chapters, appendices, bibliography, index.
Twenty-four pages of illustrations.

Fiction.

1879. Hirschfeld, Herbert. The Radiant Cross. A Novel of the
Ukrainian Struggle for Peace and Freedom. New York, Wil-
liam Frederick Press, 1963. 176 p.
   In fiction form the author presented situation of
Ukrainians in Western Ukraine under Polish domination,

attitude of Germans to Ukrainians, organization and
activities of the Ukrainian Insurgent Army (UPA). A
story of a family of German colonists in Western
Ukraine (Volynia) and its attitude to the problem of
the Ukrainian surrounding serves as background.

X. UKRAINE AND OTHER COUNTRIES AND STATES.

3. Ukraine and Russia.

1880. Bregy, Pierre. The Ukraine, a Russian Land, by Pierre
Bregy and Sergei Obolensky. Translated by George Knupfer.
London, Selvyn & Bount, 1940. 260 p. maps.
A presentation of the Ukrainian problem from the Rus-
sian point of view, claiming that it is a part of Russia.

4. Ukraine and Poland.

1881. Groth, Alexander J. "Dmowski, Pilsudski and Ethnic Conflict in pre-1939 Poland." Canadian Slavic Studies. 3:
69-91, no. 1 (Spring), 1969.
The author predominantly discusses Polish anti-Semitism
but also mentions the Polish attitude to other ethnic
minorities.
He calls Dmowski chauvinist and anti-Semite and states
that Pilsudski, who at the beginning of his career was
a liberal, later did neither express nor practice these
ideas.

1882. League of Nations. Protection of Minorities in Poland.
Petition to the League of Nations concerning the Ukrainian
minority in Poland and the question of the establishment
of the autonomous region in the territory known as Eastern
Galicia, submitted by members of the British Parliament
and other persons on October 5, 1932 together with supplementary correspondence. 11 p.

1883. Slivonski, S. Polish-Ukrainian Relations, 1919-1939. Oxford, Oxford University, 1947.
An unpublished doctoral dissertation.

XI. UKRAINE - STATEHOOD.

1. Ukraine - Statehood - General.

1884. Hrushevs'kyi, Mykhailo. The Historical Evolution of the
Ukrainian Problem, by Prof. Michaelo Hrushevsky. Tr. with
the kind permission of the Editors of Le Revue Politique

Internationale by George Raffalovich. English edition
published for S.V.U. London, Garden City Press, 1916.
58, 2 p. bibl. p. 53-58.

1885. Mandryka, Mykyta P. The Ukrainian Question. Winnipeg,
Manitoba. The Canadian Ukrainian Educational Association,
1940. 57 p. illus. map.

1886. Shumeyko, Stephen. Ukrainian National Movement. New York,
United Ukrainian Organizations of the United States, 1939.
46 p.
The history of the Ukraine briefly retold.

3. Ukrainian Independence Claims.

1887. Galicia. Ukrains'ka Natsionalna Rada. Western Ukraine--an
Independent Commonwealth. Wien, West-Ukrainian Press
Agency. n.d. n.p. 53 p.
At the head of title: Printed as manuscript. W.U.P.
no. 3. Published probably between 1919-1923. The authors,
speaking for the Western Ukraine Parliament, try to
repell Polish and Soviet demands to the Eastern Halychyna.

1888. How to Defeat Russia. ABN and EFC Conferences. Speeches,
reports and messages. Munich, anti-Bolshevik Bloc of
Nations, Press Bureau, 1969. 114 p.

1889. Stetsko, Jaroslav. The Principles of Ukrainian Foreign
Policy. International Situation and Liberation Struggle.
London, Ukrainian Information Service, 1966. 31 p.
Discusses the aims of the Ukrainian nationalists.

4. Ukraine - Diplomatic History.

1890. Dobriansky, Lev E. "China, Russia and Ukraine."
Ukrainian Quarterly. 28: 14-27. Bibl. footn. no. 1/1972.
Concerns Congressman Burke's Resolution H. Con. Res.
449, demanding that the U. S. President ask the Soviet
Ukrainian Republic and Soviet Belorussian Republic be
expelled from the U. N. and Congressman Zablocki's
resolution H. S. Res. 994 demanding that the U. S.
establish direct diplomatic relations with Soviet Ukraine
and Soviet Belorussia.

1891. Edgerton, William B. "Laying a Legend to Rest: The Poet
Kapnist and Ukrainian-German Intrigue." Slavic Review.
30: 551-560. September, 1971.
The author contends that Kapnist, a representative of
the Ukrainian gentry, who in 1795 contacted Prussian

Minister Hertzberg asking for Prussian help to regain independence of the Ukraine, was not Wasyl Kapnist but one of his brothers, an adventurer, who did not express the wishes of the Ukrainian gentry which was loyal to Russia, but merely his own wishes.

This conception has been argued against by some Ukrainian historians.

1892. Ukrainian National Council. The Ukrainians and the European War. Jersey City, N.J., Ukrainian National Council, 1915. 64 p. illus. map.

XIII. UKRAINIAN CULTURE.

1. Religion.

a. Ukrainian Church - History.

1893. Jacobson, Roman. "Minor Native Sources for the Early History of the Slavic Church." Harvard Slavic Studies. 2: 39-73, bibl. p. 70-73.
Also quotes some Ukrainian sources.

1894. Pekar, Athanasius. Historic Background of the Eparchy of Prjashev. Pittsburgh, Pa., Byzantine Seminary Press, 1968. 83 p. ports. maps.

1895. Welykyj, Athanasius, OSBM. Documenta Unionis Berestensis eiusque auctorum (1590-1600). Romae, Analecta Ordinis Basilii Magni, 1970. XVI, 540 p.
Includes documents from the Vatican archives concerning the preparation, conclusion and promulgation of the Union of the Ukrainian Orthodox Church with the Catholic Church in Brest Litovsk in 1596. Includes papal documents, letters of Ukrainian bishops, Ukrainian noblemen and laymen, letters of the Constantinopol Patriarchs and Polish kings and other governmental officials. Three hundred fifty-seven documents have been published in the following languages: old- Ukrainian, Latin, Italian, Polish and Greek.

b. Ukrainian Church - Biography.

1896. Pekar, Athanasius B., OSBM. Saint Josaphat (1580-1623). New York, Good Shepherd, Basilian Fathers, 1967. 63 p. illus. port.

c. Ukrainian Church - Miscellaneous.

1897. Catholic Church. Byzantine Rite (Ruthenian) Liturgy and
Ritual. Leiturgikon. English. The Divine Liturgy. New
Canaan, Connecticut, Byzantine Franciscanes, 1965. 101 p.

1898. Catholic Church. Byzantine Rite (Ruthenian) Liturgy and
Ritual. Leiturgikon. English. The Liturgy of St. John
Chrysostom, Ruthenian Form; Historical Background, Intro-
duction and Commentary. Collegeville, Minn., Liturgical
Press, 1961. 64 p.

1899. Gulovic, Stephen C. Windows Westward: Rome, Russia, Reunion. New York, D. C. Mullen, 1947. 208 p.
Bibliography concerning Eastern Churches p. 156-185.
The author discusses the question of the schism between
the Eastern and Western Churches. On p. 125-155 is the
history of Ukrainian and Carpatho-Ruthenian Churches in
America. The author stresses the difficulties these
churches met from the Latin Rite Catholic hierarchy and
clergy.

1900. Obriad Consecratsii i Persa Archiereiska Sluzba Boza ikh
Exellencii Danila Ivancha Episkopa-Koadjutora dla Katoli-
kov Vizantiiskoho Obriadu v Amerike v Katedralnom Chrami
Ap. Pavla, Fifth Avenue Pittsburgh, Pennsylvania, 1946.
83 p.
English t.p. added. Text in Ukrainian Carpatho-Ruthenian
vernacular printed in Latin characters and English. The
full text of all services with explanations of the consecration and first bishop's Liturgy of a bishop of Byzantine Rite.

1901. Archiepiscopal and Patriarchal Autonomy. A Symposium held
on July 15, 1972 at Lincoln Center Campus. Thomas E.
Bird (and) Eva Piddubchyshen, editors. New York, Fordham
University, 1972. 74 p.
A transcript of a Symposium concerning the right of
autonomy of the Ukrainian Catholic Church, held at Ford-
ham University. Included besides the preface and intro-
duction, remarks of National President of the Society for
a Patriarchal System in the Ukrainian Catholic Church,
Dr. M. Nawrocky and Co-editor Miss E. Piddubchyshen,
lectures held on Symposium: Wilhelm de Vries, S. J.
"The Origin of the Eastern Patriarchates and Their Rela-
tionship to the Power of Pope," "The Rights of the
Ukrainian Church at the Time of the Union of Brest and
Its Present Situation," by John Madey, "The Present
Canonical Status of the Ukrainian Catholic Church and
Its Future," by George A. Maloney, S. J. and, "The Role
of Ukraine in Recent Soviet-Vatican Diplomacy," by

Alexis U. Floridi, S. J., and of discussion after every
lecture.

1902. <u>Obriad Konsekratsii</u> X-22-1942 i Pershoi Arkhiereiskoi
<u>Sluzhby Bozhoi 10-25-1942 v tserkvi Sv. Mykolaia v Chicago,</u>
Illinois Preosviashchennniishoho Ambrozia Senyshyna ChSVV,
Epyskopa-Pomichnyka dla Ukrains'koi Katolyts'koi Dietsezii
u Spoluchenykh Derzhavakh. Chicago, Illinois, n.p.,
1942. 71 p.
Text in Ukrainian and English. Consecration of a Bishop
for the Ukrainian Catholic Church in the U. S. Full
text of all services with explanations.

1903. "Woes and Triumph of Ukrainian Catholic Church. "Birth of
Autonomy. <u>Ukrainian Quarterly</u>. 28: 5-13, no. 1/1972. Bibl.
footn.

2. The Ukrainian Philosophy.

1904. Manning, Clarence A. "Hrihori Skovoroda," in Manning,
Clarence A. <u>Ukrainian Literature</u> (See entry no. 1398) p.
17-22.

1905. Scherer, Stephen P. "The Concept of an Unlimited Natural
World in the Thought of H. S. Skovoroda." <u>New Review</u>,
12: 33-42, no. 3/48/1972. Bibl. footn. p. <u>40-42</u>.

3. Ukrainian Law.

1906. Padokh, Yaroslav. "A Concept of Humaness and Democratism
in the Criminal Law of Princely Ukraine." <u>Ukrainian</u>
<u>Review</u>, London. 19: 26-37, no. 3/1972. 19: 44-55, no.
<u>4/1972</u>.

4. Ukraine - Education and Scholarship.

1907. Flynn, James T. " V. N. Karazin, the Gentry and Kharkiv
University." <u>Slavic Review</u>. 28: 209-220, 1969, no. 2
(June) bibl. footn.

1908. Manning, Clarence A. "The Background of Ukrainian Culture,"
in Manning, Clarence A. <u>Ukrainian Literature</u> (See entry
no. 1398) p. 7-16.

5. Ukrainian Books, Libraries, Printing.

1909. Boiko, Maksym. <u>The First Cooperative Library and Its</u>

Cultural and Economic Influence. Bloomington, Indiana,
Volhynian Bibliographic Center, 1968. 100 p. Xerox.
   About a cooperative library organized and managed by
   the author in the Village Lopushno in Volynia in the
   years 1930-1935.

1910. Kalicinsky, Omelan. Psalterium Winipegense: A Cyrillic
Manuscript: Paleographic and Linguistic Analysis. Winnipeg, University of Manitoba, 1970.
   Unpublished Master's thesis. Author mentions in
   introductory chapters translation of the Bible by S. Cyril
   and Methodius, study of the Old Church Slavic Monuments
   and sources of this study and role of the Psalterium
   among the Eastern Slavs. In the body of the thesis
   author gives a paleographic and linguistic analysis of
   an undated manuscript of Psalter in possession of the
   Library of the University of Manitoba and tries to
   establish the date and area of origin of the manuscript.

1911. Sokolyszyn, Aleksander. "First Ukrainian Printer of Books
in Cyrillic on the Occasion of the 480th Anniversary of
Fiol's Book Published in Cracow." Ukrainian Quarterly.
28: 286-293, no. 3/1972. illus.

1912. Veryha, Vasyl. "Ukrainica at the University of Toronto
Library." Canadian Slavonic Papers. 14: 345-349, no.
2/1972.

   XIV. UKRAINIAN LANGUAGE AND LITERATURE.

   1. Ukrainian Language - General.

1913. Bidwell, Charles Everett. The Language of Carpatho-
Ruthenian Publications in America. Pittsburgh, Pa., University of Pittsburgh. The University Center for International Studies, 1971. 68 p. bibl. p. 67-68.
   Author discusses dialect of Ukrainian language used as
   literary language by group of Ukrainians originating
   from Carpathian Ukraine who called themselves Carpatho-
   Ruthenians.

1914. Bidwell, Charles Everett. Outline of Ukrainian Morphology.
Pittsburgh, University of Pittsburgh, 1967-1968. III, 59 p.

   3. Ukrainian Literature - General.

1915. Coleman, Arthur Prudden. Brief Survey of Ukrainian Literature. New York, Ukrainian University Society, 1930. 23 p.

1916. Trubetskoy, N. S. "Introduction to the History of Old Russian Literature." Harvard Slavic Studies. 2: 91-103.
    Notes of an introductory course on the history of literature of Kyivan Rus, given at Harvard University.

5. Monographs and Articles Concerning Single Works, Types of Works or Literary Forms
Slovo o Polku Ihoreve.

1917. Fennel, J. L. "The Slovo o Polku Igoreve; The Textological Triangle." Oxford Slavonic Papers. New Series. 1: 126-127, 1968.
    About influence of "Slovo o Polku Ihoreve," on later monuments of literature of old Rus.

1918. Iowetz-Tereshchenko, N. M. Some Problems of the "Tale of Expedition of Igor," a Russian Poem of the Twelfth Century. Oxford, Oxford University, 1928.
    An unpublished doctoral dissertation.

1919. Likhachev, D. S. "Further Remarks on the Textological Triangle: Slovo, o Polku Igoreve, Zadonshchina and the Ipathian Chronicle." Oxford Slavonic Papers, New Series. 2: 106-115, 1969.

Monographs and Articles Concerning Single Authors.

Chubai, Hryhorii.

1920. Struk, Danylo. "Hryhorii Chubai beyond All Expectations." Canadian Slavonic Papers. 14: 281-299, no. 2/1972. French resume' p. 299. Bibl. footn.

Franko, Ivan.

1921. Manning, Clarence A. "Ivan Franko," in C. A. Manning. Ukrainian Literature. (See entry no. 1398), p. 76-80.

Franko, Ivan. Works.

1922. Franko, Ivan. Moses and other stories. Translated by Vera Rich and Percival Cundy. New York, Shevchenko Scientific Society, 1973. 163 p.

Hohol, Mykola.

1923. Keefer, Lubov. "Gogol and Music." Slavic and East European Journal. 14: 160-181, no. 1/1971.
    The author discusses musical works (Operas a.o.) based on Hohol's works. Most of these works, which have been used by librettists and composers, have Ukrainian plots.

1924. Kolb-Seletski, Natalia. "Gastronomy, Gogol and His Fiction."
       Slavic Review. 29: 35-57, no. 1, 1970, bibl. footn.
            The author discusses Hohol's interest in gastronomy
       and quotes passages from his works in which he describes
       foods, meals, a.o.

                    Kosach, Kvitka Laryssa.

1925. Manning, Clarence A. "Lesya Ukrainka," in C. A. Manning.
       Ukrainian Literature. (See entry no. 1403) p. 89-95.

                    Kotlyarevskyi, Ivan.

1926. Manning, Clarence A. "Ivan Kotlyarevsky," in C. A. Man-
       ning. Ukrainian Literature. (See entry no. 1398) p.
       23-33.

                    Kotsyubynskyi, Mykhailo.

1927. Duravets, George Nicholas. Maxim Gorki and Mykhaylo Kot-
       siubyns'kyi: Personal Contacts and Literary Relationships.
       Winnipeg, University of Manitoba, 1970.
            Unpublished Master's thesis. Author tells about
       friendship between the Mykhaylo Kotsyubynskyi and Maxim
       Gorki which started when they met in Capri on June 2,
       1909 and lasted until Kotsyubynskyi's death in 1913.
            The author proves that their friendship did not
       influence either life or literary style. The integral
       part of the thesis is based on correspondence between
       both writers.

1928. Manning, Clarence A. "Mikhaylo Kotsyubinsky," in C. A.
       Manning. Ukrainian Literature. (See entry no. 1398). p.
       56-60.

                    Kulish, Panteleymon.

1929. Manning, Clarence A. "Panteleymon, Kulish," in C. A. Man-
       ning. Ukrainian Literature. (See entry no. 1398) p. 56-
       60.

                    Kvitka-Osnovyanenko, Hryhorii.

1930. Manning, Clarence A. "Hrihori Kvitka-Osnovyanenko," in
       C. A. Manning. Ukrainian Literature. (See entry no. 1398)
       p. 34-40.

Levyts'kyi-Nechuy, Ivan.

1931. Manning, Clarence A. "Ivan Levitsky-Nechuy," in C. A. Manning. Ukrainian Literature. (See entry no. 1398.) p. 66-70.

Myrnyi, Panas.

1932. Smyrniv, Walter. "Irony in Panas Myrny's Short Stories." Canadian Slavonic Papers. 14: 315-323, no. 2/1972. French resume' p. 323. bibl. footn.

Oles, Oleksander.

1933. Manning, Clarence A. "Oles," in C. A. Manning. Ukrainian Literature. (See entry no. 1398.) p. 112-117.

Shevchenko, Taras.

1934. LaPica, Larry. "Taras Shevchenko: Bard of Ukraine." Ukrainian Quarterly. 28: 146-165, no. 2/1971.

1935. Luckyj, George S. N. "The Archetype of the Bastard in Sevcenko's Poetry." Slavic and East European Journal. 14: 277-283, no. 3/1970.

1936. Manning, Clarence A. "Taras Shevchenko," in C. A. Manning. Ukrainian Literature. (See entry no. 1398.) p. 41-55.

Stefanyk, Vasyl.

1937. Manning, Clarence A. "Vasil Stefanyk," in C. A. Manning. Ukrainian Literature. (See entry no. 1398) p. 103-111.

1938. Struk, Danylo. A Study of Wasyl Stefanyk: The Pain at the Heart of Existence. Foreword by G.S.N. Luckyi. Littleton, Colorado, Ukrainian Academic Press, 1973. 200 p.
   Biography of Vasyl Stefanyk, reviews of his works by different reviewers, characteristics of Stefanyk's short stories. Added translation of 13 Stefanyk's short stories.

Vahylevych, Ivan.

1939. Brock, Peter. "Ivan Vahylevych (1811-1866) and the Ukrainian National Identity." Canadian Slavonic Papers.

14: 153-190, no. 2/1972. French resume' p. 190. bibl. footn.

Vovchok, Marko.

1940. Buyniak, Victor O. "Marko Vovchok and Lev Tolstoy."
<u>Canadian Slavonic Papers</u>. 14: 300-314. French resume'
p. 314. bibl. footn.

1941. Manning, Clarence A. "Marko Vovchok," in C. A. Manning.
<u>Ukrainian Literature</u>. (See entry no. 1398.)

Vynnychenko, Volodymyr.

1942. <u>Volodymyr Vynnychenko</u>. New York, Ukrainian Academy of Arts
and Sciences in the U. S., 1953. 70 p. illus.

Linguistic and Literary Relations of Ukraine with Neighboring Peoples.

1943. Likhachev, D. S. "The Type and Character of the Byzantine
Influence on Old Russian Literature." <u>Oxford Slavonic
Papers</u>. 13: 14-32, 1967.

7. Ukrainian Fiction.

1944. Pidmohylny, Valerian. "A Little Touch of Drama." Translated from Ukrainian by G.M. Luckyj. Littleton, Colorado,
Ukrainian Academic Press, 1972. 191 p.

XV. THE UKRAINIAN ART.

2. The Ukrainian Architecture.

1945. Cross, Samuel Hazard. <u>Medieval Russian Churches</u>.
Edited by Kenneth John Connant. Cambridge, Mass. Medieval
Academy of America, 1949. 95 p. plates.
    In the first chapters the author describes the medieval
monuments of church architecture in the Ukraine, in Kyiv
and Chernyhiv, and also in Novhorod the Great.

1946. <u>Kiev's Hagia Sophia</u>. State architectural-historical monument. Compiled and introduced by Hrihoriy Logvin. Kiev,
Mistetstvo Publishers, 1971. 47 p. 274 full-page illustrations (part. col.).
    Concerns medieval Kyiv Cathedral built by the Great
Prince Yaroslav the Wise and converted at present by

Soviet regime in an architectural monument.

7. Ukrainian Moving Pictures and Theatre.

1947. Pikulyk, Roman Bahrij. "The Expressionist Experiment in Berezil: Kurbas and Kulish." Canadian Slavonic Papers. 14: 324-344, no. 2/1972. French resume' p. 344. Bibl. footn.

1948. Revutsky, Valerian. "Mykola Kulish in the Modern Ukrainian Theatre." Slavonic and East European Review. 49: 355-364, no. 116, July, 1971.

1949. Revutsky, Valerian. "A Survey of the Ukrainian Postwar Drama." Canadian Slavonic Papers. 14: 251-268, no. 2/1972. French resume' p. 268, bibl. footn.

XVI. MISCELLANEOUS.

2. Ukrainian Folklore.

1950. Bain, Robert Nisbet, editor and translator. Cossack Fairy Tales. Selected, edited and translated by R. Nisbet Bain. New edition. London, A. H. Bullen, 1902. 290 p. illus.
   A selection of Ukrainian fairy tales.

1951. Gregorovich, Andrew, comp. Ukrainian Folk Songs. Toronto, Ukrainian National Youth Federation of Canada, 1959. 32 p.

1952. Klymash, Robert Bohdan. An Introduction to the Ukrainian-Canadian Immigrant Folksong Cycle. Foreword by Carmen Roy. Bulletin no. 234. Folklore Series no. 8. Ottawa, Information Canada, 1970. 156 p.
   Brief and concise description of the beginning of Ukrainian immigration to Canada 80 years ago. An analysis of different types of Ukrainian folksongs. An appended selection of 28 Ukrainian-Canadian folksongs in the original Ukrainian with English translation and score. Recordings of ten songs on flexidiscs are included.

1953. Klymasz, Robert Bohdan. Ukrainian Folklore in Canada. An immigrant complex in transition. Bloomington, Indiana University, 1971. 342 p.
   Unpublished doctoral dissertation. The author stresses that over the years the folklore of Canadian Ukrainians had lost its formal strength and now finds its expression in other forms like sounds, colors, forms, f. e. Easter eggs, folk dances, a. o.

1954. Klymasz, Robert Bohdan. The Ukrainian Winter Folksong Cycle in Canada. Foreword by Carmen Roy. Bulletin no. 236. Folklore Series no. 9. Ottawa, Information Canada, 1970. 156 p.

In the introduction the author discusses the factors stimulating the transformation and revitalization of these folksongs. The collection includes fifty Ukrainian-Canadian folksongs, including some old carols with traces of old Ukrainian pagan religious beliefs. Photographs of Ukrainian Christmas customs.

1955. Lord, Albert Bates. Slavic Folklore. A Symposium. Philadelphia. American Folklore Society, 1956. VIII, 132 p. port. (Bibliographical and special series of the American Folklore Society, v. 6.)

Also deals with Ukrainian folklore. Includes bibliography.

1956. Ojnas, Felix J. "The problem of the Aristocratic Origin of Russian Byliny." Slavic Review. 30: 513-522, 1971. no. 3 (Sept.

2. Supplement.

1957. Desroches, Alain. The Ukrainian Problem and Symon Petlura. (The Fire and the Ashes.) Chicago, Ukrainian Research and Information Institute, 1972. 109 p.

Translated from French original. Biography of Symon Petlura, head of the Ukrainian State, in the time of Independence and his role in the Ukrainian National Revolution.

1958. Stachiw, Matthew, Peter Stercho and Nicholas L. F. Chirovsky. Ukraine and the European Turmoil 1917-1919. Introduction by Senator Prof. Paul Yuzyk, PhD. edited by Joan L. Stachiw. New York, Shevchenko Scientific Society, 1973. 2 v. (Ukrainian Studies. English Section v. 10 and 11.)

In preface Prof. Dr. Yuzyk gives a short outline of the history of the Ukraine, discusses the influence of the Ukraine on the development of Russia and defines this book as "a documented history of the Ukraine in the crucial years 1917-1919 on the background of the political turmoil in Europe in that time."

In their book the authors discuss the history of the Ukraine in the time starting from November, 1918 because the earlier period of the Ukraine's independence has been discussed in publications of other students of recent Ukrainian history.

The authors present Ukrainian-Russian relations,

Ukrainian relations with powers of the Entente and their attitude to the Ukraine expressed best in the Versailles Peace Conference.

Short bibliography of books on the Ukraine added to the first volume, footnotes and indexes on the end of each volume.

AUTHOR INDEX.

Numbers after Names Indicate No. of Entry.

Bakalo, Ivan   1851
Balavyder, A.   1070
Bandera, Stepan   621
Bandura, Ivan   191
Baran, Alexander   492
Barclay, Clayton   1207
Barghorn, Frederick C.   844
Barr, James   962
Bauer, Isa   1680
Bayley, C. M.   275
Bedriy, Anathole   600, 643, 654, 859, 860, 861,
                                          1276, 1308, 1563, 1564

Belov, Fedor   181
Bergh, Hendrik Van   379
Berlstein, Alfred   1425
Bern, Ronald L.   1741
Besharov, Justinia   1584
Bespalov, Ivan   192
Besushko, Volodymyr   1459
Bida, Constantine   1338, 1426, 1590
Bidwell- Charles   1913, 1914
Bilash, Borislav N.   317, 1362
Bilinsky, Yaroslav   234, 662, 681, 804, 1140, 1173
Billington, James H.   466
Bilon, Petro   1213
Biloz, Michael   193
Bilynsky, Andrew   748
Birch, J.   1141
Birko, P.   194
Black, J. L.   346
Bloch-Halun, Marie   314, 1616, 1617, 1618, 1720
Blunden, Godfrey   1116
Boba, Imre   460
Bobykevych, Ostap   195
Bociurkiv, Bohdan R.   715, 729, 1232, 1780, 1843,
                                          1844, 1845, 1846, 1847, 1848,
                                          1865

Bogojavlensky, Marianna   1450
Bohachevsky-Chomiak, Martha   534
Bohdaniuk, Volodymyr   647, 845
Bohor, M.   1004
Boiko, I.   5
Boiko, Iurii, also Boyko, Yuriy,
    and Bojko, Jurij   769, 805, 1277, 1521
Boiko, Maksym   1768, 1909
Bolshakoff, Serge   716
Boresky, Theodosia   1244
Boretsky, Mychajlo   159
Borovko, Gregory   437
Borovskyj, Mykhailo   1605
Borshchak, Ilko   508, 619, 1174
Borys, Jurij   682, 1842

```
Pavliuk, Mykhailo (also Pavlyuk)        177, 214, 872
Pavlovych, Petro                        948
Pazuniak-Ishchuk, Natalia               1328, 1480
Peel, Bruce Baden                       67
Pekar, Athanasius B.                    1894, 1896
Pelensky, Euhen Julian                  40, 53
Pelensky, Yaroslav                      1414
Pennan, John                            1851
Perejda, George J.                      1223
Peters, Victor                          627
Petrov, S. S.                           1833
Petrov, Victor                          783
Petrovsky, Oleksander                   121
Pfeffer, Carl R.                        1456
Piddington, William E. H.               1000
Piddubcheshen, Eva                      1255
Pidhainy, Alexandra                     949, 1843
Pidhainy, Alexander                     677, 690
Pidhainy, Oleh S.                       568, 644, 754, 1032, 1092, 1101,
                                        1182, 1183, 1293, 1832, 1861

Pidlusky, Bohdan J.                     178
Pidmohylny, Valerian                    1944
Pigido-Pravoberezhny, Fedir             254, 901, 1838
Pikulyk, Roman Bahrij                   1947
Piniuta, H.                             298, 328
Pipes, Richard                          685
Plevako, Mykola A.                      122
Plyushch, Vasyl (also: Plushch)         703, 704, 1013, 1014, 1015
Podvesko, M.                            1371, 1372
Pohorecky, Zenon                        1789
Pohorilyi, Semen                        1400
Polonska-Vasylenko, Natalia             389, 464, 505, 539, 625, 645,
                                        746, 1169, 1239

Polovy, Hannah                          1511
Poltava, Leonid                         825, 1705
Poplujko, A.                            226
Popovich, J. D.                         1373
Porsky, Volodymyr                       555
Porter, Richard                         1786
Pospishil, Victor J.                    1224
Postyshev, Pavel Petrovich              1856
Potichnyi, Peter J.                     1142, 1871
Povroznyk, Lubov                        1716
Povstenko, Oleksa                       1650, 1651
Poznansky, Mykhaylo                     1374
Pritsak, Omelyan                        1802, 1872
Prociuk, Stepan Y. (also:               168, 179, 219, 220, 221, 227,
   Protsiuk, Stephen)                   232, 874
Procko, Bohdan P.                       155
Prokop, Myroslav                        873, 950, 1127
Prokop, Peter                           299
Prokopiv, Orysia                        310, 432
```

Shpilevych, Vira   20
Shramchenko, Mykola   1660
Shtendera, Yaroslav   572
Shuhayevsky, Valentin   659, 660
Shukhevych, Roman   1019, 1020
Shulgin, Alexander   1138, 1162
Shulgin, Antin   614
Shulgin, Basil   156
Shumeyko, Stephen   237, 1079, 1886
Sichynsky, Volodymyr   152, 157, 759, 1296, 1656, 1657,
                         1658, 1659, 1670

Siehs, Karl   691, 1437
Simmons, Ernest J.   1583
Simovych, Vasyl   1332, 1416
Simpson, George W.   127, 164, 615, 1134, 1246, 1545,
                         1687, 1769

Skochok, V.   831
Skrypnyk, Mary   1473
Skvarok, Josaphat J.   333
Slavutych, Yar   334, 767, 786, 1379, 1380, 1381,
                         1382, 1383, 1384, 1403, 1514,
                         1572, 1574, 1575, 1630

Slipyi, Joseph, Cardinal   1211
Slivonski, S.   1883
Slosson, Preston William   540
Slowacki, Juliusz   512
Smal-Stocki, Roman   128, 132, 244, 442, 459, 530,
                         560, 692, 800, 832, 833, 834,
                         857, 953, 985, 1021, 1080,
                         1144, 1515, 1546, 1547, 1736

Smart, Terry Lee   571
Smyrniv, Walter   1932
Snovyd, Dmytro   1275
Soborny, V.   969
Sokolyszyn, Alexander   41, 42, 875, 1313, 1516, 1762,
                         1911
Solchanyk, Roman   835, 1841
Solovey, Dmytro (also: Solovij)   876, 877, 909, 954
Solovii, Meletii   1227
Solovyev, Aleksander   1598
Sonevycky, Leonid C.   1184
Stakhiv, Mathew (also:
   Stachiv, Matvij)   257, 572, 580, 581, 609, 616,
                         626, 713, 1087, 1095, 1163, 1297,
                         1438, 1958

Stankiewicz, Edward   1333, 1356
Starchuk, Orest   1334, 1439
Stebelsky, Bohdan   1671
Stechishin, Julius W.   1386
Stechishin, Savello   1737, 1757
Stefan, Augustine   977, 989, 996
Stefanov, Marlene   303

- 303 -

SUBJECT INDEX